George

Fr. Charles College

February 20, 1959

Man, Morals and History

MAN, MORALS

Today's Legacy from Ancient
Times and Biblical Peoples

AND

HISTORY

CHESTER C. McCOWN

Harper & Brothers, Publishers, New York

MAN, MORALS AND HISTORY

Library of Congress catalog card number: 58-10366

TO THE TRUSTEES OF
PACIFIC SCHOOL OF RELIGION
Who have always allowed
AND TO
ITS FACULTY
Who have always encouraged
Freedom
of
Thought, Research, and Expression
IN APPRECIATION

FOREWORD

AT THE TIME of the author's unexpected death on January 11, 1958, he was in the process of reviewing certain editorial changes which had been suggested by the publisher. Since these seemed to be mainly of a routine nature, not affecting the substance of the completed book, we have taken the liberty of trying to finish the task which he had to leave undone. Of necessity there will still be errors which the author himself would doubtless have corrected. For these we and we alone must be held responsible.

At the end of the Preface the author had left a notation indicating that he had further words to add. We feel sure that he intended, at that point, to express his appreciation of assistance which he had received. Since we have no way of knowing the names of those he planned to mention, we should like, on his behalf, to thank all those who will recognize in this book the part they must have played, in particular Mrs. John Jungnickel, Jr., and the staffs of the libraries of the University of California and the Pacific School of Religion.

JOHN H. OTWELL
BEATRICE McCOWN MATTISON

PREFACE

WESTERN CULTURE in general has welcomed the unprecedented progress recently made by science in all its areas, naturalistic and humanistic, and that in spite of its novelties and dangers. A highly vocal minority, however, has turned pessimistic and antihistorist. Instead of law and order in the universe and society they see only absurdity and irrationality. Similarly, a vociferous minority within Protestantism claims to accept historical criticism yet replaces its basic principles by eighteenth-century dogmatism, ignores the spirit and the discoveries of modern science, and rivals the existentialists in their condemnation of man and all his works.

During the last three or four centuries, inquiring minds in the Western world have gathered unprecedented masses of new and revolutionary information in all areas of knowledge. Physical science has reinterpreted its world. On the foundation that Darwin laid, biology has built far beyond him. Sociological, anthropological, and cultural studies have illuminated the processes by which men learn to live together. This spate of change has gone on with unbelievable acceleration, especially within the last fifty years. Of necessity open-minded persons have thoroughly revised their conceptions of the world, of man, and of God.

Revaluation of the history of the ancient Near East is especially demanded. From that area come most of our inherited techniques, customs, and concepts—above all, our philosophical, moral, and religious ideas and convictions. That region, from Greece and Egypt to Iran, has been greatly favored by astonishing archaeological discoveries and philological advances, particularly within the last thirty-five years. Our historical-cultural inheritance must be interpreted and

ix

x Preface

continually reinterpreted by means of constantly increasing knowledge, with its new and ever-improving materials, techniques, and points of view.

Therefore it seems worthwhile to put well-known and newly discovered facts and events into relationship one with another in order to discover their meaning for morals, religion, and cultural morale. The result is inevitably a philosophy of history, a *Weltanschauung,* that differs sharply from any based on prescientific myth and superstition. This is a pragmatic test of the discovered concept of history. It does not depreciate or discard the ancient world, but explains it. Valuable discoveries made by the keen observations and experienced wisdom of the ancients, the rich materials worked out in their lives and cultures, even though expressed in antiquated myth and symbol, must be conserved and used by reinterpretation.

This study has resulted in the conviction, derived from objective research, that the experience of the past gives mankind reason for hope in the future, a hope that is not mere wishful thinking. No attempt is made to prove that Western civilization is the best attainable (quite the contrary) or that it will inevitably survive the recurring crises of its present period. The torch lighted in the Near East may pass on to others. Neither is any special form of social-economic organization proposed, although the necessity for change is obvious.

This is, rather, a perhaps too ambitious attempt to exhibit in outline developing moral and religious values that can be discovered in history and thus to present in concrete profile the nature of progress and the meaning of the historical process. It is concerned with the spirit, not the form, of culture. To present ideas in the context of the historical process may be the best way in which to set them forth.

Both the old and the new must be tested by critical scientific and historical method that is both objective (so far as is humanly possible) and empathic. The modern seeker after truth starts with no scientific, theological, or philosophical presuppositions except the hypothesis that this is a reasonable universe, that progressively it can be better and better understood, and that its God must be like it. The result of the search must be scientifically and philosophically defensible. The conceptions of history that this account illustrates I hope to state and discuss more fully in the future. Meantime a pragmatic test may well precede the statement.

Taken realistically, man's psychosomatic constitution makes him a citizen of two worlds, that of nature and that of mind, or spirit. Therefore he can learn the secrets of both the physical and the spiritual world, the two worlds of science and of history. History is a process, or combination of processes, that involves nature *and* human nature. These processes are equally objective to the seeking scientist and the seeking historian. Both the physical (*Naturwissenschaften*) and the humanistic sciences (*Geisteswissenschaften*) pass through the human mind but they are not constituted by reason, or intuition, or a priori principles. The constitution of things inheres in the physical and psychical processes themselves. The "laws" of nature and human nature develop in the evolutionary process. They are simply the way things work, ways that men must learn.

This is not a theological treatise but a historical sketch of human achievements. Though written in the language of theism, it may serve the humanist or agnostic. What matters is the recognition of order, meaning, and purpose in the universe.

Limitations must be set to such a study. Emphasis has been laid upon the development of morals and religion but not on art, philosophy, and ritual. The contributions of Greece and Rome have been little discussed, partly because of personal limitations, partly because these areas have already been more objectively appraised, and partly because they have less to do with morals and religion, though culturally they are of prime importance.

The realistic conception of history as an organic process receives its philosophical justification from Alfred North Whitehead, with inspiration from such diverse spirits as Ernst Cassirer, Wilhelm Windelband, Adolph Deissmann, Wilhelm Dilthey, and Ernst Troeltsch. The method follows (at some distance, no doubt) the principles of cultural anthropology developed by A. L. Kroeber, R. E. Lowie, and their colleagues. Naturally I have turned to specialists in various fields for materials. For historical relations and chronology I have relied upon

W. F. Albright because of his rich use of archaeological materials and his constant efforts to employ the latest information. While far from agreeing with all of his opinions and sharing his own distrust of some of his dates, I have adopted his changing chronology as the most comprehensive and internally consistent. I have referred to the Old Testament criticism of R. H. Pfeiffer as not exhibiting certain atavistic tendencies of recent years. Neither Albright nor Pfeiffer would claim to be infallible. For many years I have profited by contacts with various departments of the University of Chicago and its Divinity School. Above all I cannot omit mention of my many obligations to the American School of Oriental Research in Jerusalem and the Pacific School of Religion.

In studies carried on over long years innumerable obligations are incurred. I have tried to acknowledge those involved in this study in bibliographies and notes. Some works that are valuable, both pro and con, are not elsewhere mentioned. No doubt I have overlooked many and missed much pertinent material.

C.C.M.

CONTENTS

xiii

Contents   xvii

ILLUSTRATIONS

The illustrations are to be found following page 170.

1. Looking south toward Sidon
2. Sand dunes east of Caesarea (Stratonis)
3. Stone-built mountain village; Beit-ur il Tahta
4. From Mt. Scopus looking eastward over Wilderness of Judea and Jordan Valley to Transjordan.
5. Looking eastward on upper reaches of Wadi Qelt.
6. Qattara, "Bad Lands"
7. Wadi Sir, in Transjordan
8. From Tell Abil (Abel-Beth-Maacah) over the Jordan Valley toward Mt. Hermon
9. El-Jib (Gibeon) looking north from slopes of Nebi Samwil
10. Petra, el-Haiyeh, the Serpent, surmounting a free-standing cube of sandstone, a monument to serpent worship
11. Petra "altar," a true "high place"
12. Tell el-Qedah, ancient Hazor
13. Bedouin camp near Tekoa, some sixteen miles across the Wilderness from the Dead Sea
14. Basalt dolmen found near ancient Chorasin
15. Train of camels crossing Plain of Esdraelon on track from Egypt to Damascus

MAPS

Man, Morals and History

PART 1

THE CUP OF LIFE

The Making of Culture: Prehistory

In the beginning God
created the heavens and the earth.

GENESIS I:I

Thou art the River that created everything
When the great gods dug thee;
On thy bank they established prosperity.

AKKADIAN INCANTATION

None knoweth whence creation hath arisen,
And whether he hath or he hath not produced it;
He who surveyeth it in the highest heaven,
He only knoweth—or haply he knoweth not.

RIG-VEDA X 129

In the Beginning was the Word:
And the Word was with God,
And the Word was God.

He was with God in the Beginning.
Through him all things came into being,
And not one thing came into being without him.

What came into being in him was Life;
And the Life was the Light of mankind.

JOHN I:1-4

CHRONOLOGICAL TABLE I. FROM THE "BEGINNING" TO HAMMURABI

Abbreviations: A=Age, B=Bronze, C=Century, c.=circa (about), CL=Chalcolithic, E=Early, L=Late, M=Middle or Million, NL=Neolithic; ± Radiocarbon dates

Years B.C. (all approximate)
- 4,000 M Stellar universe, planetary system, and Earth take form
- 2,000 M Separation of moon from Earth (Gamow)
- 1,000 M Protozoic Era: Radiolaria, worms, algae
- 500 M Paleozoic Era: Foraminifera, trilobites, fishes; algae, mosses; crustaceans, mollusks, insects; trees, seed ferns, ginkgoes
- 200 M Mesozoic Era: Age of Reptiles; ichthyosaurs, etc.; birds, nonplacental mammals, conifers, true ferns, ginkgoes
- 70 M Cenozoic Era: Age of Mammals; placental dominant; modern flora
- 70 M Tertiary period: Carnivores, rodents, early horses, elephants; first lemurs, monkeys, apes; most modern genera of flora
- 1 M QUATERNARY PERIOD: AGE OF MAN

    PLEISTOCENE EPOCH: ICE AGE
- 500,000 Lower Paleolithic culture: earliest Man, Java, China, Heidelberg, etc., food gatherers *Savagery*
- 150,000 Last (third) Interglaciation begins
- 75–15,000 Last Glaciation (Wurm): M. Paleolithic: Levalloisian, Mousterian culture: Galilee, Tabun, Sukhul Man; Neandertal to H. sapiens
- 30–15,000 Upper Paleolithic: Magdalenian, Atlitian, H. sapiens

    HOLOCENE (RECENT) EPOCH BEGINS
- 15–8,000 Mesolithic culture, Kebaran, Natufian: rudimentary food production, no pottery
- L8–E7,000 "Neolithic Revolution": food growers, villages *Barbarism*
- 7,000 Prepottery Neolithic: Jericho: hogback brick phase; many floor levels; city walls, domed houses, great tower
- c. 6,000 ±6,250; ±5,850; plastered-floor stage: Tahunian; walled city, well-built houses, shrine, "statues," animal figurines (fertility cult?)

	SYRIA-PALESTINE	MESOPOTAMIA	EGYPT
±4,750	Pottery NL; Jericho IX / Dolmens	Jarmo 3 (rad.–carb. date) / Hassunah	Tasian, Fayum A
4–3,000		"Urban Revolution"	*Higher Barbarism*
3,800	ECL, Jericho VIII	Halaf	Badarian, Amratian
3,500	MCL, Ghassul, frescoes	Halaf, Eridu, Obeid	Amratian
±3,200	LCL, Jericho Tomb A 94	Protoliterate	31–2900 Dyn. I (JAW)[1]
3,000	EB I	Jemdet Nasr, Gawra VIII	*Civilization*
2,800	EB II	E. Dynastic I–II	Dyn. I–II (WFA)[2]
2,600	EB III Ai Temple	Mari, Akkad. Dyn. 26–25C	Dyn. III–IV Pyr. Age
2,500	Megiddo: large altar of unhewn	Royal Tombs at Ur	Dyn. V
2,450	stones; 2500–1800	Uru-kagina at Lagash	2350–2175, Pyr. Texts
2,300	EB IV	2360–2180, Akkad. Emp. Sargon, Naram-Sin	Dyn. VI (2250–2200, JAW)[1] / First Intermediate
2,200		L22C, Gudea of Larsa	Social, gnomic literature
2,100	MB I	Dyn. III, Ur: Ur-Nammu, Shulgi; oldest code (Sum.)	
2,000	Egypt: cultural influx		Dyn. XII
1,900	MB II A	Isin, Larsa Dyns.: Ishme-Dagan, Lipit-Ishtar;	Rise of Assur: Cappadocian colonies and tablets
19–13C	'Apiru mentioned in many lands	c. 1870, Sumerian Code / 19C Eshnunna Code (Sum.)	18–15C Second Intermediate

[1] JAW = John A. Wilson   [2] WFA = W. F. Albright

CHAPTER I

In the Beginning

1. *Human Beginnings* The twentieth century had run almost one-third of its course when a unique discovery was made in Palestine. In the spring of 1931 a small British-American expedition was excavating in Old Stone Age (Paleolithic) remains at the western foot of Mount Carmel about two miles from the Mediterranean. It is a picturesque, romantic spot. To the northwest a little over three miles away at Athlit there rises from the water's edge the plundered remains of the last and most beautiful of the Crusader buildings in Palestine, the Pilgrims' Castle, and a little to the south lay a small settlement of Zionists, representing a Hebrew reconquest of the Promised Land. The level plain running to the shore is checkered with fields and olive groves.

At the foot of the mountain a rough scarp of limestone rock rises sharply from the plain, broken, just at the point where the expedition worked, by a narrow gorge, or wadi, that runs back into the mountain. The center of interest was a large cave, Mugharet el-Wad, just south of the gorge. From the cave and the terrace of human occupation in front of it a multitude of stone and bone tools and more than sixty skeletons of early man were found in a Middle Stone Age (Mesolithic) culture. Below them were flint tools and other remains, including bones of animals used as food, but no human skeletal material aside from a few teeth.

A short distance away, up the little wadi, Mugharet es-Sukhul (the Cave of the Kids), a small cave with a terrace in front of it, was found to contain flint tools and animal bones embedded in a kind of breccia

5

resulting from the mixture of decayed limestone with the remains of human activity. When excavation began there, for day after day nothing was found but basket upon basket of tools and bones that were similar to the Levalloiso-Mousterian type already known in Europe. That is, they belonged to the middle of the long central portion of the Old Stone Age (Middle Paleolithic). Since the large cave had already produced an enormous quantity of exactly the same material, the excavation seemed fruitless. However, in hopes that something more exciting might appear, the apparently useless labor was continued.

One afternoon, just before the close of the season, the American School of Oriental Research in Jerusalem, which had been following the excavation with interest, received a telegram saying, "Neandertaler found." The skeleton proved to be that of a small child, tightly flexed, with knees drawn up to the chin. The following year, 1932, the complete or partial remains of ten more skeletons were found there. Eventually another almost complete skeleton was excavated, with parts of still another, in a third cave, Mugharet et-Tabun, that lay just south of the larger one.

These discoveries marked an epoch in prehistoric studies for they brought to light the first abundant and well-preserved remains of the Neandertal type of primitive man outside of Europe. Actual priority belongs to a skullcap found in 1923 near the Plain of Gennesaret. Unfortunately there was too little of it to allow positive classification. Yet the late Sir Arthur Keith had noted certain peculiarities that distinguished it from the Neandertal type. "Galilee man" was now reinforced by "Carmel man."

Paleanthropus palestinensis, as it was called, was a hominid form that clearly differed from the Neandertal race in certain features, although resembling it in others. Indeed, the skeletons differed greatly among themselves. The Tabun skeleton was that of a typical Neandertal woman. One of the Sukhul men was practically Cro-Magnon—that is, like modern man. This was a taller race than Neandertal man with a larger brain and beetling eyebrows, but with a chin. There is difference of opinion as to whether it was a hybrid form or was unstable and plastic owing to evolutionary mutations, and whether it belongs to the stem of the human family tree or to a noncontributing branch. Later discoveries near Nazareth, when fully published, may throw further light on the early development of man in Palestine. Flint cultures that go still farther back, perhaps to 500,000 years ago, have been found. The beginnings of man in Palestine hark back to the mists of dawn.

Where man originated no one can yet say. Piltdown man has been proved a fraud. Java man and Pekin man are much earlier than Carmel man, for they go back to 500,000, perhaps 750,000, years ago. In Africa various forms of early man have come to light, including one that a number of scholars regard as an important (not necessarily *the*) missing link. Man originated in Africa or Central Asia, possibly in both. However, the discoveries of Paleolithic man in little Palestine, along with cultures that can be matched in Europe and farther east in Asia as well as in Africa, put it in the full stream of human physical and cultural evolution from an extremely early period.

Palestine, therefore, makes a unique contribution to history. History did not begin there, but, in the present state of knowledge, Palestine provides a long and a continuous survey of the development of Western culture such as can scarcely be found elsewhere in the world. It has been said that without ruins and memories a land has no history. If the converse is true—and it surely is—Palestine, a land of ruins and memories par excellence, is above all a land in which to study and relive history. The three religions that have most directly and powerfully affected Western civilization arose in Palestine (Judaism and Christianity) and near it (Islam). Because three monotheistic religions, each claiming to be the hope of the world, center there, Palestine has more to offer and has been more intensively studied over a longer period of time than any similar area.

Its central situation put it in a position to profit by the cultural developments of all the great civilizations of antiquity. Even India was not entirely outside the circuit. Palestine received constant cultural impulses from the Tigris-Euphrates Valley, which was in touch with the Indus Valley. Egypt, that hothouse of culture in a more isolated area, was close enough to affect Palestine deeply. Central Asia and

Arabia, two prolific fountains of human energy, constantly poured their multitudes and their products into and across it. The Mycenaean and Greek civilizations reached it by land and sea. Palestine and Syria gave the Western world mythology, the alphabet, and how much more! Because Palestine became for many centuries a part of the Hellenistic and Roman empires, it made, through its monotheistic faiths, an incalculable contribution to Western culture.

Another outstanding contribution of Palestine is particularly important in the study of the meaning of history. Judaism adopted from its Semitic environment the first theory of history, revised it in the light of its own historical experience, combined it with elements of an Indo-European conception received from Iran, and passed it on to Christianity and Islam, where it is still developing. That theory, as modified by subsequent experience, is essentially the subject of this discussion. A sketch of the history of Palestine, therefore, and a concomitant discussion of the conflicting Hebrew-Jewish-Christian interpretations of history, form one necessary approach to the present problems of history and Christianity. Such a discussion will at least make clear what the alternatives are as an attempt is made to understand history and the hope it holds out for the future of mankind.

After Sir Arthur Keith announced the discovery of the fragmentary human skull close to the Sea of Galilee, a popular preacher delivered a sermon on "Galilee Man and the Man of Galilee." The central theme of this discussion is the current of moral thinking within the stream of history from Galilee man to the man of Galilee. One of the Carmel skeletons held within its arms the mandible of a wild pig, apparently provision for a wholly materialistic life after death. It is unexpected testimony to some conception of the dignity of man. The concept of life after death holds little moral implication. The concept of an ideal future society is a much more difficult and a highly moral achievement. Faith in the future eventually became an important, if ambivalent, element in the notion of a reign of God, which is the final formulation of the Iranian, the Jewish, and the Christian ethical ideal.

In the artifacts of preliterate cultures very little of man's intellectual and emotional life can be discovered. The earlier sections of this study can deal only with material culture. Even that examination can find in prehistory reasons for hope, since material culture is basic to expanding life. But the essential element in hope is spiritual, in the large sense; it is a matter of moral, not merely material, values; it is a question both of morale and of morality. Toward an appreciation of all the elements of culture this study is intended to lead.

There are certain preliminary questions to be considered before the problems of culture can be profitably discussed. The reliability and value of history have often been questioned. Therefore its nature, the materials for writing it, and the techniques of research must be noted. Misapprehension and misunderstanding on this score must be removed in advance, if possible. This discussion proceeds on principles that are accepted by historians but are not commonly observed or even known by the public at large. They must be briefly set forth.

2. *What Is History?* The word "history" has two meanings: (1) history as such—what actually happens, or develops, among men, that is, all human activity and experience; and (2) history as known— what is remembered, recorded, and handed down about what has happened to human beings and what they have done. It is not the doings of kings and courts and armies that constitute history in any genuinely useful sense. It is rather what happens to people to make them what they are; what makes their customs, their laws, their institutions, their attitudes and reactions, their total way of life as individuals and as social groups. History is a process, a long process, of cultural development.

What has come about in the process is recorded and handed down, not solely in oral tradition and written documents, but also in men's genes and their multitudinous combinations; yet even more in their tools, utensils, weapons—in everything they have made. Their ways of doing things, their social customs, their proverbs and popular sayings, their language, their very gestures, their institutions, and particularly their rituals, their ethics, and their religions—culture in the largest sense—tell the chief part of the story. What is written by and about them, by their contemporaries, is of course of great value. But, although usually regarded as the real history, it is actually only a small part of the total. History is a cultural process.

Only cultural history has genuine value for understanding man and what has happened to him. According to A. L. Kroeber, its materials have four aspects, or may be grouped around four centers of overlapping circles: (1) reality culture, which includes all material, technological aspects of man's activities and is "diffusional" and accumulative; (2) value culture, which includes religion, ethics, philosophy, and art and is "ever re-creative"; (3) societal culture, which includes social, political, and economic institutions and structures and is neither specifically accumulative nor creative; and (4) language, which fundamentally differentiates man from animals.

Without excavation and archaeological investigation, written history may be sadly misunderstood, for reality culture is almost inevitably slighted by dependence upon the written word. What the ancient chronicler thought magnificent and significant may appear very poor and uninteresting to modern eyes accustomed to brighter scenes. It may have been utterly commonplace and inconsiderable in comparison with what other contemporary peoples were producing and enjoying. This is a matter to be remembered in reading many biblical accounts: the glories of Solomon, for example. Racial pride and ignorance of the rest of the world caused to be handed down fantastic stories regarding Israelite heroes, populations, armies, national wealth, and the productivity of the Promised Land. Visible evidence corrects innumerable errors of written history.

Written history has had a low reputation with many people, off and on, for centuries. This may be due to mere ignorant anti-intellectualism, of which a well-known American industrialist gave a notorious exhibition in his offhand judgment that "history is bunk." It may arise from unhappy recollections of history badly written and poorly taught. At the moment it is in part due to the recent phase of historical writing that so exaggerated scientific objectivity as to deprive history of both interest and meaning. Inaccurate historical writing and disputes among historians gave rise to Voltaire's saying, echoed by Napoleon, that history is a mere collection of *fables convenues*. Some theologians distrust and fear the historical temper because it is antidogmatic. It teaches evolution and progress in religious and moral ideas and thus promotes moral and religious relativism. It actually compares Christianity with other religions.

Again, a crisis of history was said to arise after World War I because the oncoming generation wished to make a fresh start in a "brave new world" after a clean break with the horrors of the past. Yet there has been in recent years a constantly growing interest in the discussion of the meaning and philosophy of history.

Violent or supercilious reactions against history exhibit radical misconceptions of its nature. Written history should be a record of human experience. What chiefly distinguishes man from the animal is his capacity for history, his ability to remember his past and to hand on its accumulating accomplishments to his successors, not by instinct, but as a reasoned body of knowledge and skills to be studied, interpreted, and used. No scientist loftily discards the work of his predecessors. He tests all things to hold fast what is good, but to discard the mistaken and useless. So science progresses, each man standing on the shoulders of those before him. The historian, as a social scientist, must do the same.

As an area of scientific study, history, like all science, accepts one presupposition only: that there is order and coherence in its processes and that man, since he is a historical being, can discover that order. The historian, to borrow a phrase applied generally by George Santayana, rests upon his "animal faith," his "instinctive trust in the consistence and consecutiveness of a world in which [he] moves." But history, as recovered, reconstructed, and written, is also a work of art, an often tragic epic of conflict. All history as such, being actual human experience, is drama and pageantry, but also, as written, it is philosophy.

In the long perspective of the ages, the genuine drama of history is not Alexander drinking himself to death, Brutus stabbing Caesar, Socrates calmly submitting to anti-intellectual envy and legalized injustice, but man's long conflict with nature and human nature, and his upward struggle from primitive savagery to our present, still dismally low level of civilization. As Dionysius of Halicarnassus said, following Thucydides, "History is philosophy teaching by examples." Its instruction is primarily, not for individuals, but for peoples, for society. With Henry Brooks Adams we may say, "All experience is an arch, to build upon."

3. *History and Time* In any consideration of history, time, as a symbol of continuity and measure of change, is an essential element. Timeless history does not exist. No matter how bitterly many a student may dislike dates, they are indispensable, for time is the essence of history. Exact dates are not always necessary, but sequence dates are. Full comprehension of the passage of time and of the succession of events is fundamental. History cannot reverse the time machine.

Many dates in history are uncertain, and the length of prehistoric periods cannot be precisely known. Yet within the last few years, one might almost say within months, new methods of determining approximately the lapse of time and the antiquity of geological and archaeological finds are promising to bring order into many a confused historical situation. It is impossible (and undesirable) to enter here into technical details, but something must be said regarding the new precision now becoming possible. Only one who carefully surveys the development of historiography during the last fifty years can appreciate the advance that has been made. There is no room for that story, but only, so to speak, for a few illustrations.

Even dated documents require careful study and interpretation, for ancient methods of determining and recording the passage of time were so varied and inaccurate as easily to lead astray. It is enough to point out the ridiculous error in the date given the birth of Jesus. How can he have been born in 4 b.c., or, still better, 8 b.c.? The error stems from much later attempts to work out the date from different types of reckoning. The farther back, the greater the difficulty. The famous archaeologist Sir Flinders Petrie once dropped a thousand years out of his long-defended chronology of prehistory without mentioning the fact, and even so his chronology is longer than that now generally accepted. Within the last quarter of a century discovery and publication have been so active in reference to the history of the ancient Near East that constant revision has been demanded. Until recently, prehistoric, geological, and evolutionary timetables have been mere guesses.

In 1946 Frederick E. Zeuner published his *Dating the Past,* a remarkably complete and critical summary of all modern scientific methods for determining the lapse of time. To mention only a few, dendrochronology, or tree-ring analysis (developed since 1901), has been found very useful in forested areas and where wooden buildings are preserved, as in the western United States, among the Zuñis, and in Scandinavia. Varve analysis, developed in Sweden, counts the laminations (varves) of silt laid down in summer on lake beds by melting glaciers. The analysis of pollen from peat bogs and other deposits makes it possible to discover the types of plant life connected with various layers, to determine the climatic changes, and eventually to date objects such as flint tools by the pollen in the earth that clings to them. Paleontology notes the kind of prehistoric and usually extinct animals connected with geological strata and archaeological materials and thus dates periods and human artifacts.

For comparative chronology, the study of human artifacts is extremely useful. In prehistoric times, communication between western Asia, Europe, and Africa seems to have been fairly continuous. Therefore it is possible to build up and apply to extensive areas a succession of cultures characterized by the kinds of implements used and the techniques employed in making them. For the Paleolithic period flaked implements of flint, in the Late Paleolithic and Mesolithic bone tools also, serve as chronological indices. In the Neolithic period polished stone tools and pottery are added, and the latter becomes one of the most useful products of human labor for establishing relative chronology. Later, metals and other man-made articles enter into the picture.

When flint tools are found in connection with the bones of prehistoric animals or with geological formations, the combination adds greatly to certainty. When pottery occurs in connection with some object that is more precisely datable, a Sumerian inscribed brick or door socket or a Pharaonic scarab, it becomes valuable not merely for comparative but for precise, or absolute, dating. Thus archaeological chronology merges eventually into historical chronology, in which written documents establish, not merely the succession and relations of cultures, but their exact period. All this applies to postglacial times. For earlier ages some of the same methods may be used.

Attempts to correlate the pluvial periods of Palestine, southern Asia, and Africa with the ice ages of Europe and America have been made, but as yet with uncertain success. Rates of sedimentation in lakes and seas, of erosion (e.g., the rate of the wearing away of Niagara Falls), evidences of climatic change (e.g., glacial moraines), volcanic activity, mountain making, and, indeed, a great variety of geological activities are useful. All are combined with paleontological and evolutionary phenomena.

What has been attempted in the past has now come to be combined with two new techniques that promise to be of great value for both comparative and absolute chronology. The date now given for the beginning of our solar system and of the whole ordered universe, as we know it, is based upon the decrease of radioactivity discoverable in igneous rocks, such as pitchblende and basalt. The rate of emanation and of the resulting formation of lead and helium is known. Therefore, intrusive igneous rock in sedimentary strata fixes their dates within a small ratio of uncertainty. The method also allows the determination of the time when the earth had taken its present form and begun to solidify as about two billion years ago. That is the minimum age of the universe as calculated by astronomical methods based upon the rate of the expansion of the universe (still a moot theory). The results are, therefore, still tentative, but the radium technique promises much for the future.

Research in this field is progressing so rapidly that Zeuner's authoritative work, finished in the summer of 1945 and published in 1946, had to be revised and republished in 1950 and again, fully revised, in 1952. One method, which is of the greatest value to the student of prehistory and ancient history, the Carbon[14] technique, was not even mentioned in the first edition and is very briefly described in the second. The results have not always agreed with those reached by other trustworthy methods, and the new method is being further refined. New determinations are constantly appearing in various publications, with discussions of the difficulties.

The method is based on the fact that organic matter contains minute portions of radioactive Carbon[14]. In dead organic matter, the proportion of C^{14} diminished at a determined rate. Wood, paper, parchment, clothing, anything organic can be used if the quantity is sufficient. One of the spectacular applications of the method was in settling the date of the extremely significant Dead Sea Scrolls, putting them almost exactly at the date already determined by paleography and the pottery index: the first century A.D. or somewhat earlier. Dated documents discovered later have confirmed the result. Bones are less useful with the C^{14} method, but a fluorine technique can be applied to them. All of these methods that make for scientific accuracy combine with a constant stream of newly discovered written and unwritten documentation of human activity to make history more precise, more instructive, and more dramatic.

4. *When Did History Begin?* When in these two billion years does a people's history begin? That is another problem to be noticed. There are two parts to the answer. One has to do with the land in which they live, the other with the people themselves. What has happened to make people what they are goes back to the beginning of things. The land is a product of ages of geological change; the people are the product of biological and historical processes that are only slightly less impressive in length of time and are far more momentous in complexity and results. History cannot be understood without some theory as to all that lies behind it.

The Hebrews were not concocting stories out of mere idle curiosity or playful fancy when they developed their cosmography. Their conception of the work of God in history depended upon the beginning of things. They had some vague idea of the religious and philosophical import of all such questions and of their answers when they began Genesis (1:1, 27) with "In the beginning God created the heavens and the earth. . . . God created man in his own image . . . , male and female created he them." The meaning of history cannot profitably be discussed until the two questions are answered: How was the earth created and how did it become what it is? How was man created and how did he become what he is?

Anything that affects man's experience becomes necessarily a part of his history. In one sense, then, the beginning of the earth is the beginning of history; and the whole process by which the earth became what it is, including the evolution of plants and animals and eventually of the human race, with the entire story of the development of culture, belongs to history. To consider it all is an overwhelming task.

In point is a story Washington Irving tells to explain why he did not begin *The Knickerbocker History of New York* with the Creation. He said that a renowned Dutch tumbler of antiquity undertook to jump over a hill. But he took such a long run to get up sufficient momentum that, when he reached the foot of the hill, he was completely exhausted. So he sat down to rest and then walked over the hill. With this warning in mind, one must still start at the beginning.

The Hebrew author divided the universe into two parts: the material world, including all things inanimate and animate, and secondly, man, as a separate, special creation, not merely spoken into existence, but personally formed by God. Today, not being animists, we naturally make two grand divisions: the physical universe and the world of living things. Physics, chemistry, geography, and astronomy study the physical universe. Because of our legitimate human interest, we divide the world of living things into biology, paleontology, and anthropology. What the Hebrew cosmographer compressed into thirty-one repetitious and oratorical, but impressive, verses now becomes libraries. What he crowded into six days becomes an infinitely complex process of two, three, or possibly four billion years. So to expand the process is not in the least to detract from the glory of God or to belittle the marvels of his handiwork, but rather to magnify both beyond all imagination.

No educated person now sets 4004 B.C. in his Bible's margin opposite "In the beginning," as did the devout and learned Archbishop Ussher. But if, as the ancient Hebrews saw, human history does go back to the beginning, man's understanding of the tremendous process determines his diagnosis of his current predicament and his prognosis of the future.

CHAPTER II

What Happened in the Beginning

1. *The Making of the World (Cosmogony)* A large number of scientists affirm that, according to present evidence, some two to four billions of years ago "something happened" to start the making of the ordered world as we know it. The birth of the stellar universe was followed by the formation of our planetary system. Then, according to one theory, the moon was thrown off from the earth and left a great chasm into which the waters that practically covered the earth's surface flowed to form the Pacific Ocean. So the continents appeared, and, in the ooze of the ocean shores, eventually life had its origin, perhaps much more than a billion years ago.

Beginning in microscopic protozoa, simple bits of protoplasm that left no trace, more and more complicated forms developed. Perhaps a billion years ago algae, primitive water plants, left the first visible remains. Beginning with the Foraminifera, tiny supports, or skeletons, of lime were produced and left behind to appear as fossils in the rocks. Aquatic forms of life, vegetable and animal, were followed by the development of land plants and then of land animals. There was a succession of fishes, amphibians, reptiles, birds, and mammals, all of which are known from the fossil records. Successive structural disturbances of the earth's crust raised mountains. They were in turn eroded by unbelievably heavy rains that built sedimentary rocks in which the fossils were preserved. Thus was formed the mighty book of nature, with its leaves of stone in which the geologist and paleontologist read the story of the making of the earth and its living creatures long before man appeared.

2. *The Fact of Evolution*   The theory of evolution is anything but new. The Greeks, especially Anaximander, Empedocles, and Aristotle, suggested the idea in their conception of a sequence of organic types. But their methods were neither scientific nor fruitful, and they found no data to awaken the concept of development. Their idea was not historical and, therefore, not evolutionary. It was, on the contrary, a static pattern, a logical, systematic classification, like Linnaeus' botany. Combined with the biblical concept of special creation, it dominated Western civilization for two thousand years, and, becoming a dogma, religious as well as "scientific" and philosophical, it raised a solid mental block against the recognition of the evidence for evolution when eventually it became available.

After Descartes, who held evolutionary views but suppressed them because of "distaste for hell-fire and respect for the church," a series of scholars, down to Erasmus Darwin (grandfather of Charles), Lamarck, Wallace, and eventually Charles Darwin himself, brought the evidence together in such a form as to convince those who were capable of considering it without dogmatic prejudice. Within the last half-century the science of genetics, using modern tools such as a vastly improved microscope, has been able to explain much of the mechanism of inheritance and evolution. Darwin's theory has been revamped and refined and the whole hypothesis placed upon a firm foundation of observed fact. It is no longer correct to speak of a theory, or hypothesis, of evolution, but of the fact. There are still differences of opinion on many details of the process. But, while explanations differ, there can be no doubt as to the fact. Beginning with lowly protozoa in ocean slime a billion years ago, a succession of living forms has developed, one out of another, down to the present time. All living things upon earth, including human beings, are the result of that long process.

3. *The Nature of Evolution*   This brief account of what happened in the beginning in the process of evolution does not necessarily imply that progress has followed a gradual, glorious march upward from the beginning. Among those who believe in evolution, there have been widely different views as to its course. Many have denied that evolution has any connection whatever with progress. At the opposite extreme,

many have assumed that evolution involved linear progress, so to speak, a series of changes each for the better, resulting in steady and inevitable advance. Neither of these extreme conclusions can be drawn from the evidence in the solid pages of the book of geology, nor from the equally trustworthy biological data.

Experiments of geneticists indicate that mutation has no definite regularity. Plants and animals with a very brief life span will evolve at a different rate from those with a long and productive adult life. The paleontological record indicates that there has been explosive evolution —periods of extremely rapid change, followed by apparent quiescence. Again, throughout the period when plants and animals were evolving, there continued a succession of catastrophic convulsions in the earth's crust and alterations in its climate. Mountains were reared and then washed into lakes and seas by torrential rains to form new strata of rock. The continents were adrift, according to a widely held theory. Even down to less than 25,000 years ago, the climate of all the present Northern culture lands was going through the fluctuations of the ice ages. It would have been impossible for the process of evolution to proceed quietly under such radically changing external conditions.

There has been deterioration as well as improvement, retrogression as well as progress. Time and time again a form of life that seemed to dominate the earth and to represent, from many points of view, a climax in evolution (e.g., the titanic beasts) has disappeared and been replaced by some other apparently inferior type that then went through its long period of development and expansion until it also reigned supreme, only to fail and fall as catastrophically as its predecessors. Evolution seems to have been a random process. It has appeared as if only lucky accidents have saved life on earth from extinction and produced what we now have and are. Not so!

New theories of the process suggest that there is a law of disorder in nature's methods that might be likened to that discovered by probability calculus. Darwin established the fact of evolution, but his conception of the process has not stood the test of subsequent discoveries. To describe nature as "red in tooth and claw" is an exaggeration. The struggle for existence and the survival of the fittest are not the chief mechanisms by which evolution works. Mutations through recombinations of the genes in the chromosomes make new forms of life possible, and these new forms, these mutations that Darwin left unexplained as spontaneous generation, are the real source of evolution.

4. *Criteria of Progress* Can the process be said to have produced progress? The great majority of biologists, holding that they are objective scientists and are thereby estopped from philosophizing or passing value judgments, insist that evolution is not to be taken as equivalent to progress. They are concerned only with the process and its mechanisms; it is not for them to decide what is good or bad, what is better or worse. They will not take sides in a debate as to something so evanescent as progress. Now, admittedly, change is not necessarily progress. It may as well bring deterioration as amelioration. Progress has various meanings and is tested by various criteria.

Increase in size is not evidence of progress. If it were, the *Sequoia gigantea* would be the highest, as it is the tallest and possibly the most impressive, form of plant life; the whale would be the highest type of aquatic animal, and the elephant king of beasts. All three are limited in range and lack many qualities which other types of flora and fauna possess. If size alone is considered, then evolution reached its apogee in the titanotheres, and the Cretaceous period marked the end of evolutionary progress. But size became a handicap for the ichthyosaurs, the dinosaurs, and similar gigantic beasts, and for this and other reasons they eventually ceased to be. One might pause to consider the social gigantism of buildings, business, industry, and cities with which present-day culture is afflicted.

Herbert Spencer set down increasing complexity as a chief mark of progress. But beyond a certain point complexity, like size, proved a handicap to adaptation, and simpler forms of life supplanted those that proved to be too highly developed. Undue specialization, likewise, prevented adaptation to changing conditions. Progress in specialization is "in inverse relationship to the possibility of further progress." As an analogy it is to be noted that modern industry continually seeks simpler machines to replace the complex and often prefers an all-purpose tool to one that is specialized.

Adaptability (not adaptation) is one factor in both plants and animals that played a large role. Those forms of life that could accommodate themselves to the largest variety of conditions have always stood the best chance of survival. The survival value of an organism is indispensable, but it is far from the only desideratum. Otherwise the lowly protozoa, the earliest form of life and still one of the most numerous, would be the crown of creation. The oyster has persisted for 200,000,000 years, so it is said, almost unchanged. But who would be an oyster? Insects are the most numerous class, or phylum, of fauna. But who would be an insect? Survival is anything but a criterion of progress.

From the point of view of cultural anthropology, A. L. Kroeber denies the eighteenth- and nineteenth-century faith in spontaneous, inherent, and inevitable progress, but, since Paleolithic times, he insists, there has been some kind of progress. It is marked by the growth of societies in size, allowing differentiation in function and increase in skills and the accumulation of knowledge. Advance is now more or less proportional to (1) the total quantity of culture; (2) the ability to distinguish subjective from objective phenomena—e.g., the atrophy of magic, supernaturalism, and psychopathology; (3) the diminishing influence in social situations of anatomical considerations and physiological events (birth, puberty, etc.), and increase in humaneness; (4) the growth of science and technology, of reality culture; (5) to these may be added, as a part of humaneness, the development of value culture, religion, ethics, philosophy, and art. To an anthropologist, such as Kroeber, social and cultural change is due to a complex and shifting causality, affected by environment and individuals but composed largely of sociocultural factors.

The discussion of progress, then, inevitably raises the question of values. Thus it goes beyond the limits of pure science. The answer to the question must be, to a certain extent, subjective, for values are relative. But the recent progress of science, which no one will deny, has brought chemists and physicists face to face with the problem of values, human values. And their almost unanimous conclusion seems to be that, in the large, human values must not be overlooked by pure science. This may be a subjective reaction due to the fact that scientists are human beings, but if they were merely animals, they would not be scientists. It is certain that no other member, even of the hominid group, has ever dreamed of the problem. A science that destroys men might be stigmatized as too thoroughly objective.

Certain, not wholly subjective, criteria to be used in the testing process can be discovered. One characteristic that involves life as a whole is the tendency to expand. There is the old saw, Nature abhors a vacuum. Expansion is a feature that has its drawbacks because the earth and its bounties are not unlimited. However, any group that contributes largely to the total sum of existence may, *ipso facto,* be said to contribute to progress. Protozoa, insects, and men make large quantitative contributions to life. But, though incalculably numerous, protozoa and insects cannot be compared with men in capacity to fill the earth with life. The human race is the one group that incorporates the most material—in itself and in the vast bulk of its domestic plants and animals; and in all of this it is expanding as is no other group.

Dominance and control of environment are other objective criteria. They are not the same but are related. Various groups give their names to the ages in which they were dominant: the Ages of Invertebrates, Fishes, Amphibians, Reptiles, and, last of all, Man. Only by a better adaptation to environment is dominance over other forms of life achieved. Evidently certain types of environment gave to the various groups, each in its turn, an opportunity to dominate for the time being. Other factors are involved. In the list no strict succession of dominance appears. Protozoa, mollusks, and insects have even now a certain dominance within their own orbits. Also the matter of descent, a time element, enters into the calculation. In some cases one dominant form replaces another, but that is not always true.

5. *The Superiority of Man*   With all classes of plants and animals, adaptation to environment is essential to survival. The more easily and completely any type of organism adapts itself to environment and uses it, and the larger the range of environment which it can use, the more probable is its survival. Now, out of all the groups that have ever appeared, only man controls environment to any significant degree.

Man's body does not instinctively adapt itself to so wide a range of conditions as do some other animals, even though the human body does make some adaptations to heat and cold, to humidity and aridity, and to various kinds of food and drink. For example, man can be either carnivorous or herbivorous. And, by his intelligence, man can protect and educate his young and enlarge his own capacity almost without limit to use all parts and products of the earth to promote his physical and cultural well-being.

This being so, it is wholly natural and legitimate for man to regard himself as the criterion by which to judge values and so to measure progress. Happiness, ease, comfort, security, survival—these are not in themselves the highest goods to seek. Many animals have reached those goals as truly as men have. Some men ask no more; they are ready to live a purely animal existence. But that is not true of all or of a majority, if a better alternative becomes possible. Something within men drives or lures them to a life better than that of any animal. Man, therefore, is by right both criterion and critic.

Any progress that man can now make is possible only within human society and only if he differentiates himself more and more from his animal ancestry. Man's "biologically unique capacity for tradition," to use Julian Huxley's phrase—in other words, his knowledge and use of his past—is the basis of his potentiality for progress. It makes possible his advance in material well-being and also in intellectual, aesthetic, ethical, and religious concerns. This increase will be numerical and quantitative in the sense that more and more individuals will share it and that the items making for physical and cultural well-being will be more and more numerous. Yet it will not be merely quantitative as to either persons or possessions, but also and chiefly qualitative.

Animals live to eat, to exercise their muscles, and to reproduce their kind. Such physical functions have no stigma attached to them, but they are only means to purely physical and animal ends. They need not and should not occupy more than a modicum of man's time and attention. Human progress involves and depends upon the increase of intelligence, the rise of the level of the whole population in perception, synthetic grasp, analytical capacity, balance, and judgment. It depends upon more co-operation and less competition. Combativeness was essential to survival in the earlier stages of mankind's existence and even still has its values, but it should undergo sublimation into effort for others' weal, not woe. Intelligence involves greater disinterestedness and fuller control of the emotional impulses, since the latter easily damage the individual who harbors them, as well as other individuals and the whole fabric of society. Man has these capacities that other animals lack. By exercising them he can make himself less an animal and more a man.

6. *Evolution and Culture*   The word "evolution" is used advisedly and with full knowledge of the objections urged against the concept of social evolution. It is not for a moment to be assumed that the laws of biological evolution apply directly and fully to the analogous processes in society. But it is unfortunate and unscientific to deny that there is a close analogy between the two processes, just as it is to go to the opposite extreme and apply the concepts of genetics and biology without modification to social groups. (If it please the scientist to regard the language of cultural evolution as metaphorical and anthropomorphic, that may be granted. Unfortunately but inevitably all language describing human intellectual, emotional, and volitional activity is metaphorical.) The dissimilarities demand attention.

One outstanding difference between biological and cultural evolution is that between inherited genetic traits and acquired characteristics that must be imitated or taught and learned. To use an illustration from Gordon Childe, the baby mammoth was born with a tendency to grow a hairy coat and therefore it could survive in the ice ages. The human baby has no such inborn capacity; man had to learn to build a fire and clothe itself in skins. Largely because the human parents could talk and teach and the child could learn, the species *Homo sapiens* could adapt itself to new and changed environment and survive the end of the ice ages, while the overspecialized *Elephas primigenius* (the hairy mammoth), which depended upon physically inherited traits, disappeared, in spite of his imposing bulk. He could not shed his hairy coat. *Homo sapiens* has hardly altered his general and psychical characteristics since the tall Cro-Magnon and the faintly Negroid Grimaldi men appeared, more than 25,000 years ago. How different the case is as to cultural change!

Social and cultural inheritance is a fact that no person can escape any more than he can his physical heredity. Edmund Burke expressed it in eighteenth-century terms.

"Society is indeed a contract," said Burke; not a "subordinate contract" for trade in coffee and calico, "to be dissolved by the fancy of the parties," but an enduring and inescapable contract, "to be looked on with utter reverence, . . . a partnership in all science, in all art, in every virtue and in all perfection. As the ends of such a partnership cannot be obtained in many generations, it becomes a partnership not only between those who are living, but between those who are living, those who are dead, and those who are to be born."

The language of social contract derived from economics has changed in the twentieth century to that of an equally inept social mysticism, which is also equally metaphorical when it uses such terms as "social mind" and *Zeitgeist*. It may turn aridly mechanistic in behaviorism as it reduces conduct to conditioned reflexes. Yet the fact remains that every infant from its first breath is subjected to a conditioning from which it can never fully escape, no matter how rebellious the adolescent or cynical the man may become. And everyone inevitably contributes to the acculturation, or conditioning, and so to the shaping of society in future generations.

Language—its structure, vocabulary, emphasis, and tone; gesture, facial expression, and bodily posture; type of housing, kinds of food, habits of eating, sleeping, and other personal matters; the relations among members of the family and with outsiders—all of these apparently trivial and external factors subtly condition the child. The illustrative list could be expanded indefinitely. In different societies, Louisiana and Maine, Bavaria and Prussia, the Highlands and Lowlands of Scotland, to name a few familiar examples, different temperaments, different ways of reasoning, different ethical and aesthetic evaluations, and different volitional reactions develop through social conditioning. "Bad company corrupts good morals" (1 Cor. 15:33) can be legitimately generalized into "Society makes manners, morals, and man." Culture, in the anthropological sense, makes man.

Yet man makes culture. The ability of man to remember the past, to learn from it, and to control and alter his physical environment, his social organization, and his cultural inheritance in the light of what he has learned, makes progress possible. Vague desires for better things and more or less haphazard efforts to make improvements in past societies have produced progress. If it has been and remains all too slow, yet time has brought an increasing tempo and also increasing hazards. Whether progress continues without intervening catastrophe depends upon each succeeding generation. Human culture, said Ernst Cassirer, is "the process of man's progressive self-liberation," a process by which he comes to "know himself." In the process he discovers "a new power, the power to build an 'ideal' world."

7. *Progress a Reality*   The denial of progress in times such as the present, like the recrudescence of adventism and millennialism, is not based upon thoughtful consideration of past experience and human potentialities but arises from profound emotional disturbances due to the seemingly insoluble problems confronting man at the moment and to consequent personal fears and frustrations. It comes from lack of objectivity and control of the emotional impulses, when it is not due to crass ignorance of the past. Pessimism always thrives in times of trouble.

When one looks back upon the long road along which the universe has come from the great convulsions of billions of years ago to the minor disturbances, seismic, meteorological, political, and social, of the present time, when one considers even *Paleanthropus palestinensis* lying, more than 25,000 years ago, in the protecting breccia before his cave home with a wild boar's jaw in his arms, any ability to analyze evidence and synthesize results must admit the fact of progress as well as of evolution. It may be granted that evolution does not necessarily imply progress. A science that ignores values is not bound to believe anything connected with ethics or culture. But it is difficult to consider human values, as every human being has the right and obligation to do, and not reach hopeful conclusions that are much more than mere wishful thinking.

From its emergence the human race, because of its adaptability and intelligence, had the possibility of dominating and controlling all other forms of life and of using the inanimate world also to enhance its own powers and potentialities. The human race and society have progressed and will continue to do so. There are different opinions as to the future of physical evolution. Some biologists and geneticists hold the view that there are no existing forms of life that have within them the capacity for further physical evolution. Others keep the possibility open, even for the human race. However, no one who believes that there has been progress in human society during the past can doubt that there are further possibilities of advance. We do not live in a perfect or a perfectible world, but in one that can be continually made better.

A glance back over the progress of mankind deepens the impression of the quickening of its rate in recent times. The emergence of Pekin man and the first eoliths is set at perhaps 500,000 years ago, Neandertal man and *Paleanthropus palestinensis* at 50,000 years ago. If Pekin man be placed at the far end of a five-inch scale, Neandertal man is only half an inch from today, Neolithic man only one-twelfth of an inch, and the beginning of literacy but one-twentieth of an inch away. In that small fraction, one-hundredth of the human race's total span, all that is usually called history has come to pass.

In retrospect another characteristic of the process makes an indelible impression. Cultural development, like biological evolution, has not proceeded in a straight line. On the contrary, there have been periods of appalling deterioration. Often progress in one direction has been nullified by retrogression in another, gain offset by loss. Apparently hopeful variations have proved ineffectual. If one can put himself in the midst of the process, he will find many periods when the future must have seemed hopeless, when culture seemed destroyed, when insignificant creatures followed the magnificent leaders of former periods. Yet the insignificant and worthless have not infrequently proved the beginnings of unbelievable advances.

In the past lies hope for the future. But what is the nature of that hope and how is it to be realized? These questions must be considered, for we wish to know what our relations and obligations are to past, present, and future. One approach to these problems that, because of its historical importance, must not be overlooked and that must be considered because of what it promises is the study of Jewish and Christian conceptions of history and its goal. Violently conflicting interpretations of Hebrew history deeply influence segments of Western society, from Marxist communism to Second Adventism. What can one make of them?

The study of Hebrew and Jewish history within the frame of the cultural history of the ancient Near East has another interest. More detailed consideration will make clearer the peculiar values, already noted, that set Palestine and its religious history apart as especially appropriate for study. Hebrew history from the beginning, even as the Bible relates the story, documents the nature of social development and progress in a case study that can hardly be duplicated in any other nation or religion. Recent attempts at discovering a philosophy of history have analyzed the history of many nations in segments. They have dissected and dismembered many corpses and piled analogous parts together in an attempt to reconstruct a typical cadaver. It is simpler and perhaps more rewarding to consider the story of one living and growing historical entity in all its many relations and through all its multiform transformations.

The preceding pages outline the conclusions reached in the study of the historical materials presented in the succeeding chapters. A selection has been made as fairly illustrating the actual nature of history: its complexities, the difficulties and uncertainties, but also the reality, of progress, and the future possibilities of world culture.

CHAPTER III

Palestine: The Two Cups

1. *The Inner Cup: The Land as a Whole* A California Indian, a Christian and a leader in introducing modern ways and ideas among his people, expressed his conception of life to Ruth Benedict in words that reflect the concrete and picturesque thinking of his ancestors. "God," he said, "gave to every people a cup, a cup of clay, and from this cup they drank their life." He was referring to the ethos of his people, their ways of living and their attitudes toward life.

A people's way of life is made for them, in no small part, by its geographical context, by the land in which they live and by their neighbors. In the large, to express it less picturesquely, a people's attitude toward life and their life itself are the product of three factors: (1) the land in which they live, (2) their relationships with the peoples around them, and (3) their reactions to these two sets of external features. The first two constitute the challenge they face; the third is their response. The cup of life, like the Holy Grail, consists of two parts, an outer and an inner cup. The inner cup is the people's own land; the outer, all the nations that surround them. The contents of the cup include all their cultural attainments, institutions, and attitudes, the national ethos. It makes the national life blood.

Palestine, then, the inner cup, is about 135 miles long from Dan to Beer-sheba (the Hebrew phrase for its full extent). Dan, at one of the headwaters of the Jordan, was 25 miles from the Mediterranean, and across Beer-sheba from the Dead Sea to the ocean is 70 miles. Allowing for irregularities in the trapezoid, the area comes to about 6000 square miles, or 3,840,000 acres. Only Rhode Island, Delaware, and

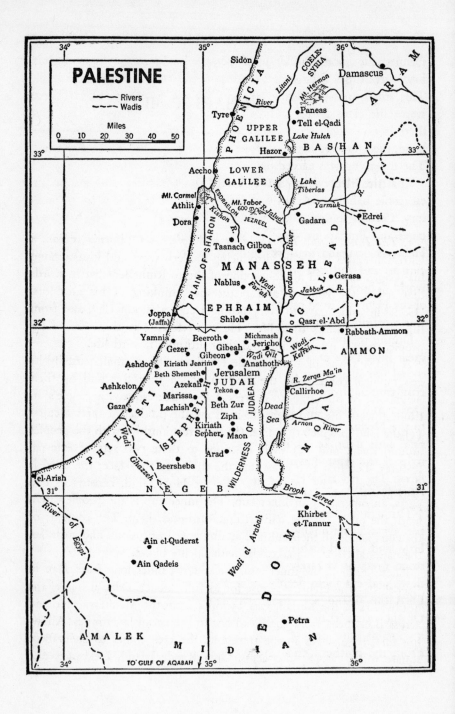

PALESTINE

— Rivers
-- Wadis

Miles
0   10   20   30   40   50

Sidon
Litani River
COELE-SYRIA
Mt. Hermon
Damascus
PHOENICIA
Tyre
Paneas
Tell el-Qadi
UPPER GALILEE
Lake Huleh
Hazor
BASHAN
Accho
LOWER GALILEE
Lake Tiberias
Mt. Carmel
ESDRAELON
Mt. Tabor 600 m.
R. Jalud
Yarmuk
Athlit
Kishon R.
JEZREEL
Gadara
Edrei
Dora
Taanach Gilboa
GILEAD
PLAIN OF SHARON
Jordan River
MANASSEH
Nablus
Wadi Farah
Gerasa
Jabbok R.
Joppa (Jaffa)
EPHRAIM
Shiloh
Ghor
Qasr el-'Abd
Yamnia
Beeroth
Michmash
Jericho
Gibeah
Jerusalem
Wadi Qilt
Anathoth
Rabbath-Ammon
AMMON
Gezer
Gibeon
Wadi Kefrein
Ashdod
Kiriath Jearim
Beth Shemesh
Azekah
JUDAH
Tekoa
R. Zerqa Ma'in
Callirhoe
Ashkelon
Marissa
Beth Zur
Dead Sea
Gaza
Lachish
SHEPHELAH
Ziph
Kiriath Sepher
Maon
MOAB
Arnon River
Arad
WILDERNESS OF JUDAEA
Beersheba
Wadi Ghazzeh
PHILISTIA
NEGEB
Brook Zered
el-Arish
River of Egypt
Khirbet et-Tannur
Ain el-Quderat
Wadi el Arabah
Ain Qadeis
EDOM
Petra
AMALEK
MIDIAN
TO GULF OF AQABAH

Connecticut among the United States are smaller. Texas is more than forty-three times as large and California over twenty-six times as large. This small area practically accounts for the Promised Land. There were elite clans living at times on the east side of the Jordan, but there is no evidence as to the extent of their territory. On the other hand, the Israelites never occupied any large part of the coastal plain. The inner cup was exceedingly small.

That the Hebrews possessed a very small territory was not an inescapable handicap. Attica had only 700 or 800 square miles of territory. Certain unique characteristics of Palestine gave it both advantages and limitations. That portion of its 6000 square miles that the Hebrews occupied most continually was one of the most varied in climate and tortured in terrain of all the similar-sized areas in the world. Those rugged limestone mountains where the major portion of the Hebrews lived offered only small areas for cultivation. Palestine was woefully lacking in other sources of wealth.

During the forty or fifty million years of the Cretaceous period, the great inland sea of Tethys laid down thousands of feet of limestone strata. Eventually the Arabian Peninsula, a great block of the earth's crust running from the Taurus and Armenian mountains to the Indian Ocean and from the Tigris-Euphrates Valley and the Persian Gulf to the Mediterranean and the Red Sea, was tilted up at the western side until it broke its high mountain crest and dropped a narrow strip of the crust down to form the rift valley in which the Jordan flows. The rift runs all the way from the Taurus Mountains to the Gulf of 'Aqabah and then through the Red Sea into eastern Africa.

Through succeeding millions of years torrential rains of pluvial periods and continually repeated earthquakes in this precariously tilted little land caused such fissuring and twisting and carving of the limestone strata as is rarely seen, with erosion that wore the mountains down and cut them deeply on their fissured flanks, while it partially filled the inland sea that had established itself in the rift valley. Of the ocean that once covered all the land west of the Persian mountains, the Sea of Galilee and the Dead Sea alone remain. From the northern end of the Dead Sea, with its tropical heat, to the subarctic snows of Mount Hermon is only 100 miles. From Banias at 1300 feet above sea level and near-by Dan at 600, the chief sources of the Jordan, the river runs down its 100 miles to the Dead Sea surface at 1286 feet below sea level and 2600 below at its lowest sounding.

2. *Regional Differences* Taken from west to east, Palestine has four narrow north-south strips: a coastal plain varying from nothing at Ras en-Naqurah and again at Mount Carmel to some thirty miles at Gaza. Next comes what is called the Central Mountain Range. At Ras en-Naqurah it is about twenty-five miles across; at Samaria, twenty miles; across Jerusalem, twenty-five miles if the Wilderness of Judea is included; south of Hebron it begins to disappear, but reappears in a detached mountain block half way to the Gulf of 'Aqabah and again in the Sinaitic Peninsula. West of the Mountains of Judah there is a considerable area called in the Bible the Shephelah, or lowlands. It was economically and politically important because its low hills and wide, open valleys provided a richer agriculture than the mountains and yet it could be held and ruled from either mountain or plain. East of the full length of Judea was the steppe, or wilderness.

The Jordan Valley forms the third strip. It is too narrow and deeply eroded, by the wandering river and the flash floods that roar into it from the mountains on both sides, to offer a home for any considerable number of people. The fourth north-and-south strip is to be found in Transjordan. It is a high plateau, lying two to three thousand feet above sea level and cut by three major river gorges, the Yarmuk, the Nahr ez-Zerqa, or Jabbok, and the Wadi Mojib, or Arnon. Many small gorges drain into the rivers, the Jordan, and the Dead Sea, and the three rivers have dug deep into the plateau. Yet as a whole the surface is far from being so rough as in Galilee and especially Judea. Its broad upland plains, its forested hillsides, and its clear, deep-flowing streams make it a far more attractive land than Judea. Many a modern has wondered how, in preference to the wide fertile acres of Bashan, Gilead, and Moab, Moses could have chosen the rugged mountains on the west side.

The width of the habitable land of the fourth strip varies. From

the Jordan to 'Amman, the ancient Rabbath-Ammon, which is practically at the eastern limit of agriculture, is only twenty miles. Northward the line between the desert and the sown runs much farther to
the east, up to sixty or seventy miles from the Jordan. Southward,
arable land ceases some distance southeast of the Dead Sea. Beyond
all of it stretches the great Arabian steppe, rich in agricultural possibilities but, because of lack of rainfall and rivers, condemned to
remain steppe and desert. The scant rains of winter produce grass
enough to satisfy the flocks of its nomadic inhabitants during winter
and spring. Its occasional oases and water holes serve them as they
wander in search of pasturage. In summer they often have to come
to the borders of the sown lands for both food and water.

From north to south also there are regional variations. The Leb-
anons and Anti-Lebanons, with their forests and fertile valleys, were
beyond the Hebrews but provide the main sources of the Jordan,
while they served as a hinterland that made the Phoenician coast richer
than that of Palestine. Upper Galilee, though mountainous, is relatively
rich, for it has a rainfall of above twenty-five inches. Lower Galilee,
the section west of the Sea of Galilee, is more open, with lower and less
rugged mountains and many wide valleys and small plains and but
slightly lower rainfall.

Then follows a significant feature, the Plains of Esdraelon and
Jezreel, which formed a wide gate through the mountains between
Mount Tabor and Mount Gilboa, past Beth-shan, and across the
Jordan, eastward into the wide and fertile fields of southern Bashan,
the center of the Decapolis. Southeastward this pass through the
central mountain range opened into the rich hill country of Gilead.
It served not only caravans and armies but also moisture-laden winds
from the Mediterranean that enriched the land all the way to the
Jebel Druze. At one point the watershed between the Mediterranean
and the Ghor was only some 200 feet above sea level.

The southern border of Esdraelon and Jezreel was dominated by
Mount Carmel at the west and Mount Gilboa at the center. South of
Carmel lay the Plain of Sharon; south of Gilboa, the high mountains,
low hills, and wide valleys of Samaria. One commercially significant

feature was the narrow pass through the mountains between the two great peaks of Ebal and Gerizim at ancient Shechem, modern Nablus. It connects eastward by Wadi Far'ah with Gilead and the Transjordan country and so with the caravan route to southern Arabia. Farther south, in Samaria, the terrain becomes rougher, the mountains not higher but more rugged, and the valleys narrower, leading eventually without any clear geographical boundary into the much more barren mountains of Judea.

For students of biblical religion and the Hebrew contribution to history, Judea is the most significant area. It may be described as consisting of the Shephelah, the mountains of Judah, and the Wilderness, or steppe, of Judah. Protected on the west by its mountain wall, which could be entered only through the narrow gates of its deeply cut wadis, and on the east by the deep moat of the Jordan rift valley and the still narrower wadis through the forbidding Wilderness, its heart was the most isolated and most nearly impregnable area in all Palestine. It was approached from the north and the south more easily, but not without danger and difficulty. However, an often traveled road led along the watershed north and south; another, equally traveled by caravans, passed across it through Jerusalem by the upper end of the Dead Sea, and up one or another wadi into the highlands of Gilead and Moab. The narrow Judean plateau on both sides of the watershed (on which Jerusalem stood) offered scant opportunities for agriculture. The maximum width of arable land in Judea is hardly more than sixteen or eighteen miles, and this is deeply cut by wadis on both sides. Two or three miles east of the watershed a series of villages following a fault line marked the end of settled occupation until the Jordan Valley is reached at Jericho.

The extent of Judah north and south varied greatly in Old Testament times. Its northern boundary during the period of the Divided Kingdoms ran perhaps between Tell en-Nasbeh (Mizpah) and Ramallah-Beeroth, eight and ten miles north of Jerusalem. Up to the Exile it included Hebron and usually Beer-sheba and its dependent villages of the Negeb, forty-five miles southwest of Jerusalem. With the Shephelah, the Wilderness, and the Jericho Plain, it might have had an area of 1200 or 1300 square miles at most, but often, in periods of weakness, very much less. A width of eight or ten miles must be taken off of its entire east side to allow for the almost barren Wilderness. After the Exile the Edomites occupied the district of Hebron almost up to Bethlehem and thus cut Judean territory nearly in half.

The diminutive size of the area from which such decisive influences have come upon subsequent ages is most noteworthy. In another respect it was peculiar and quite unlike Galilee and Samaria. On the east and south it was bordered by steppeland. Beginning about ten miles north of Jerusalem it ran southward without a break until, to the east of Beer-sheba, it coalesced with the Negeb, or "South Country," the great steppe and desert area that finally ends in the Sinaitic Peninsula. The Wildernesses of Judah, of Tekoa, of Ziph, of Maon, as they were variously called from the nearest region or town, lay on the eastern side of the watershed, beyond the reach of the rains, except when cloudbursts filled the steep, narrow gorges, or wadis, with flash floods. The area was broken by many faults and flexures due to the rift valley of the Jordan and the Dead Sea, which it overlooked. The quick torrents of many a winter had cut its tortured surface into fantastic gorges and into rugged peaks and precipices, and percolating water had hollowed out a multitude of caves (like those about Qumran) in its tilted and twisted limestone strata. Except for a rare spring, it was waterless.

The Negeb had great stretches of beautiful, slightly rolling acres where immense quantities of grain could be raised if there were water. But precipitation gradually decreases from about eight inches a year at Beer-sheba to almost nothing some miles farther south. Evidence of occupation during the Hebrew period has been found only around a few springs.

The maritime plain and the Plains of Esdraelon and Jezreel are the areas where intensive cultivation could have been carried on. In some parts this was effected by irrigation. Unfortunately the maritime plain was never fully occupied by Hebrew settlers and during much of Hebrew history was in other hands.

The Jordan Valley never played an extensive role in either the political or the economic history of Palestine for one very simple reason: it is extremely narrow. At some points it is no more than two miles across. Where it is widest, in the southern part over a length of some fifteen miles, the old lake bed through which the Jordan flows has been dug out by the spring freshets of the meandering river and eroded into numberless gullies by the torrents from both sides. None of it, except about Beth-shan, gets a sufficient rainfall, and save in the north the Jordan is too far down in its eroded stream bed to provide irrigation except at considerable expense. There are a few garden spots: the little Plain of Gennesaret (perhaps a thousand acres), level land on both sides of the river just south of the Sea of Galilee and near Beth-shan, a smaller area at the mouth of Wadi Far'ah, and again at Jericho, at all of which irrigation is possible. The wide level stretches of the Plains of Jericho and of the Plains of Moab on the other side of the river are partly ruined by the salts left by the drying up of the Dead Sea, partly eroded into hills of marl, partly without water for irrigation because of ancient lack of engineering skill.

The Transjordan plateau does not enjoy heavy or regular rainfall owing to its position behind the mountain range in western Palestine. But it is usually able to export wheat from southern Gilead, Moab, and Edom, as they were called in antiquity. The Bashan-Hauran region enjoyed an even more adequate rainfall. Gilead was an attractive land, with mountains but fair valleys, excellent for olives and grapes. The rainfall was not heavy but sufficient in average years; there were abundant springs, as at Jerash (ancient Gerasa).

3. *Climate and Its Consequences*   Along with terrain, climate makes a land whatever it is. The climate of Palestine, like the climates of California and Florida, was both a blessing and a curse. It served the prophetic writer with many a hortatory moral. The Deuteronomist (11:10–12) made the best of a bad situation as to Palestinian rainfall. He called Palestine a "land flowing with milk and honey," for it was not like Egypt, from which the people had come, where they sowed their seed and watered it with their feet, but it was a land

of hills and valleys that drank water by the rain of heaven, a land that God cared for. The eyes of the Lord their God were always upon it, from the beginning to the end of the year. Then he went on to point out the blessings of rain and abundant crops that they would enjoy if they loved and served the Lord their God, and the drought and famine that would follow disobedience. The climatic zone in which Palestine lies offered the moralist many a happy opportunity to sharpen his objurgations.

Palestine falls between 31° and 33° north latitude, the same zone as southern California and northern Baja California. Like Los Angeles, El Paso, Marrakesh, ancient Babylonia, and Lahore, it lies on the northern edge of the great desert belt that encircles the earth. With its Mediterranean climate of winter rains and summer drought, it may well be said that each summer moves the desert in to occupy the land, and on recurrent occasions it comes for the greater part of the year, sometimes for years at a time, with resulting poverty and famine.

In more than one sense Palestine is marginal land. It is on the margin of the tropics, on the margin of the desert, on the margin of productive agriculture. Like the Dust Bowl in the United States, it produced richly when the rains came at the proper seasons and in sufficient amounts. But the failure of either the former (early, or autumn) rains or the latter (spring) rains could always be even more disastrous than a partial failure of the heavy winter rains. Storms could be destructively severe. Hail was a not infrequent menace. Locusts, even in the face of modern methods of fighting them, can still bring widespread ruin. Biblical writers refer repeatedly to the blasting of crops by the *khamsin,* or sirocco, in May or October, and the mildew from long-continued rains or too-heavy fall of the otherwise blessed dew that ruined crops and stores. There were innumerable occasions when the superstitious peasant could feel the heavy hand of an offended God upon him.

On the other hand, the climate of Palestine is health giving. Diversity of terrain and marginal situation as to latitude, with the sea on one side and the desert on the other, give it a stimulating variety such as makes for resilient health and for physical and intellectual vigor. The hundred miles from the subtropical heats of the Ghor at Jericho to the subarctic cold of Mount Hermon included, it would seem, all the climates of the world. Summer resorts and winter resorts were always close at hand. There were salubrious hot baths near Tiberias and at Callirrhoe by Wadi Zerqa Ma'in near the east shore of the Dead Sea.

The invigorating dry air of the mountains, the prophylactic heat of the sun, the grateful coolness of the breezes that blow daily in summer from midmorning to sunset from the Mediterranean over the mountains, the stimulating variations in temperature, all combine to make Palestine a healthful country. It is true that many persons find Jerusalem too stimulating. Its atmosphere seems to produce a nervous tension that makes for quarrels and schisms. The land produces men and women of health, vigor, and initiative in abundance, far more than its meager acres can support. Since the days of the Patriarchs, probably since long before, its scant harvests have sent its sons out to neighboring lands and eventually all over the world to seek opportunities for better living. They have gone, some to remain in richer countries, but many to return, with whatever wealth of things and ideas they may have found, to enrich the culture of their fathers. The high productive capacity of the people and the low productivity of crops are of central significance historically, both in general and in particular as the basis for an understanding of the relation of the Hebrews to ethics and religion.

4. *Material Resources* In passage after passage the J source in the Pentateuch (Exod. 3:8 *et passim*) and other writers speak enthusiastically of Palestine as "a good land and a large, a land flowing with milk and honey." A section of Deuteronomy (8:7–10), probably written in the seventh century, continues, "a land of brooks of water, of fountains and springs flowing forth in valleys and hills," and it proceeds to boast of its wheat and barley, its vines and fig trees and pomegranates, its olive trees and honey, "a land whose stones are iron and its hills hold copper," where there will be no scarcity of food or lack of anything.

If the words had been spoken to nomads fresh out of the steppe, as the assumed situation presupposes, their extravagance could be understood. But the writers were descendants of fifteen or twenty generations of farmers, and their enthusiasm is difficult for the modern visitor from genuinely productive lands to understand. It is probable that the land is not so fertile or attractive now as it was before it had suffered 2500 years of erosion and wasteful, unskillful cultivation. But, as compared with Egypt, Mesopotamia, and Syria, it was anything but a rich country. Possibly the phrase "flowing with milk and honey" comes from a myth describing the ambrosia of the gods in some happy paradise and is to be understood metaphorically. It may be interpreted as a nomad's idea of paradise. A peasant would speak of wine, oil, and grain instead. As to the Deuteronomic boast, it can only be described as hermeneutic hyperbole.

The 5700 square miles of western Palestine (excluding the Negeb) include something over 1,000,000 acres of arable land in its plains, along the coast, in Esdraelon and Jezreel, and the Jordan Valley. The cultivable area in the mountains, north and south, is variously estimated at from 875,000 to 1,300,000 acres. Of this, much the larger part is in Galilee and Samaria; Judea was far more pastoral than agricultural. The steppe along its eastern side offered some grazing during winter and spring. In the summer after the early harvest that began in May, the stubble, which the sickle always left long, served as pasturage for the flocks and herds. Western Palestine seems never to have produced enough grain to feed itself. Its chief crops were olives and grapes. Of them alone was there a surplus for export. Milk and honey, wine and oil, were properly mentioned, but the remainder of the Deuteronomic blurb was sadly exaggerated.

The Deuteronomist's language actually suited Transjordan better than western Palestine. There are many springs in Galilee, Samaria, and Judea (in descending order), but there are few running brooks, whereas on the eastern side there are several besides the rivers already mentioned. More pomegranates are now to be seen on the east side than on the west. (It perhaps should be said that citrus fruits were unknown in the Near East in antiquity.) The sea was far away and the Jordan shallow. Except near the Sea of Galilee fish seem to have been little used.

No metals have ever been found west of the Jordan. Iron was once mined in Gilead along the Jabbok. Both iron and copper were found at several places in the 'Arabah, especially south of the Dead Sea, and at Ezion-Geber at the north end of the Gulf of 'Aqabah, Nelson Glueck excavated a well-planned smelter of considerable proportions. Slag heaps and other evidences of ancient mining and smelting have been noted at a number of spots along the Wadi 'Arabah. Pottery found at Ezion-Geber and other mining and smelting sites points to the reign of Solomon as a time when full use was made of these mines, with less use indicated during the reigns of Azariah in Judah and Jeroboam II in Israel. Indeed, these kings may have owed some of their prosperity to the exploitation of this source of wealth. But only when the Israelite kingdoms were strong could they control this territory. As to other mineral products, salt and pitch were always available at the Dead Sea. The land was rich in fine limestone for building. (There is no marble.) Here and there were supplies of potter's clay sufficient for local use. But the chief resource of Palestine's population was always pastoral and agricultural, with the addition of what they could glean from the very considerable caravan trade that passed along its camel tracks.

Unhappily even for pastoral and agricultural pursuits the fissured and eroded limestone mountains where the majority of the Hebrews always lived offered only small areas for cultivation and good pasturage. Fields were often so small that they hardly allowed room for turning the diminutive wooden plows with their diminutive oxen. Often they lay in little hollows where the soil had to be retained by stone dams. Hillsides were terraced in strips often only five or six feet wide following the contours of the limestone strata, and the earth was held in place by long dry-stone walls. The walls were always washing away with the winter rains. They required an immense amount of labor to build and maintain.

Orchards were planted on the shelving limestone strata by digging holes large and deep enough for the tree roots. Soil was brought up from the valley below, doubtless as it is done today, in baskets on the women's heads. There was so little level ground and so little surplus water that irrigation in the mountain areas was usually out of the question. There was one fortunate feature. The constant disintegration of the limestone compensated in part for the lack of artificial fertilizers. Probably, then as now, the pasturing of flocks on the fields in summer and the observance of a regular routine of fallowing saved the land from complete exhaustion. But, again, the necessary fallowing cut down the available acreage for crops to a serious extent.

When the Hebrews entered Palestine, the mountains were probably heavily wooded and the population was sparse. The relatively few cities allowed the invaders to find unoccupied land on which to settle. As the Hebrew population increased, the forests were cut down for domestic uses and thus the rapid run-off of rains and the erosion of the soil were promoted. The result was a slow and steady deterioration in productivity. The priestly tradition referred to the seventy years of the Babylonian captivity, when the land supposedly lay idle, as an enforced fine, so to speak, levied by God for the failure of the nation to fallow its fields as the law demanded.[1] Perhaps there was sufficient reduction of population to relieve somewhat the pressure of cultivation and to assist in the rehabilitation of the land when the Restoration occurred.

At best, however, Palestine could never compete with the rich valleys of the Nile and the Tigris-Euphrates region, or even with Syria. Palestine may have had its earliest agriculture at Jericho and Teleilat el-Ghassul in the Jordan Valley. But the Jordan was much too far below the level of these villages to serve them with water for irrigation. It is as ridiculous to compare their economy with that of Egypt and Mesopotamia as it is to discuss a Jordan Valley Authority as if it could be on the scale of the Tennessee Valley Authority. The little irrigation that was possible above and below the Sea of Galilee and in a few other spots could feed no multitudes. Use could not be made of the *qanat*, the ingenious shallow underground storage of water and irrigation that enriched more favored lands in the Near

East, because of Palestine's broken terrain and shallow earth above its backbone of limestone.

This rapid survey, it is hoped, will assist to an understanding of the Hebrews' economic and cultural problems.

5. *The Outer Cup: Surrounding Lands*   If the inner cup was plain, the outer cup, Palestine's external relations, was as rich as any diamond-studded chalice ever shown to gaping tourists. Poor as the land was, it was still much richer in sources of human comfort than the steppes that partially encircle it. The Arabian Peninsula is one of the breeding places of the human stock, a hive from which human swarms have poured forth again and again into neighboring lands, into Mesopotamia, Syria, and Palestine, and at times into northern Africa. What combinations of circumstances led to these mass migrations that left their traces in the third, the second, and the first millennium B.C., and again in the seventh century A.D., probably never can be specified. Almost certainly they were connected with economic difficulties, with scarcities of food and population pressures. The process of infiltration, in addition to mass migration, by nomadic tribes from the steppe into Palestine has been continued up to recent generations. Arab villagers speak of their grandfathers as having come from across the Jordan. According to the dominant tradition the Hebrews thence entered Palestine. And there were nomadic cultural elements as well as nomadic sibs, family groups like the Rechabites, for example, that persisted for centuries.

However, the Arabian steppe was not the only direction from which peoples and cultural influences flowed into Palestine. One of the most significant features of Palestine's physical situation has often been overlooked. Indeed, just the opposite of the fact has been loudly maintained. The comparative seclusion of Judea and the isolationist policies of later Judaism have been expanded into a dogma applied to the Israelites and their culture throughout their history. It seems to have been thought that the unique quality of Israel's revelation of God must be demonstrated by insisting upon their isolation from the rest of the world. As a pure and unmixed race, so the argument appears to run, protected by God from contacts with other races and religions, Israel produced a pure and uncontaminated religion that came directly from God himself, speaking immediately to the law-givers and prophets of his Chosen People. The historical and geographical facts indicate that God had a very different way of revealing himself.

The lines of contact between Palestine and the rest of the world were multitudinous. The road from Gaza to Memphis has been called the "oldest road in the world." From Egypt it branched out into all Africa. From Gaza northward one branch ran along the coast into Asia Minor. Another went by way of Megiddo and the west foot of Mount Tabor across Galilee and the Jordan to Damascus, and thus on to all interior Asia. From Gaza an important caravan route crossed the 'Arabah below the Dead Sea and from Petra branched in various directions, while still another ran southeastward to the Gulf of 'Aqabah and on to Arabia Felix. From the coast various wadis led up across the central mountain range by way of Jerusalem, Bethel, and the Shechem pass to Transjordan to join the north-south roads on the edge of the steppe. From Phoenicia a much-traveled caravan route led across Lower Galilee to the Jordan near Beth-shan and so to all Transjordan and Arabia. The Jordan Valley itself was an easy route by way of the extension of the rift valley between Lebanon and Anti-Lebanon into the interior of Syria and out into the northern and eastern segments of the Fertile Crescent. Lying at the southwestern tip of the Crescent, Palestine was at the small end of a funnel through which all of the cultural goods of the Crescent flowed.

The inner cup which held Hebrew life was unique in its climatic and topographical variety, in its combination of austerity and luxuriance. No features better illustrate that characteristic than the burgeoning forth of acres upon acres of flowers in spring, only to fade and wither within days to apparent nothingness. The silvery sheen of its olive groves, the overwhelming brilliance of its little Galilean Sea under the midday summer sun, the sullen gray of its Sea of Death under the winds of a wintry sky, the brief splendor of a Mediterranean sunset, the severe dignity of its mountain skylines, the unbounded mystery of its silent steppes, stretching endlessly into the beyond—no description can do justice to these. But, historically speaking, the outer cup is far more significant. The one decisive geographical feature of Palestine is not its peculiarity or its isolation, but its intricate relations with all of the ancient world.

The stones that so liberally sprinkle Palestine's fields and speak of the chisel of an ancient mason, the potsherds that cover its *tells* to reveal the touch of women's fingers, the columns that spring from the midst of briars and brambles to proclaim the presence of ancient cities where now no human being or building survives—all this must not be forgotten. But the paths of Palestine tell a more romantic and significant story; stony paths that, fixed by the terrain, cannot have altered their courses greatly since Abraham, Isaac, and Jacob stumbled over them; paths of the armies of Thutmose III and Ramses II, Nebuchadnezzar and Cambyses, Alexander and Pompey, Richard Coeur de Lion and Napoleon. Even more important, for such a study as this, than kings and conquerors were the humble merchants and the migrating tribes that wandered along these paths of Palestine or came to settle in it, for they brought, not rapine and destruction, but cultural goods that enriched the people of Palestine with myths and customs and concepts that went to form the content of the cup, of which eventually Western culture drank deeply. If it is not stretching the metaphor too far, it can be said that the shape of the inner cup, the form and color of the outer cup, gave to the content itself something of its unusual characteristics.

CHAPTER IV

The Contents of the Cup:
Culture in the Making

1. *At the Center* Jerusalem stands for many different ideas and ideals. One aspect of its historical values is too little mentioned. In the center of the Greek Catholicon in the Holy Sepulcher in Jerusalem stands a small stone globe carved in a stone vase. Pious Greek Orthodox worshipers still go to it and kiss it on entering the church for they believe that it stands at the geographical center of the world and symbolizes the rule of Christ over all the earth.

In a sense of which they do not dream, it represents historical fact. The drama of Hebrew and early Jewish history was played at the center of the oldest and one of the most virile and productive civilizations that the world has ever known. Sumerians and Semites, Egyptians and Mycenaeans, Babylonians and Hittites, Phoenicians and Persians, Greeks, Romans, and Parthians, all made their contributions to the manifold matrix of modern Western culture. Even China, India, and unnamable Aryan tribes had a part in enriching the historical experience of the Hebrews and the Jews of Jesus' day. History did not begin in Palestine, but that land serves marvelously as a watchtower from which to observe the long drama.

The archaeological discoveries of the last century and particularly of the last half-century have continually emphasized the fact that Greek literature and philosophy and Hebrew and Christian ethics and religion, in both the Old Testament and the New, show dependence on the currents of historical experience among all of these widely scattered peoples of the Near East. The resultant richly complex culture, with its philosophical, ethical, and religious notions, was handed down to us through Greco-Roman and Hebrew-Christian writings, traditions, and institutions. Judaism and Christianity were born at the center of the ancient Near Eastern and Mediterranean cultures. Jerusalem was at the center of the ancient civilized world.

Living thus at the center of civilization, inescapably interdependent with other cultures, the Hebrews developed their unique and original contribution to history. Later they preserved it by isolation and by social, religious, and political ideas that are now very generally regarded as mistaken and evil in their ultimate consequences. They partially fossilized themselves by chauvinistic nationalism, vainglorious racialism, and haughty religious pride. Strangely enough, in the alchemy of history, these unattractive and even repellent ideas, base metal if ever there was one, were transmuted into what, for modern thinking, is pure gold. The nature of these historical processes is a problem that brings to the student unsolved difficulties, but also endless interest and enlightenment.

Students of the origins of Western civilization, as well as of the Old Testament, must keep fully aware of the new contributions which, in these years, archaeological research and linguistic studies in the Near East are making to the ancient history which forms the background of Hebrew and, indeed, all Western history. Henry C. Rawlinson and his brother, the historian, George R., Austin Henry Layard, George Smith, and Hormuzd Rassam have been succeeded in the twentieth century by a host of excavators, linguists, and historians, among whom any selection of names would be invidious. The explorations and excavations of anthropologists and prehistorians, many of them recent or still in progress, have made possible astonishing advances in understanding the evolution, not only of the human body, but also of society.

Present results are far from final. Indeed, all of our questions will never be answered. Yet the studies in early cultures have progressed far enough to throw a great deal of light on the problems to be discussed here: how the Hebrews came to be what they were; how Near

Eastern society developed, became what it was, and influenced them. To consider these problems, it is necessary to go back to the beginning, at whatever risk, in order to exhibit the progress that preceded the achievements of the Hebrews. The following brief sketch will show, to all but the most querulous and unreasonable skepticism, that society has progressed in all that makes for genuine human values. It will also clarify the nature of evolution and of progress in society. A society that consists of human beings will never reach perfection. Too much cannot be expected of any kind of evolution in a finite world.

It is a useful convention of prehistorians to speak of the savagery of Paleolithic and Mesolithic times, the barbarism of Neolithic agricul-tural man in his villages, and the civilization that emerged in the city-states of the Near East at the close of the fourth millennium. If the etymological meaning of "civilization," as the product of the *civis,* or city, be taken, and no pejorative connotations be attached to "savage" and "barbarous," the usage can be accepted in labeling suc-cessive stages of social and cultural progress provided also that "stages" be understood as implying no sudden steps upward and no universal strait jacket into which to fit all societies. What this slow movement upward brought to mankind is worth noting.

2. *Prehistoric Savagery* Even the Middle Paleolithic Neander-talers and their contemporaries had developed techniques in the mak-ing of flint tools that required forethought and planning. They hunted big game, such as the mammoth and woolly rhinoceros—game large enough to demand organization into packs for the purpose. They had burial rites that included some kind of ritual, special treatment of corpses, and the provision of food for a life after death. Evidence of a sense of form and beauty appears in the careful chipping of their flint tools and traces of magical rites in connection with their hunting.

In the Upper Paleolithic, when modern man appears, data ac-cumulate to prove that a revolution had occurred between Middle Paleolithic Mousterian and Upper Paleolithic Aurignacian. It in-volved an expansion and enrichment of culture second only to the Neolithic revolution that was to come later. It included a still further development of superstitions, of sacrifices to deities and spirits, along with the engravings and paintings in the French caves, which reveal the beginnings of art and religion and the development of systems of belief, rightly called ideologies.

What V. Gordon Childe calls a "dazzling culture" with a numerous population arose in the last phase of the Ice Age among the Magdalenians. But when the glaciers retreated and forests began to cover the tundras and steppes, the herds of reindeer also retreated northward. The mammoth, the bison, and the horse migrated or died off, and there was a distinct recession of culture in Europe while man learned to adapt himself to a new set of climatic conditions.

As the forests spread and the desert belt, moving northward, made itself felt, an economic revolution came upon society in humbler groups less highly specialized than the Magdalenians. While the men hunted the gazelle and antelope, which now became the chief sources of food, the women began to collect the seeds of wild shattering cereals by stick and basket and eventually to cultivate (instead of depending on nature's sowing) and reap the ancestors of our wheat and barley. In the Mesolithic strata at Mugharet el-Wad were found sickles of curved bones set with small sharp flints showing a polished edge such as would be produced by rubbing against stalks of grain. The unusual feature was that no pottery was discovered nor other accompaniments of agriculture. Elsewhere along with sickles the bones of domestic animals appear. Thus man learned to supplement his hunting and fishing and collecting of food by controlling nature to a certain extent, and savagery gave way to barbarism, which increased its food supply by cultivating edible plants or domesticating animals, or both. Thus, very gradually through hundreds of years, came the Neolithic revolution.

3. *Prehistoric Barbarism*   Where wheat and barley originated is a moot question. Probably it was somewhere in the Near East, just possibly in Palestine. All known evidence points to the Near and Middle East as the region in which Neolithic culture, with the cultivation of grains, the domestication of animals, and the making of pottery, began. Palestine entered the Neolithic phase of culture along

with the rest of the Near East. How widely spread and how numerous the population was cannot be determined. Flints are found on the surface and in excavations in many parts of the country, but excavation has also revealed them still in use at the beginning of the Hebrew monarchy. Unless located in stratified deposits, they are, therefore, no evidence of Neolithic occupation, but only of a cultural lag in a poverty-stricken country.

All over North Africa and the Near East the Neolithic expansion of food supplies brought increase of population. The severe fluctuations of the Glacial period ended about 22,000 years ago. There may have been a gradual desiccation for 12,000 to 14,000 years, but only minor fluctuations in rainfall. In Palestine and neighboring countries a relatively dry climate had prevailed with no greater variations in rainfall and temperature than in historic times. An agricultural and pastoral economy kept a considerable and growing popuation alive in villages and tents, with a few still dwelling in caves.

Villages probably were very small and perhaps at first impermanent. Childe cites a Thessalian village that covered one acre. The mound of Jarmo, the "earliest available village" in the Fertile Crescent, covered three acres and its mound was twenty-five feet deep. How much of it was occupied at one time is uncertain. Flint tools, stone bowls, pottery bowls and jars, occasional female figurines, painted pottery with geometric designs in well-marked bands and with an occasional angular human figure are found in the earliest villages yet excavated in the Tigris-Euphrates area. The Carbon[14] date for Jarmo is tentatively set at 4756 ± 320 years.

Though never completely excavated at any level, prehistoric Jericho, lying beside its bountiful spring under tons of debris, has the distinction for the present of being the oldest walled city known. Its well-constructed walls and a round tower with an interior stairway go down to a level much below a radiocarbon dating taken from materials in the prepottery Neolithic strata of at least as early as 6000 B.C. That is, it had long been a walled city before that date. More than one culture had come in from elsewhere and occupied the attractive, well-watered site.

Much later a somewhat different culture developed at Teleilat el-Ghassul some ten miles away across the Jordan. It consisted of rectangular mud-brick houses in small groups of two or more, all together covering an area half a mile long by a quarter of a mile wide. It was impossible to determine how many of the structures were occupied at one time during the several hundred years of the settlement's existence, archaeologically dated to *c.* 4000–3400. There was no enclosing wall or other perceptible means of defense.

Among Jericho's most remarkable discoveries were two groups of three clay figures molded on "skeletons" of reeds; each apparently represents a triad: man, woman, and child. They were about two-thirds of life size. Viewed full face, they were remarkably lifelike. From the side, the heads looked like disks. But the limbs were rounded and exhibited some realistic observation, although far from perfect proportions. To the same period belong a half-dozen lifelike heads, made by modeling marl on human skulls. None of these was found *in situ,* and their use can only be surmised. At Teleilat el-Ghassul three highly artistic frescoes were found painted on plastered mud walls. In one of them four concentric eight-pointed stars, accurately drawn, each a remarkable sunburst, are surrounded by now-fragmentary human figures. In another, a man faces seated figures of which only the feet remain, one pair with embroidered shoes. A third wall has a bird painted with remarkable verve and naturalism. Nothing has remained by which to interpret the paintings but what they themselves reveal. Magic or worship is suggested.

Various objects supposed to have magical value, especially female figurines in clay, the so-called mother-goddess amulets or fetishes, are much more numerous in the Neolithic than in the Mesolithic period. In Jericho a building with polished floor resembled a Homeric megaron with a hexastyle porch. It had no domestic furniture and no hearth, but a central post to support the roof. In its neighborhood were numerous small clay figurines of animals: the cow, goat, sheep, pig, and possibly the dog. Other objects seem to represent a cobra head, the male organs, and small cones. The building was possibly the center of a fertility cult. It was found in stratum XI, early in the Neolithic period (before 4500). The painted building at Teleilat el-Ghassul may have been a thousand years later.

In Mesopotamia buildings that can be recognized as temples come late in the Neolithic, at the earliest in the Halaf period, about 4000, at Tepe Gaura in the north and at Abu Shahrein (ancient Eridu) in the south. At Tepe Gaura and Arpachiyyah, *tholoi* were found, large round buildings, exceptionally well built. Since no other use can be suggested, they are taken for temples—a poor but plausible argument. However, there can be no doubt that the dead were buried there with the expectation of some kind of future life and that supernatural powers were invoked by those in need, in danger, or in distress. The great temple-building period coincided with the beginning of literacy.

The Neolithic period, then, in Palestine and elsewhere developed agriculture, pottery, and the domestication of animals. The plaiting of mats out of reeds comes early; the weaving of textiles, i.e., cloth out of wool and flax (cotton in India), eventually supplied substitutes for the skins of animals as clothing. The many uses and varieties of pottery, pots, bowls, jugs, cups, even hard-baked sickles and axes of clay, along with polished stone tools and bowls, and tools of wood, bone, and ivory, all contributed to make life and the means of supporting it more rich, varied, and secure. The artistic impulse expressed itself in a great variety of colored designs on pottery, as well as in diverse shapes, and in carvings of different kinds. Wall paintings may have been common, but they are rarely preserved, for arid regions like that at Teleilat el-Ghassul are not often inhabited. The storage of food, in pits lined with stones or clay or baked bricks or in bins built of these materials, contributed greatly to security between harvests and in times of drought. The Tigris-Euphrates and Nile valleys were made much more productive by the extension of irrigation. From Egypt through Palestine and all the way around the Fertile Crescent, over the mountains into Iran to Tall-i-Bakun near Persepolis, to Tepe Hissar and on to Anau, to Baluchistan, and finally to the Indus Valley, essentially the same level of culture, with local variations, prevailed.

In the absence of writing, the modern historian can discover no political, but only cultural, connections among all these widely separated communities. They vary in their pottery, tools, houses, and other attainments. No two show exactly the same assemblages. Yet in spite of their varied geographic and climatic conditions, there is the same basic agricultural-village culture. They are in the main small, unwalled villages. Perhaps the normal size was three or four acres, with sixteen to twenty houses and a population of from 200 to 400 persons. Yet the pottery shows that there have been migrations, importations, and borrowings, from Persia into the Tigris-Euphrates Valley, from Palestine into Egypt, and vice versa.

It must not be supposed that there was gradual, linear growth from the crudities of the Neandertal cave dwellers at Mugharet el-Wad to the relative advancement of Jericho houses with painted and polished floors, and from the unbaked pottery of Neolithic Jericho to the high artistry of Samarra and Tall-i-Bakun ware. One village went up and another went down. At one time Tell Halaf spread its wares from Lake Van and Mosul to Alexandretta. At another 'Obeid pottery appeared at Carchemish and Gaura. Type after type of pottery prevailed and was succeeded by others. Techniques consistently improved for a long period but declined when metals seized the public interest.

The Neolithic period shades imperceptibly into the Chalcolithic. In Palestine it is customary to speak of a Subchalcolithic phase beginning about 4250 and followed by Early, Middle, and Late Chalcolithic periods, each lasting some 250 years. The Subchalcolithic period exhibits the sporadic appearance of copper ornaments or bits of copper of unknown use; the full Chalcolithic begins with more abundant remains of the metal but has few useful tools. Stone for tools was still a successful rival of metal. Vessels and other useful copper objects come to light in Mesopotamia in the Protoliterate ('Obeid-Uruk) period, the Palestinian Late Chalcolithic. At about the same time the use of tools of hardened copper or bronze introduced higher agricultural productivity, and the beginning of writing prepared for an increased population and the building of cities. Thus came another peaceful revolution, or, better, another step in social evolution that introduced civilization.

It may seem that a disproportionate amount of attention has been given to the somewhat shadowy figure of prehistoric man. It is disproportionate only because we know so much more and can write so much more glibly about historic times in the Near East from, say, 3200 to 1200. Actually, if "historic" be understood in terms of "what actually came to pass," of what was discovered and invented in techniques that made civilization possible, in terms of social evolution as well as of lapse of time, the accomplishments of prehistory were more difficult and culturally more fruitful than what was achieved in the first 2000 years of "civilization." With the sole exception of the linear alphabet, in the previous 20,000 years the Near East acquired all of the essential characteristics which marked it from 3000 to the flowering of Greek and Persian culture and Hebrew religion in the middle of the last pre-Christian millennium.

4. *The City Revolution*   The fourth millennium came to a close in both Egypt and Mesopotamia under very different conditions from those of the fifth. In Egypt, predynastic separatism, attacked by the Scorpion and Narmer, gave way to Menes and the First Dynasty about 2900. In Mesopotamia, the Sumerian, or Protoliterate, Age—that is, the period marked by the first writing and the use of the Sumerian language—was succeeded by the Early Dynastic period about 2800. In both countries scattered peasant communities were succeeded by organized city life. The organization, however, was very different in the two countries.

In Egypt it was not organized city life that marked the difference so much as a national organization that combined Upper and Lower Egypt and gradually consolidated the two during Dynasties I and II (2900–2700). In Mesopotamia there was no general organization until Sargon of Akkad (*c.* 2340) made an empire out of a large number of conquered cities. However, toward the close of the Protoliterate period began the organization of cities into states that resembled those of Greece in the first millennium much more closely than they do our urban communities.

Even so, in neither land was there a distinct urban civilization based on trade, commerce, and industry, nor was there a sharp and sudden change in the nature of the economy. The basis of living still was agriculture. Every citizen, even the soldier and the city official, was still a farmer. John A. Wilson remarks that Gordon Childe's theory of an urban revolution is just and acute as a theory but only if understood as neither urban nor a revoluton. However, a gradual but marked increase in the material goods available for living was accompanied by a rapid growth in population, by its concentration in much larger units, and by various changes in the techniques of production. Which was cause and which effect is difficult to determine. Doubtless all changes derived from preparatory developments in Neolithic, non-writing times.

Various factors combined in the millennium between 3500 and 2500 to make for progress. Among them were writing, bronze, technical specialization, economic organization, and commerce. It would be a serious error to emphasize a sudden expansion at either 5000 (the Neolithic revolution) or 3000, when the city revolution is set down in the chronological charts. Slowly acquired ability to write and record business transactions made a much more ambitious and complicated economy possible, but certain accidents dominate written history.

A minor and, let us hope, temporary handicap is the small number of prehistoric sites penetrated by archaeology, since they are so often buried under the heavier remains of later generations. More important is the fact that written records are not so necessary for a rich culture as modern man thinks. Memory among those who do not write or read has uses and values that the literate has lost. Think of the business transactions an old-fashioned Chinese merchant carried in his head! The less paper work the more time for business. Written documents give the historian such a sudden enlargement of horizon that it has been customary to make the beginning of (written) history a landmark of the utmost significance. In real history (that is, the actual course of events) the introduction of writing can have brought about change and enhanced progress only almost imperceptibly, because culture was already high and writing could have been neither invented and perfected all at once nor learned quickly, and then only by an inconsiderable number of persons. Nevertheless, the expansion of civilization when cities eventually developed out of Mesopotamian peasant villages was enormous.

Actual business records show that the temple owned the tillable land of many cities and apportioned land, labor, and sustenance according to certain fixed rules. The temple officials were masters of life and death. Yet this Sumerian hierocratic socialism apparently long maintained a satisfactory balance between the individual and the state. It did not entirely disappear until the time of Hammurabi.

Agriculture in the village communities had been enlarged and made secure by irrigation. Through fuller co-operation under the larger city organization, it was further expanded to make the "land between the rivers" still more productive and safe from drought and inundation. The use of copper and bronze tools helped pay for their importation by rendering labor easier and more productive. The improved plow, the the wheel, and increased use of asses (or small horses) were labor-saving devices. The somewhat complicated and detailed records of the communal use of temple lands reveal an economy that would have suffered seriously without writing or, indeed, would have been impossible.

The socialization of land and of other economic goods may have discouraged individual initiative, but it contributed to the security of the individual and the city-state. Irrigation from the rivers would have been severely limited and even extremely difficult without some authority representing the entire community, just as water is now provided in our cities by public authority. The Tennessee Valley Authority is a modern analogue to practice in ancient Mesopotamia and Egypt. At the same time, in Mesopotamia individual ownership of properties of individual use and concern was conserved, while the temple management seems to have been fairly equalitarian. Specialization in the crafts and arts made for technical proficiency and enlarged productivity.

In spite of communized agriculture, the political and judicial democracy of the ancient city-states is notable. Actually it goes back to preliterate times, as is demonstrated by myths of the gods in which judgments and decisions are rendered by the whole body of deities. The senior gods often act, but final decisions are made in the assembly, which includes both male and female deities. Various documents indicate that the same kind of government prevailed in the city-states: a council of elders and the assembly of the people. (Whether women were included is uncertain.) The assembly settled conflicts within the community, decided upon war and peace, and, under stress of attack, could delegate supreme authority to one member for a limited period.

With increasing wars among the cities and invasions from without, this primitive democracy was succeeded by more or less permanent dynasties. The famous Sargon of Akkad seems to have settled his own followers on the common lands that belonged to the city (or the temple) and thus to have put an end to equalitarian socialism, which had once insured the life and promoted the good of every citizen. The speech put into Samuel's mouth by the theological corrector of 1 Samuel (8:11–18) had a fitting illustration in the tyranny of the kings of Mesopotamia some 2000 years earlier. The urge for security triumphed over the joys and responsibilities of primitive democracy. Authority shifted from people to monarch, and private property became the rule, not the exception.

In Mesopotamia the hegemony shifted from one city to another, and dynasties changed from century to century.The Amorites infiltrated the Sumerians peaceably and later took over certain cities by force. The Kings of Sumer and Akkad brought a Sumerian renaissance. The Gutians, followed by the Hurrians and the Elamites from the mountain barrier east of the Tigris, invaded and destroyed one and another dynasty in the river plains, while the Amorites from northern Mesopotamia and Mari on the middle Euphrates pressed upon them from the other side. Yet civilization continued and even the short-lived dynasties became tremendous builders.

One of the evidences of the prosperity of the Sumerian and Semite city-states is the enormous energy put into temple building. A beginning had been made in Protoliterate times, but it was immoderately expanded within the next few centuries. The great earthen mounds of the ziggurats that they piled up came almost to rival the Pharaonic pyramids, in size if not in durability. The frown and favor of the gods were taken seriously. Also the institution that played so large a part in the economic life of the community would naturally wish to glorify itself. At the same time, its business organization demanded enlarged facilities and quarters, and its control of the economic life of the city gave it command of the city's resources. Bank and "church" were one.

It is not possible to determine how far mundane and cynical incentives were responsible for the apparent enthusiasm that built and rebuilt. When kingly rule at least nominally replaced that of the priests, the same policy continued. Perhaps temporal wealth only made possible an intensified quest for communion with the unseen forces of the universe through closer contact with the divine, or at least supernatural, Power that resided on some mythical mountain.

As time went on, the kings built for themselves even as they built for the gods. Early excavation has made Assyrian palaces familiar. They were anything but singular. Zimri-Lim of Mari in the eighteenth century had a palace that covered fifteen acres, and the palace records in thousands of Akkadian tablets tell a story of wide commercial relations and active business. It was an international period. Zimri-Lim received a present of a gold vase from King Yantin-'ammu of Byblos, whom the Egyptians knew as Entin. But his magnificent palace and his royal prestige brought him no security. About the time of his death Hammurabi of Babylon captured Mari and made an end of his dynasty. A little later the Hyksos and then the Mitannians swarmed over his country. A century and a half after Hammurabi a chance raid of the Hittites from far-off Asia Minor and then occupation by the Kassites (Cossaeans) from nearby Luristan put an end to the dynasty of Hammurabi and to Babylonian cultural progress for two centuries.

The patriarchal age, which may be thought of as beginning about the time of Hammurabi (*c.* 1728–1686), is a period when the Near Eastern world as the Hebrews knew it was beginning to take form. Later, for many centuries Babylon was in eclipse. For two centuries or more there was a catastrophic interruption of written records in both Egypt and Mesopotamia and apparently of other civilized activities in the whole Near Eastern area. However, excavation in Palestine, Syria, and Mesopotamia has recovered the material remains of the cultures of this interregnum. Fragmentary records along with the comparison of what preceded with what followed make it possible to reconstruct the general course of developments. In the fifteenth century the darkened picture begins to come into the light once more, and materials are abundant for the two or three crucial centuries that prepared for the settlement of Canaan by the descendants of the Patriarchs.

CHAPTER V

The Hebrews: Racial and Cultural Inheritance

1. *Artifact and Tablet* Out of ninety millennia of savagery, seven millennia of barbarism, and two of civilization, Near Eastern society emerged as the cultural inheritance that came to the Hebrews when they settled in the Promised Land. For the person who is now trying to discover what actually developed in the ancient world, a feature of outstanding significance, in the two millennia immediately preceding the Conquest, is progress in the art of writing. During 1500 years the complicated little groups of wedges of Sumerian-Akkadian cuneiform ideographs and syllables had been pressed into a sufficient multitude of clay tablets for the outlines of political and social history in the Near East to become clear to the modern scholar. But a better device was discovered shortly before the Hebrews entered Palestine.

Alphabets were invented by inhabitants of Syria-Palestine itself. At about the same time, while the Mycenaean Greeks were carrying on business with their crude Linear A and B scripts, two systems arose. A cuneiform alphabet of some twenty-eight or twenty-nine characters was put into use in Ugarit (Ras esh-Shamrah) on the northern coast of Syria, and the immediate predecessor of the Hebrew-Phoenician-Greek linear alphabet was developed, possibly in southern Palestine, probably under the stimulation of Egyptian hieroglyphs and the difficulty of their use.

The linear Phoenician alphabet proved to be so practical that, beginning in the thirteenth century, it came into general use throughout Syria and Palestine. It displaced the Ugaritic cuneiform alphabet and other recently invented scripts. Eventually it supplanted the Akkadian

58

syllabic cuneiform that had been employed in Palestine (in the Amarna tablets and other sporadic pieces) for official purposes and was the medium of communication in the second great international period, the Late Bronze Age. The linear alphabet, which appears in Palestine and at the Sinaitic porphyry mines in the Middle Bronze Age (before 1500), was slow in gaining acceptance. But long and wholly intelligible inscriptions, as on the Ahiram sarcophagus, show it in full use in the late eleventh and early tenth century, at the beginning of the Hebrew monarchy. Some Canaanite, who knew a little of Egyptian hieroglyphs, had conceived a brilliant and extraordinary idea that never had occurred to the learned priests of Egypt or the scribes of Babylon. The Hebrews never needed to learn those hundreds of crabbed characters used in the great centers of ancient learning, but could keep the records of the Hebrew monarchy from the beginning and write down their ancestral traditions in twenty-two easily learned, simple letters.

The linear alphabet was not suited to the clay tablet, but it could be readily inscribed with a reed pen and ink on skins or the abundant papyrus of Egypt. Doubtless one reason why no contemporary records remain from the early Hebrews is that they became writing-conscious when pen and ink and papyrus took the place of stylus and tablet. Fortunately the unglazed pottery everywhere in use would also take ink from a reed pen, and specimens of early Hebrew script have come down to us on the lowly potsherd (*ostrakon*), which was as common as waste paper is with us and rather more durable. The Moabite Stone, the Siloam Tunnel inscription, and a few other brief documents cut or scratched in stone or pottery, and short notes of capacity and ownership impressed or written on unburnt pottery are building up a useful paleographic record of the development of the alphabet. They also testify to a considerable literacy during the later monarchy.

Archaeology and the artifact must not be forgotten in the avid search for written documents and for their decipherment and interpretation. How poor our conception of Periclean Athens would be if we had no Parthenon or Athenian vase paintings! How dull our picture of Babylon without ziggurat and Ishtar Gate! Putting artifact and tablet together, the student can live the life of ancient Ur or Babylon over again. Words may have no meaning without the artifact to which they refer.

There is a verse in 1 Samuel (13:21) telling the cost to the Hebrews of going to the Philistines to sharpen their tools. It was meaningless until, one day in a souvenir dealer's shop in Jerusalem, George A. Barton picked up a small stone weight and saw *pim* carved on it in ancient Hebrew characters. He remembered that the word appears only once in the Hebrew Bible, in that verse in Samuel, and that no one knew what it meant. Even the Septuagint translator (before 200 B.C.) could not unravel the mystery. Many such weights have since been found and the knowledge that *pim* means a weight (of one-fourth to one-third of an ounce) has made it possible to unravel the meaning of the sentence (see RSV).

How slowly archaeological information travels is illustrated by the still-continuing use of "plowshare" (for *eth*) in the same verse and elsewhere. Nothing resembling a modern plowshare, or coulter, has ever been excavated in Palestine. The word *eth* stood for a short tube of iron hammered down to a point, which was thrust over the pointed lower end of the wooden stock of the plow. This "plow point" does not cut but digs, or better scratches, through the ground. It is one of the reasons yields have always been small in the Near East. Not merely in such minor matters, but much more in the large terms of total atmosphere, knowledge of the culture of the ancient Near East assists in understanding the religion of the Bible. Of these matters more later.

2. *Language and Race* A significant historical factor in Near Eastern history is the mixture of races and languages. The racial character of the Israelite population and the neighboring states is not closely determinable. That is not strange. Where in the world is such knowledge possible? Only in a few isolated racial islands. Certainly in all the Near East there was a large variety of strains. The original inhabitants of the Tigris-Euphrates Valley, the Sumerians, were an unclassifiable race with an unclassifiable language. The majority were Semitic in speech, consisting chiefly of Canaanites and Amorites (the Amurru of northwest Mesopotamia). To them large Aramean and Arabic elements from the steppe were added before 2000, and repeatedly later.

At the beginning of historical records, a chieftain of the Amorites was at Mari on the Euphrates over 200 miles northwest of Babylon and across the desert from Byblos and Palmyra. His race spread northward, westward, and eastward and settled among the Sumerians until gradually it conquered and absorbed them and their culture. The Amorites replaced the Sumerian language with their own (Semitic) Akkadian, which they had learned to write in cuneiform characters adopted from the vanquished. But they were not left undisturbed. Minor and major intrusions from the mountains to the north and east and from the nomadic Semites of the Arabian steppe constantly disturbed peaceful progress. Palestine, like Mesopotamia, was never quiet for any long period.

There were at least three major non-Semitic racial and linguistic intrusions into the Near East, in addition to the Sumerians: the Hurrians, the Mitannians, and the Hittites. About 2400 the Hurrian race appeared to the east of the Zagros Mountains and northward toward Lake Urumiah. They spread into southern, northern, and eventually northwestern Mesopotamia and became a principal constituent in the population from Nuzi in the east to Harran and beyond in the west. Some of them followed the Hyksos into Syria and Palestine and formed a distinct group there from the seventeenth to the fifteenth century. They were so numerous that some Egyptian documents call Palestine "Hurru land." They were absorbed into the Canaanite population and eventually formed an element of the Israelites, whose occasional Armenoid features may stem from that race. By a false etymology their name was equated with Hebrew *hor,* "cave," and they appear in the Bible as Horites, "cave dwellers," as the poor and depressed often still are in the Near East. Their language was neither Sumerian, Semitic, Elamitic, nor Indo-European. However, progress is being made in interpreting it.

Hurrian words and documents almost always appear in connection with some other language, for the Hurrians seem always to be secondary or subject to others. They have been found at Amarna and Boghazköy, in the Ugaritic tablets, and at Mari. Their names crop up everywhere from Nuzi to Jerusalem. Abdi-khipa, or Abdu-kheba, of

Jerusalem in the Amarna tablets has, in turn, been thought a Hittite, a Mitannian, and now a Hurrian, worshiper of the Hurrian goddess, Kheba. Their name, Hurri, was first recognized in 1915, and their emergence as a factor in history has been slow and uncertain, but they must be accepted as a part of the Hebrew cultural, as well as racial, heritage.

The Mitannian kingdom, another fairly recent archaeological discovery, appeared in northern Mesopotamia in the sixteenth century or earlier. The rulers were Indo-European in language for they worshiped Mithra, Indra, Varuna, and the Nasatyas. Their migration into Mesopotamia was probably an offshoot of that *Völkerwanderung* that sent the Aryans into India and the Iranians into Persia. Probably they followed in the wake of the Hyksos (see below). They established an empire across northern Mesopotamia that at one time ranged from the Mediterranean to the Zagros Mountains. Driving in on their chariots, they submerged the Hurrians and other inhabitants and ruled over them as a warrior caste; but, since they were small in number, they did not deeply affect the total culture of the region.

Meantime, another power, the Hittites (Kheta), had slowly arisen in eastern Asia Minor, with Cappadocia as its core. They were a remarkable mixture of racial and linguistic elements, but the dominating strain again seems to have been Indo-European. They came, perhaps before 2000, from Europe into Anatolia in two waves. The first crossed to the south and settled all along the coast; the second stopped in the north-central part about the Halys River. They absorbed various previous inhabitants of the region and set up the "Old Empire" in the seventeenth century under three kings, father, son, and grandson. They had a hieroglyphic system of writing, but they learned, doubtless from the Assyrian merchant colony at Kanish (Kül-tepe) on the Halys, to write their language in cuneiform. The latter was deciphered with relative ease, but the hieroglyphic, having no Rosetta stone, is only now slowly yielding its secrets. The "Old Empire" exploded in a raid that crossed all Mesopotamia to destroy Babylon and its First Dynasty about 1600. Thereafter it was in turmoil and for nearly two centuries it played no international role.

In the Late Bronze Age, during the eighteenth Egyptian dynasty, the Hittites appear again as an empire that reached from the Black Sea to the Mediterranean and Aleppo and from west of the Halys to the Euphrates. In attempting to extend the "New Empire" south into Syria, they came into conflict with Ramses II and, in spite of Ramses' boasting, it is clear that the struggle ended in a stalemate and a marriage between the eldest daughter of the Hittite king and the Pharaoh.

Although the Hittites never penetrated farther south or east, the Hebrews could be supposed to appeal to them for military aid even in the days of Ahab (2 Kings 7:6). Numerous references to the children of Heth in the Old Testament (from Genesis 10:15 to Ezra 9:1) point up their part in the history of the lands of Syria and Palestine. They seem to have been an important constituent of the population. That Uriah the Hittite (2 Sam. 11) had a Hurrian, but also apparently a Yahwist, name suggests the absorption of many of his like by the Israelites. Arauna the Jebusite (2 Sam. 24:18) has been supposed to be a Hittite also. But a Mitannian prince of that name has been found in Syria four centuries earlier. This and other similar evidence have been put along with the fact that, while all the other towns in the mountains of Judah, all doubtless Semitic in language, fell to the Hebrews on their entry into the country, Jerusalem held out until David could rally an army sufficient to capture it. In other words, the city was in the hands of non-Semitic intruders, Mitannian, Hurrian, and Hittite, who would not surrender until a bold stratagem broke their defense.

All parts of the Fertile Crescent were open to attacks, from within by the hungry nomadic peoples of the steppe, from without by hardy and often hungry mountaineers, who ringed it on the north and east, and from sea raiders on the west. Sporadic raids that merely carried off booty constantly weakened the cities of the Tigris-Euphrates Valley. The Elamites were a threat to southern Babylonia, the peoples behind the Zagros Mountains to those farther north. About 2180 the dynasty of Akkad was overthrown by the Zagros mountaineers of Gutium. Elamites and Amorites put an end to the Third Dynasty of Ur *c*. 2025. Hittites from the far northwest and Kassites from the near-by southern Zagros Mountains overthrew Hammurabi's dynasty. The stela containing Hammurabi's laws, found at Susa, may serve as a symbol of the quenching of the torch of culture at Babylon for centuries. It was one of the tragic accidents of history.

For Palestine, the most significant of these invasions was that of the Hyksos. It had a quite different effect. The language, origin, and racial composition of the Hyksos are still undetermined, and their place in history is a problem only partially solved. However, the discoveries of the last generation have clarified the general character of their influence on culture in Syria, Palestine, and Egypt. There was a nucleus of chariot-driving warriors whose great rectangular camps, surrounded by ramparts of beaten earth (*terre pisée*), have been traced backward from Tell el-Yehudiyeh, near Heliopolis in the Egyptian delta, to the Shantung province in China, through Tell el-'Ajjul (Gaza), Tell el-Far'ah, Tell ed-Duweir (Lachish), Tell Beit-Mirsim (Kiriath Sepher), Tell el-Hesi, Askelon, Jericho, Tell Balatah (Shechem), Tell Ta'anek, Megiddo, Tell Keisan, Tell el-Qedah (Hazor), Tell el-Qadi (Dan), and half a dozen places in Syria, to somewhat similar fortifications found in Transcaspia and Iran. Whether their origin was central Asiatic is uncertain. Indeed, beyond northern Syria their track is conjectural.

There were non-Semitic elements among them, in part doubtless Hurrian. But, aside from some names borrowed from Egyptian and others which were those of Egyptian quislings, their names are chiefly Semitic. The evidence is now taken to indicate that there was Semitic infiltration into Egypt at the beginning of the Second Interregnum at the end of Dynasty XII (*c.* 1780). About 1730, with the aid of the invading chariot riders, the Fifteenth Dynasty was established at Avaris (later Tanis) in the northeastern Delta, and an empire was built up that ruled Palestine and a large part of Syria. Its control over Egypt was loose. Its real center seems to have been Palestine, with nominal control from southern Nubia to the Euphrates.

While Egypt languished, Palestine was superficially more prosperous than at any time before or after for many centuries. The scarabs of officials, used for sealing documents and jars, are more numerous than at any other period and attest their dominance in Palestine from *c.* 1700 to 1550. It was a time of enlarging cities, growing population, and increasing feudal luxury, as city walls and buildings and the contents of tombs of the period, but especially the booty that Thothmes III took at Megiddo, demonstrate. The most attractive conjecture attributes the growth of wealth to widespread commerce, of which there is sufficient archaeological evidence, for Palestine at the center would profit by trade throughout the great extent of territory controlled by the government. The character of ornaments, weapons, and other artifacts suggests that fertile and industrious Egypt, with its hinterland on the Upper Nile, was one source of Palestinian wealth.

3. *Egypt and the Hebrews* In view of the proximity, power, and high culture of Egypt, Palestine and the Hebrews would be expected to owe much to the land of the Pharaohs. They derived little linguistic material. As to racial contribution, the evidence is uncertain. As to culture, especially art and literature, the situation is different. The story of the Sojourn in Egypt and the Exodus suggests high expectations. The political history of the contacts between the two regions adds to them. The "wretched Asiatics" had entered the Delta during the First Intermediate period. The Twelfth Dynasty (c. 1989–1776) had close relations with Palestine, according to Egyptian records, and probably dominated the coastal area and its trade. The Second Intermediate period and the following Hyksos regime are now seen to mean the enrichment of Palestine and its people at the expense of Egypt. The Eighteenth Dynasty, having driven the Hyksos out, followed them up into their heart land, Palestine, overthrew their power there, and finally followed through to their great north Syrian fortresses at Qatna and Kadesh, where the Egyptians came into contact with the empires of the Hittites and Mitanni. The Hyksos power was completely destroyed.

During the next four and a half centuries the tables were turned, and Palestine enriched Egypt (1550–1100). "When Egypt ruled the East," to use Steindorff and Seele's expressive title, the tablets from Amarna and tablets, reliefs, and other records in cuneiform and hieroglyphic found in Palestine demonstrate the dominance of Egypt. Not only in the south along Wadi Ghazzeh but at Jericho, Megiddo, Beth-shan, in the Hauran, by the Sea of Galilee at Tell el-'Oreimeh, and elsewhere, the Pharaohs built fortresses, left their inscribed monuments, and deposited evidence of their conquests. They were still in nominal control during the period of the biblical Judges and almost up to the time of the monarchy. But except for an occasional city (e.g., Jerusalem) their monuments do not include the mountains of Samaria and Judah. Consequently the Hebrews were able to enter and settle there while the Egyptians ruled the roads and the plains. Only the famous stela of Mer-ne-Ptah mentions Israel as a nomadic people in Palestine (*c.* 1230).

Solomon's alliance with a Pharaoh of the Twenty-fifth Dynasty (1 Kings 3:1) and marriage to an Egyptian princess, followed by the gift of Gerar (or Gezer) to Solomon, points to the interest of Egypt in her small neighbor to the northeast. Jeroboam's flight to Egypt for refuge with Shishak (Sheshonk), when Solomon sought to kill him (1 Kings 11:40), and Shishak's later expedition into Palestine to establish his control confirm the continuance of that interest. Egyptian intrigue at Jerusalem went on in Isaiah's day. Finally Josiah's tragic death at Megiddo at the hands of Necho illustrates Egypt's need to control this buffer state.

The contacts between Egypt and Palestine after the rise of the Hebrew monarchy, however, were quite different from those of Dynasties XVIII and XIX. Ramses III (1195–1164) never went farther north than southern Phoenicia. His statue was found at Beth-shan, and at Megiddo a notice of his rule remained. Egyptian documents tell of his building a temple for Amon in Palestine and mention the payment of dues by nine Palestinian towns to the god. But he was called upon to meet a new threat, an invasion of the Sea Peoples, Philistines, Sicilians, Teucrians, perhaps Achaeans and Danaäns (Greeks).

4. *The Philistines* The Sea Peoples seem to represent the last, far-flung spray of the wave of migration that wracked southern Europe and Asia Minor in the second half of the second millennium. Hebrew tradition had the Philistines coming from Caphtor (Crete), but according to the contemporary Egyptian records they came down the coast with their wives and children riding in oxcarts. Since they were ac-

companied by ships, which engaged the Egyptian fleet, some may have come by way of Crete. The painting of their defeat by Ramses, somewhere on the Palestinian coast, is remarkably dramatic and also instructive as to the character of the invasion. It was no mere raid. That Ramses was able to defeat them saved Egypt, but his failure to destroy them or drive them back brought a new racial and cultural element and a new era to Palestine.

The Philistines occupied the seacoast plain and for a time the Plains of Esdraelon and Jezreel, the richest part of Palestine. From the coast they were never dislodged, and they condemned the Hebrews to becoming permanently mountaineers, with only brief and small opportunities to emulate their Phoenician cousins as seagoing merchants. They brought with them a distinctive style in pottery; they introduced the use of iron and for a time this technical advantage reduced the Hebrew to vassalage (1 Sam. 13). Perhaps they introduced new architectural ideas also. The legend of Samson's death suggests such sports as the Cretans enjoyed in their palace areas. Apparently they were illiterate and shortly abandoned their own language and religion for those of their subjects. Philistine pottery, made in Palestine in imitation of that which the invaders brought with them, disappeared after 150 years (1150–1000). The conquerors were swallowed up by the conquered.

Nevertheless, brief as their heyday was, they deeply affected Hebrew development. They interposed a strong barrier between the Israelites and the stream of commerce that followed the "oldest road in the world" along the coast, and they held the coast open, as a bridgehead, for the incoming Western culture when the Greeks began to sail the seas and seek room in the East. Their threat to Hebrew independence produced the monarchy in Israel and the epic figures of Saul and David. They had another effect upon the Hebrews. The story of David indicates that Hebrews and the seacoast peoples could be friends when it seemed politic. Moreover, the Carites, Cherethites, and Pelethites were Carians, Cretans, and Philistines. As foreigners, they could be trusted to take the part of their employer against his subjects. They add a drop of still-different blood with strange genes to the racial inheritance of the Hebrews.

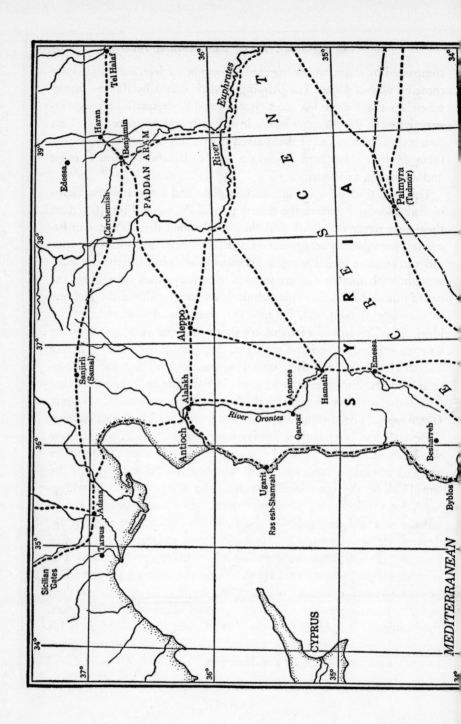

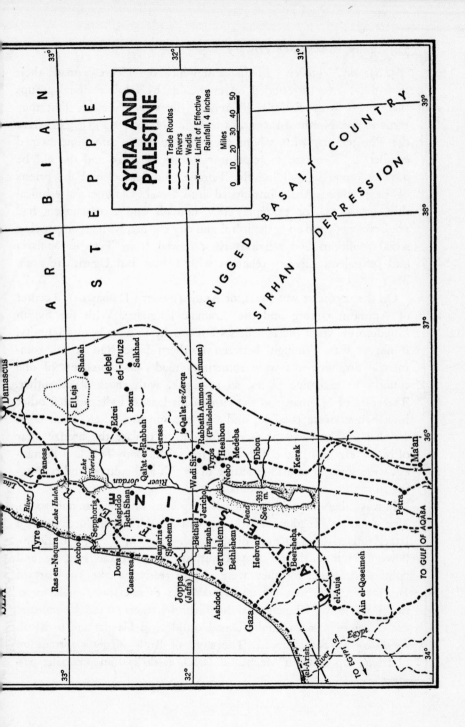

SYRIA AND PALESTINE

- Trade Routes
- Rivers
- Wadis
- Limit of Effective Rainfall, 4 inches

Miles
0 10 20 30 40 50

ARABIAN STEPPE

RUGGED BASALT COUNTRY

SIRHAN DEPRESSION

Damascus

El Leja

Shabah

Jebel ed-Druze

Salkhad

Edrei

Bosra

Qalat ez-Zerqa

Gerasa

Rabbath Ammon (Amman)
(Philadelphia)

Qalat er-Rabbah

Wadi Sir

Tyros

Heshbon

Nebo

Medeba

Dibon

Kerak

Ma'an

Paneas

Lake Huleh

Lake Tiberias

River Jordan

Tyre

Ras en-Naqura

Accho

Sepphoris

Megiddo

Beth Shan

Dora

Caesarea

Samaria

Shechem

Bethel

Mizpah

Jericho

Dead Sea 393 m.

Petra

TO GULF OF AQABA

Joppa (Jaffa)

Jerusalem

Bethlehem

Hebron

Beersheba

Ashdod

Gaza

el-Auja

Ain el-Qoseimeh

el-Arish

River of Egypt

TO EGYPT

5. *Syrian Neighbors* In the land which the Hebrews made their own they were surrounded on every side by small national groups that spoke, with dialectic differences, the same language that they came to use. North of them, in the region of Byblos and Ugarit were the Phoenicians, with whom they almost never came into armed conflict. It is enough to remember Hiram of Tyre and the aid he gave Solomon in building the Temple, and Jezebel and the priests of Baal whom Ahab introduced into Israel. Commerce, technical skill (masonry, for example) that nomads and mountaineers had not developed, and an agricultural and city culture, with accompanying social traditions and religious rites, flowed from Tyre to Samaria and Jerusalem. Literary relations with Byblos and Ugarit are notable.

On the northeast was Syria, or Aram (modern Damascus), a center of Aramean culture and the Aramaic language. With the Syrian kingdom of Aram the Israelites seem usually to have been at enmity, if not at war, although, between northern Israel and Aram, commercial arrangements were sometimes made for merchants of one country to exchange places, so to speak, with those of the other. The story of Naaman and the cure of his leprosy indicates that other interchanges were possible; and this is confirmed when Ahaz takes an altar in Damascus as model for one to replace the bronze altar of burnt offerings in the Temple at Jerusalem. Both Tyre and Damascus were superior to arid Palestine in wealth and culture, and borrowing from them was to be expected.

It was otherwise with the small kingdoms on the east and south. The Amorite kingdom which lay east of the lower Jordan when Israel entered Canaan soon disappeared. Ammon, Moab, and Edom, however, remained and played various parts in the military and political situation, for they were always ready to take any part of Israelite territory that lay undefended. As these nations spoke practically the same language as the Hebrews, there could be cultural exchanges of various kinds. David could send his parents to Moab for safety (1 Sam. 22:3 f.). The story of Ruth suggests a tradition of friendship between Moab and Israel, as do certain postexilic passages.

According to the archaeological and historical evidence, the recently nomadic tribes of Ammon, Moab, and Edom were settling down in Transjordan at about the time when the cities of southern Palestine, for example, Lachish and Kiriath-sepher, were destroyed and rebuilt, evidently by the Israelites. That the invaders of western Palestine were also nomads is clear from the sharp drop following the invasion in the size and culture of the captured cities. In other words, the non-Israelite settlers on the east side of the Dead Sea were culturally closely related to the Israelites, whatever may be made of the genealogies and traditions of Genesis about them. Their language, the few inscriptions known, and their pottery are much alike although they make distinctions possible.

Other nomadic tribes still remained in the Negeb and the Sinaitic Peninsula to trouble and influence the Hebrews. The Amalekites and Midianites made dangerous raids. Beyond the Edomites was a prolific source of nomadic culture that, in the fifth century, sent forth the Nabateans to drive Edom into southern Palestine and to usurp the caravan trade from the Mediterranean to Yemen. Thence eventually came the Islamic Arabs. The part that the Negeb played in Israel's political, cultural, and religious history is a significant subject to which it will be necessary to return.

6. *Nomadic Neighbors* The discussion of the races and languages that made the cultural matrix in which the Israelite nation took its shape requires a further word regarding Arab nomadism, to which frequent reference has been made. In spite of the contradiction in terms, nomads are not *ipso facto* uncivilized because of the lack of fixed habitation. Cities are not the necessary index of culture. The culture of the nomads from the Arabian steppe who throughout the centuries have sought to enter and settle in Palestine must not be undervalued.

Nomadic life does not lend itself to the perpetuation of written records. Consequently, although there is ample evidence that the Sabaeans and others in the first millennium were highly literate, almost nothing had been found, until recently, to vouch for the Arabs of the northern steppe in earlier times. The inscriptions now being found in the steppe of Hashimite Jordan, as well as in Nabatean territory, indicate the possibilities. The South Arabian alphabet was an early derivative from the linear Phoenician alphabet. Except for the Rub' al-Khali, the Empty Quarter, the peninsula was criss-crossed with caravan routes. There is no evidence of the use of camels in caravans until the eleventh century. All earlier nomads could use only the ass as a beast of burden, a slow and limited means of travel and commerce, with which the Patriarchs were per-force content. Yet the Arabian Peninsula was in touch by land and sea with all the great cultural lands of antiquity and was thus sub-jected to exciting stimuli from many directions. With the general use of the camel, commerce must have greatly increased just when the Hebrews were building up their settled culture. Amorites, Ara-means, Hebrews, Moabites, Edomites, Nabateans, and the Moslem Arabs all came from that great fountain of humankind, and all very quickly demonstrated their ability to acquire civilization.

PART 2

WHAT THE MOVING FINGER WROTE

WHAT ACTUALLY HAPPENED

Said the Eternal unto Abraham, "Leave your country, leave your kindred, leave your father's house, for a land that I will show you; I will make a great nation of you and bless you and make you famous for your bliss."

GENESIS 12:1–2 (MOFFATT)

Listen to this charge of the Eternal against you, sons of Israel, against the whole race that I brought up from the land of Egypt:

You alone, of all men, have I cared for;
therefore I will punish you for all your misdeeds

AMOS 3:1–2 (MOFFATT)

Bring me my bow of burning gold!
Bring me my arrows of desire!
Bring me my spear! O clouds unfold!
Bring me my chariots of fire!

I will not cease from mental fight,
Nor shall my sword sleep in my hand,
Till we have built Jerusalem
In England's green and pleasant land.

WILLIAM BLAKE

Chronological Table II. From Hammurabi to the Exile

Abbreviations: B=Bronze (Age), C=Century, *c.*=*circa* (about), E=Early, I=Iron (Age), L=Late, M=Middle; (e.g., I i a=Iron, part i, phase a.=10C)

	SYRIA-PALESTINE	MESOPOTAMIA	EGYPT
1830–1530	Babylon, Dyn. I	Hammurabi, *c.* 1728–1686; Code, *c.* 1690	
1700	MB ii b E. Hittite Emp.	Mari: Amorite Age	Hyksos rule, 1710–1550
International Age:	Yantin-Ammu (Syria)	Zimri-Lim (Mari); Hammurabi	Nefer-hotep
1600	MB ii c Hittites ruin	Babylon: Kassite Dyn. 1600–1150	
16C	Sinaitic Alphabet	Mitannian Emp. 16–14C	Dyn. XVIII, 1570–1310
16–13C	"First Internat. Age" (Breasted): Babylonians, Assyrians, Hittites; Arzawans, Cypriotes, Hurrians (Hyksos); *cuneiform the lingua franca*		
15–11C	Egyptians at Megiddo and Beth-shan		Ramses II 1290–1224
15–13C	Israelite infiltration		Thut-mose III, 1490–1435
1500	LB i *Ugaritic Alphabet*	New Hittite Empire	Amen-hotep III, 1406–1370
1400–1350	Amarna Period	Assyrian revival	Akh-en-Aton, 1370–1363
13C	Israelite occupation	Shalmaneser I, 1280–1250	Dyn. XIX, 1310–1200
1220	Mer-ne-Ptah stela	Tukulti-Ninurta, 1234–1197	
1200	I i a; Alalakh ruined		Dyn. XX, 1200–1065
1167	Sea Peoples defeated		Ramses III, *c.* 1175–1144
12C	I i b; Philistines	Tiglath-pileser I, 1115–1056	
1125	Song of Deborah; Gideon		
1050	Fall of Shiloh		
1020	Saul: United Monarchy		
1000	David		
961	Solomon	Tiglath-pileser II, 967	Dyn. XXII, 935–720
922	Division of Monarchy		Shishak I 935
913	Asa in Judah	Adad-nirari II, 912	Osorkon I 914
876	Omri in Israel	Assur-nasir-pal II, 884	Takelot I 874

JUDAH	ISRAEL	ASSYRIA
873 Jehoshaphat	869 Ahab	
849 Jehoram	853 Battle of Qarqar	859 Shalmaneser III
842 Athaliah	842 Jehu; Tribute 841	
837 Jehoash	(8C Hesiod)	811 Adad-nirari III
783 Uzziah (Azariah)	786 Jeroboam II	
750–700 Amos; Hosea; Micah	745 Menahem	745 Tiglath-pileser III
735 Ahaz; Isaiah (740–700)	737 Pekah; 733 Galilee taken	727 Shalmaneser V
715 Hezekiah	722 Samaria taken	722 Sargon II
701, 688 Assyrian attacks on Jerusalem		705 Sennacherib
687 Manasseh; Deuteronomic "Code"; "canonized" 621		681 Esarhaddon
640 Josiah; Zephaniah; Jeremiah 626–580; Reform 621		669 Assur-bani-pal
Nahum before 612; Habakkuk before 600		612 Fall of Nineveh
609 Death of Josiah; invasion of Necho		605 Nebuchadnezzar
598–587 Zedekiah; 598—after 561 Jehoiachin		
598,587,581 Deportations		
593–571 Ezekiel; during Exile, Job		

CHAPTER VI

Who Were the Hebrews?

1. *The Nature of the Problem* The long ages of prehistory and the two millennia of history already sketched may be taken as the matrix in which the Hebrews and their world took form. The outer and the inner cups, the physical factors and the cultural products of the long aeons before the Hebrews emerged into the stream of known history, provided the matrix and in a sense also the content. If the metaphor were continued, the life which the Hebrews poured into the cup would be its content. But neither matrix nor cup is a satisfactory figure; both suggest a mistaken static conception of history and culture.

History is movement. "The moving finger writes and, having writ, moves on." Many a line lost to posterity was written indelibly into the genes of the race and woven into the fabric of its culture. Like a partly defaced inscription, only a portion of the writing can be recovered by the keenest and wisest reader. Yet one of the reasons for following the history of the Hebrews is that, in their case, the moving finger wrote with a fullness covering a longer period than in any contemporary nation, and it moved in shapes and directions not elsewhere recorded. They made history in the culture that they produced and in their record of its production. Best of all, they wrote as they moved. The Bible is a travel book, a vivid record of an intellectual, ethical, and religious pilgrimage. What can now be recovered of its record, and how is it to be understood? These are the pressing questions. In other words, what was the course and meaning of Hebrew national history?

2. *The Hebrew People and Their Language* If the racial composition and the linguistic equipment of the peoples of the Near East are

77

complicated and confused problems, still there is a growing mass of material that makes general conclusions fairly safe. As to the Hebrews, racially considered, the situation is much the same. One thing is certain. Contrary to their official theory, but according to their own genuine traditions, they were hybrid, like hybrid corn and like all of the most prolific and productive cultural groups.

Their traditions are clear and emphatic. Abraham, as they believed, started out from Sumerian Ur when it had long been under Semitic (Akkadian, Amorite) influence. He moved to Harran, high in the west-central part of the Fertile Crescent where Hurrians, Amorites, and other peoples were already living together. He passed on to Canaanite Palestine. But he sent back to get a wife for Isaac from the family of the Aramean Bethuel, his nephew. Rebekah's son, Jacob, went back to her brother's house to find his two wives. It is not strange, then, that in Deuteronomy the Israelite was taught to say, "A roving Aramean was my father." It is entirely possible that Abraham and his group learned Aramaic before going on to Palestine. When there, they had to learn the Canaanite dialect. A change of language of course does not involve a change, or even a mixture, of race, but it may bring a considerable alteration in culture. It is quite unlikely that the Patriarch's herdsmen would have been more careful than Esau was in the choice of wives. Under the given conditions, eventually the Hebrew people as a whole must have been composed of numerous racial elements.

When the Hebrew group learned the Canaanite language, they at once put themselves into communication with all the various tribes that divided Palestine, its mountains, and its surrounding steppes among them. It was as a group of tribes among many other tribes that they later settled in Canaan. In outward appearance they probably did not differ from their neighbors. According to their own story they came in from the steppe on the east side of the Jordan, as the Canaanites had done perhaps a millennium and a half before them, as the Amorites went into northern and eastern Mesopotamia, and as the Arameans less than a thousand years earlier had gone into the northwestern sector of the Fertile Crescent. According to the accepted tradition, they entered all at the same time; thousands upon thousands of them conquered all who opposed them and took over the whole land within a man's lifetime (Josh. 10–12).

It is hardly necessary to say that this account is contradicted by the primitive records in Judges and by the later history of the people and the country and even by the Book of Joshua itself. After long lists of kings whose cities had been taken, there follows a description of the land that yet remained to be possessed (13:2–6). Various passages in Deuteronomy (e.g., 7:1) and other books emphasize the mixed character of the population after the Conquest. One example of amalgamation between the incoming Israelites and the previous inhabitants, one out of many in all probability, is the case of the little tetrapolis of Gibeon, Chephirah, Beeroth, and Kiriath-jearim (Josh. 9:3–27), who tricked the Israelites into making a treaty with them. The Septuagint translation calls them, not Hivites, as in the Hebrew text, but *Chorraioi,* Hurrians, reading an *r* that, in the Hebrew square character, could easily be read as a *wau,* transliterated *v.* The upshot of the matter is that the Gibeonites and their allies, true to their traditional position in the population, became "hewers of wood and drawers of water" for the Hebrews. At Shechem, in Jacob's time, the Israelites made a pact with a group who are also called Hurrians in the Septuagint, but Hivites in the Hebrew Bible (Gen. 34).

If one turn from the romanticized account of the Conquest in Joshua, even the more sober Book of Judges plainly contradicts itself. Indeed, the statement that the "men of Judah" captured Jerusalem is made and denied in the same chapter (1:8, 21). Not only so, but with monotonous repetition it is said that Manasseh, Ephraim, Zebulon, Asher, and Naphtali "did not drive out the inhabitants" of the land that fell to their lots, "but the Canaanites dwelt among them," or they "dwelt among the Canaanites." In some cases it is reported that the Canaanites were subjected to forced labor; in others, that clause is omitted (1:27–33). In the words of Psalm 106:34, "They did not destroy the peoples, . . . but mingled with the nations." It was a period when they could easily absorb a mass of Canaanite myth and religious conceptions.

Not only the Bible itself but information from other sources raises many questions as to the nature of the Conquest. The date of the entry of the Israelites is still uncertain. As to the date of Joshua and of the fall of Jericho, W. F. Albright seems to have abandoned hope of certainty. However, it is safe to say that even conservative critics are accepting the position that the entry and conquest were not accomplished in a single campaign, no matter how long, and certainly not within any man's lifetime. Biblical and nonbiblical evidence agree in that conclusion.

The famous Amarna letters, written by Palestinian kinglets and chieftains reporting the state of affairs in Palestine to their suzerain at Amarna, tell of groups of intruders who are roaming through the country like bandits and endangering Egyptian rule. These 'Apiru, or Khabiru, have been taken to be the equivalent of the Hebrews, and the date of the entry into Palestine has been set in the fourteenth century. However, the word has a much wider application. It appears in cuneiform and hieroglyphic texts of the nineteenth and eighteenth centuries, as well as in Nuzian, Hittite, and Ugaritic documents. Besides appearing in the Amarna tablets, it is found in texts of Dynasties XIX and XX as late as the twelfth century. A stela of Seti I (1308-1291), found at Beth-shan, seems to refer to " 'Apiru of the mountain of Jordan." It is applied to people who are sedentary sometimes, nomadic at other times, sometimes to soldiers, bandits, raiders, or rebels against authority, sometimes to impressed laborers and slaves, apparently to groups of no definite ethnic origin. Ramses IV (1144-1137) used 800 'Apiru (Hebrews?) as quarry men.

Attempts to interpret these puzzling data have been many, and none has won common consent. The term could have been applied to the Hebrew Patriarchs as they wandered from Harran through Syria and Palestine and down into Egypt. It suits their slavery in Egypt and their warlike entry into Palestine. It is a plausible hypothesis to suppose that the Hebrews accepted for themselves this designation, which, originally, was not racial and was anything but tribal (in spite of 'Eber, Gen. 11:16-26), but rather a derogatory epithet, something like the "roving Aramean" of Deuteronomy (26:5). The word, then, has only quite hazy value in determining the time when the Israelites entered

Palestine, and none as to their racial origin. It does mean that, before they entered the Promised Land, they were essentially nomads, although not averse at times to settling down, as the Israelites are said to have done in Goshen.

Another set of data, small in bulk and uncertain of interpretation, indicates that a portion of the "tribes" had been in Palestine for some time before the "official" Exodus and Conquest. References to Asher and Zebulon in Egyptian and, possibly, Ras esh-Shamrah texts seem to place these two tribes in Palestine as early as the fifteenth century, possibly earlier. Jacob-el and Joseph-el are used as place names on the walls of the temple at Karnak in the time of Thothmes III (*c.* 1479), and Jacob-el and Jacob-baal appear as names of Hyksos chieftains. However, now that the Hyksos movement is known to have included numerous Semites, the appearance of these names proves nothing as to the southern Israelites.

Mer-ne-Ptah's stela (*c.* 1220) gives one definite date for the presence, not of 'Apiru, but apparently of still nomadic Israelites in Palestine. This agrees fairly well with archaeologically determined dates for the destruction and rebuilding of Kiriath-sepher and Lachish. If this somewhat unsatisfactory evidence be taken with that discovered in the various inconsistent traditions of the Old Testament accounts, it all adds up to fairly positive conclusions. The "Conquest" was a long process. There was continued infiltration into unoccupied areas. It involved various roving tribes, some of which had been in Palestine long before the others arrived. Some may have antedated the 'Apiru, or Khabiru, of the Amarna period. Others may have come in the time of Ramses II (1291–1224), when, according to the archaeological evidence, cities in southern Palestine were destroyed. In a sense, this was the final phase.

3. *Nomads and Peasants* A reasonably certain assumption puts the main groups of Hebrew, or Israelite, tribes in Palestine before the end of the thirteenth century. What were their political, economic, and cultural conditions? When they arrived, according to their traditions, they found the whole land divided among a very considerable number of cities ruled by kings and without any over-all authority, much as in the Amarna Age. It is interesting to note how fragmentary the records

actually are. The vast majority of the cities mentioned in Joshua 1-12 and Judges 1-2 are south of Bethel. In what became the mountains of Samaria south of Gilboa, two are named in Joshua and one in Judges. The number north of Esdraelon and Jezreel is small.[1]

According to the archaeological evidence, at Tell Beit Mirsim, for example, the invaders at once took over the cities they destroyed and rebuilt the walls. They brought a sharp drop in culture and in numbers. They were presumably seminomadic and easily learned the agricultural practices of the Canaanites. They were accustomed to the care of sheep and goats, perhaps also of cattle. Viticulture would be new to them. They would have much to learn of the refinements of crop raising, now that it had become the major part of their support instead of being a mere auxiliary, and a part of the new lore would be religious, or magical. They would have to learn the practices that insured the blessing of the storm god who was the Baal of this or that region. With all this would go the myths and the superstitions of the Canaanites.

In such a land as Palestine it would have been impossible for people who had just abandoned nomadic life to lose entirely the attitudes and mores of nomadism. No part of the central mountain range is without grazing land. Especially from above the northern border of Judea running southward until it merged in the steppe of the Negeb, there was steppe which could not be escaped and which must be used. There is much rough land in the hills of Palestine, land that cannot be cultivated because of the thinness of the soil or because of protruding boulders and *balat,* or flat stretches of stone with little or no earth, where hardly enough grass grows among the rocks to tempt a half-starved goat.

Consequently, until the most recent years, it was possible to find the black "houses of hair" of the Bedouin among the sand dunes of the coast, on Mount Carmel, and by the Sea of Galilee, as well as here and there in the Wilderness of Judea, of Tekoa, and southward to the Negeb. Many Arab peasant families left their stone huts in their villages in March and wandered about until October with their flocks, living the life of the Bedouin as to food, clothing, and the amenities of the goat's-hair tent. Being farmers, they followed the wheat harvest, perhaps from its early onset in the hot Ghor to the slightly later crop in the warm maritime plain and still later to the colder mountains—wherever any members of the group had bits of cultivated fields. The line of villages that follows the fault marking the border between the sown and the steppe from Ephraim by way of Michmash, Anathoth, Bethlehem, Tekoa, Ziph, and Maon on to Arad always had shepherds watching their flocks by night. Pastoralism has ever played a large part in their activities, and pastoral life easily shades into nomadic.

Nomadism had an influential role, not only in the economic life of the Hebrews and as an unconscious substratum in their culture, but consciously in their religious thought and practice and in their politics as well as in their complicated concept of culture, for example, in the stories of Abel, Cain, and the Patriarchs. For reasons about which there is great difference of scholarly opinion, the Hebrews regarded their religion, the worship of Yahweh, and their birth as a nation as connected with Mount Sinai in the original home of the persistently nomadic tribe, the Kenites, and the Kenites thought of themselves as the true worshipers of Yahweh.

Entering Canaan, the Kenites settled near Arad in the Negeb but, of course, still lived in their tents as did Heber the Kenite, who, in the days of Deborah, had wandered as far north as Kedesh Naphtali. It is significant that Heber had friendly relations with Jabin, king of Hazor, but Jael, his wife, felt a higher, or at least a stronger, loyalty to the Israelites, and became for Deborah "of all tent-dwelling women most blessed." Saul in turn respected the bond when he attacked the Amalekites but saved the Kenites. Presumably Jehonadab the son of Rechab, who met Jehu and joined him on his way to the bloody task of massacring the worshipers of Baal, was descended from Heber or some other Kenite who had wandered from the south to the north. When the northern kingdom came under the control of Assyria, Kenites were found in Judea, and Jeremiah could use them as an example of faithfulness to tribal tradition. The nomadic ideal will appear later as a powerful formative element in the ethical attitudes of the Hebrew people.[2]

4. *Egyptian Relations* In view of all the evidence, both archaeological and literary, it is impossible to accept the once-popular biblical

view that the whole Israelite nation was descended from twelve men who, with their families and retainers, went down into Egypt (somewhere about 1700) and returned to the Promised Land (some 300 years later) as a multitude of hundreds of thousands of people. But since the Sojourn in Egypt is woven so tightly and fully into Hebrew tradition, it must be accorded a prominent place in the story of the nation's origin. The most plausible theory, now accepted by many scholars, both liberal and conservative, is that an important portion of the nation, one that was able later to become more or less dominant in its literary and religious life, was for some generations in the eastern delta of the Nile and left it, perhaps before the middle of the thirteenth century, to wander for a time in the Sinaitic desert and then emerge later as leaders in a final wave of nomadic invasion that practically overwhelmed the Canaanite population in southern Palestine.

The group that had been in Egypt, possibly as early as the time of the heretic Pharaoh Akh-en-Aton, had had opportunities to become acquainted with the higher culture of the Egyptians and could have brought with them religious ideas that blossomed into the Tabernacle and Temple cult. In other words, they could have become the source of the Aaronic priesthood and the ritual ministry of the Temple. Possibly they brought with them also the protomonotheism, if it may be called that, or at least the idea of a high and all-powerful deity, that later was combined with or applied to the worship of Yahweh.

5. *Mesopotamian Relations*   If the story of the Exodus and its implications have raised questions about which many hypotheses and differences of opinion have developed, how much more so the patriarchal legends, in spite of their lack of historical importance. That they are legends, traditions handed down by word of mouth for five or six centuries before they were put into writing, probably late in the tenth or in the ninth century, is a widely accepted critical judgment. That they were originally told, or were edited, for the etiological purpose of sanctifying and so reinforcing certain social customs, ethical concepts, and religious ideas, such as circumcision, intertribal solidarity, avoidance of human sacrifice, the Chosen People idea, and the Covenant concept, is patent.

Radical critics have denied the stories all historicity and regarded Abraham, Isaac, and Jacob, as well as the last's twelve sons, as tribal names, not those of individual persons. The elaborate genealogies of Genesis (chap. 10), which include the names of tribes, give excuse for this conclusion. However, there are so many features of the legends that suit the conditions in Mesopotamia, Syria, and Palestine in the second millennium that a completely skeptical judgment is hardly warranted. Just as excavation at Troy, Mycenae, and Boghazköy has convinced many classical critics that the stories and heroes of Homer rest upon a solid basis of fact, so the heroes of Israelite legend need not be purely the product of imagination and rationalization but are in part historical characters, not merely historical names.

That they are historical names has been proved in the case of a large percentage of them by their discovery in documents of various countries. The genealogical lists that bore the Bible reader prove to be mines of linguistic and historical information. The chronological schemes of Genesis are partly traditional, partly calculated on the basis of the generations of the lists. It is neither possible nor important to relate such chronology closely to the facts of history. What is needed—and possible—is a chronological scheme that connects Israelite tradition and history with that of the remainder of the Near East in a general way. Recent archaeological discoveries and concomitant linguistic progress supply valuable assistance in this enterprise.

Whatever relations the ancestors of Abraham had with Ur of the "Chaldeans," or "the land of the 'Chaldeans,'" as the Septuagint reads the text, many connections with Harran and northwestern Mesopotamia are discoverable. Abraham is a good Amorite name from southern Babylonia. Names of ancestors and relatives of Abraham belong to places near Harran, and the name Jacob and a tribe of Benjamin are found there. No traces of the Patriarchs have been found; it would be a minor miracle if they had; but the names are not later inventions, nor were they in common use in later times. According to Albright, the early chapters of Genesis reflect also traditions of Nuzi and Mari in the time of Hammurabi (c. 1728–1686) and a little later. The customary laws of the Nuzian documents correspond to the practices of the patriarchal stories. C. H. Gordon argues for the fourteenth-century connections between the Patriarchs and Nuzi and the Hurrian kingdom of Mitanni. He cites Ugaritic, Babylonian, and Egyptian parallels also, all from the Amarna age, which for him is the patriarchal age.

The data regarding those puzzling nomads the Khabiru, or 'Apiru, cover the same centuries as the patriarchal legends. The Patriarchs do not fit into the situation, along with the Khabiru, of the nineteenth and eighteenth centuries, as formerly supposed. But, appearing as the Khabiru do in Nuzian, Hittite, and Amarna documents of the fifteenth and fourteenth century, they connect with the Hebrews not only in name and social and historical function but also in chronological position. Like a large number of scholars, Albright connects the three Patriarchs with the Hyksos, although he agrees with Gordon in the main as to fourteenth-century parallels. The Amarna age is equally possible for the story of Joseph, for then Syrian influence was strong at court. Such details are extremely interesting historical problems, but exactitude in such matters does not affect the eventual outcome in Hebrew history.

6. *Historical Reconstruction*   A reconstruction of the prehistory of the Hebrews may be suggested that combines the various and sometimes contradictory data. The family may have come from south Babylonian Amorites living among the Sumerians. In the time of Hammurabi, when Amorite influence was strong in northwestern Mesopotamia, they would have migrated to that region and lived in the cities whose names Abraham's supposed ancestors bear. Here, in Paddan-Aram, the Plain of Aram, the family, now a sib, dwelt long enough to acquire the Aramaic language and the customs of that part of the world. Abraham was thus a roving Aramean in both language and folkways. Sometime during the Hyksos period Abraham moved down into Palestine. Both he and Isaac visited the Delta region in Egypt as, according to Egyptian evidence, Bedouin tribes from Palestine had been doing at least since the time of the First Intermediate period.

Since the Hebrew Conquest does not appear to have been consummated until late in the thirteenth century, it suits the data best to begin the Sojourn in Egypt in the Empire period, when connections were strong between the reigning dynasty and Syria. The group of Hebrews who later told the story of the deliverance from Egypt and who, as priests and Levites, eventually became the cult leaders of the nation were those who, presumably, had connections with the learning and religion of Egypt in the Amarna age, and they came out with advanced ideas about the nature of God. Coming in contact with related sibs in the steppe, they attached their conceptions of God to the tribal deity and created what has variously been called monolatry, henotheism, or, to be precise with W. F. Badè, mono-Yahwism, a mongrel but expressive compound.[3]

The time for the Exodus of this group is best set in the early part of the reign of Ramses II, the entry into Canaan toward its end. In the steppe south and east of Palestine and in Canaan itself, as the Amarna letters show, there had been groups of Khabiru, some of whom had already made themselves at home in the land. These all combined, or coalesced, as time went on, to make a nation, with the religious leadership in the hands of the half-educated Levitic group, at whose head stood the Aaronic priesthood. It was this group that Mer-ne-Ptah's forces found, still as nomads, in southern Palestine in 1220 and knew as Israelites. As groups of loosely related tribes, the nomadic Hebrews settled in Palestine and slowly conquered and absorbed the populations of its mountains. It was long generations before the Aaronic group, centered at Jerusalem, managed to dominate the numerous cult leaders at sacred sites throughout the country.

CHAPTER VII

From Tribe to Nation (c. 1025–587)

1. *The Times of the Judges (c. 1250–1025)* The biblical history of the world from the Creation to the conquest of the Promised Land was written with a highly specialized interest. The preceding chapters are intended to place the story within its larger context. Whatever the historian's viewpoint, to understand the story in its reality the little Hebrew caravans, with their burros and sheep and goats crawling over the steppe, the roving bands of Khabiru, the rude tribal groups thrusting their way, unnoticed by history, into the forested hills of Palestine must be seen against the background of world history, so much of which can now be recovered from the written and unwritten records of the thousands of years behind them. Their role in history was already chosen for them by the past. An outline of what actually happened to them in Palestine is the task of the succeeding chapters.

Unfortunately the story of Israel as a nation is a polemical subject. Ideas concerning it vary so greatly that it must be regarded from three points of view: (1) what actually happened, or how the nation met its limitations and opportunities and developed, considered as objectively as possible; (2) how the Hebrews themselves read and interpreted their history as seen in the Bible; (3) how the modern historian can understand and interpret that process. The task of this and the two following chapters is the first: how the roving Aramean, the vigorous and warlike Khabiru, developed into a peasant nation and finally into a cult community, a city-state centered about a temple and ruled by priests (chap. IX).

The weakness of Egyptian rule, beginning in the fourteenth century, allowed the 'Apiru, as the Egyptians called them, to settle in the mountains and take control of cities here and there, as already noted. After Ramses III's victory over the Sea Peoples (*c.* 1167), a race developed between the Philistines and the Hebrews as to which could occupy the larger amount of territory. The conflict led to the consolidation of a large proportion of the land from Dan to Beer-sheba in the United Monarchy.

Warring among themselves, with Canaanite remnants in the land and nomadic tribes on its outskirts, the Hebrews in one or another area had to pay tribute from time to time to a stronger neighboring group or "king." The Judges seem to have exercised few judicial functions, but rather were local sheikhs who aroused enough spirit to lead to victory over the oppressors. One outstanding figure among them was a woman, Deborah. One bond uniting the tribes seems to have been the sanctuary at Shiloh. Some of the evidence for it is late and doubtful, if not apocryphal. But it is permissible to call the tribes a loose amphictyony.

During the period three tribes emerge as strongest in numbers, leadership, and initiative: Judah in the south, Ephraim and Manasseh in the central mountains, the latter two taking the place of "Joseph," from whom they were supposed to be descended. The putative descendants of Levi, as priests and cult servitors, never obtain a "lot" in the land. Benjamin is the tribe of the first king. Simeon, Reuben, Gad, and Dan disappear. Gilead is sometimes named as if a tribe. The other tribes, Asher, Zebulon, Naphtali, and Issachar in Galilee, which are merely lay figues as sons of Jacob, are important only in the earlier years. The purely theoretical character of the distribution of the land among "Twelve Tribes" is evident. Actually Hebrew history is the story of Judah and "Joseph," and "Levi."

The stories of Abimelech, Jethro, Samson, and the Benjamites, if not historical in detail, doubtless have enough truth in them to document the final sentence of the Book of Judges: "In those days there was no king in Israel; every man did what was right in his own eyes." The Judges, who were often Ibn Sauds, each with seventy sons riding on asses (seventy being a perfect number), indicate the conventional standard of well-being.[1] Even if all possible allowance be made for the difficulties of the Israelite situation, the period of the Judges was an inglorious era. Licentiousness, murderous brutality, human sacrifice, shameless deceitfulness, not merely to outside enemies but among the tribes one toward another—all this was taken for granted, with one serious protest in which the communal punishment seems far worse than the original sin, brutal as it was (Judg. 17–21).

There were many places of worship in the land; sacrifice could be offered wherever a theophany or an unusual incident occurred. The Tabernacle and the Ark, so elaborately described and so often mentioned in Exodus, Leviticus, and Numbers, play no important role in the Books of Deuteronomy and Judges. The appearance of the Tabernacle at Shiloh in Joshua (18:1, *et al.*) is plainly fictitious. However, the Ark was in the possession of Ephraim at the end of the period (1 Sam. 4). Samuel, an Ephraimite, became the chief national leader, a judge, not a prophet, at the beginning of the next period.

According to the arrangement of incidents in the Book of Judges, the Philistines became a serious menace only toward the end of the period, sometime after 1100. Doubtless it took time for the Sea Peoples to establish themselves before they could attack the Israelites. After the weak reign of Ramses VI (*c.* 1133–1129), the Egyptians were in no sense a menace and the Philistines were free to consolidate their power and undertake further conquest. For such a time, Israel found leaders in Samuel, Saul, and David.

Centuries twelve to ten offered a favorable interlude for the growth of the little ethnic groups in Palestine and Syria. Solomon might think it politic to marry an Egyptian princess. Shishak (*c.* 918) was able to set up a stela at Megiddo and plunder the Temple and royal palace in Jerusalem. But, after Ramses III, Egypt carried no weight north of her border. The great days of the Mitannian empire and of Egyptian power were gone. Aram and Assyria were yet to rise.

In this hiatus, when all the great culture centers that ringed the eastern Mediterranean were inactive, Byblos, Phoenicia, and Aram (Syria, or Damascus) had their opportunity. Philistia, Israel, Ammon, Moab, and Edom had their chance to develop agriculture and trade and, in conflict among themselves, be driven to abandon purely tribal organization for royalty, as the city-states of Babylonia had done two millennia earlier.

2. *The United Kingdom (c. 1025–922)* Samuel, the last of the Judges, was a very different individual from any who preceded him, for he played the prophet and priest, not the warrior, role. He was intimately associated with the cult at Shiloh. The loss of the Ark to the Philistines and its later return, not to the tribe of Ephraim but to the territory of Judah, along with the migration of Samuel to Ramah in Benjamin, were events of prime importance. The destruction of Shiloh (probably by the Philistines), although not mentioned in contemporary literature, has been dated to this period on archaeological evidence. The only biblical mention of its fate, by Jeremiah, takes it as a punishment for Israel's sins.[2] It was natural, therefore, to transfer the Ark to a different place. At Ramah and Mizpah Samuel was only from three to five miles from Gibeah, the home of Israel's first king, whom he was to anoint, and some ten or twelve miles from Bethlehem, where he was to find the second. He never mentions Shiloh and the Ark.

Here for the first time an Israelite prophet-priest appeared, and he at once became also a politician in an active sense, as Elisha later was. The greatest prophets were all deeply concerned with national policies and politics, but they did not often enter into intrigues to promote the fulfillment of their desires and predictions. When Samuel anointed Saul, he doubtless thought he was following a command directly from God. So also when he anointed David. But he had actually become a religious kingmaker. How far was Saul's failure due to the domineering personality and offended dignity of the prophet-priest? A "holy man" who is confident that he knows God's will can be a sore trial to other people. Whether there is any historical fact in the Samuel stories or not (there doubtless is some), they reveal painfully primitive conceptions of God and religion.

Nathan plays a more circumspect and honorable role in dealing with David. There is no good reason for not taking the sections of 2 Samuel, where he appears, as genuine history (save for small editorial additions). The parable of the poor man and his "little ewe lamb" is a notable monument to the prophet's courage and the deep democratic sense of justice that pervaded Hebrew thinking at its best. If Nathan eventually joined Bath-sheba in an intrigue to place her son, Solomon, on the throne, he may be excused on the ground that he thought he was carrying out David's wishes.

When Ahijah inspired Jeroboam's revolt against Rehoboam and the Davidic monarchy, he played much the same role that Samuel had. Ahijah was from Shiloh and one cannot but wonder whether sectional and cult-based jealousy of the Davidic house and the Solomonic Temple may not have stimulated his treasonable action. On the other hand, Solomon's regal magnificence and oppressive exactions to sustain it were sufficiently contrary to the nomadic-democratic tradition of Israel to justify a prophet in protesting. He should have been a Nathan to Solomon. But he was that to Jeroboam, when the latter departed from the aniconic worship of Yahweh. In the end he was true to his vocation.[3] His was a pattern that prophets too often have had to follow when their resort to direct action has gone wrong.

In the persons and prophetic practices of Samuel and Saul there are elements of shamanism that need not be thought surprising in view of the common beliefs of their age. Saul goes to a man of God, a seer, who, for a price, may be expected to tell by some occult means where to seek for straying asses. What the seer sees is not only the asses, already safe in Gibeah, but the young man Saul as the king of Israel. These are surely most contradictory concepts of the prophetic office, the petty almost eclipsing the noble.

The ecstatic episode in Saul's career immediately following his anointing calls attention to another shamanistic element in prophecy as it was understood throughout the pre-exilic period. When Saul meets 'a band of prophets . . . with harp, tambourine, flute, and lyre before them, prophesying," he joins them and prophesies, to the astonishment of all who had known him. It was evidently an ecstatic seizure induced by music and probably dancing. Samuel's word, that the Spirit of God would "fall upon," or "rush upon," him indicates the nature of the experience, as then understood.[4] In the Wen-Amon story, a court page of Zakar-Baal, king of Byblos, falls in an ecstatic trance while the king is making a temple offering, and he proclaims a message that is accepted as divine and rescues the much-harassed Egyptian envoy from still worse troubles that threatened him. The incident, which belongs a generation or so earlier than Saul, indicates the general prevalence of this conception of divine action upon chosen human beings. God could speak through Balaam's ass, as well as through psychotic humans.[5]

So far as the biblical statements go, Samuel's vaticination derived from less violent inner experiences, and so did those of other prophets. But bands of prophets, mentioned in the Bible from time to time, seem to have been of the ecstatic, or pseudo-ecstatic, type. The priests of Baal who opposed Elijah on Mount Carmel exhibit a dervish-like frenzy that was calculated to attract the attention of an indifferent deity, quite in contrast to Elijah's quiet assurance. Outwardly at least they paralleled the "sons of the prophets." [6] Whether Saul's erratic conduct later was due to emotional instability is another unanswerable question.

As to cult, the transfer of the great national religious symbol, the Ark, from Shiloh to Jerusalem and its eventual establishment in the Temple is the outstanding event of the period. There is evidence to support the hypothesis that Mount Moriah, or Zion, had long been a sacred spot. In any case, the fame of David and Solomon and of the centuries of its subsequent history, accompanied by zealous propaganda by its naturally interested priesthood and dynasty, established Jerusalem as the Holy City for Western civilization above all the rest of the world. As such it has been a place of personal and political intrigue, religious strife, undisguised ritualism and formalism, theological fundamentalism, and human slaughter that has few parallels down to this day. The fortunes of the priesthood and of individual priests fluctuated according to their ability to please the reigning monarch. The Temple was for generations the king's private possession and it shared the fortunes of the Davidic line that built and maintained it. Vested interests of both priesthood and dynasty that were to play a major role in Hebrew religious history were established.

The lack of factual accuracy in the traditions of the grossly exag-

gerated glories of the reigns of David and Solomon unfortunately did
not affect their influence on subsequent historical thinking among the
Hebrews. A gorgeous lie is much more acceptable and powerful than
bare truth. All down through their history, Hebrew and Jewish reasoning has deduced from the Davidic and Solomonic legends the conclusion that similar wealth and power were possible again in a glorious
future.

3. *Israel and Judah: A Divided People (922–722)*   The fortunes of
the two little monarchies fluctuated wildly during the period of the
Divided Kingdom. For the problems with which this study is concerned, the alternations of war and peace, of prosperity and misfortune
through which they struggled during the two centuries from the
disruption of Solomon's empire to the fall of Samaria are hardly more
significant than the stories of the Judges.

Their periods of prosperity were due largely to temporary lack of
pressure from weakened neighboring nations and from Assyria and
Egypt. Their misfortunes arose in part from invasions from without,
but even more from their wars one with the other and with Syria
(Damascus), Moab, and Edom, as well as from internal strife within
each. Northern Israel was much the larger, richer, and stronger, but
suffered from its exposed position and from the instability of its
dynasties.

Omri set the policy of the northern kingdom when he built his
sumptuous capital among fertile valleys on the lovely, rounded hill of
Samaria, and when he married his son, Ahab, to the Princess Jezebel of
the Tyrian royal family. He thus thrust Israel into the swirling stream
of international politics. He had his reward: he was immortalized in
Assyrian annals, which always refer to Israel as Beth-Omri, the house
of Omri. Even Jehu, who massacred his descendants to the last man,
was ben-Omri, son of Omri. His people suffered corresponding disasters.

After a half-century of war, the two minute kingdoms were allied under Ahab and Jehoshaphat, the latter as vassal. For a brief
period both nations enjoyed prosperity but their joint attempts at
conquest ended in disaster. In his famous inscription Mesha, king of

Moab, admits that Omri and Ahab had occupied his country, but, he boasts, "Chemosh restored it in my day." Judah lost both Edom and Libnah. Worst of all, Jezebel's efforts to introduce Tyrian Baal worship and her highhanded injustices, as illustrated in the story of Naboth and his vineyard, brought internal catastrophe. Jehu's revolution, with the massacre of hundreds of Baal worshipers and nearly all the members of both royal houses, could not have contributed to the strength of either kingdom. It ended their alliance, but, in Judah, it had the contrary effect of allowing the Baalist Athaliah (Jezebel's daughter in spirit, if not in fact) to seize the throne. With her assassination by the high priest, Jehoiada, the threat of Tyrian Baalism seems to have vanished. Yet there is no evidence of a genuine purification of Yahwism in either land. When the long and disastrous war with Syria ended (*c.* 800), a period of prosperity ensued under Amaziah and Azariah (Uzziah) in Judah and under Jehoash and Jeroboam II in the northern kingdom. For over sixty years Syria was occupied with Assyrian inroads and could no longer harass her weaker neighbors.

Under Jeroboam II Israel enjoyed an autumn sunshine that quickly faded. Within twenty-two years after his death, the northern half of Israel had been plundered and half depopulated by Tiglath-pileser III, and then Samaria, which had been regally adorned by Ahab and Jeroboam II, fell before the the armies of Shalmaneser V and Sargon II. Judah survived because Ahaz (Jehoahaz) accepted Assyrian overlordship and made Assyrian religion officially preferred to Yahwism. It was an inglorious end for the northern kingdom, which had every apparent advantage, above all in comparison with its smaller sister state. It was an equally inglorious survival for Judah. But it was a survival.

The period is celebrated for the pernicious influence of women, especially three of them, Maacah, grandmother of Asa, Athaliah, mother of Jehoram of Judah, and Jezebel. There is no need to repeat their stories. These foreign women seem to have been piously devoted, but to Baal, not to Yahweh. They are offset by one courageous princess, Jehosheba, daughter of King Jehoram of Judah. When Athaliah was killing all of the king's sons, she saved Joash, her infant nephew, and hid him in a room in the Temple itself, for, according to 2 Chronicles (22:11), she was the wife of Jehoiada, the high priest, who later killed Athaliah and set Joash on the throne.[7]

The story of the Temple at Jerusalem during this period is brief and inglorious, except for Jehoiada. As the king's private chapel, so to speak, it contributed again and again as a treasury from which to take funds to buy off an enemy or purchase a friend. Only in the case of Joash and Jehoiada does it openly influence the course of Judah's history. Possibly the Temple acted also as a place of refuge for the editors of the J and E traditions, and thus served a day that was yet to be.

The problem of the nature of prophecy emerges again and again. The kings, especially in northern Israel, had prophets whose predictions were calculated always to please the monarch. Often, it would appear, they fell into an ecstasy in order to demonstrate their divine inspiration. Even Elisha sought a minstrel to bring the power of the Lord upon him. Judah, on the other hand, is represented as served by men who did not speak to please the king. Only in the last years, just before the Exile, does a prophet, Jeremiah, face the opposition of prophets who were kept by the king.[8]

Outside the Temple, according to both the biblical and the archaeological evidence, popular worship went on as it always had. In the business records of the Samaritan ostraka, personal names compounded with Baal are to those with Yahweh as two to three. It seems strange that Athaliah should have been named as a worshiper of Yahweh; therefore the usage in names cannot be allowed too great significance. However, there is a contrary indication of the general attitude (at least among women) that can hardly be gainsaid. Every excavation of strata belonging to this period has uncovered numerous Astarte figurines, crude little nude female statuettes with special emphasis on the female organs. They are usually scattered over the whole of a mound and, it would appear, were to be found in nearly every house. They can hardly be anything but representations, sometimes so crude as to be merely symbols, of *dea nutrix*. In other words they are fertility amulets. The peculiar anxieties and superstitions of uneducated women play no small part in the history of religion.

Cult places belonging to the Hebrew period are extremely difficult to discover. None that can unquestionably be identified as in use in this period has come to light, even in places that have been fully excavated, such as Megiddo, Beth-shemesh, and Tell en-Nasbeh.

Apparently the "high places" were in the open air and had a minimum of fixed or permanent furniture. Altars of earth or of un-hewn stones (Exod. 20:24 f.) could hardly be preserved or recognized if found. Sanctuaries, distinctly recognizable, have been uncovered in earlier strata at numerous sites, but they disappear when Hebrew oc-cupation begins. Doubtless there were open-air sites for sacrifices in every considerable village and at sacred spots in the open country, just as the Moslems of today have the *weli*. But there would have been nothing to distinguish them.

As to objects connected with cult, the only unquestioned example is the horned altar, of which eight were found at Megiddo, several of them certainly in Israelite strata. At Tell en-Nasbeh only fragments of two or three were preserved. In both places they were scattered in various parts of the mounds and marked no building that could be proved to be a sanctuary. The standing pillars that were long taken to be *massebhoth* are now known to have been roof supports. Conical stones of some size were found, one at Tell en-Nasbeh and one at Beth-shemesh. They might have been *massebhoth,* but that cannot be proved, as neither was *in situ.* Thus there is still no clear evidence as to the nature of a "high place."

The period of the Divided Kingdom is one of growing tension in Hebrew culture and religion and of developing literary activity and religious thinking. There is no reason to doubt that, from David's time on, the court kept records of various kinds, including chronicles of events. The linear Phoenician script had been in use for centuries and surely could be written by many persons. It should be remembered that it is found scrawled freehand on unbaked pottery vessels, scratched on vessels already fired, and written with reed pen and ink on sherds (ostraka). The legends of the Patriarchs could have been written down (though probably they were not) in the fourteenth or thirteenth cen-tury, before their times were too long forgotten. It seems strange that the prophets of the two centuries when Solomon and his immediate successors were breaking away from the old ways had nothing to say that demanded recording. Perhaps papyrus rolls were lost. Perhaps the apparent glory of the enlarging kingdom and the wealth that was accruing to king and people clouded the prophetic vision.

On the one hand there were faithful worshipers of Yahweh in country towns such as those from which Elijah and Elisha emerged. The Rechabites appear unexpectedly now and again to illustrate faithfulness to the better traditions. Elijah is said to have been reminded that he had a "perfect host" (7000) behind him in his battle with Jezebel and Baal. There were men who could work up the traditions of "J" and "E" to strengthen the national sense of unity and destiny under Yahweh. The emergence of the writing prophets in the eighth century and of the Deuteronomist in the seventh along with such prophets as Zephaniah and Jeremiah is evidence enough of the reserves of steadfastness and courage, as well as of literary ability, that preserved the national ideals and the nation.

There was need enough for strength and courage. What called forth Amos, Hosea, Micah, and Isaiah was the failure of the kings and the people to keep God's laws and the fear that the time was ripe for punishment, even of the people whom God had chosen. Two centuries of political, ethical, and religious frustration, along with the growing war-fed luxury of the rich and the complementary poverty and neglect of the poor, gave bitterness to the protests of Amos, Isaiah, and Micah, while neglect of Yahweh and the continuing, perhaps increasing, popularity of Canaanite Baalism drove Hosea into action. It is notable that all four of these first "writing" prophets appeared just after both Israel and Judah had reached the height of prosperity under Jeroboam II and Uzziah.

For over a century the two little kingdoms in the Palestinian mountains had been shivering before the approach of Assyria, the most ruthless power the Near East had yet seen. With Ahab at Qarqar in 853 spending 2000 chariots and 10,000 men in temporary opposition to the advance of Shalmaneser III and with Jehu, followed by his tribute bearers, groveling before the same king in 841, Israel entered into the historical records of Assyria as Beth-Omri. It would be interesting to compare the Israelite and Assyrian accounts. Both exaggerate, the Assyrian scribes boasting of the wide lands devastated and their populations removed. The Hebrew accounts admit enough to prove that there was wealth to be plundered, as the excavation of Ahab's "ivory palace" at Samaria has demonstrated.

The lively but wearisome details of Israelite intrigue, assassination, and rebellion may be passed over. The effects of Assyrian deportations are important. In 733, the Galilean section of the northern kingdom, the wide land of Naphtali, was taken by the Assyrians and many of its people were deported. In 722–721 the wide land of Beth-Omri was taken. Its capital, Samaria, was not destroyed, but its population suffered extensive deportations at the hands of Shalmaneser V and Sargon II. Further abortive revolts brought repeated punitive measures. But Yahweh worshipers remained amid Arabs and other, imported followers of various gods. The Assyrians even encouraged Yahweh worship on the grounds that the territory belonged to him and could prosper only if he were properly worshiped—an early version of *cuius regio, huius religio*. Thus the most beautiful two-thirds of the land were lost to Israel (2 Kings 17:24–41).

4. *Judah Alone (722–587)* The details of Judah's social history now become matters of importance. Judah and Jerusalem come late into the purview of the Assyrians. More than a century after Ahab's unfortunate venture at Qarqar, Azariah of Judah (*c.* 742) headed a coalition (including Menahem of Samaria) against Tiglath-pileser with equally unhappy results.[9] A decade later Ahaz appealed to Assyria for aid against the "two stumps of smoking firebrands," Rezin of Syria and Pekah of Israel, who attacked him. The result was that Judah became a vassal of Assyria;[10] and in twenty years Samaria was captured. Now that the northern kingdom was a half-heathen dependency of Assyria, Judah lay fully in the hot sunlight of Assyrian imperialism.

Sennacherib repeatedly mentions "Hezekiah the Jew" with venom, because he "did not submit to my yoke" and had aided Ekron to revolt on the death of Sargon. The Assyrian annals reveal aspects of the Judean royal menage that the Bible leaves quite unsuspected. Not only did the Assyrians take forty-six of Judah's walled cities and many villages and carry off 200,150 (?) persons and animals without number, but, when "his Arabs and other picked troops fled," Hezekiah was driven to pay a ransom of 30 talents of gold and 800 talents of silver, besides "gems, antimony, jewels, couches and chairs of ivory, elephant's hide, elephant's tusks, boxwood, all kinds of valuable treasures" and "his daughters, his harem, his male and female musicians," all sent to Nineveh. But Jerusalem was not taken, either then or during Sennacherib's sixth campaign, when "the wide province of Judah" was devastated again and "the strong proud Hezekiah" was forced into submission. Jerusalem remained inviolate as Isaiah had promised in the name of God.[11] It is another of those significant events that eventually made Jerusalem "the unholy city." The city became an idol.

Hezekiah is the first king who is credited with removing the "high places" and destroying the symbols of Baal worship. The Chronicler enlarges upon Hezekiah's piety and success, with what warrant one cannot say. That his piety can have deeply affected the people of the former northern kingdom, as the Chronicler avers, seems doubtful. Possibly it had values and results that appear only later.

On the other hand, the reign of Hezekiah's son, Manasseh, although he himself was an apostate, is usually credited with the chief work of the Deuteronomist, for the Book of Deuteronomy came to light in the almost immediately succeeding reign of Josiah. Yahweh worshipers could be found in the southern country districts lost to Judah. A considerable nucleus of the faithful must have survived in Samaria and northern Palestine for some three centuries at least, until the Pentateuch was completed in its present form and accepted by the Samaritans. Indeed, Albrecht Alt believes that Deuteronomy was written there.[12]

The renegade Manasseh, by yielding, like his grandfather Ahaz, to Assyrian influence and domination, saved his country from the fate of Samaria and secured for his people a period of comparative rest and prosperity while the Transjordan territories were being inundated by new masses of nomads seeking ease and security in the sown land.

According to 2 Kings (21:1–18), he restored the worship of Baal at the high places that his father had destroyed and made a complete reversal of his father's policies. Doubtless his long reign contributed largely to the anti-Yahwist tendencies with which Josiah and Jeremiah had to deal, but it also made the work of the Hebrew writers of the seventh century possible.

The death of Josiah at the hands of Pharaoh Necho is an enigma. The purposes of neither the Egyptians nor Josiah are clear. The results are plain enough in one regard. The man who had done most to restore the worship of Yahweh had futilely lost his life at the hands of a supposed enemy of God's people. Strangely 2 Chronicles (35:21–22) quotes Necho as claiming God's support for his campaign and blames Josiah for not heeding "the words of Necho from the mouth of God," a remarkable expression, to say the least.

Manasseh's grandson had had an opportunity to undo his grandfather's work. Various historical factors affected the course of his reign. The important point is that he attempted to rehabilitate the Temple and the cultus and, when the book of the law, which was doubtless Deuteronomy in its essential elements, was discovered, he was ready to carry through a thoroughgoing reform. The decay of Assyrian power allowed him a liberty of action that none of his immediate predecessors had. He is reported to have exercised sufficient authority to destroy the high places, not only in Bethel, but in all Samaria. Whether tradition has added unhistorical details to his story it is impossible to say. It is strange that the Book of Kings gives much more attention to Hezekiah than to Josiah, and Chronicles reduces his story slightly while expanding that of Hezekiah. He seems to have lived under an evil star.

Back of his unhappy end lie the problems of a small nation that could not escape being the plaything of great powers. The difficulties are compounded for a conscientious monarch who is trying to follow religious principles. The Egyptian party and the Assyrian party had both intrigued for Hezekiah's support, and the prophetic advice had been to keep clear of entanglements and trust in God. Josiah's problem was triple, for he had the strength of Assyria, Babylon, and Egypt to estimate. Whatever his motive and purpose, his error was fatal to him and his nation and, with other current influences, fatal also to reform.

His sons had small opportunity to show either piety or ability. They were caught in the same dilemma, and they failed to foresee that, for over half a century, Babylon was to be the dominant power in the Fertile Crescent. Jeremiah, who advised submission and, quite naturally, was branded an appeaser and collaborator, was, wisely, a neutralist. He made his situation worse by giving an unpopular reason for it. He insisted that the nation's difficulties were due to neglect of Yahweh and his law. The answer of his opponents was sustained by Josiah's fate. During Manasseh's reign they had enjoyed comparative security. Josiah's reforms had been followed by repeated disasters. Jeremiah had the longer vision, but how could his contemporaries know it? (Jer. 44:15–23)

In the words of Amos, God said, "You only have I known of all the people of the earth; therefore will I visit upon you all of your iniquities." Following Amos' logic, Jeremiah warned that the Day of the Lord was coming as "a day of darkness, and not of light," as Amos had said. Yet he saw light beyond it if they repented. After seventy years restoration would come.

CHAPTER VIII

From Nation to Cult Community (587–516)

1. *A Critical Period in Jewish History* For the person interested in modern religion and its future, the seven or eight hundred years from the seventh century B.C. to the second century A.D. are perhaps the most significant in history. During these centuries, practically all of the religions that have meant most and still mean most to the world (except Islam) had their origins and developed their basic forms and ideas. What is of immediate and special significance for this discussion is the fact that during this period Judaism crystallized the welter of ideas, ideals, and hopes that gave birth to the two religions that have most deeply affected Western culture, the Judaism of the Law and the Prophets and the Christianity of Jesus and of Paul.

The great age of original religious thinking among the Hebrews, so far as recorded, began in the eighth century. It continued into the fifth and perhaps the fourth century, with occasional flashes of inspired writing in later times. The remarkable coincidence, or convergence, of great religious writers and founders of religions in the sixth and the three or four following centuries has often been remarked. Preceding all of them, as in the case of Judaism, there were long histories of religious development. Like discoverers of fire and metals and inventors of plow and wheel, unknown thinkers had struggled with the problems, not of man's food, but of his fate and of his relation to his fellows and to supernatural powers and persons. Their ideas were absorbed and proclaimed by their known and unknown successors for uncounted thousands of years before the ferments of the sixth century brewed new and richer draughts of religious thought. In all the important culture areas the further developments of the period under consideration had extraordinary significance, nowhere more than in the Near East and the eastern Mediterranean area, where the matrix of Western civilization was taking shape.

What the convergence of religious and philosophical thinkers in the eighth, seventh, and sixth centuries implies as to theories of cultural history is a moot question. Did subtle influences flow between China, India, and the West over the already ancient trade routes? Or is there some rhythm of cultural development that brings about analogous results more or less coincidentally? Whatever the answers to these questions, the Jewish people and Palestine, often disparaged as among the most isolated and backward of Near Eastern areas and nations, marched, not with the rest of the world, but rather a little in advance in producing its great constellations of prophets in the eighth and sixth centuries. These men cannot be ignored by any student of religion, for their innovating originality and their penetrating ethical vision made them pioneers for all the world.

What is too often ignored is the influence of Assyria, Babylonia, Persia, Phoenicia, and other neighbors, as well as Egypt and Greece, upon Jewish religion in the exilic and postexilic periods, when its literature was receiving its final, classical form in the Old Testament. The noncanonical literature that appeared subsequently, in the latter part of the period, reveals foreign influences even more clearly and must receive due attention in its place. During this era all these various streams of tradition poured for the time being into one channel to make the vigorous and turbulent torrent that divided into two branches before it flowed out into the ocean of world civilization in the Roman and Parthian empires.

The period gathered up diverse concepts of morality and religion into two chief lines of religious thinking: the racial religion of ritual, law, and ethics known as Judaism and the universal religion of judgment and individual salvation, of prophetic morality, enthusiasm, and eschatological hope that produced the innumerable varieties of Christianity. Because of the basic and immediate importance of this era for the origins of Judaism and Christianity, it must receive fuller treatment than the previous ages. Not only did both religions originate in this briefer period, but the sources available are more numerous, and the complications of the Jewish situation sharply increased the dangers to the nation and its religion.

2. *A Complicated Situation*   The dangers to Judaism were multiple in number and in kind; they were physical, political, and cultural. No period in the history of Israel was more challenging and more perilous than the relatively unknown Persian era, and none was more significant in the development of Jewish literature and religion. In the vast indifferent or hostile empire, the faithful Yahwists of the southern kingdom might have been swallowed up, as most of the "Ten Tribes" had been, or they might have been so diluted as to be practically lost, as the remnants of northern Israel were in Samaria.

However, there were factors in the historical situation that were favorable to their survival. One was the tolerant and generous attitude of the Persian regime. In contrast to that of the Assyrians, wide latitude was allowed to subject states and particularly to dissident religious groups. A second was the abandonment by the Persians of the Assyrian policy of mass deportation, which was by intention and in practice genocide.

Another favorable item, a corollary of the first and second, was the large body of prosperous Jews in the Tigris-Euphrates Valley and in Persia, who were finding it possible to live well outside Palestine, to serve the Persian monarchs, and even to play influential roles in the administration (e.g., Nehemiah and Mordecai) without sacrificing their ancestral religion. Two periods are almost a blank in biblical history, from 582 to 538 and from 516 to about 444 or a little later. But in Babylonia it is becoming possible to reconstruct from cuneiform documents some significant items.

From one discovery, an item in 2 Kings (25:27-30) receives unexpected illumination. The verses record that (in 561) Jehoiachin was released from prison and restored, by the new monarch, Evil-Merodach (Amel-Marduk), to a position as a royal pensioner. That he had held such a position is documented by tablets found in the royal palace in Babylon and only recently published. Written about 592, they give Jehoiachin the title of king and record him and his sons as receiving allowances from the royal stores, just the privileges restored by Evil-Merodach. The Jewish princes were royal hostages for the good behavior of their subjects in Palestine and lost their freedom on account of some Judean revolt. Their originally favorable position is confirmed by discoveries in Palestine, at Beth-shemesh and Tell Beit Mirsim, of three jar handles stamped with the seal of Jehoiachin's steward (*na'ar*). As king, he still received income from his private estates in Judea, at least for a time.[1] Later Cyrus, who posed as the legitimate successor to the kings of Babylon, merely followed the kindly practice of his Babylonian predecessors, which coincided with his own lenient attitude toward subject peoples.

Like the royal family, the other Jewish captives, at least a large body of them, had been well treated and were settled in the busiest and most fertile part of the great alluvial plain between the rivers—for example, at Tel Abib (the "hill of the storm cloud," or "of the Flood") on the "Grand Canal" (*Nehar Kebar,* Ezra 3:15) and, as many tablets show, at Nippur, also on the "Grand Canal." Before a hundred years had passed Jewish names begin to appear on business tablets in various connections. They were working in private and public offices in numerous capacities. The "Jewish firm of Murashu and Sons" is famous in Persian business annals as loan sharks.

Within a couple of generations the Jewish captives in Babylon were well on their way to a position of influence and affluence. As business tablets prove, the process began early that eventually produced a cohesive community under exilarchs of the Davidic dynasty. The relative security of their exilic home led to the active prosecution of literary and historical studies that produced the nucleus of the Old Testament. Babylonian Judaism developed rabbinical experts who could vie with those of Palestine and actually preserved a complete Talmud, whereas that of Palestine is lacking certain sections. Babylonian Jews were able to exert as much influence on the development of their faith as Palestinian Jews, partly, perhaps, because of their relative freedom from priestly conservatism and corruption and from nationalistic politics and intrigues.

A less-known non-Palestinian group of Jews that may have affected their homeland originated in the last years of the Babylonian Empire. For reasons unknown, Nabonidus early in his reign left Babylon to Belshazzar and, building himself a palace in Teima, lived in this desert oasis and caravan center. In Jewish folklore it was the land of the fabulously wise Bene-Qedem. It may be supposed that Jews followed him there and engaged in the trade that flowed from Medina, Mecca, and South Arabia through Teima to the Fertile Cresent.[2] Such Jews may easily have played a part in the political intrigues of changing dynasties.

At least since the sixth, perhaps since the seventh, century a group of Jews had been living on the opposite side of the wide empire, in Egypt. Two collections of papyri, found at Elephantine (Assuan) between 1906 and 1908, were published, one in Germany, the other in England. A third, after lying in a private collection unstudied for fifty years, has now been published in this country. Written in Aramaic (the lingua franca of the time and the language of the Jews) during the fifth century in a colony of Jewish mercenaries who were defending the Egyptian frontier at the first cataract of the Nile, these very considerable documents afford most valuable information regarding this unusual Jewish group and throw light on Judaism and the Persian administration. Other Aramaic documents from Egypt, recently published in England and centering about the well-known satrap Arsames, who also appears in the Elephantine papyri, provide supplementary information.

The Jewish military colony at Yeb the fortress, (*Yeb birta*) was in a very different position from the exiles in Babylon. Its members were restricted to an island in the Nile on the border far from the richer and busier sections of the land, quite in contrast to the Jews in rich and populous Babylon. These people formed a vigorous little group, but they had their own interests and troubles, for their Egyptian neighbors were hostile. They made and wrote little history. As to Judea, they mention few names that are already known, but, to our joy, their dated letters make it possible to place the persons named, especially Sanballat and his sons, in their proper historical context.

They also throw welcome light on the religious syncretism of the time.

As these contemporary documents clearly reveal, the Elephantine Jews were religiously pre-Deuteronomic. They had built a temple (unfortunately destroyed by Egyptians in a riot) and were openly worshiping two females deities, or hypostases, some would say, along with Yahweh. In common speech they used the names of both Semitic and Egyptian deities. Whether or not they include the refugees who took Jeremiah to Egypt, they may be taken as an unexpected and welcome example of the kind of Yahwism that prevailed in Palestine, perhaps in Samaria, in the seventh and sixth centuries, outside the influence of Josiah and the priestly and prophetic circles in Jerusalem. Fortunately, they seem to have had no close ties with Jerusalem, nor could Jerusalem control them, even with the aid of the Persian government.

Jews as well as other Aramaic-speaking people may have begun to penetrate Asia Minor even before the Persian period. Inscriptions in Aramaic and other evidence of later date demonstrate their presence there. However, it is in the period after Alexander that the prosperous Hellenistic Diaspora in Alexandria, Asia Minor, and lands farther west became influential, partly through their financial contributions to the mother country, partly through the fresh winds of ethical and philosophical speculation that they brought into the somewhat stagnant air of Palestinian Jewry.

3. *Theological Effects of the Dispersion* One aspect of the new situation after the Exile affected the Jewish conception of God with unexpected but profound results. When monotheism arose among the Hebrews is a vigorously but futilely debated question. Perhaps the incipient monotheism, or monolatry, of the Amarna Aton worship had suggested a vague conception of universal deity to some of the Hebrews who sojourned in Egypt. Amos is the first definitely dated writer to use phrases that may seem to embody the idea. Universal empire must raise questions in inquiring minds.

The ordinary Jews in Palestine could think of Yahweh as dwelling and acting in his own land only. They could say that the exiles in

Babylon had "gone far from Yahweh," as Ezekiel quotes them (11:15). The claim of the Assyrian monarchs that Assur gave them authority over all lands was a challenge to Yahweh's authority. The Persian monarchs, Darius and Xerxes, claimed universal dominion for Ahura-mazda and intimated that all the old deities were demons. Moreover, Jews were living in many lands, from Ecbatana to Assuan and, possibly, Athens. Since they found it possible to maintain their allegiance to Yahweh though living in far-distant lands, he could no longer be pictured as going forth from Seir and marching out of the land of Edom (Judg. 5:4) to succor his worshipers. Even ordinary Jews had to rethink the role of Yahweh in the world.

The vague monolatry of the Aton cult, the earliest known step toward universality, arose when, for the first time, Egypt became a world power, and a truly international situation developed. The Persian Empire introduced a much more inclusive international situation, and with it a universal deity. This critical period brought Judaism into contact and competition with the noblest of ancient religions, Zarathushtrism, monotheistic, without images, highly ethical, and with a definitely universal God, as well as a historical theory and a future hope. Judaism had to grow to meet the challenge, and it was ready. The implied universalism of Amos and Isaiah became outspoken and unequivocal.*

The first chapter of Genesis could hardly have been written in Judea or by a Jew in any land before the Babylonian captivity. Even Second Isaiah seems more at home in Babylonia than in Palestine. Of course not all Jews became monotheists by traveling abroad, just as many Americans imbibe no cosmopolitanism with French wines. But communication that went as far as India and China must sooner or later affect the outlook of the intelligent. While the bitter nationalism forged in the tribal conflicts of little Palestine still fettered the feet of religion

---

* Editorial Note.   At a number of points through this book, the author speaks variously of Zarathushtrism, Zoroastrianism, and Mazdaism. Each term has a specific meaning, as used in this book. Zarathushtrism refers to the religion in its purest state, as originally founded by Zarathushtra. Zoroastrianism refers to a later, somewhat debased form, and Mazdaism is employed to indicate a still later stage of degeneration.

in Judah, elsewhere Judaism seemed to be on the way to become a universal religion.

4. *The Exile*   The political history of the Jewish people is not easy to follow after the record of the Book of Kings comes to an end. Many books were written, but, aside from Haggai and Zechariah, no certain dates were given, for those of Ezra and Nehemiah are indefinite and confused. The little province in the Judean hills was too unimportant to rate mention in Persian official inscriptions. Archaeological evidence is meager since no Jewish cities or villages have been excavated that persisted from 600 to the Christian era. What is known of narrative history can be briefly summarized. It gives some assistance in making clear the cultural trends that become visible in the literature as it emerges from editorial hands in the third and second centuries along with the fuller documentation of the Hellenistic period.

According to a brief and apparently trustworthy document appended to the Book of Jeremiah (52:28–30), there were three captivities: in 598 (when Jehoiachin was taken), in 587 (when Jerusalem was destroyed), and in 582 (possibly following the murder of Gedaliah). In these deportations 4600 persons all told were taken away, a much more reasonable figure than the 10,000 (including all Jerusalem) and the rest of the multitude deported according to 2 Kings (24:14; 25:11). There is much room for difference of opinion as to the population after the final deportation in 582. The archaeological evidence, such as it is, indicates that a large number of Judean cities had been destroyed, but inhabitants remained in sites that have been excavated, such as Bethel and Mizpah (Tell en-Nasbeh), and of course in many other places.

There had been officers and men in the country when Jerusalem was destroyed; many people had fled to Moab and Ammon and Edom to escape the Babylonians. One of the officers, Jaazaniah son of the Maacathite, had died, perhaps murdered with Gedaliah; his artistic seal, with a marvelous little fighting cock carved on it and inscribed "officer (slave) of the king," was found in a Tell en-Nasbeh tomb.[3] In spite of the emphatic statements of both 2 Kings and the Book of Jeremiah, it cannot be supposed that actually all the people left in Judea went to Egypt after Ishmael's murder of Gedaliah.

The Jewish writers exaggerated. If no Jews had remained, the Edomites, who occupied the land up almost to Bethlehem, would have taken it all, or other neighbors would have moved in. Undeniably the remnant was a sorry show, and the territory available extremely small. It reached Tell en-Nasbeh on the north, but apparently not Bethel. From there to the Idumean border was but fifteen or twenty miles. Judea no longer included the cities on the edge of the Shephelah but probably retained Jericho. It would seem that, until the time of Nehemiah, it was under the governor of the province of Samaria, for he was able to stop the building of the Temple for twenty years after the first Return.[4] From 582, when the third deportation took place, until 538, when Cyrus decreed the return, Jewish and Palestinian history is a blank, except for the incident of Jehoiachin's release from prison.

Jehoiachin's acknowledged royalty, his interest in the revenues from his Judean estates, and the prosperity of the Babylonian Jews point to a different situation that arose after the first deportation, that presumably continued, and that exacerbated class distinctions within Judaism for at least 200 years. The people left in Palestine looked upon the exiles in Babylon as no longer real Hebrews. Having gone far from Yahweh, they had forfeited their citizenship, as we would say, and with it their property rights. The land belonged to those who remained. The fact that the exiles enjoyed special privileges emphasized their defection in the view of their suffering brethren left behind in ruined Palestine.

This gave a solid economic basis to the religious conflict between the two groups. Jeremiah, relaying a "word of the Lord," called the exiles "good figs," but Zedekiah, his princes, and the remnant in the land, "bad figs." The oracle goes on to promise solemnly that the exiles should be gathered from all over the world and brought back to Jerusalem (24:1–10). Ezekiel repeats a similar promise of return. He had already described the worship of the sun-god Shamash, pagan mystery rites, and women mourning for Tammuz-Adonis in the

Temple itself (8:5–18). His bitter denunciation of the faithless Jeru-
salemites is a fitting antiphony to his enthusiastic prophecies of return
and restoration for the exiles (36:22–36).

The religious situation was precarious. After the death of Josiah,
the reformer who had championed Yahweh and his law, it is not
at all surprising that leaders and people turned to other deities, as
both Jeremiah and Ezekiel report. Josiah's brief reign of thirteen years
after his reform began could make little change in age-long practices,
all the more because both prophets and people agreed that the deity
worshiped ought to give his worshipers all possible prosperity. The
evidence was all on the side of the pagan gods.

As the refugees in Egypt told Jeremiah, they would worship the
Queen of heaven as their fathers had done, for then (in the reign of
Manasseh) they had plenty of food and prospered and saw no evil.
Since they had left off burning incense and pouring out libations
to the Queen of heaven, they had lacked everything and had been
consumed by the sword and famine (Jer. 44:17–19). By a series of
unfortunate coincidences, every word they said was true. The Egyptians, robber bands from among their neighbors, and finally the Chaldeans had wasted the land from end to end. Jeremiah had no reply
but wild and empty threats in Yahweh's name.

It is significant that the Baalim, once the hated rivals of Yahweh,
had completely faded from sight. Their worship may have continued
at country high places. But the leaders, like Ahaz and Manasseh, with
the Jerusalemite patricians, were turning to foreign cults and exotic
practices learned from their conquerors. The gods of the strong battalions were about to prevail. On the accepted premises, the poor people
of Judea can hardly be blamed.

5. *The Day of Yahweh*　A generation later (actually about forty
years), the Restoration was undertaken, and, as Jeremiah and Ezekiel
had predicted, the exiles began to return. The situation into which
they came was a trying one. It is improbable that either economic or
religious conditions in Judea had materially changed. No written
records or archaeological data on such a matter are available. But
in such a land, at so low a cultural level, sacred places are rarely for-

gotten, even when a new race enters, and that was not the case in this instance. Except at the ruined Temple, worship probably went on as before, as did sowing and reaping, tending flocks, and building hovels. Yet in Babylonia much had taken place among the captives from Judea. Out of disruption, deportation, and despair a new spirit had been born.

There were many reasons why an optimistic Jew might believe that a new day was dawning for his people, when he saw the mighty Babylonian Empire destroyed by the greater might of Cyrus. The changes caused by the Persian conquest were particularly auspicious for the Jewish people. Whether for want of time or want of will, the Babylonians had not followed the Assyrian custom of settling displaced persons in Judea to fill the void left by the removal of the upper-class Jews, nor were the deported Jews settled in similar voids elsewhere in the empire. The Jews and Judea were left in an undetermined, provisional status, which could be readily altered. This allowed the Return and Restoration to take place without undue complications.

When, therefore, the Persian Great Kings, with their humane and liberal principles, succeeded the Babylonians, some Jews quickly grasped at the opportunity to reclaim their geographical heritage and re-establish their racial and national integrity. On the whole the Persian period was most fortunate for the larger part of the population of the immense empire that, "by favor of Ahuramazda and the other gods" and by Darius' vigorous action, he and his successors received and maintained for 200 years. The empire was better organized and more equitably governed than its predecessors; yet it was not an organism, but a vast conglomerate of peoples and tongues and religions. There was great variety in the forms of government, since local autonomy was allowed and the satraps enjoyed no little freedom of administration, provided only the assessed tribute was forwarded. Toward its subject peoples the imperial government was liberal and tolerant. Isocrates thought its inhabitants to be more prosperous than those in the Greek cities.[5]

From a later point of view, it is difficult to understand the en-

thusiasm with which, in Second Isaiah, the conquest of the Babylonian
Empire by Cyrus was welcomed. How could the Lord be supposed
to call Cyrus "his anointed, whose hand I have grasped"? How could
he say, "He is my shepherd, and he shall fulfill all my purpose"? [6]
Yet, in the beginning, the new regime did differ in a marked degree
from both its predecessors, the Assyrian and the Babylonian empires.
The rigors of the Assyrian regime and the sternness and then weakness of the Babylonians were succeeded by strength and firmness, with
some consideration for the ruled.

There is an interesting parallel to Second Isaiah from Babylon.
A damaged tablet contains a poem contrasting the evil deeds, the
pride, and the ignorance of Cyrus' predecessor, Nabonidus, with the
good deeds of the new king and it describes the joy of the Babylonians
at their "liberation" by Cyrus. A clay barrel, the famous Cyrus cylinder, carries a much better preserved prose text and a more explicit
statement. Following the same familiar pattern that may have been
standard in preliterate days and is still followed in modern political
campaigns, it describes Nabonidus' faithlessness to the gods and his
oppression of the people. Upon their complaints, Marduk, in great
anger, "scanned and looked through all the countries, searching for a
righteous ruler. Then he pronounced the name of Cyrus, king of
Anshan, and declared him ruler of all the world."

The tablet continues: Cyrus always endeavored to treat the black-
headed people with justice. Marduk beheld his good deeds with
pleasure and gave the city of Babylon and Nabonidus into his hands
without a battle. All the people received Cyrus with jubilation and
happily greeted him as a master through whom they had come from
death to life and had all been spared damage and disaster. In a long
description of his principles of government Cyrus says that he does not
allow anyone to terrorize any place and that he restored the sanctuaries
of cities in many lands and gathered all of their inhabitants and returned them to their habitations. He strove for peace in Babylon and
all of Marduk's sacred cities.[7]

Here was all that the Jewish exiles could wish. Their great prophet
insisted that it was Yahweh, not Marduk, who had called Cyrus, who
had grasped his hand to aid him in subduing the nations (Isa. 45:1),

and who had called him by his name (v. 4), even though the Great King was entirely unaware of Yahweh's commission to him. The passage reinterprets the Babylonian proclamation to set the event into the frame of the prophetic conception of history.

With high hopes the exiles returned, fortified by the decree of Cyrus and by the unreserved encouragement of one of the most beautiful and inspiring prophecies in the Bible. The great Unknown Prophet of the Exile had, in effect, announced that the Day of Yahweh, the day of judgment and punishment threatened by all of the great prophets from Amos and Isaiah to Jeremiah and Ezekiel, was now long past and that a new Day of Yahweh, a day of recompense and return, a day of rebuilding, was at hand, for the nation had received double for all of its sins.[8]

Perhaps with these glowing words ringing in their ears, the first to return began to rebuild the Temple. But their leader, Sheshbazzar, the Prince of Judah, who probably was Sin-ab-usur, the youngest son of Jehoiachin, suddenly and mysteriously disappears from the story. Their neighbors, after seeking to join them in building and being curtly repulsed, began to oppose their efforts and succeeded in preventing any progress until after the death of Cambyses. Then, while Darius was fighting for the throne of the empire, the hopes that had been frustrated for two decades bloomed again under the leadership of Zerubbabel, the nephew of Sheshbazzar, and Jeshua, or Joshua, the high priest.

The disturbances that preceded and followed the suicide of Cambyses in 522 were so serious that it took Darius more than two years to reduce all the provinces to submission. Doubtless it looked to dissatisfied subjects as if the empire were falling to pieces. In 520, while the issue was still in doubt, the prophets Haggai and Zechariah began urging Zerubbabel and Joshua to complete the rebuilding of the Temple. Three months later Haggai quoted God as announcing to him, "I am about to shake the heavens and the earth and overthrow the throne of kingdoms; I am about to destroy the strength of the kingdoms of the nations. . . . I will take you, O Zerubbabel, and . . . make you like a signet ring." He is the Davidic prince about to come into his kingdom.[9]

The fate of Zerubbabel, like that of Sheshbazzar, is one of the mysteries of the postexilic period. Long before the Temple is dedicated (March 12, 515), both he and Haggai disappear from view. Perhaps Haggai's too exuberant language had been reported at court. So much seems to have been expected, so little accomplished. The prophecy of Haggai closes with unlimited promises to Zerubbabel.

Zechariah, a priest turned prophet, is more interested in Joshua, the high priest, than in Zerubbabel; but he combines the two in the famous *menorah* vision (4:2–14), with the promise, in God's name, that Zerubbabel's hands that had laid the foundation should complete the Temple, "not by might, nor by power, but by my Spirit, says the Lord of hosts." The two olive trees suggest a kind of diarchy, Temple and palace, priest and king. But in Zechariah's next chapter mysterious symbols of iniquity appear, and a little later four men set a crown on the head of Joshua the high priest. He is the "man whose name is Branch . . . and he shall build the Temple of the Lord" (6:11–14). Symbolism could hardly be clearer. The crown had passed from the line of David to that of Aaron. The priest had replaced the prince.

Judea was to remain a hierocracy, a priest-ruled cult community, as long as it maintained a national entity and retained a semblance of autonomy. For 600 years the Hebrews had looked to a king as ruler (1125-515). For 600 years again they were to be under priestly rule (515 B.C.–70 A.D.). The steps taken when Josiah introduced the Deuteronomic law and Ezekiel planned his priestly utopia had now reached their inevitable end. The Exile altered the form of the state completely. Formerly the palace controlled the Temple; now the Temple controlled the nation. The palace was no more. Unfortunately, the prophets, who had exercised a measure of control over the monarchy, disappeared in the fetid atmosphere of priestly rule. There were no checks and balances for the priesthood until Pharisaism arose, some four centuries later. The monarchy had failed, as Samuel was supposed by some priestly writer to have warned. Now the priesthood had its opportunity.

CHAPTER IX

The Hierocracy of the Second Temple (516 B. C.–A. D. 70)

1. *Problems of the Restored Community* The complexities, both internal and external, of the situation in which the infant restored community found itself were beyond the powers of the priestly group upon whom leadership devolved. They were part of a vast, sprawling political aggregation. Semitic groups had worn themselves out trying to govern it. Leadership had now fallen to a very different and wholly inexperienced non-Semitic race. It is remarkable that the Persians governed as well as they did. The returning Jews found themselves surrounded by suspicious neighbors and in the midst of putative brethren with a very different set of ethical standards and religious opinions and with hostile economic interests.

The eloquent Prophet of the Exile might celebrate Cyrus, but succeeding Great Kings proved to be uncertain factors. One king readily reversed what his predecessor had decreed. Only influence at court, such as Nehemiah had, could insure continued favors. The Persian system of taxation was so burdensome and unjust that it eventually brought widespread ruin. In general the dynasty exhibited a gradual decline. Under Artaxerxes II, who reintroduced Mithra worship, it almost expired.

Problems for those who returned were the exiles who preferred the richer life of Babylon and the permanent Jewish inhabitants of Judea who wished to keep the land for themselves. Josephus says that the Babylonian Jews "did not wish to leave their possessions."[1]

So it is today with many both orthodox and liberal Jews of England and America. So also the orthodox Jews who had already lived for years in Palestine eyed the irreligious, nationalistic Balfour Declaration Jews askance, even though they came bearing gifts.

As to religion, however, the roles are reversed. The Babylonian exiles came back with an orthodoxy and a religious enthusiasm that were quite alien to the lax and syncretistic Jews in Palestine, who preferred their easy liberty and their friendly relations with their neighbors. They could hardly welcome the Babylonian Jews with their claims to land and the supercilious superiority of the "good figs." It is little wonder that the Return brought little Restoration.

Moreover, when the new priestly state was reinvigorated as a result of Haggai's and Zechariah's efforts, the little province was under twenty miles long, north and south, and fifteen miles wide, plus over a hundred square miles of useless steppe east of the watershed and a few hundred acres of irrigable land near Jericho. Albright estimates the population at 20,000. In a community made up largely of the permanent inhabitants and with hostile neighbors on every side, the returned exiles, in their minority status, were gradually worn down until they lost their enthusiasm, once the Temple had been built. They learned to accommodate themselves to the situation and, perforce, to make friends and intermarry with the people of the neighboring states. For a century more or less, no information is available —that is, from the time of the dedication of the Temple to the coming of Nehemiah. A new chapter in Judea's history began with his arrival.

2. *The Second Restoration (450–400)*   Nehemiah and Ezra appeared in Jerusalem sometime during the second half of the fifth century.[2] Their exact time and their mutual relations are relatively unimportant. Their information regarding the community is priceless. Their complaints make clear how completely the first Return had failed. The child had almost died shortly after birth. In both ritual and morality the embryo kingdom of God had fallen to an extremely low level. The Sabbath was not observed; the Temple sacrifices were neglected; the prescribed offerings were not brought in. The rich were over-

reaching the poor, seizing their lands for debt, and actually selling Jewish children into slavery to aliens to satisfy their fathers' obligations. Worst of all, priests, Levites, and people were intermarrying with "the peoples of the lands." Samaria, Ammon, Ashdod, and Moab are specified.[3]

As in modern Zionism, the use of the Hebrew language was specially stressed in this second Return. An amusing touch is Nehemiah's complaint that, owing to the foreign marriages, half the children spoke the languages of these aliens and could not speak the language of Judah. The irony of his remark cries to heaven, for at this very time the Jews everywhere in the Persian Empire were learning to speak Aramaic and were losing the use of the sacred Hebrew. Nehemiah wrote his memoirs in Hebrew, and that for him was no doubt the language of Judah. But when the Chronicler compiled the Book of Ezra he put into it Aramaic documents along with Hebrew. The Jews in Elephantine used Aramaic exclusively throughout the fifth century. At Jericho, Jerusalem, and Tell en-Nasbeh, stamped handles of jars for taxes carried the legend *Yehud,* the Aramaic word for Judea, in Aramaic letters quite similar to those of the Elephantine papyri. Since the settled occupation of Tell en-Nasbeh probably ended nearer 400 than 350, these jars must have come into official use in the little province Nehemiah had made internally independent at the latest shortly after his sharp protest.[4] Nehemiah was trying to sweep the tide back with an antiquated broom.

Nehemiah's linguistics may have been confused, but his intention is clear. His overmastering concern was the purity of the racial stock and of religious practices. The two were inseparable. By isolation from their neighbors God's Chosen People would be kept clean from all ritual defilement and from alliances that threatened their religion. He was oblivious of the fact that such isolation was impossible and he forgot that it was not practiced in Babylon. He himself was a court official. As a eunuch, wife and children meant nothing to him. The inherent baseness of a demand for the ruthless divorce of women who had married in good faith might have been in the mind of Malachi (2:11–16), but he is pleading for Jewish wives abandoned for "the daughter of a foreign god" (v. 10). "What does God desire? Godly offspring." (v. 15). Malachi's concern is the same as Nehemiah's: a pure race.

The reading of the Law by Ezra and the covenant accepted and signed by leaders and people seem to have been just as effective as were like actions taken under Josiah.[5] The aggressive measures of Nehemiah and Ezra with regard to alien wives, which form a bizarre climax for both books, were equally ineffective, if one may judge by subsequent practice among patrician families. It required centuries of discipline and education and the final threat of extinction, religious and national, to produce a law-abiding and partly integrated community, with both ideologies and institutions firmly established.

3. *Society and Politics* To understand what happened during the two following centuries, from which we have almost no historical records, it is well to take stock of conditions as Nehemiah left them. The total Jewish population may be supposed to number just under 50,000, of whom 7000 were slaves and, last and lowliest of all, 245 were male and female musicians.[6] The territory could have been little larger than it was a hundred years earlier, when the Temple was built. Many Jews from beyond Judea were included in the census and came to assist in the building of the city walls, as subject to the religious authority of the high priest. The jar handles stamped *Yehud* and coins with the same legend indicate a status for Judea such as other sacerdotal states, of which there were many in the empire, enjoyed. Certainly they place Tell en-Nasbeh, Jericho, and Jerusalem in a truly microscopic territory.

The Day of the Lord had been indefinitely adjourned. The rocky backbone of the Judean mountains provided a precarious living for the inhabitants of an almost infinitesimal priestly state that seemed like its neighbors. Because it was so small and so circumscribed, its resources were pitiably meager, even less than those of any of its rival neighbors, Samaria, Ammon, Ashdod, and the "Arabs."

Both Ezra and Nehemiah were interested chiefly in rebuilding Jerusalem and establishing the Temple cultus according to the prescriptions of the Priestly Code. But the internal conflict between rich landlords and poor peasants and the constantly recurring catastrophes that menaced the rural population could not be escaped. Nehemiah (5:1–13) met one such crisis by trying to enforce the Pentateuchal laws forbidding interest on loans, the enslavement of Jews, and the permanent alienation of anyone's land. But that could not solve the problem of sufficient production for even a minimum standard of living. As to well-being, the Jews could hardly compete with their neighbors.

From Nehemiah's point of view the great danger was that they should become like their neighbors, and that was exactly what their neighbors desired. Actually they were different. Behind them the Jews had written records of an inspiring history, greatly exaggerated it must be granted, but nevertheless a past of which they could be proud, as the mixed populations of Samaria and the coast (Ashdod) could not. Even the more homogeneous Moabites and Ammonites had never had a David or Solomon. Worst of all, from their neighbors' point of view, they had a theory of history and a national and racial hope, a world-embracing political theory, that promised them eventual universal dominion. Their neighbors all possessed territory that had once belonged to the Hebrew empire. Therefore they feared the revived Jewish state as the Arab states fear modern Israel. When nationalism, racialism, and religion unite on an imperialistic foreign policy, neighboring peoples may well dwell in fear. Moreover, like modern Israel, the Jews had rich and energetic groups of coreligionists abroad that could influence the imperial administration and also send them help in men and wealth when needed. It is little wonder that they were viewed with suspicion and hostility.

The strategy of their neighbors was based upon a real, if self-interested, policy of friendship. The motives of Geshem the Arab and of the Ashdodites were doubtless purely selfish. Geshem may have had the Jewish merchants of Teima in mind. But, in the case of the two men whom Nehemiah most feared and hated, religious considerations played a part and made them all the more dangerous.

Sanballat had a Babylonian name, Sin-uballit (but so had Zerubbabel and other Jews of the period). The worst that Nehemiah could say of him was that he was a Horonite, from Horonaim in Moab (Isa. 15:5, rather than Beth-Horon), and therefore of dubious ancestry. He does not say that Tobiah was an Ammonite, but "the Ammonite Commandant," with an intentional play upon the word *'ebed,* literally "slave." [7] He must have been the Persian-appointed governor of the district of Ammon, as Sanballat was of Samaria. Yet both men could claim a share in the Jewish state because they were, at least formally, Yahwists. Tobiah is shown to be such, not only by his own name, but also by that of his son, Yohanan (Neh. 6:8.), as well as by the subsequent romantic history of his house. Sanballat proved his allegiance by giving his sons Yahwist names, as is known from the mention of "Delaiah and Shelemiah, sons of Sanballat, governor of Samaria" in the Elephantine petition to Bagohi (Bagoses), dated 25 November, 407, for permission to rebuild the Jewish temple there.[8] Apparently Delaiah had succeeded his father as governor, for he joins Bagohi in sending approval of the proposed rebuilding.

The history of Samaria in this period is otherwise blank. When would the Samaritans have adopted the Pentateuch? It must have happened during the period of friendship between the two little states, probably after Nehemiah's final departure, for there is no reason to believe that his brutal measures were immediately and permanently successful. At the end of his governorship, or at least of his memoirs (13:28-29), his last act was to "chase from him" the high priest Eliashib's grandson (named Manasseh by Josephus), who was married to a daughter of Sanballat and refused to divorce her. This seems a suitable time for Josephus' variant story, that Sanballat undertook to build a temple on Mount Gerizim for his faithful son-in-law and that friends of the young high priest followed him to assume office under him in Samaria.[9] At such a time the Pentateuch would have been taken by the ambitious priest as a symbol of authority. Time rapidly embittered cultic and ethnic animosities.

As to the relations between the Jewish community and the mighty but slowly failing empire after Nehemiah's time, no record or even hint has been left except for two minor exceptions. The small ethnic group, ruled *de facto* by its priesthood, but subject *de jure* to the

Persian governor, lay wide open to intrigue and abuse of power. Josephus reports an item that does the hierocracy no credit but is, perhaps, characteristic. Yeshua, brother of the high priest, Yohanan, was a favorite of the governor, Bagoses. Out of jealous fear, Yohanan killed his brother within the Temple itself. This gave the governor occasion to enter and thus violate the sacred area and to impose a heavy fine on the Jews.[10] Whether this Bagoses (Bagohi, Bigwai) and Yohanan were the governor and high priest of the Elephantine letters is uncertain, but the identity is plausible.

Eusebius reports a revolt of the Jews against Artaxerxes that led to the destruction of Jericho and the deportation of many Jews.[11] This could have happened *c.* 353–345, for at that time there was a Phoenician, or Sidonian, revolt, which the Jews might well have joined. The decrepitude of Artaxerxes II in his old age suggested possibilities of freedom. Unfortunately he died unexpectedly, and Artaxerxes III showed remarkable vigor in resuscitating the moribund empire and suppressing revolts with a cruelty and deportations that were Assyrian rather than Achaemenian in their heartlessness.[12] Some scholars discover effects of this episode in the complaints of various postexilic documents.

In such times as these, Jews like Sanballat and Tobiah, syncretist and sympathetic to pagan culture, if not religion, could have been found in all the lands around Judea. To men like Ezra and Nehemiah they were pestilential centers of infection. Liberalized Jews of un-questionably good ancestry were ready to make friends with the gentiles and inclined for various reasons to compromise the strict re-quirements of the Law. Business opportunities were attractive to some and, what was much the same, political intrigue to others. Some were drawn by natural curiosity and by dissatisfaction with the isolation of strict Judaism, some by the freer and more colorful life of other peoples. The priestly groups seem to have been especially open to temptation. Perhaps Eliashib, the high priest whom Nehemiah hated, was persuaded that, as titular head of the state, he was providing for its safety by outside alliances, as David and Solomon had done. The story of Tobiah and his family illuminates the problems, the dangers,

and the effects of the conflicts and intrigues within the Jewish state
and with their neighbors, although it is an extraordinary and perhaps
unique example.

4. *The Story of the Tobiadae (c. 450–c. 170)*   The Tobiads are unusually interesting both for the sinister part they played in Jewish history during more than two centuries and for the remarkable documentation of the story. Bene-Tobiyah appear in the lists of Ezra
(2:60) and Nehemiah (7:62) among families from Babylon which
could not prove their Israelite descent. Presumably the Tobiah Nehemiah hated belonged to that family. Two letters of a Toubias who
was military governor of Ammon were preserved among the famous
Zenon papyri. Josephus relates with relish and at length fabulous
stories of two Tobiadae who, a half-century later, were prominent
figures in Syro-Palestinian history and in Jewish priestly intrigue as
publicans, tax farmers for the territories of the Ptolemies in Syria
and Palestine.*

Most remarkable of all is the archaeological documentation. In all
of Palestine the only Jewish name that still remains carved upon the
family dwelling place is that of a Tobiah. High in the western mountains of Transjordan, looking out southwestward through Wadi Kefrein toward the Dead Sea, is a mountain peak in which, in a limestone
scarp, a most unusual establishment was excavated: large and small
living rooms and stables sufficient to accommodate a considerable
entourage. Twice deeply carved in well-formed Aramaic characters
on the smooth-cut rock frontal, the name Tobiyah stares out on an
area of ruins. A short distance away are the remains of a castle, or
villa, of which the one white-limestone wall that still stands carries
"beasts of gigantic size" (a slight exaggeration), which Josephus mentions. Josephus' unusually accurate description of the structures would
have been denounced as pure romance if they had not been preserved.
The barbaric mixture of Oriental and Occidental styles and the
Aramaic characters could belong to the fourth or the third century.

---

* Editorial Note.   In this section the name Tobias is spelled in four different
ways. These various spellings seem to be reflections of the forms used in the
source which the author was employing, and hence intentional.

By a strange coincidence the Arab names for the places, 'Araq el-Emir, "the Prince's Peak" (or "Caverns"), and Qasr el-'Abd, "the Slave's Castle," are reminiscent of Nehemiah's enemy, who was both a "prince," a royal officer, and a "slave" of the Persian emperor. Is it a mere coincidence? The carved name and Josephus' description defy any question as to the identification.

Much less is known of the Tubias of the Zenon correspondence. He addressed Ptolemy II with the customary obsequious formulas. He wrote to Apollonius, the king's powerful finance minister, as an equal. His occasion was a present to the king of wild animals from the steppe and a gift to Apollonius of a eunuch and four well-bred slave boys. Tubias was neither an "Ammonite slave" nor an "Ammonite sheikh," as some have called him, but a Hellenistic gentleman of wealth, rank, and authority. There is nothing in his letters to indicate that he was a Jew; there was no call for such an identification. His name is sufficient. He was well known as military commander and governor of Ammon with his seat at Birta, the "Fortress." [13]

A generation later his son and grandson, or a grandson and great-grandson, Joseph and Hyrcanus, were successful and powerful tax farmers under the Ptolemies. The mother of Joseph was sister of the high priest, Onias II, and she must have been the wife of the Ammonite Tobiad, since Joseph is called "son of Tobias." Josephus tells (with great relish) a gorgeous series of fantastic tales about the father and the son and their dealings with the monarchs whom they served, to show how Jews could charm and outwit the gentiles.

It was a wonderful success story until Antiochus IV Epiphanes recovered Palestine from Ptolemy VI. Hyrcanus' jealous half-brothers had turned against him. In a brawl between them, some of the brothers were killed, and Hyrcanus fled to his "strong fortress" in Ammon and busied himself fighting the "Arabs." When Antiochus was ready to take Palestine over, Hyrcanus committed suicide in fear of him. His brothers had combined with the high priest, Onias-Menelaus, their cousin, to offer Antiochus assistance in Hellenizing the Jewish people. A decade later Judas Maccabeus had "Tobiad Jews" to defend at a fortress in Ammon.

The Tobiad story in a sense covers the blank period between Nehemiah and Judas Maccabeus. It even goes back to Zerubbabel. The Bene-Tobiyah, returned but rejected exiles, might be expected to migrate to Ammon when they were refused full status in Israel. With the ability, religious flexibility, and energy shown by their descendants, they could have won wealth and position that partially erased the blot on their ancestry and made them seem to the harassed high priests in Jerusalem to be worth cultivating. As Yahwists they had a deep interest in Jerusalem, although they were syncretists and assimilationists. The history of the Tobiad family fully justifies the apprehensions of Nehemiah and Ezra as it also demonstrates the futility of their countermeasures.

Elijah and Elisha had tried political intrigue, with disastrous results. Beginning with Isaiah, the prophets had warned against foreign alliances. Pacifism and neutralism were the only safe policies for a little buffer state caught between great nations. So Isaiah and Jeremiah warned. The Isaian inviolability of Jerusalem seemed to point in the pacifist direction. But, repeatedly relying on the broken reed of foreign aid, the nation had again and again suffered a pierced hand but had learned nothing. Nehemiah's legal measures proved equally futile. The struggle between isolationist and assimilationist reached its climax when Antiochus Epiphanes, misled by intriguing Tobiads, tried a premature policy of forced Hellenization.

5. *Hellenism in Judea (c. 500)* Foreign cultural influences were always at work throughout the Fertile Crescent. For the Chosen People manifest destiny could not combine with magnificent isolation in a country like Palestine. What could be expected in a land that formed a bridge between continents and a portage between the ships of the sea and the "ships of the desert"? Numerous artifacts from all the world found in ruins of every period abundantly demonstrate the fact. Language and tradition bound them to the Orient. But archaeologists have registered the impression that, in pottery for example, it was the West rather than the East that contributed the most numerous and most artistic models. The sea offered a smoother path than the land. Every excavation, be it noted, that covers the Middle Bronze and Late

Bronze periods finds Cypriote "milk bowls" and "wishbone handles." "Philistine pottery" is the only distinctive and highly decorated ware indigenous to the country, and that, without a doubt, was of foreign inspiration—from the West. Foreign importation continues throughout the Iron Age. In the sixth century Greek ware and coins begin to appear. In the second century the cities were flooded with Rhodian wine jars. Quite naturally this western influence is very strong in cities on the coast and in or near the maritime plain, such as Gezer, Azekah, Marisa, Tell Abu-Hawam, and Samaria. Yet it went inland also.

How early and how strong Greek commercial influence was is shown by a piece of a Clazomenian bowl and several fragments of Attic red- and black-figure ware dating from 540 to 500 found at Tell en-Nasbeh, an insignificant country fortress in the mountains. Some twenty-five different vessels were represented. One imitation Attic bronze tetradrachm of 409–393 tells the same story of trade with the Aegean.[14] Within a small excavated area Beth-zur had similar evidence dating from about 400. In view of the fact that no extensive excavations have been carried on in Judea elsewhere, except at Jerusalem (comparatively fruitless), it is not surprising that there is no evidence except from the two border towns of Persian Judah. That Attic wares should have been found at two little mountain fortresses, such as these two places were, speaks loudly for the extent of Greek penetration into Judea long before the armies of Alexander marched down the "oldest road in the world" to Egypt. Ideas came later, but they came.

The coins found in the citadel of Beth-zur offer an epitome of Judah's political and cultural history in the Hellenistic period. There are ten Greek or imitation-Greek coins that belong to the last century of the Persian period. Fifty-one come from the century of Ptolemaic overlordship, ending in 198, and two, of Ptolemy VI (182–181), suggest lingering Egyptian influence and commerce after the country fell to the Seleucid dynasty. That line, which made Beth-zur one of its fortresses, is represented by 173 coins, at least 110 of them bearing the head of Antiochus IV Epiphanes (176–165). They soon disappear after John Hyrcanus came to the throne (135–104).[15]

The growth of Hellenistic influence on all sides of Judah left it, as before, an embattled enclave in the midst of enemies. Cities with all the appurtenances of advanced civilization were all about: Gaza, Ashkelon, Ashdod, Jamnia, Dora, Ptolemais, Samaria, Sepphoris, Scythopolis (Beth-shan), and, on the east side of the Jordan, the cities that later became the Decapolis. Rabbath-ammon had been refounded and given its Greek name, Philadelphia, in the time of Ptolemy Philadelphus (283–245). Under the imposing Roman remains at Gerasa there is evidence of a Greek city that goes back into the second century, probably to earlier times. In the time of Zeno and Tubias, Marisa, with its rectilinear city plan, had its Sidonian colony, its painted tombs, its columbarium, and it was an active center for the slave trade.[16] The full flowering of Hellenistic civilization came later, when Pompey again founded the cities and gave them Greek "democratic" constitutions. But an excellent beginning had been made under the Ptolemies and the Seleucids.

The painted tombs of Sidonian Marisa, the grotesque symbolic sculpture of Nabatean Khirbet et-Tannur, the synthetic architecture and carving of the palace and the rock-cut living rooms and banquet halls of Tobiad Birta, the tasteless combination of styles in the tombs along the Kedron Valley at Jerusalem, all are indicative of the maelstrom of cultural change in the Persian and Greek periods. Perhaps most startling and significant of all, certainly the most impressive, are the tombs and dwelling places, the tremendous façades of temples, and the mountaintop and underground sacrificial triclinia and altars of Nabatean Petra, the "rose-red city," carved in the variegated sandstone of the mountains of Seir. These remains testify to the vaulting ambition, the crude artistic taste, and the synthetic culture of families and cities, both Jewish and gentile, that found themselves caught in the new world created by the Macedonian and Roman conquests.[17] The stories Josephus tells of the Tobiads and the high priests are social and political reflections of the cultural conflicts and changes that are so spectacularly illustrated by the archaeological remains.

The office files of Apollonius, preserved by the meticulous Zeno, with their carefully docketed and dated documents and letters, draw a brief but illuminating sketch of another basic phase of culture, the commercial life of Palestine and Syria in the latter half of the third century. It is a record that can be extrapolated to suggest conditions all through the Hellenistic and Roman periods. Zeno, his agents, and his business correspondents travel all over Palestine, Syria, and Anatolia, apparently in comparative safety. They direct commerce by land and by sea.

There are very few references to Judea and Jerusalem. Doubtless that area was too poor, as well as too inhospitable, to offer opportunities for making money. But elsewhere trade was vigorous in many commodities: myrrh, frankincense, perfumes, and other luxuries that came overland from South Arabia through Palestine; grains, oil, wine, and in Palestine especially slaves. Zeno purchased a seven-year-old slave girl in "Birtha of the Ammanitis" and several men in "Marisa of Idumea." Toubias' gift to Ptolemy included horses and dogs, but the asses of peculiar breeds, wild and half-wild, were hardly articles of commerce, although all were broken. Of the slaves sent to Apollonius, two were circumcised, two uncircumcised. In other letters are references to escaped slaves and to fraudulent slave trade. The devious workings of the customs system are mentioned. It is a vivid and informative revelation of active business on a large, international scale.[18]

The stories that the Books of Maccabees and Josephus tell of intrigue and strife among the priests, especially in this period, make a sorry picture. They tried to get the most possible for themselves and their families through bargains, first with their Egyptian and then with their Syrian overlords. Defection was worst in the higher, that is, the richer, circles of the priesthood. Yet there were honest, patriotic, and pious high priests, such as Simon the Just. No one doubts that there were great numbers of the rank and file who did not play in with their oppressors. There were many who were willing to adopt Greek hats, dress, manners, and morals, even Greek religion, in order to get on in the world and enjoy the freer air and larger pleasures of Greek society. They set no value on race, nation, or religion. But there were many more who were ready to resist to the last extremity, as became evident enough, to the astonishment of both Greeks and Jews, when the brave old priest Mattathias rebelled against the attempt of Antiochus Epiphanes to replace the worship of Yahweh with that of Zeus, to put pigs instead of lambs on the Temple altar.

On the other hand, the Hellenistic period and perhaps still more that of the Persians made tremendous changes in the thinking, the theology, and the social attitudes of Jews of all classes. Since so much of the best biblical literature, in the prophets and the Psalms, cannot be securely placed as to date, it is impossible to determine in detail what internal experiences and external influences produced the various phases of change. The most startling innovations, that is, ideas new and strange to the Old Testament, come to light in the pseudepigraphic writings that are usually dated after 200. To these it will be necessary to return before attempting to assess the trends of thought that produced the New Testament and Christianity, on the one hand, and Talmudic Judaism, on the other. The new did not suddenly spring up, blossom, and bear luxuriant fruit without sowing and without depth of earth. It is sufficient here to refer to these problems before passing on to discuss the general political and social situation under the Maccabees and the Romans.

6. *The Maccabean Revival of Nationalism*   It has often been said that, if Antiochus Epiphanes had not attempted to force the abandonment of the worship of Yahweh, the permeating acid of Hellenistic thinking would have destroyed or denatured the Jewish faith within another generation. So far as any historical might-have-beens can be accepted, the saying is probably right. At least so it seemed then to Antiochus' Jewish advisers and so it appears to the modern student. However, as so often happens, undue haste and the use of force produced just the opposite of the intended effect.

The result was epoch making, in the exact sense. It produced a new age in Judaism—one might say, a new Judaism. It is difficult to believe that the isolation decreed by Ezra's laws, forbidding exogamous marriage, for example, could have been strictly observed or enforced when the leading families were themselves so deeply involved in the affairs of the Ptolemies and then the Seleucids, as well as of the neighboring states. In the Book of Ruth the Old Testament canon itself preserved a charming and idyllic protest, how effective one cannot say, against the social and racial exclusiveness of Ezra and Nehemiah, just as Jonah clearly criticized religious exclusiveness and hatred of gentiles. But the bitter struggle to preserve their religious documents and their faith created among the Jews a new atmosphere of deep hostility to all things Greek. Proselytism was not excluded, but there were Jews who did not accept the more generous attitudes of some of the prophets.[19] According to a Christian source (Matt. 23:15), the Pharisees were famous for proselyting zeal. But, although Ruth the Moabitess had been an ancestress of David, no priest whose mother was not an Israelite could serve in the Temple.

The same historical circumstances that produced a new sense of difference between Jews and all other nations revealed new cleavages within the isolated group itself. They centered first about nationalism. When the faith was in danger, all Jews (except some patricians) rallied to the side of the Maccabees. As soon as religious freedom was offered by the Seleucids, some of the Hasidim, the strict observants of the Law, who were not interested in the political organization and independence of their country, fatuously abandoned Judas to make peace with Alcimus, the Syrian appointee as high priest. The Pharisees later broke with John Hyrcanus, and, as the Maccabean dynasty became more clearly warrior kings rather than priests, the parties of the Pharisees and Sadducees took definite, antagonistic form.

The threat of annihilation to its religion brought to the fore another division within the nation. Those who trusted in God rather than arms to save his people took refuge in the wild visions of apocalyptic literature. The Day of Yahweh was to be, not a historical event, or the culmination of historical events, but a purely miraculous, catastrophic interference in the course of history. Prophetic historicism became apocalyptic eschatology. The "last events" in history were just at hand —whence the use of the word *eschaton* and the term "eschatology." With the priestly Sadducees holding only to the Torah, the five books of Moses, and the Pharisees in the main adding to the Law only the prophets and the other canonical writings, those who accepted the apocalypses, whether they were Pharisees or others, made a notable addition to the sacred writings and created still further divisions within the nation.

There was a time when the Maccabean rulers could be regarded as fulfilling the prophecies of a happy future for the restored nation. Simon had introduced a brief idyllic age of peace and prosperity, when, as the historian wrote,

> They tilled their land in peace,
> The land yielded its increase,
> And the trees of the plains their fruits. . . .
> Everyone sat under his own vine and fig tree
> With none to make them afraid.[20]

John Hyrcanus united within himself, says Josephus, the three most excellent offices, the supreme command of the nation, the high priesthood, and the gift of prophecy.[21] The dynasty was fortunate in having four strong and worthy men at its beginning. It went out in complete disgrace under Alexander Janneus and his two warring sons, the stubborn Aristobulus and the half-witted Hyrcanus. The reign of Herod was better, that of the Roman procurators still better for the nation as a whole. But the people's national and racial hopes had again been ground to pieces under the heels, not of foreign oppressors, but of their own ineffective and perverse rulers.

7. *Under Roman Rule* When, in 63, Pompey made his famous survey of the eastern Mediterranean countries, all of those lands, Judea no less than the others, entered a new political era. However strong the Hellenizing influences that flowed over Palestine and Syria, that area was still occupied by Aramaic-speaking peoples, with a strong infusion, indeed, of Greeks and Hellenized Orientals, but still facing toward the Semitic East. The rule of native dynasts did not at once come to an end; the evils of colonial administration for which the cupidity of Roman senators was responsible still continued for thirty years, and the Roman civil wars left their trail over these lands also. But a new sun was arising, in the west. If it burned it also blessed. It brought the end of the nationalistic revival.

The situation of Palestine under Hyrcanus II, whom Pompey made ethnarch and high priest, even when the steadying hand of the Idumean Antipater was added in 55, was most unhappy and was greatly embittered by the attempts of his more vigorous brother, Aristobulus, to replace him. But in 40 the Parthians unexpectedly solved the problem by invading Palestine, capturing Hyrcanus, and allowing his nephew, Antigonus, to mutilate his ears, which made him ineligible to act as priest. In 37 Antony beheaded Antigonus. Herod had become king. Thus the Maccabean dynasty came to a sorry end.

Herod the Great, at least to outward appearance, determined Judaism and Christianity for the West. Once, at a lightly attended Sabbath morning service that coincided with the Fourth of July, I heard an eloquent rabbi assure his audience that but for Judas Maccabeus "and his friends" there would have been no Fourth of July. They had saved freedom and monotheistic religion with its ethics, without which Western civilization never could have developed. It is another of those historical might-have-beens that are plausible and thought provoking.

It is just as appropriate to say that but for Herod the Great Western Christianity never could have been. Until Alexander the Great marched eastward, Palestine had always been within the Eastern orbit, even if on the western edge of it. Parthia, the one power that could challenge Rome, captured and beheaded the famous Roman consul, Crassus, and his son, and destroyed his Roman army in 53; in 40 they took possession of Palestine. With remarkable energy and resourcefulness, the Idumean Herod, with the aid of a couple of Roman legions, drove out the Parthians and saved Palestine for the West. Otherwise, Jesus might have been born on the outskirts of the Oriental world with its eyes toward Asia, instead of in a far-eastern province of the Occidental world with its eyes toward Europe. An Aramaic-speaking Paul might have stormed Seleucia and Ecbatana instead of Corinth and Rome.

How serious the grievances of the Jews against Herod were it is difficult to say. They certainly had reason to prefer a Roman procurator to Herod's son, Archelaus. But under neither could they have been worse off than they had been under the last Maccabean kings. Augustus had decidedly altered the abominable methods by which the provinces had been plundered under the Republic. The rapacity of proconsuls and procurators that Cicero so vividly portrays had been put under control. Even provincials could appeal to the emperor. Stupid and arrogant governors like Pontius Pilate might deeply offend their sub-

jects, yet there were limits to their injustice and tyranny. In Egypt
there were also stirrings of revolt, but no native population made such
trouble for the Romans as did the Jews. The reasons for this were only
in part derived from Roman misgovernment. They arose rather from
Jewish racialism and nationalism.

Unfortunately the only full account preserved of the events leading
to the "Jewish War" comes from Josephus, renegade Jewish general
and collaborator with Rome who, when he became a prisoner of war,
went over to the enemy. But Josephus as writer does not entirely
falsify the historical situation. He does avoid direct mention of the
messianic hope. He calls patriotic Jews brigands and bandits. He appeals to the personal and financial feelings of Roman equites and
senators when he tells how the rebels burned the public archives that
contained moneylenders' bonds, an item that reveals other sores in the
body politic aside from any Roman misgovernment. Yet he cannot tell
the story without revealing the deep-seated aversion of the Jewish
people to their Roman overlords and to any foreign rule.

An unsolved problem of first-century Judaism is the actual number
and influence of the "fourth sect," which Josephus places beside the
Sadducees, Pharisees, and Essenes. He gives them no name but elsewhere refers to *zelotes,* "Zealots" (Aramaic, *qan'ana,* "zealous," not
"Canaanites"), and sometimes to *sicarii,* "dagger men, assassins." The
"fourth sect," who seem to include all "activists," believed that God
expected them to do something about the evil situation and that, when
they acted, he would assist them. They were, therefore, for revolt because they believed, not that they could overcome the Romans, but
that God would do it for them if they showed themselves brave and
resolute. They "have an inviolable attachment to liberty," says Josephus, "and say that God is their only ruler and Lord." In other
words, they wished complete independence in a "reign of God," doubtless with themselves as administrators and executors of God's will.[22]

The Essenes make their appearance in the records of Josephus and
the writings of Philo. Both authors' generalized and rhetorical accounts
are now remarkably supplemented and corrected by the Dead Sea, or
Qumran, Scrolls, with a mass of materials that will take years to in-

terpret and evaluate. Such groups provided for those who, as Pliny expressed it, were weary of life's struggle with the waves of adversity.[23] They were ascetic, communistic, messianist, and in revolt against current Jewish practices. There are striking resemblances between their beliefs and those of early Christianity, but equally striking differences, whether compared with Jesus or with Paul.

Very different is the picture of simple, quietistic Jewish piety drawn in Luke's account of the families of John the Baptist and Jesus. Doubtless it is idealized, but there are parallels in some of the Psalms and Old Testament prophetical utterances. The new documents will help the modern student to understand better the complex movements and trends within Judaism that brought Christianity to birth and then repudiated it. Some of this material must be reserved for the analysis later on of the Jews' interpretation of their own history and for the evaluation of the beginnings of Christianity.

The aristocratic Sadducees were so far out of touch with the general population that they could exercise little leadership. The Pharisees were the leaders of thought. But they were from the upper middle class and the group of artisans, or skilled laborers. They encouraged a reasonable interpretation of the Scriptures and, aside from some undue legalism, a reasonable interpretation of religion. Yet there was nothing especially attractive, no release, no "salvation," in their way of life and their ideas. They offered no leadership to the multitudes and no hope for the present—or the future.

A great mass of Jews on the lower social and economic levels— poverty and want must have been great—were alienated from the Pharisees, for, although they could not but approve their religious and moral system, they found their unrealistic legalistic demands impossibly difficult and their dogmatism harsh and repellent. They already belonged to what the later rabbis called *'Am ha-'arets,* the "people of the land," ignorant or neglectful of the Law and therefore accursed. Accordingly they were ready to follow personally attractive and dynamic leaders like John the Baptist and Jesus and to accept their warmer and more inspiring conceptions of God and duty and above all their confident assurance that the reign of God was near.

Amid all these mental confusions and party conflicts, the profound unrest and dissatisfaction of the great majority, along with exaggerated memories of the past, mythical hopes, and continued frustrations, led finally to three epoch-making events: the Roman war with its destruction of Jerusalem and the Temple, the development of Talmudic Judaism, and the birth of Christianity by fission. That Judaism should have survived the destruction of the supposedly inviolable city and Temple, and that out of the ruins two great religious movements should have arisen testifies to the invincible vigor and the indestructible values that had evolved in the 1200 years of Hebrew-Jewish history. How, then, is that history to be interpreted? How were such values created? These questions are to be considered in the succeeding chapters of this discussion. Did the moving finger as it wrote "make the vision plain upon tablets so that he may run who reads it"? Hardly! Some of the various readings of that long historical experience follow. First, the orthodox Jewish interpretation, as seen in the Old Testament and the sects of the Second Temple period.

PART 3

WHAT THE RUNNER READS:
THE INTERPRETATION OF HEBREW HISTORY

*That so strange and so passionate Jewish race, . . . a race
that lived on prophecy and hope, and believed in its tran-
scendent destiny.*

SANTAYANA

*The hidden issues of the future are with the Eternal our
God, but the unfolded issues of the day are with us and
our children for all time, that we may obey all the orders
of this law.*

*I have put life and death before you, the blessing and the
curse: choose life, then, that you and your children may
live, by loving the Eternal your God.*

"MOSES," DEUTERONOMY 29:29; 30:19
(MOFFATT)

*"Yes, and through stammering lips and in a foreign
tongue will God talk to this people. . . So 'law upon law,'
it shall be, 'law upon law, line upon line, line upon line,
a little here, a little there,'" . . . to make them trip and
tumble backwards.*

ISAIAH 28:11-13 (MOFFATT)

JEWISH HISTORY AND LITERATURE	NON-JEWISH HISTORY	POLITICAL BABYLON
587–538 Exile	7–6C Solon	605 Nebuchadnezzar
587 Fall of Jerusalem	6C Pythagoras	587 Gedaliah, governor
587–517 Temple in ruins	Zarathushtra	
581 Third deportation		581 Murder of Gedaliah (?)
570–560 Lamentations 2, 4; Obadiah; Gen., Exod., Deut., Josh.-Sam. re-edited		562 Amel-Marduk
560–500 Book of Kings; Job, 2 Isaiah, Lamentations 5	6–5C Buddha, Confucius, Heraclitus	560 Nergal-shar-usur
		556 Nabonidus
		Persia
538 Edict for Jewish Return		539 Cyrus
520 Haggai, Zechariah 1–8	Aeschylus	530 Cambyses
Rebuilding of Temple		522 Darius
515 Dedication (March 12)	Pericles	520 Behistun Inscription
Messianic hopes blasted		Persepolis begun
c. 500 Micah 6:1-7:6	5C Sophocles, Euripides, Herodotus, Thucydides, Socrates	486 Xerxes
500–450 Holiness Code, Lam. 1	480 Thermopylae, Salamis	
500–400 Priestly Code, 3 Isaiah, Obadaiah, Malachi, Ruth	448– 380 Aristophanes	465 Artaxerxes I
445 Nehemiah in Jerusalem	450– 175 Tobiad dyn. in Ammon	465 Artaxerxes I
Eliashib, high priest	5–4C Xenophon, Plato	
428 Ezra, Nehemiah in Jerusalem	431–	423 Darius II
Tobiah, Sanballat, Geshem	22 Peloponnesian War	
L5–4C Elephantine (Yeb) papyri	Ahikar and Behistun inscription at Yeb	

419 Passover papyrus to Yeb	410 Temple at Yeb destroyed	
L5–E4C Samaritan schism	408 Order to restore temple	
	404 Athens dismantled	404 Artaxerxes II
	400 Anabasis	
	399 Death of Socrates	
4–3C Large parts of Psalms, Proverbs; Jonah, Joel Beginning of synagogue? *High Priests*	4C Demosthenes, Aristotle Manlius defends *plebs*	
	345 Sidonian revolt crushed	359 Artaxerxes III *Macedonia*
	4–3C Epicurus; Zeno (Cypro-Phoenician, Stoic) Menander, Euclid Berossos Alexandrian Library	
330 Joiada, Jonathan, Jaddua		330 Alexander
		323 Death of Alexander *Egypt and Syria*
		323 Ptolemy I, Soter
300 Onias I, Simon I	312 Seleucid era	312 Seleucus I
3C Lamentations 3	3C Birta at 'Araq el-Emir, Qasr el-'Abd	285 Ptolemy II, Philadelphus
300–250 Song of Songs, Jubilees Eleazar b. Onias, high priest Manasses, high priest	Zeno archives, Fayum Manetho	280 Antiochus I
	259 Tubias, letters to Ptolemy II Chrysippus, Cilician	262–246 Apollonius, "controller"
250–150 Greek translation of O.T. (LXX) Onias II, b. Simon, high priest	250 Babylonian, Sudines introduces astrology	246 Ptolemy III, Euergetes
	3–2C Hannibal, Scipio Africanus, Cato Major	246 Seleucus II
		223 Antiochus III
	c. 210 Joseph b. Tobiah, tax farmer	221 Ptolemy IV, Philopator
200 Close of Prophetic canon Simon II, b. Onias, the "Just," high priest	c. 190 Hyrcanus b. Joseph, tax farmer	203 Ptolemy V, Epiphanes and Cleopatra
198 Antiochus III conquers Palestine	Polybius	187 Seleucus IV
190–160 Koheleth; Tobit	Pergamon Library	181 Ptolemy VI, Philometer

CHAPTER X

The Hand of God in History

1. *The General Framework of Hebrew Thought*   What the runner reads depends upon what is in his mind. To understand the Hebrews' reaction to their historical experience, it is necessary first to see it as they understood it. "In the beginning was the Word," said the Christian mystic, thinking of the first chapter of Genesis and of what other "beginnings," Babylonian, Egyptian, Platonic, Aristotelian, Stoic, or Gnostic, we do not know. The Hebrew also put God and his spoken word at the beginning. The Greeks had begun with Chaos, out of which came Ouranos and Gaia, Heaven and Earth. From them were born the gods, and the gods eventually created man. In Sumero-Babylonian myth, the world resulted from the struggles of the gods against the powers of chaos. Only Enlil, god of storms, or his vice-gerent, Marduk, could by the might of his inherent powers conquer Ti'a-mat, dragon of the deep, and out of the body of this demonic representative of evil and disorder (unhappy thought) create the heavens and the earth.

In the Hebrew myth, God in solitary grandeur presides over *Tehom*, the abyss, while his spirit moves upon the face of the waters. Unlike Enlil and Marduk, he needs no sweeping floods, no thunderous storm winds, to master chaos; his creative word brings all things into existence. The Hebrews' interpretation of history was an achievement as remarkable and original as their conception of its beginning. The parentage of ideas leaves an indelible birthmark. The Hebrews saw history in the light of this omnipotent creative monotheism.

A theory, called a hypothesis if a scientist proposes it, is an attempt to discover order in the big, buzzing confusion that experience thrusts upon man. His experiences are the result of the immediate impact of nature, society, and his own body upon his mind. He interprets his sensory impressions according to what he has previously experienced and according to what he has learned from society. Order seems to be a natural demand of the human spirit, easily degraded or dispelled, but always at least latent. By ordering his experiences into a supposedly coherent system, man renders himself somewhat more capable of meeting the challenges of life and of living with his constant frustrations. The Old Testament is not a mere chance collection of experiences and their resulting emotions and ideas, but comprises attempts of numerous inquiring minds to find order and meaning in their world, both in their physical and their social experiences.

Under the impact of conflicts with their immediate neighbors and then with the Assyrian, Babylonian, and Persian empires, the Hebrews became self-conscious, history-conscious, and world-conscious. As we have it, therefore, in the Old Testament, Hebrew thought puts the history of the nation and the world within the framework of a creative monotheism. God was in the beginning; from the beginning he was master of the universe. The heavens declared his glory and the firmament showed his handiwork. The winds were his messengers, fire and flame his ministers. He gave snow like wool, he scattered hoarfrost like ashes. He cast forth his ice like morsels. Examples might be multiplied. God not only created; he also sustained and directed whatever happened in the universe.

God was equally the maker and director of history. Whatever happened he willed or allowed, although he took no responsibility for sin and the serpent or for the devil and his demons. It was not merely that God's miraculous hand was at work in the childhood of the race, in the primitive folklore of the beginnings of the universe and of the nations, the confusion of tongues and the Flood, in the call of Abraham, and in the rescue of the Hebrews from slavery in Egypt. God's hand continued to rest upon all peoples and all history. "The Most High gave the nations their inheritance and fixed the bounds of the peoples." He "brings princes to naught and makes the rulers of the earth as nothing." [1]

A long series of prophetic "woes" upon the national enemies of Israel emphasizes this faith of little Judah in the days of Amos, Isaiah, Jeremiah, and Ezekiel. Moreover, Yahweh roused up "the Chaldeans, that bitter and hasty nation . . . to seize habitations not their own." Yet "woe to him who builds a town with blood, and founds a city with iniquity! Behold, is it not from the Lord of hosts that people labor only for fire, and nations weary themselves for naught? For the earth shall be filled with the knowledge of the glory of God as the waters cover the sea." Strange combination of ideas! God even called Cyrus and "anointed" him, took his hand, and sent him "to subdue nations before him, for the sake of his servant Jacob." [2]

The priestly material (P) in the Pentateuch, used to cement together and interpret its three variant traditions (J, E, D), is especially significant, and it became the most influential element in Hebrew social and national thinking. It has been said that the priestly document is like Augustine's *City of God*. It is not historical but dogmatic. It pictures a utopia, for which Ezekiel (40–48) had prepared a preliminary fragment. According to some interpreters of the document, God from the very beginning proposed to make for himself a holy nation unlike any other on earth. According to others, God made a good world, but man fell, and agriculture and childbearing became painful punishments. Cain built cities and fathered the arts of civilization, which plunged men into worse sins and evils. When the Flood failed to cleanse the world, God tried a new plan. He selected a family through which all the nations of the earth should be saved.

Under God's mighty hand, the Chosen People was brought by Moses and Joshua into the land that God had selected and promised to them. The story of the monarchy and the Exile was a sad one, but, after the Exile's purification of the nation, a theocratic state was to be established, not by a miracle, as in the later apocalypses, nor was it left to the distant future; it was to come at once, by historical processes. It would not conflict with a temporary overlordship of the Persians, but it did separate the Hebrews as God's people from the rest of the world. The priestly document provided the constitution of this ideal theocracy. It outlined the utopia that normative Judaism always hoped to see transposed from blue print into actuality. [3] Since theirs was the only God and he was all powerful, such a hope was not at all fantastic. As the primitive monotheism of the Aton cult arose under the Egyptian Empire and the philosophical monotheism of Greece developed with the Athenian Empire and the spread of Hellenism, so Hebrew monotheism developed under the great Oriental empires. The doctrine had a historical and social connection.

The monotheism of the Greeks had a theoretical, philosophical cast. It was an intellectual product. The Hebrews' monotheism, on the contrary, was not the outcome of logical or philosophical deliberation. It was the result of organic thinking, a spontaneous recognition of the relevance of their concepts of the Covenant and Chosen People to the activity of God in the world and in history. Thus Hebrew monotheism had a practical social and historical aspect. But, although historically, not philosophically, conditioned, it had an important philosophical corollary. It implied personal rule, not the rule of law. God could do what he would. He made the law; he could break it. God was the law.

When a complete and thoroughgoing monotheism began to be accepted in the more intelligent circles of Judaism and when the people as a whole came to adopt it are two very different but equally difficult questions. Answers to both depend upon definitions of monotheism as contrasted with monolatry and henotheism. Answers to the first derive from highly uncertain data, such as the dating of documents and the interpretation of sentences in the lyrical outbursts of psalmists, the impassioned sermons of prophets, and the exhortations of moralists and lawgivers, all of them far from intending precise theological definitions. If Moses was a monotheist, it mattered little to the rest of the people. Amos is the first datable evidence for the type of thinking that logically and organically suggests monotheism.

Genuine monotheism, or even henotheism, was far from the thought of the multitude and even of the leaders of the nation in Jeremiah's time, as his controversy with the worshipers of the Queen of heaven, Ishtar, fully demonstrates. People of the better classes were insisting that it paid to worship Ishtar rather than Yahweh. The poor remnants of the population, according to Ezekiel, believed that the exiles could not worship Yahweh in a strange land, just as the deportees in Samaria reached the conclusion that they could not farm successfully unless they did worship Yahweh, the god of the Samaritan hills. Jeremiah, Ezekiel, and many more of the exiles in Babylon had no such views of Yahweh's limitations.[4] The literature of the subsequent periods and the reported prayers of the Maccabees, for example, prove nothing as to the populace, even as prayers in a modern legislature do not prove that its members are God-fearing believers. Only the Gospels, at length, demonstrate that monotheistic belief can be assumed for the majority of the Jewish population. Even so, polytheistic survivals, like the Moslem and Catholic worship of "saints" in India, the Near East, Italy, Spain, and Latin America, were doubtless widespread. Educated Jews had long been monotheists.

However, it was a prescientific monotheism. The kind of world in which the ancient Hebrews and nearly everyone else lived up to the eighteenth century can best be described as animistic and dynamistic. Everything that happened, including many events that to us are quite clearly due to easily observed natural causes, was ascribed to invisible beings and potencies. We speak of the personification of abstract ideas. This ancient attitude of mind was no rhetorical personification. It is not quite correct to speak of animism and dynamism, but rather of animistic personalism. It was not a belief that spirits animated rocks or trees, but that rocks, trees, and fetishes were persons of a sort, but of a different kind from human beings, and so were animals also. Furthermore, human beings, animals, and, indeed, any object could be possessed by spirits that were otherwise disembodied.

This is not to say that the Hebrews' thinking was prelogical, nor was it mystical. They had a great deal of knowledge of a practical kind based upon keen and accurate observation. But they lacked any scientific theory, any empirical attitude. This was a mysterious, miraculous world, where, as one of Apuleius' characters announced, anything could happen. Besides the invisible gods, or God, there were innumerable other invisible beings all around every human being, in springs and streams, in rocks and trees, in the planets and the stars, all able to affect human destiny. What happened did not happen according to natural laws. No such law was known, except to the few who came into contact with Hellenistic scientific thought, and even there it was sadly obscured. What happened was chiefly the result of the actions of personal agents, human or nonhuman.

From the beginning, the Jews' interpretation of experience contained other elements that determined its outcome. For one thing, their notions of life were thoroughly materialistic. Theological and metaphysical speculation was outside the circle of their thought. If one may use terms that would have been incomprehensible to them, they had a psychosomatic, not a dualistic, view of the world. Until after their contacts with Zoroastrianism and Hellenism, they had no idea of a resurrection or of immortality. The body returned to the dust. The divine element returned to God. A "shade," the individual element, went down to sleep in Sheol outside of God's world.[5] All of God's dealings with man were reckoned in terms of the present material world.

Since they were deeply moralistic, virtue must be rewarded. The concept of virtue as its own reward had not occurred to them. What could God do but reward those who served him with long life and prosperity? Those who disobeyed, who neglected the rites of worship, who disregarded tabus, who broke the divinely sanctioned laws and customs of the community, must be punished by misfortune and early death. No religion could be more thoroughly hedonistic, materialistic, and this-worldly than that of the Deuteronomist. He promised, to the obedient, blessings in the city and in the country, blessings in the fruit of the body and of the ground, in the fruit of beasts and the increase of cattle, in basket and kneading trough. On the disobedient corresponding curses were pronounced and, in addition, disease, fiery heat, blasting, and mildew, blindness, madness, and utter confusion.[6] The life of the individual and the history of the nation were interpreted in the light of this conception of rewards and punishments.

Another determinant in the interpretation of God's dealings with man and nations was the conception of revelation, of communication between God and man. Since the Hebrews' notions of God were consistently anthropomorphic and their view of the world was utterly simple, they conceived of God as communicating directly with man by voice, by omens and portents, and by dreams, even as their neighbors expected their gods to do. Any unusual ideas were modestly—or belligerently—ascribed to God, or to some other being outside of man, like the serpent in the Garden of Eden, or, later, to angels or evil spirits. God was so dominant that even the evil spirits obeyed him. An "evil spirit from the Lord tormented Saul." [7] Satan could attack Job only with God's consent. The Spirit of God could seize a man, and then he spoke words that were not his own, but God's. Moses and the prophets communicated directly with God and relayed his commands to men. The Hebrews, therefore, claimed to have an unimpeachable revelation from God himself covering everything necessary for living according to the will of God.

This revelation had been acquired not without doubts and difficulties. There were false prophets. Were they merely conscious deceivers, or could they sometimes be self-deceived? Evidently the latter alternative was thought possible if God could send a lying spirit to speak through a prophet (1 Kings 22:23). The problem of distinguishing true from false prophecy was never solved except by comparing prediction and fulfillment, and that criterion gave a decision too late to avoid the consequences of error. [8] As to prophetic ideas of religion and ethics, history, then as now, spoke with no clear voice. How decide between all-too-human imagination and the divine word?

The Hebrews were as utterly oblivious as literalistic moderns are of the inescapable fallibility of all language and all interpretation. They were equally oblivious of the evident inclusions in the Torah of long-current commercial customs and conventions that had been recorded centuries before in the law given to Hammurabi by his god, Shamash. Sumerian and Hittite, Ugaritic and Hurrian laws, as well as Babylonian, embody ideas that reappear in the various Hebrew codes and that occasionally seem to us more humane than those of the Hebrews. For example, the *lex talionis,* derived from the harsh culture of the nomad, had long been modified in other cultures. The Hebrews speciously evaded it through the establishment of cities of refuge. But it still stood in the Torah—to be repudiated by Jesus. Critical scholars may reject the idea of a literal, verbal, or even plenary inspiration of the Scriptures, but, when they write biblical theology, they may accept what fits their dogmas as the divine word. The ancient Jew did the same.

2. *The Hebrew Theory of History*   The general framework of Hebrew thought was much like that of the neighboring peoples. Within it and shaped in part by it, the Hebrews added certain novel ideas and emphases that set them and their conception of the world and history apart as thoroughly original. God created a good world, good materially and morally. Sin came and befouled both matter and morals. Man and the world must be cleansed from sin. The means finally chosen for this truly Herculean task were the Chosen People. The idea of God's covenant with them as his Chosen People dominated their conception of their nation and of history. When they were henotheists, one people among many with one god among many, the idea hardly distinguished them from the many. But when, perhaps with David's conquests, the idea came that they had a mission to save the world by ruling it, the Chosen People idea ceased to be innocuous. It is a common saying among Jews that their worst misfortune was the assumption that they were God's Chosen People. A sense of mission may be extremely dangerous both in individuals and in nations. Nazism and Soviet communism are pertinent examples. Other nations have suffered from the same megalomania. The idea of a "white man's burden" laid a heavy burden on the "lesser breeds without the law." The disease was endemic in the United States for over a century and a quarter and is not yet entirely eradicated. The concept of "manifest destiny" has unfortunate results for those who hold it and for many others.

The henotheistic, or monolatrous, conception of deity is so common that it may be regarded as an artless product of social evolution, as a folk idea natural at a particular stage of cultural development. The concept of manifest destiny, whether for an individual or a nation or a race, may also come more or less spontaneously. It may thus be also a folk idea. If, in the culture of the nation, or of the individual, there is sufficient critical irony, some sense of the comic, the disease may be cured before it becomes chronic. If there is national self-criticism, the idea can be sublimated into that of social and international responsibility.

Unfortunately these saving graces were lacking in the majority of the ancient Hebrews, just as they are in too many Americans and British. They had a better excuse. The idea of a national God and a national destiny was no mere diffuse tradition. Their God and his choice of them and covenant with them had been revealed through two great national heroes at particular times and places during the national infancy. The revelation was a recorded historical fact, an act of God that had brought their nation to birth, so they believed.

For families, tribes, and nations in a lawless world, covenants were the equivalent of nonaggression treaties to prevent mutual destruction. The Bible is full of them, as was that ancient society. This different kind of covenant, presented to them by supernatural power and assuring them of everything heart could wish, was naturally a favorite idea. As Adolphe Lods pointed out,[9] the historical character of Hebrew religion was based upon the (supposedly) historical fact of divine election and a divine covenant. The Hebrews, unlike other nations, did not merely accept a traditional religion; they adopted one at a definite time and place as a result of known historical occurrences.

According to the biblical record, there was a succession of covenants at specific times and places: two at Mount Sinai under Moses' leadership, one validating the legal and ethical Covenant Code, and one connected with a ritual, sacrificial code. There was another under Joshua at Shechem, described simply in Joshua but with dramatic trappings in Deuteronomy. There came one again under the high priest Jehoiada, after Athaliah's overthrow, and still another under Josiah accepting the Deuteronomic law. Then, finally, came the acceptance of the (completed) Torah under Ezra.[10]

According to priestly tradition, however, long before any of these, God had repeatedly promised Abraham to make his descendants a Chosen People who should rule the world. One covenant was guaranteed by eerie supernatural sacrificial rites. A Noachic covenant, with the rainbow as its symbol and perpetual guarantee, was discovered, another with circumcision as its symbol, and still another with the

Sabbath as its symbol. The entirely unconditioned promises that God is reported to have made to David and his dynasty eventually came to play a role almost as significant as that of the covenant with the nation.[11]

For the Hebrews these convenants were actual historical events. Since they so believed and held that God had miraculously rescued them from Egyptian bondage and preserved the nation in Palestine, their history had an ineluctable religious interpretation and their religion an unshakeable historical basis. God's free and gracious act in choosing them for a great destiny and the ethical, legal, and ritual conditions under which the covenant was given became facts to reckon with always. They colored all conceptions of the past and created indestructible hopes for the future. Upon this supposedly historical basis developed the tenacious national and racial feeling of solidarity and the later prophetic interpretation of Israel's God and Israel's mission. This manifest destiny was formally ethicized by the divine promise to Abraham, "I will make of you a great nation, . . . so that you may be a blessing" (Gen. 12:2). This hope and ambition must be as early as the time of the United Kingdom (*c.* 950–900). God's covenant with them insured their future.

3. *Hope and Frustration* The checkered course of Hebrew history after Solomon's time was a sad problem for the prophets. Their solution was that Israel's failure to obey God's commands resulted in the repeated inroads of enemies and subjection to their rule during the period of the Judges and that of the divided monarchy. But God's promises must stand. Therefore, the Day of Yahweh, when he would take full control, destroy sinners (that is, the enemies of Israel), and fulfill his original promise to Abraham, became the national hope. A recurrent theme in prophetic literature was the goodness and power of God in choosing the Hebrew people, saving them from bondage in Egypt, and giving them the Promised Land. According to the prophetic moralists, this goodness of God should move them to obedience; his power could give them confident hope.

The problem was not merely the frustration of nationalistic hopes. God's own character was at stake, in two ways. His promises to the nation must be fulfilled. More than that, the righteousness of his rule over men was in question. As a psalmist asked in plaintive tones, "If the foundations are destroyed, what can the righteous do?" Many a harassed worshiper of Yahweh demanded, "Shall the righteous fare like the wicked? . . . Shall not the Judge of all the earth do right?" Here was the prophetic dilemma. It was a standard problem for the psalmists. How could the ways of God with men be justified? Was there actually a just God in the heavens? Then "why should the nations say, 'Where is their God?' " [12]

The Day of Yahweh was the answer. When the phrase first appears in Hebrew literature, in Amos (5:18-20) *c.* 750, it was already the slogan of thoughtless patriots who trusted blindly in God's supposed promises. It presupposes long disappointment of national hopes of conquest and consequent national wealth and power. Amos turned it around and so reinterpreted the covenant idea. The promises were conditional; the covenant involved obligations that Israel had not discharged. To those who were "at ease in Zion, . . . who lie on beds of ivory, . . . and eat lambs from the flock," the Day of Yahweh, when it came, would be "darkness and not light" (Amos. 6:1,4). God's choice, flouted by disobedience, turns to a curse. Yahweh says, "You only have I known of all the families of the earth; therefore I will punish you for all your iniquities" (3:2). Isaiah, Jeremiah, and Ezekiel consistently urged the people to submit to the Assyrians and Babylonians as due punishment for the nation's sins. Since the king and the people did not submit, the punishment was to be long and hard, so long that the exiles were urged to accept their lot and make the best of it (Jer. 29:1-14). Yet this was not the end.

There was still light back of the dark Day for Jeremiah. By divine command he purchased property, even while the Babylonians besieged Jerusalem, to leave to his offspring (32:1-15). It might be seventy years, but return was certain. When one who had escaped out of Jerusalem came to Ezekiel saying, "The city is smitten," his prophecies of doom ceased. God would sprinkle clean water upon the people of Israel and cleanse them from all their filthiness. He would give them a new heart and a new spirit.[13] A new covenant, a covenant written on the heart, which Jeremiah (31:31–34) had foretold, would be given them, and they would return and dwell in the land of their fathers.

Among the most magnificent passages in the Bible are the chapters in which, fifty years later, Second Isaiah portrayed the glory of that Return and Restoration. Yet how miserable the reality! Sheshbazzar and Zerubbabel disappear; Joshua, the priest, builds the Temple, and then stagnation! Nehemiah reveals how low the nation had sunk. Over two centuries after him, centuries of priesthood and Torah, are punctuated by possible participation in the Sidonian revolt, by the murder at the hands of the high priest of his own brother in the sanctuary itself, by the Samaritan quarrel and defection, by the Tobiad tale of greed and intrigue. Finally, a nation ready for Hellenization is saved by the brief glory of the Maccabean uprising. And that seeming sunrise turns into a blood-red sunset.

The Jewish state ended in the irresponsible tyranny of Herod the Great and the calculated but regulated tyranny of the Roman procurators. The Jews were probably better off than under the Hasmoneans, but they were ruled by gentiles. The result was a little nation that seethed with frustration and hate. Abroad, during the Hellenistic period, there were three groups, one in Babylonia and Persia speaking Aramaic, two speaking Greek, one in Alexandria, the other in Asia Minor and spreading continually farther westward. They assisted not a little, by their offerings to the Temple and their remittances to relatives, in softening the economic hardships of the country. But, perhaps all the more because of the prosperity and liberal tendencies of the Hellenistic groups, the Jews in Palestine felt the contrast between hope and experience. Unable to accept the fact that Palestine never could be the basis of world empire, they beat their heads against their cage, until at last they committed national, though not racial or religious, suicide.

4. *Ways of Living* For the time being there were the four recognized, standard adjustments to the seemingly hopeless situation: those of the Sadducees, the Pharisees, the Essenes, and the revolutionaries. And there was the fifth, which was historically even more satisfactory to many in the other groups (aside from the Sadducees), that of the

messianists and apocalyptists. To all appearances the first three were reasonable and fairly successful, *ad interim*. In any event they involved no open violence to either society or intelligence. They all accepted the *status quo,* the rule of Rome, as the great prophets had advised their fathers to submit to Assyria and Babylonia, and they did not seek national freedom and sovereignty, for they recognized the impossibility of Jewish independence in the shadow of the Roman and Parthian empires on this side and on that. They were willing to trust God and wait.

In the event, only two of the five, apocalypticism and Pharisaism, survived to preserve anything of the Hebrew past and to allow the Jews a continued existence as a race, a religion, and an enduring factor in history. The religious basis of Saducean policy was too narrow. The Temple and the Torah did not present principles and ideas strong enough and flexible enough to carry the traditions and values that Judaism had developed. The Samaritans illustrate the weakness of a merely Pentateuchal foundation for religion. Saducean aristocratic social organization was too narrow, its compromising political policy too broad and weak to provide depth and vitality. Revolutionism was equally lacking in solid principles and social stability, the more so as it was a political, racial, and economic movement that depended, like apocalypticism, upon an illusory religious faith, the expectation of miraculous divine intervention to provide victory for armed revolt. Essenism failed because it was chiefly monastic and celibate, and hence antisocial. It was deeply ethical, but it was impractical since it was economically communistic and theoretically apocalyptic and thus depended upon miracle. It was mere escapism.

Apocalypticism (of which more later) was, be it noted, an element in all of these ideologies except Saduceeism. It was one of the chief weaknesses of revolutionism and Essenism. It drew its adherents largely from Pharisaism. From Pharisaism Christianity sprang, but from its most thoroughly apocalyptic elements. Why, then, if revolutionism and Essenism failed, did Pharisaism and Christianity succeed?

They succeeded in spite of their apocalypticism certainly, but also because of it. They might believe that "this age" was ruled by Satan.

But they saw hope in history because it was in God's hands. They preserved other religious and ethical concepts and principles that made it possible for them to serve men in society. Both laid strong emphasis on devotion to God and his will, and that attitude provided the basic ethos that gives religion vitality and stability.

In the first century of our era, as the period of the Second Temple was coming to an end, the Pharisees were religious, not political, leaders. They were spiritual descendants of the Hasidim of the Maccabean period who refused to fight for political independence, once religious liberty was assured, and so they represented also the prophetic point of view. But they belonged to the middle class; they were plebeians in Finkelstein's analysis of Jewish society, and they rarely had political power or responsibility. They were willing to leave history in God's hands. Their responsibility was to prepare the nation to meet his ethical and cultic demands. He would take care of the rest.

The Christians, although Pharisaic like the majority of the people, were from the lower classes where economic needs bulked larger in interest than cultic rites and observances. Jesus stood much closer to the prophets than to the lawgivers. Being convinced that the reign of God was close at hand and that, in God's view, love and justice were infinitely more important than Sabbaths and sacrifice, he was bitterly critical of the legalistic technicalities of the scribal interpreters of the Law. He was even less politically minded and much less racial and nationalistic in his thinking than the Pharisees. He combined the ethical and religious fervor of the prophets with the contagious enthusiasm of the apocalyptists. Anger at a biting critic and fear of a too-popular preacher and possible insurrectionist led to his rejection by the Jewish leaders and his execution. So Christianity parted company with Judaism.

It took with it the Jewish conception of history, minus its racialism and nationalism, and it absorbed also the best cultural values that Judaism had created. It arrogated to itself the title of "the true Israel" and all of the promises and covenants of the Old Testament. Unfortunately, in adapting itself to its Hellenistic environment, it sublimated

the social-ethical message of the prophets and Jesus into a weak individualistic moralism and mysticism; and it replaced the self-immolating
devotion and vital enthusiasm of Jesus and Paul with a pagan magico-
mystical ritual and eventually with a typically Roman hierarchical
ecclesiasticism.

Unswerving allegiance to the Torah and fear of Sadducean assimila-
tionism led the Pharisees to redoubled emphasis on isolation. Having
seen God's hand in the destruction of the Temple, they magnified
emphasis on dietary restrictions and ritual regulations. They saved
their heritage, but they made it impossible for them to bless all nations
as God's covenant with Abraham had promised.

The foregoing sketch of Jewish historical thinking notes merely
outstanding features. But for its superficiality, it might be called a
skeleton. It may serve as a rough scaffold. Its chief value is to call
attention to the problems that historical experience set for the race and
to the more facile and superficial answers that became popular. It
does not do justice to the profound and searching, often importunate,
reflection of Jewish leaders of thought.

For the modern student questions still remain. How did the little
barren country of Palestine come to produce such a people with such an
intellectual and religious history and with such a unique interpretation
of history? How close to reality is that interpretation? What are its
values and what the genuine cultural values of their history as compared with their interpretation of it?

To answer such questions, the various phases and features of the
Jews' cultural history must be considered with careful attention to
their contributions to total world culture. The answers are partly
implicit, partly explicit in their literature and institutions. Out of the
same matrix of historical experience came the Judaism of the apocalypses, Pirke Aboth, the Mishnah, and the Talmud. Out of it came
the various diasporas, the Judaisms of Yemen, India, and China, of
Russia, western Europe, and Spain, of Great Britain, South Africa, and
North America, to mention only a few. Out of it came also Chris-

tianity, with its multitude of sects, its national and its free churches, its Orthodox, Roman, and Protestant divisions, with multicolored Islam in addition.

These questions are beyond fully satisfactory answers. Partial explanations can be discovered by a different formulation of the problem. What were the methods and results of the educational process through which the Jews learned? What actual values in customs, institutions, and ideas did they create and pass on to the world?

CHAPTER XI

God's Education of the Hebrew People

1. *The Unique Conditions* For the vast majority of pious, law-abiding Israelites as the Old Testament canon came to its close, the chief lesson derived from their history was that God had guided history from the beginning of creation and had finally made choice of Abraham. He had watched over them since Abraham's departure from Ur of the Chaldees and down to their own time. Their land, their national existence, and their law were all the result of his guidance. His alternating loving-kindness and chastisement had made them what they were and would still follow them until the promises of the Covenant were fulfilled.

In the light of their anthropomorphic conception of God and their prescientific idea of the world and of history, this seemed a satisfactory conclusion. But from a modern point of view, a less simple and naïve analysis of God's "tender mercy and chastisement" is demanded in order to understand the outcome. How had God's education of their nation through his self-revelation in nature and history actually functioned? What had they learned and what should they have learned? It is the purpose of this study to discuss the nature of the historical process and its cultural results as illustrated in Hebrew history.

It is hard to consider *how* they learned without including *what* they learned; the two are inseparable. But, for analysis' sake, the emphasis of this chapter is on the process, while those that follow turn more to results. In both cases not a cross section, not a slice for a microscope slide, but a longitudinal section, a study of the process of change and growth is the intention. History is a living thing.

In a sense every situation, whether geographical or historical, is unique, just as every individual is unique, even to the papillary ridges on his fingertips. But there are individuals who stand apart as others do not. There are unusual geographical situations and nations with outstanding achievements to their credit. Among unusual lands and peoples are Judea and the Hebrews, none more so.

The historian's task is to indicate, as clearly and fully as he can, in what the peculiar genius of his subject consisted and how conditions affected its development and its contribution to the values that constitute civilization. Before turning to a discussion of the various competing Jewish and Christian conceptions of the meaning of Hebrew history, it is imperative, for the sake of clarity, to bring together in a general conspectus a summary of the components of the Hebrews' culture at the close of their independent national history, when they had completed and canonized the Old Testament, their great literary and religous contribution to civilization.

In order to emphasize and analyze this unique contribution and to show how their history enabled them to make it, it is intended now to focus attention on the only teacher and curriculum through which men can receive a genuine education. The teacher is experience and the curriculum is history—not history as written, but history as such. Historical experience is the school in which men learn to live, where alone they can live, in society.

The effort has been made to note the distinguishing features in the education of the Hebrew people through the centuries, and their characteristic responses to the total changing environment. It has been the description of a process. It is not intended to be, and indeed cannot be, a complete and final "explanation" of their contribution to the life of mankind. Who can "explain" life? All that anyone, even the most inspired theologian, can honestly do is to record what happened, how the historical process developed, and to note the apparent relations and concatenations of economic, social, and cultural events. An understanding of the developments in Hebrew history in all their ramifications makes the Hebrew achievement all the more impressive and astonishing. It gives the ethical and religious ideas that eventually emerged a commanding claim upon the ideal aspirations of all men everywhere.

The physical habitat under which the nation developed constitutes an important formative aspect of its historical experience. Conditions are not causes; they are factors in causal relationships; they condition, but do not determine, ultimate results. The geographical situation with which the Hebrews struggled was a distinct challenge and limitation on the physical side. Yet Palestine offered as wide and stimulating a variety of climates and of regional differences within its 6000-square-mile area as can be found anywhere on earth. Not only in physical conditions, but in political, economic, and indeed all aspects of culture, their situation provided stimulation, challenge, and enrichment from all of the older, more highly developed, and more opulent cultures in the midst of which the Hebrews struggled with the crises of their fate.

2. *Nomadism in Hebrew History*   Inevitably the most diverse and contradictory currents of thought are reflected in the relations and the characteristic emphases of Hebrew literature. Among them are no-madic, agricultural, and commercial ideals that echoed phases of social development. A Marxian theory of economic determinism defies both scientific method and historical data. But the influence of varying types of economic activity and organization on Hebrew cultural development in both thought and practice must not be overlooked, as too often it is. Hebrew history is unusually instructive because religion and ethics were consciously interwoven with all phases of life and activity. The physical conditions under which the Hebrews lived were most signif-icant, the more so because they were restricted, unusual, and marginal and also anything but autarkic. They therefore made an indelible im-pression on Hebrew conceptions of God, man, and the world and con-ditioned their emotional and volitional responses to experience. Ideas derived from the simple life of the nomad persisted throughout the history of the Hebrews in Palestine, not only because of their highly developed historical consciousness and memory, but also because no-madism was all about them.

Hebrew historical piety preserved both good and bad from the no-madic tradition. A fierce and narrow tribalism always remembered bat-

tle songs in honor of the relentless war god, Yahweh, who went forth
from Seir and marched out of the land of Edom to the trembling of
the earth and the quaking of the mountains. One can condone and
admire the primitive vigor and ruthlessness of the Song of Deborah.
But what can be said for Psalm 137? It begins so plaintively and appeal-
ingly,

> By the rivers of Babylon, there we sat down and wept
> When we remembered Zion. . . .

They remembered Zion—with venom for her despoiler:

> O daughter of Babylon, you devastator. . . .
> Blessed shall he be who takes your little ones
> And dashes them against the rock.

It is like the helpless hissing of a snake. Is it surprising that Dean
Inge, in his own ruthless way, protested against the singing of the
war songs of Bedouin tribes in Christian churches? Primitive tribalism
and the highly sensitive nationalism of the Chosen People combined
to produce the bitter invective of the powerful doom songs on enemy
nations that rhetorically glorify and morally disfigure the prophetic
books.

Tribal mores produced also admirable qualities that the Hebrews
never lost: open hospitality to friend and stranger, a sense of honor
that swore to its own hurt and would not change, an aristocratic sense
of personal worth, an individualism that never could submit to a stable
social bond, a democracy that resented all autocracy, hot and ruthless
jealousy of personal prerogatives, an indestructible love of personal freedom, strong and rigid, if elementary, standards of justice. These in-
compatible traits, coupled with tribal jealousies, prevented the amalgamation of the tribes into a strong nation. Divisive individualism exacerbated the class and sectarian conflicts of the post-monarchical
period.

The primitive vigor and confidence of nomadism tended to disappear
under the benumbing routine of agricultural labor and the sobering

weight of personal and landed possessions. Yet the tradition lingered on, in language and deed. Still in the monarchy, to "go home" was to "go every man to his tent," although they had lived for generations in stone houses.[1] It was always possible for the Hebrew to flee to the "wilderness," to wander "in deserts and mountains and dens and caves of the earth" (Heb. 11:38), as in Maccabean and Roman times, when conditions in town and village became intolerable. Not only could those who were in distress or in debt or discontented flee their difficulties and their obligations to join an outlaw gang, but the representatives of the nation's highest traditions could escape from tyranny and oppression and gather strength in the maze of wadis and caves in the "wilderness" for attempts to restore the nation's fortunes. Thus David escaped from Saul, and Jonathan the Maccabee from the Syrian armies.[2] Thus also the Essene and other ascetic and revolutionary groups and, later, Christian ascetics and monks sought the solitudes of the wilderness above the Dead Sea in order to escape the evils of their age.

Hebrew history is often written as if the only conflict between Canaanite and Hebrew religion were that which centered about Baal worship and its fertility cult. Hosea makes it so appear. Quite the contrary was true. From the beginning the conflict was between nomadic and agricultural mores and standards of conduct in general, in which the fertility cult was only a part. The nomad knew no landlordism and very slight social distinctions. In both kinds of life there was both good and bad. This the prophets tended to forget. As moralists so often do, they looked back with nostalgic longing to the youth of the nation and demanded a return to the primitive simplicity of the steppe and the times of the Judges (save the mark!) as a means of purifying the nation of the evils of city life.[3]

3. *The Pastoral-Agricultural Ideal* Life in the Promised Land demanded that the nomadic tradition should give place to the agricultural-pastoral ideal. Abraham had been a nomad. Isaac and Jacob, confined to Palestine, were seminomads, with flocks and herds, but also with land to till. So also their descendants. With so much of uncultivable pasture land all about them even in the plains, sheep and goats,

oxen and cows must have been a part of every prosperous peasant's possessions. With flocks and herds doubtless taken for granted, the agricultural ideal was that every man should own a plot of ground (his "lot") and "dwell in safety under his own vine and fig tree" and "drink the water of his own cistern." It was one of the marks of the idealized reign of Simon the Maccabee.[4]

The early Yahwist writer (J) might represent both agriculture and city civilization as under a curse, as Hosea did. Yet Amos, Micah, and Isaiah fulminate against the luxury of the court and the cities, but not against agricultural life. The Deuteronomist and the priestly writers rejoiced in pictures of flourishing grain fields, sparkling vineyards, and bountiful olive orchards. In spite of the primitive curse on labor, post-biblical works, Ecclesiasticus, the Testaments of the Twelve Patriarchs, and the Letter of Aristeas, glorify labor, especially in the fields. A Hebrew should "not hate hard work or farming, which the Most High had created," but "bow down his back unto husbandry and toil in labors of all manner of husbandry."[5]

Numerous passages in Deuteronomy exhibit an uninhibited (and unjustified) glorification of the agricultural and mineral resources of the Promised Land and extend an invitation to the apparently unrestricted enjoyment of material abundance and purely physical delights, which are promised to the obedient.[6] The Letter of Aristeas (112–115), whose firsthand acquaintance with Palestine is doubtful, may be merely echoing the Deuteronomic exaggerations or biased reports when it greatly overpraises the land for its wealth of population and of cereals, olives, date palms, and other fruit trees, as well as of cattle. Such boasts may be discounted as enthusiastic sales talk, patriotic, but representing no basic social ethos or moral principles. No doubt they picture the attitude of a considerable and influential portion of the Hebrew people.

That moral manual for the would-be successful man, the Book of Proverbs, is more circumspect, or perhaps more confused. It offers no sharp denunciation of wealth or of the rich as such. Some of the rich man's wicked ways are pointed out but so are his advantages over the poor man. The fear of the Lord is the beginning of both wisdom and wealth. Righteousness leads to success, wickedness to destruction.

Wealth is not too loudly praised; if acquired unrighteously or even too hurriedly, it is evil. While the rich man has in his riches a strength and a defense that the poor man lacks, yet a good name, wisdom, and righteousness are better than riches. All this, however, is overshadowed by the repeated promises of riches and honor to the wise and the righteous. Even three of the "beatitudes" in the Psalms frankly offer the blessings of wealth, prosperity, and long life. "The meek shall possess the land and delight themselves in an abundance of prosperity." [7]

Yet there is a strong countercurrent in many portions of the Old Testament. Denunciation of the greedy rich is by no means confined to the prophets. There is a distinct distrust of wealth and, in contrast, an attractive ideal of moderation repeatedly expressed in various writers. Not only does the agricultural ideal of a plot of ground, a vine, and a fig tree reveal a rather modest conception of desirable comfort; admonitions to contentment with little are numerous. "Better a little that the righteous has than the abundance of many wicked," appears in the Psalms (37:16). In Proverbs (30:8 f.) Agur son of Jakeh (perhaps an Edomite) prays, "Give me neither poverty nor riches; feed me the food that I need; lest I be full and deny thee, or lest I be poor and steal." The Deuteronomist feared that Israel would become rich and forget God. The saying in the swan song of Moses, "Jeshurun waxed fat and kicked," was a warning after the fact. Both Hosea and Nehemiah accuse Israel of exactly this sin. In spite of the doctrine of material rewards for the righteous, wealth was as much a menace as a blessing.[8]

4. *Commerce in Hebrew History* There is a nomadic and an agricultural ideal and a combination of both in the Old Testament, but no ideal of life with either industry or commerce as its basis. The one was impossible, the other wrong. Josephus was correct in theory when he said, toward the end of the first century of our era, that, since the Hebrews lived inland remote from the sea, they avoided commerce and devoted themselves to the cultivation of their productive land.[9] Ancient Judaism never gave an official blessing to commerce. Quite the contrary! Hosea of Samaria, which was then luxuriating in com-

mercial prosperity, proclaimed that a Canaanite, a "trader" (cutting *double-entendre*), inevitably used false balances and loved to take advantage of his customers. He accompanied his judgment on merchants with the accusation that Ephraim (Northern Israel) had turned trader and was amassing wealth that could never offset the guilt she had incurred (12:7–8). Zephaniah of Jerusalem (1:10–11) saw all merchants and traders destroyed and the seacoast become a pasture for the flocks of the remnant of Judah in the great Day of the Lord. So also Hosea (12:9) saw no hope and no remedy except in a return, not merely to the land, but to the steppe. Jesus ben-Sira' almost echoes him. A merchant could hardly keep himself from doing wrong; a storekeeper would not be acquitted of sin. "Between buying and selling sin is ground out." [10]

Situated as they were, no exhortation could save the Jews from commerce. Ancient Palestine never developed industry beyond immediate needs, largely because no sufficient natural resources, no raw materials, aside from wool, wine, and oil, were available for manufacture. But commercial enterprise was inescapable for a land at the center of the ancient world. Wine and oil, possibly at times wool and textiles, were in sufficient surplus to make commerce possible. But it was as a great mart for the interchange of goods that Palestine served the ancient world of commerce. Not only must the caravans of the great cultural centers pass through it. It was more than a mere highway. The Letter of Aristeas overpraised the land but was correct in telling of the great volume of spices, precious stones, and gold brought into the country. With the Nabateans and their caravans on the one side and the ships of all the Mediterranean plying from the ports of Gaza, Ashkelon, Joppa, and Ptolemais on the other, commerce with the farthest ends of the earth was inevitable.

The most prosperous periods in Hebrew history, the reigns of Solomon, of Ahab, and of Jeroboam II and Uzziah, were made so by the development of commerce, the building of fleets, and traffic with non-Israelite countries. Solomon not only engaged in commerce but also exploited the mineral deposits in the Wadi 'Arabah and built smelters, as is known both from the biblical records and from archaeological discoveries. His horse trading with Egypt made a special impression on his contemporaries, as also did the gifts that came to him from foreign countries.[11] The opportunity and its glories were ephemeral, for they depended largely on temporary immunity from enemy attacks.

The reign of Ahab was marked by a similar increase of commercial activities, this time with Phoenicia and Damascus. Damascus had had a concession for its merchants in Samaria and Ahab forced Ben-hadad to make a similar grant to Israelite merchants in Damascus (1 Kings 20:34). The remains of the royal palace at Samaria give evidence of a great increase in wealth and luxury, either then or in the reign of Jeroboam II. Both kings are credited with "ivory houses" in the Bible.[12] The historical books say nothing about commercial enterprise in the days of Jeroboam and Uzziah. Uzziah's wealth is described at some length as pastoral and his capture of Elath on the Gulf of 'Aqabah is mentioned, nothing more; but the prophets, Amos, Hosea, Isaiah, and Micah, make bitter protests against wealth and luxury and the accompanying oppression of the poor. The port of Elath suggests both mining and shipping.[13]

The kings and the courts from the beginning seem to have followed the example of Solomon and preyed upon the people instead of protecting them. The priests proved no better, even worse perhaps. Interestingly enough, the very insistence of the Pharisees upon obedience to the letter of the law involved the meticulous payment of "all the tithes into the storehouse" (the Temple), along with gifts and offerings, plus another tithe that had to be spent in Jerusalem. The whole amounted to far more than a 20 per cent income tax. (The government tax came in addition.) The Pharisees assisted in the enrichment of their Sadducean enemies, the priests, who had to spend all of two weeks a year in the Temple to earn their incomes. Such taxation made the economic situation almost impossible.

Every advance had its recession, due, not to a business cycle, but to a weak or vicious king, a period of drought and famine, or, most frequently, war. The most serious recession of all came with the Exile, when, for nearly seventy years, the Temple, a large banking

institution and commercial asset according to ancient custom, lay
waste, the city walls, an indispensable protection for wealth, were
broken down, and the royal family, the court, the propertied people,
and the artisans of the city and the country were far away.

At the first Return rebuilding began, and gradually, with the improvement of conditions in the Persian Empire, Judea also began to
recover. The open world and relative peace of the Persian Empire
encouraged the migration of an energetic and prolific race, such as
the Jews were, and promoted commerce. Their strong sense of racial
solidarity made it easy for them to set up commercial relations all over
the empire, and taxes, which were absurdly heavy under the Persians,
could be avoided by a merchant far more easily than by a farmer.
The wars of Alexander's successors must have brought ruin in their
wake, but all the evidence, which is considerable, goes to indicate that
commerce continued to expand. How unfortunate that no Zeno kept
the records of Jewish merchants in Alexandria and that no Jewish
merchant in Joppa left behind him tablets like those of the Murashu
family of Nippur! Papyrus was too cheap and too convenient and
alphabetic writing too practical.

5. *The Social Structure*   In spite of nomadic democratic traditions
and of prophetic and gnomic moralists, chance, as well as individual
ability, created inequalities from the beginning. After the establishment of the monarchy, these differences of status were accentuated.
The royal princes and the court favorites destroyed the equilibrium.
Trade, commerce, and war brought wealth to the adventurous and
unscrupulous. The priestly families acquired special status. So also
did elders and other men of substance in the country towns and villages. The original Canaanite inhabitants were partly absorbed and
were eventually accepted as Hebrews, though remaining as day laborers or tenant farmers. Some Hebrews fell from a higher to a lower
status.

There could hardly have been such a permanent stratification as
later developed in European countries and Great Britain, nor were
there ever such masses of slaves as in Greece or of "proletarians"
and slaves as in Rome. Yet, from the eighth century on, there were

perhaps five classes: (1) a considerable propertyless group of workers and slaves in city and in country; (2) a large group of peasant landowners; (3) rich landowners who ran estates and rented land; (4) the court; and (5) the royal family.[14]

After the Exile the chief priestly families, a specially privileged Brahmin caste, took the place of the court and the royal family and represented business interests as well. The Levites and Temple singers come into some prominence as a depressed landless group. Eventually a class of the moderately well-to-do, less influential priests, Levites (many of them scribes), small landowners, and craftsmen, gathered around the Torah. They distinguished and impoverished themselves by taking its rules seriously. They were the "moderates" of Proverbs and the Psalms. From them the scribes and Pharisees were later recruited. From among them those who protested against the evils of society, the "poor and needy" of the Psalms and the writers of apocalypses, must have come.

In the postexilic community Nehemiah (5:1–13), a man of independent means and authority, could accept and act vigorously upon the complaints of the farmers who were suffering from the oppression of the "nobles," the "officials," and the "priests." But when the high priest was himself the chief official, the commonalty had no protector. It is significant that Nehemiah called upon the priests separately to take oath to correct the economic abuses from which the people were suffering. The Psalms are less specific in naming those from whom the "poor and needy" suffer. But Josephus' accounts of the intrigues with which he as a priest was familiar point to the priests and their underlings as the class of persons in later Judaism who were chiefly guilty of despoiling the poor and causing the needy to groan.[15]

Analysis of the social structure in Hellenistic-Roman times by Louis Finkelstein gives a complicated picture: lay and Temple nobility in the upper class, priests and lay patricians in the middle class, Levites and Temple servants, traders and artisans in the lower classes, with a submerged group of paupers and slaves in Jerusalem. In the country in Judea and Galilee the upper class were landowners and provincial priests; the middle class, small landowners, with artisans and traders in the towns; the lower class, tenant farmers and shepherds, with a submerged group of hired laborers and slaves. The women of the upper and middle classes were emancipated, those of the lower class only so in part, and those of the submerged groups not at all.[16]

To sum up the evidence: The data gathered from the Bible and later Jewish writings and from archaeology suggest a gradual development of complexity and a rather rapid departure from the simplicity and democracy of nomadic mores. The succession of nomad tribes that entered Palestine in the fourteenth and thirteenth centuries reduced many of the Canaanite inhabitants to an inferior status as serfs and landless laborers. They were slowly assimilated, not without affecting the total culture. The Conquest at first produced serious cultural deterioration from the feudal splendor of the Late Bronze Age, but, as conditions gradually became stabilized, a marked advance in total population and in culture is revealed by excavation. There were, however, repeated periods of recession.

The ideals of the nomad settlers gradually altered to those of pastoral agriculture, with theoretical economic and social equality for all families of the conquering race, each of which was to possess its own plot of ground. But this ideal was never realized, and beginning under the early monarchy it was flouted or forgotten. As population increased the many factors that operate in a competitive society resulted in irritating social divisions, with the rich becoming richer and the poor poorer. The gap between the extravagance of the patricians and the forced austerity of the poor was enormous.

Finkelstein sees the whole history of the Hebrew people as a struggle between plebeian and patrician; between submerged landless groups and their oppressors, the great landowners; between the followers of Yahweh and the worshipers of Baal; between the equalitarian peace-lover and the class-conscious militarist, the democratic Hasid and the aristocratic Hellenist, the universalistic Pharisee and the nationalistic Sadducee.[17] Out of external and internal conflicts Judaism and Christianity were born.

6. *Society as an Educational Institution*   Human progress consists

in learning to control environment and use it to promote human values. Even if the success of the Hebrews was far from complete, still they did produce, not only an enduring society, but also values that have enriched the whole world. It would be possible to discuss endlessly the causes that produced such an indestructible people and a literature of such perennial value that, after 2000 years, it does not diminish, but rather increases, in its appeal to all nations.

Around the Hebrews, with apparently even better chances of survival, were the great culture centers, any one of which seemed more fortunately situated and unquestionably at times in their various careers was far more imposing. Only Greece and Rome are still named, along with Judea, as chief sources of Western culture. Although geographic Greece and Rome, like Judea itself, long ceased to be influential in world affairs, it is the combination of the three cultures that has made the Occident what it is. Above all, no people, not even Greece, has produced such a literature as the Bible. Some of the factors in that productivity are worthy of consideration in a study of history, even if they do not fully "explain" the result. How did the Hebrews meet the challenge of other cultures and of their own physical environment?

The most powerful educational institution in any society is the society itself. Communal mores, institutions, and ideas are a major part of culture; they are both products and producers; they are teachers, silent, indeed, but more effective educators than those who talk. This is true of any culture, all the more so when schools and official teachers are unknown.

A loosely knit, highly diversified society, if full of many divisions and competing opinions, produces people of divided minds and unsteady characters, although it may also develop genius and originality. Its culture may be rich and its opportunities varied, but it will not favor solid and steadfast individuals, even as it will not conduce to cohesiveness and resilience in the social structure. On the other hand, a society of small, closely knit groups, such as the Hebrew villages were, with small differences of status and wealth and a long history behind its traditions, customs, and dominant ideas, naturally develops conservatism and strength. The family and the social group teach twenty-four hours a day. Schools and foreign contacts interfere with the conservative function of the family and society. But, especially when children live and work with their parents and grandparents and participate in all group affairs, as they do in village life, they are inevitably conditioned to preserve and perpetuate the group inheritance without rapid change and on a relatively low level.

Before the Roman destruction of the Second Temple, Israelite society enjoyed a combination of stimulant and sedative that produced both originality and genius and also stability and solidity. It took 1100 years to produce Hillel and Jesus. After the Maccabean era Judaism veered toward isolation and stability, still more so after the destruction of Jerusalem, the Second Temple, and nationalism. However, throughout the history of the Jews they have not lacked men of genius and independence of thought. Among reasons for this was the development of certain unusual educational institutions.

7. *Three Unusual Educational Institutions*   In groups or associations of persons the Hebrews produced three specialized educational institutions that their neighbors lacked: priests, prophets, and scribes. The priests and the scribes preserved the nation and its faith; the prophets made them worth preserving. No one can explain why the Hebrews alone among the nations of antiquity produced prophets of such commanding and enduring influence. Out of the soothsayer, the clairvoyant, and the half-crazy ecstatic there came, beginning with Nathan, Amos, and Hosea, a succession of clearheaded, high-minded men who viewed life and their nation in the long perspective of past and future history, under the eye of God. They speedily abandoned locating strayed asses to guide lost and bewildered men.[18] Unfortunately the majority of men preferred to wander, but a valuable nucleus was saved.

Some of the prophets were priests, some were peasants. Some came from the country, some from the city. Some were courtiers, some were rebels. There were false, as well as genuine, prophets. Even the genuine prophets were sometimes wrong—as it appears in our perspective— in their message and advice. But the genuine prophets were con-

Looking south toward Sidon.

Sand dunes east of Caesarea (Stratonis), often four to six miles wide.

Stone-built mountain village; Beit-ur il Tahta. Fuel (thorn bush) on roof. Probably much like its ancient forerunner, Lower Beth-horon.

From Mt. Scopus looking eastward over Wilderness of Judea and Jordan Valley to Transjordan.

Looking eastward on upper reaches of Wadi Qelt.

Qattara, "Bad Lands." Limy clay in the Zor, or flood plain, of the River Jordan, eroded into curious shapes; extremely slippery when wet.

Wadi Sir, in Transjordan. Hills covered with oaks seventy years ago; now denuded and reforested with poplars by Circassian immigrants. A lusty stream turns mills and waters gardens.

From Tell Abil (Abel-Beth-Maacah) over the Jordan Valley toward Mt. Hermon. Fertile slopes lie all about the tell. Near northern border of ancient Israel.

El-Jib (Gibeon) looking north from slopes of Nebi Samwil. A typical Judean landscape: terraced hills, sparse trees (chiefly olives).

Petra, el-Haiyeh, the Serpent, surmounting a free-standing cube of sandstone, a monument to serpent worship. About one-third of the base of
the Pinnacle is not visible.

Petra "altar," a true "high place." Actually a *triclinium*, Greek fashion, for ritual meals, with altar at the center. The four sacred places illustrate the changes and mixture of religions.

Tell el-Qedah, ancient Hazor; beyond the imposing mound is an immense lower area surrounded by a *terre pisée* ramp, a possible Hyksos camp, but shown by recent excavation to have been later a large city.

Bedouin camp near Tekoa, some sixteen miles across the Wilderness from the Dead Sea. Meager cultivation to be noted.

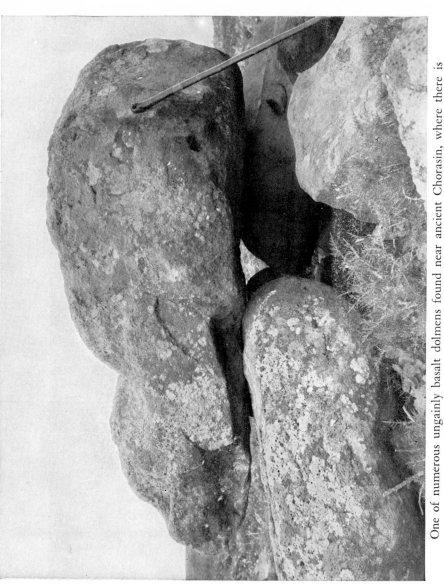

One of numerous ungainly basalt dolmens found near ancient Chorasin, where there is no limestone. The side walls collapsed under the cover block. The walking stick serves as a measure. Probably Chalcolithic (c. 4000 B.C.).

Train of camels crossing Plain of Esdraelon on track from Egypt to Damascus. An unusual sight. Camel trains are usually led by a man on a donkey. *Photo by D. E. McCown*

scientious men who believed that God spoke through them. They tried to look at life, politics, economics, morals, and religion as they believed God would view the human scene. Thus they achieved a certain objectivity, and—again under the long view of history— they spoke truth that has not yet lost its validity and its vitality. Strangely enough, they claimed to be calling their countrymen back to the old ways. Yet they were innovators from the standpoint of the majority. They were men who did not follow the mores of the group. Consequently they sowed seed that bore fruit in the distant future.[19]

The history of the priestly families and of the Levites, who ultimately were associated with them, is most complicated. It is widely assumed that, when the "high places" were definitely suppressed by Josiah, the country priests who had functioned at them were included among the Jerusalemite Temple servants. If so, the Levites and Aaronic priests constituted a motley group. The fires of the Exile probably purified it to some extent. But its postexilic history is anything but flattering.

According to the Law the priests were the custodians and teachers of the Law, and they may have played their part as both prophets (Jeremiah) and scribes (Ezra). But there is little evidence of it. They were essentially conservative, as most official religionists are, and they probably acted chiefly as conservators of law and custom. The Temple at Jerusalem is one of two places (the other the palace) that could have preserved written documents in pre-exilic times and the only one after the Exile. The story of the finding of the Deuteronomic law by Hilkiah is quite in keeping with the situation. What the priests accomplished as teachers is unrecorded. After the Exile they apparently became too deeply immersed in the mere routine of ritual, in managing the estates that they amassed, and in political and intra-Temple intrigue to carry on the teaching function. That fell to the scribes.

The "scribe" (sopher) appears as such with a name and identity as a writer concerned with religion first in Jeremiah's amanuensis, Baruch (36:26), and then in Ezra (7:6; Neh. 8:1) and Jesus the son of Sira'. The Gospels gave the word currency as the designation of interpreters of the Law, whom the Evangelists and the early Christians disliked. But the scribe, or "secretary," first appears as a court recorder of the early monarchy.

Whether the men who wrote out the traditions of J, E, D, and P were court recorders or priests (or both) turned historians no one can say. In any case they were much more than copyists. Their interest in legal institutions proves that some were priests; some were deeply imbued with the prophetic spirit. Many of them might— in other cultures—have been dramatists, for they wrote with epic and dramatic imagination. How much of prophetic originality they contributed to their narratives one cannot say. Certainly, as conservators of Hebrew tradition, ethics, and religion, they played a role of the highest value to posterity, to their own people, and to all the world. Beginning as priests, as royal secretaries and recorders, the scribes became historians, littérateurs, and eventually the official interpreters of the sacred Scriptures. They created, or at least preserved, the Hebrew theory of history. From among them came the rabbis.

In postexilic times the scribes as a rule came from the social level that Louis Finkelstein calls "plebeians." As famous a rabbi as Hillel had worked as a day laborer (a porter), and the rabbis, true to their class, insisted that every Jewish boy ought to learn a trade. They came, not from among the patricians and landowners, but chiefly from among the middle classes, from the poorer priests, the Levites, and the artisans.

The fact that the prophets arose from all levels of society and that people of middle-class background assembled and edited the books preserved as sacred explains the "proletarian" ethos of the Old Testament. Distrust of the rich, the proud, the powerful, care for the poor, the needy, the fatherless, and the widow—these social attitudes were natural in men who continually saw need about them and suffered it themselves. They wrote and they preserved the Psalms that make the "poor and needy" the most exigent and the most favored of the clients of God.

8. *Cult Institutions and Education* The continued existence and influence of Hebraism are due primarily to the centrality of its religious ideas and institutions and to the men who put its ideas into words. The institutions played their large part. Israel became a nation as an "amphictyony" centering around some kind of Tabernacle, possibly (despite critical doubts) first in the steppe, certainly later at Shiloh. The destruction of the Tabernacle and the transfer of the Ark, as an aniconic symbol of the divine presence, to Judea and Jerusalem, and the contemporary choice of a king from a southern tribe combined to make Jerusalem the sacred center, first of a kingdom and later of a hierocratic state, euphemistically called theocratic to enhance sacerdotal prestige. Though long confined almost to the precincts of the sacred city, the little state remained the religious center and symbol of its nationals, although they were scattered to the four winds.

There is evidence to indicate that Jerusalem had been a sacred city long before the Hebrews arrived in Palestine. In the processes of history, Judaism became so conditioned to it as a racial and national symbol that, for Christians as well as for Jews, the words "Jerusalem" and "Zion" in their symbolic meanings have survived the destruction of the Temple and the occupation of the city by gentile powers, Roman, Christian, and Moslem, down to the present moment. For Christians, as well as for Jews and Arabs, the"Holy Land" has been at one time or another *terra irredenta*. Unholy as it has been, destructive of genuine moral and religious ideas as the very idea of a "holy city" has proved to be, as actuality and as symbol Jerusalem has been one of the chief bonds holding the Hebrew race together. Its repeated mention in the Psalms and in Jewish prayers has preserved the idea of national unity until, even for today's nonreligious Zionists (note the word), it becomes a sentimental shibboleth that outweighs all practical, economic considerations.

Among other cult institutions that assisted in educating the Hebrews, some of the most notable for promoting racial solidarity have been their festivals, all of them ostensibly religious, but all, or nearly all, adaptations of heathen festivals, like those of Western Christians. For each of them special rites in the home and the synagogue were prescribed, and they were so interpreted as to wipe out any suggestions of paganism. To each of them one of the five Megilloth, or Rolls, was attached: to the Passover the Song of Songs, to Pentecost Ruth, to the ninth of the month Ab (the anniversary of the destruction of the Temple in 587) Lamentations, to Tabernacles Ecclesiastes, to Purim the Book of Esther. Later Hanukkah, the rededication of the Temple by Judas Maccabeus, quite naturally called for telling the story of the Maccabees. Where the connection of festival and roll is not obvious, it could be made so by allegorical interpretation, as when Canticles was interpreted as portraying Yahweh's love for his people. With uncanny wisdom the devotees of the Law made each festival serve a semireligious, seminationalistic purpose.

The Passover was to be accompanied by instruction to children regarding the escape from Egypt. The Feast of Booths was to remind them of their wanderings in the wilderness. Purim, the merriest of all, was a reminder of the race's miraculous escape from massacre as the story is told in Esther. Hanukkah, the latest festival, celebrated the temporary Maccabean triumph over the Seleucid armies. Its lights are strangely reminiscent of festivals of lights observed elsewhere (in Hindu India, for example) at the time of the winter solstice. But, even if a festival was an adaptation of a secular or heathen custom, like Christmas candles, it was adroitly used to further national and religious interests.

The greeting of each new moon with blasts of a ram's horn served notice that the calendar itself was within the purview of religious instead of secular interests. The priestly calculation of the times of the feasts, depending as it did upon empirical observation, was an added monition that times and seasons were sacred. The very abstention from work and the various rites on the Sabbath in a sense hallowed the whole week.

In itself the Sabbath became one of the most important adjuncts to the educational system since it made an opportunity for a religious gathering in which instruction could be given. It seems to have played a minor social role until after the Exile. But, so far as the evidence goes, it developed *pari passu* with the use of the synagogue. In the last two or three centuries of the Second Temple, according to the evidence of Maccabees and the Gospels, rest on the Sabbath had become obligatory on all good Jews. Indeed, it became a kind of tabu, to be observed regardless of consequences to individuals.

9. *The Scriptures* Other indispensable ideas and institutions were perhaps more substantial and more effective. Foremost were the sacred Scriptures. There are actually four "peoples of a book," Jews, Christians, Moslems, and Zoroastrians. All four have maintained a certain integrity (amid vast changes) because of that fact.

It seems incredible that the destruction of the Temple and the cessation of the supposedly indispensable sacrifices and offerings should not have involved the disintegration of Judaism. But, in the course of the five preceding centuries, two institutions had arisen to fill the void created by Jewish intransigence and Roman arms: the Scriptures and the synagogue. Following the Exile, the Torah, the Law, had come to take a dominant place in orthodox Jewish thinking, and, under the influence of the prophets, who had urged the superiority of ethical and spiritual sacrifices and offerings, the bloody rites at the Temple could come to an end without, as it seems, at all seriously affecting the loyalty of the people to their God. Jews of the two Diasporas, east and west, had long ceased to receive any personal benefit or emotional uplift from the worship in the Temple. It was hardly a genuine means of grace to them, except by imagination or on a pilgrimage.

Long before 70 A.D. a psalmist had written,

> Sacrifice and offering thou didst not require;
>   But thou hast opened my ears.
> Burnt offering and sin offering
>   Thou didst not ask.
> Then said I, Lo, I come,
>   In the roll of the book it is written of me;
> I delight to do thy will, O my God;
>   Thy law is within my heart.[20]

The sacrifice acceptable to God was a broken and a contrite spirit.

He desired "steadfast love and not sacrifice, the knowledge of God rather than burnt offerings." When, at Jamnia, Yohanan ben-Zakai found his disciples wild with sorrow at the news that Jerusalem had fallen and the Temple was burning, he told them that charity and the love of mankind would replace burnt offerings.[21] The boast of the Diaspora Jews had been their Book rather than the Temple; and, after the terrors of the Jewish-Roman wars, Palestinian Jews turned more than ever to the study of their sacred writings.

A question that is often overlooked must be considered. How large a proportion of the population of Judea knew the Law? How many could read the sacred rolls? It is a question that cannot be definitely answered, but aspects of it should be explored. The problem of the actual influence of the higher, more spiritual elements of the culture within any racial or national group is interesting and important but almost insoluble. This is especially true of the general literacy and intelligence of ancient societies. How many inhabitants of Athens could or would read Plato and Herodotus? How deeply did Athenians understand Aeschylus and Euripides and truly participate in Greek culture at its higher levels and in the progress of Greek thought? The execution of Socrates illustrates the backwardness of the Athenian electorate as Huey Long and Joseph McCarthy document that of certain sections of the United States, and evidently of many persons in all areas.

The problem of the extent of literacy and intellectual culture among the Hebrews, that is, of ability to read and understand progressive ideas, is most difficult. They never had even an opportunity to vote. However, it is safe to say that before Solomon's time very few persons knew how to read and write even the briefest, most conventional records of business transactions. In the ninth century Mesa of Moab must have counted on some readers of his boastful inscription. In the eighth, receipts on potsherds, though standard practice, and the later rather numerous graffiti do not prove wide literacy. The number that could read and understand Amos and Isaiah or the Deuteronomy that Hilkiah found in the Temple was constantly growing larger, but such skill was far from general. The Exile must have lowered the level in Judea but may have raised it in Babylonia. By the time the Hellenistic age was reached, the number was doubtless much larger, but now the difficulty arose that the common language of everyday speech was Aramaic, and the Hebrew Scriptures were no longer intelligible. The later rabinic hatred of the *'Am ha-'arets* may have arisen from popular revolts against the Law as well as from illiteracy.

However, the modern age, with its emphasis on literacy, may easily underestimate the intelligence of the unlettered. Among the villagers and even the Bedouins of Palestine, at the end of the First World War, when schools, books, and newspapers were almost unknown, a very considerable knowledge of the outside world and a keen intellectual ability could be found. Both Moslems and Christians, as well as indigenous Jews, were usually living still in that ancient, prescientific world of magic, miracle, and jinn. But a day and a night spent in the Judean steppe at an Arab judicial council of leading citizens from all the villages from 'Anata to Mukhmas revealed the possibilities of culture among people of whom probably few could write more than their names. They were roughly clad peasants. Yet they were politeness personified. They knew their social and legal customs and precedents. They could enforce their arguments by quotations and stories from traditional literature. They spoke dignified and forceful Arabic. They illustrate the intelligence and the conservative forces of oral tradition and social custom.

So the peasants Amos and Micah spoke classical Hebrew, even as did the Jerusalemite Isaiah. The prophets could go from village to village in little Judea and, "in the gate," by the stone benches where the elders sat and all men—and women— came to buy and to sell and to talk, they could proclaim the "word of Yahweh" to people who were far from ignorant of Hebrew law and tradition. In so small a land the great mass of the unlettered villagers would have some opportunity to hear Amos and Isaiah and would be able to comprehend the import of their message, especially as it touched their poverty and the oppression of their rich landlords, who "added house to house and field to field." When the Persian Empire and then the Greek made travel easier, and there was communication with the Dispersions, east and west, literacy and general intelligence must have increased. Papyrus from Egypt was doubtless generally accessible, and biblical rolls might have been found in many villages.

One characteristic of the Old Testament is especially to be noted, for otherwise its significant quality is not appreciated. It was preeminently a book of the people. A large proportion of its authors remain anonymous. So far as they are known, not one came from a patrician family. Isaiah is sometimes taken to be an exception because of his free entry to Hezekiah, but that is extremely weak evidence. Prophets were privileged individuals, as holy men still are in Moslem, Hindu, and Buddhist lands—and even clergymen in Christian countries. Some of them, Jeremiah and Ezekiel, for example, were priests, and priests had much to do with the writing and editing of the books, Ezra, for example. The one king named, aside from legendary ascriptions to David and Solomon, was not a Hebrew, but an otherwise unknown Lemuel, "king of Massa," perhaps an Edomite. One powerful official, Nehemiah, left his memoirs for use. There can be no doubt that most of those who, especially in postexilic times, wrote and edited the books and fought for the observance of the Law were, as Finkelstein says, plebeians (that is, what might be called *petite bourgeoisie* and artisans) and "scribes of the Temple," to use the phrase of the rescript ascribed to Antiochus III.[22] The Old Testament is a folk book because it was written by the folk. There could hardly be a more striking contrast than between Greco-Roman literature and that of the Hebrews.

The "Great Synagogue," or "Great Assembly," is supposed to have been called together about 200 to give the "plebeians" a part in the Council that later became the Sanhedrin. At the same time regulations were established regarding the worship of the Temple, the synagogue, and the conduct of justice by the judges in the villages. They were admonished, "Be deliberate in judgment, set up a hedge about the Law, and make many disciples."[23] Thus a mass indoctrination of the country population was attempted. All of these measures were a part of Simon's effort to counteract the assimilationist policy that had been followed by the priestly caste and to replace it with the "plebeian" doctrine that Judaism was a Torah, a philosophy greater than any other, because it emanated from God. This eminently praiseworthy undertaking must have functioned largely through the second major postexilic institution, the synagogue.

10. *The Synagogue*   The Book itself would have been far less effective but for the synagogue. Along with the Book, about which its activities centered, the synagogue was responsible above all other factors for the indestructibility of Judaism. It embodied prophet and scribe. Without it the Scriptures could have influenced only the literate few. One cannot but wonder how modern Israel in Palestine, where the majority have abandoned both Book and synagogue, can survive; certainly only as a political state, "like all the nations."

The synagogue is a unique institution. When and where it arose is wrapped in the mists of the Persian period, but it was in existence four or five centuries before the destruction of the Second Temple, and, when that occurred, it had become sufficiently established as an indispensable element in Jewish culture to take the place of Temple and sacrifices as the foundation of Jewish life. Until the Christian church imitated it in its Sunday services, it was the only institution for general religious education that had ever come into existence.

Official city and imperial cults in the Greco-Roman world and the mystery religions had their myths, their rituals, and their festivals, but no rehearsal of a body of law, ethics, and history like the Old Testament. The philosophical schools had their processes of instruction and discussion, but without religious motivation and only for the few. The Gnostics had instruction of an esoteric nature, also only for adepts. No other religion or nation had an institution remotely resembling the synagogue.

It was a thoroughly democratic institution, conducted, not by priests or rabbis, but by laymen, and for all the people who would, or could be induced to, come. There the illiterate heard the Law and the Prophets read and discussed Sabbath after Sabbath. They could assist in the repetition of the Psalms, at the least in the responses. But it was also an official community center, where the interests of the whole congregation were considered. The elders of the synagogue were the ruling body in the Jewish community. Therefore the synagogue was an eleemosynary institution, where aid was given to the poor. It was Red Cross, community chest, and social security office, and city hall and courtroom, as well as a social center. There was every reason why all Jews should attend its services.

It was also, and primarily, a religious institution, a place for worship as well as instruction. Accordingly, it gave instruction under the most favorable conditions for effective indoctrination. The lesson read brought every Jew into the presence of God's whole revelation to mankind, and to it everyone, in the responses, assented. In Deuteronomy (6:9; 11:20) it had been ordered that God's law should be written on the doorposts of the houses and on the gates, and that they should be like a sign upon the hand and like frontlets between the eyes of every Israelite. No doorposts so inscribed have ever been unearthed in Palestine or elsewhere. In the *tephillin,* or phylacteries, the little boxes which it became the custom for every Jewish man to wear on his forearm and forehead while praying, and in the similar *mezuzah,* hung upon the doorpost, a few significant verses of the Law were placed. But for educational purposes this literal observance of a figurative requirement was worse than futile. For the majority, the *tephillah* and the *mezuzah* became mere amulets, as the meaning of the New Testament term "phylacteries" indicates.

What the verses in Deuteronomy were intended to accomplish was done by the synagogues. It provided for bringing the divine word to the people in constant reiteration. If pre-exilic Israel had had the Book and the synagogue, its history might have been very different. That Judaism had become a more or less closely knit community in the first century of our era and survived through the second century was due largely to the synagogue and to the body of sacred literature that it held before its worshipers.

11. *National and Religious Self-Confidence* Without any attempt to weigh the relative merits of all the Jewish notions that made for solidarity and survival, isolationism and a sense of superiority, with the illusion of a misunderstood "manifest destiny," must be emphasized. The Law, the Prophets, and the Writings were full of both, and

the synagogue, with its readings, continually inculcated them. Both centered about the Jews' conception of Yahweh as superior to all other deities and later of him as sole deity, displacing all others. They were a peculiar people because their deity required of them certain conduct that set them apart. Their tabus as to food and sacrifices (for example, avoidance of swine in both cases) made them different. Yahweh's covenant and choice making them his Chosen People set them apart and gave them additional grounds for their sense of superiority. Consequently, as long as they had faith in him, they had an unconquerable confidence in the national future, and that confidence held them together with indissoluble bonds.

The very certainty and satisfaction with which that belief was held, however, eventually by reaction to historical fact, created an insoluble problem. One way of expressing the difficulty is to say that the justice of God became doubtful when generation after generation passed away without realizing the rewards promised to faithfulness. Why should they, a righteous people, continually suffer from the attacks of enemies and the oppression of heathen rulers? Or, to express it differently, why should the heathen triumph over God's Chosen People, to whom he had covenanted to give the rulership of the world? Was God impotent, or was he unjust?

The answers to the questions were various. John the Baptist and Jesus accepted and applied the prophetic explanation. The nation was not righteous; it had not fulfilled the stipulations of the Covenant—a most unpalatable solution of the difficulty. The different ways of living with the dilemma, discussed above, suited different situations and types of mind. The bitterness of the people's disillusionment is registered in the virulence of the quarrels between the parties. The dissatisfaction was far from being purely political. It was greatly exacerbated by social and economic inequities and the resulting conflict between rich and poor.

So implacable were the internecine hatreds that poisoned the little body politic and so irreconcilable the antagonistic points of view that Judaism almost committed racial suicide. It did destroy itself as a nation. In the outcome the race survived as a cult group that was still held together by faith in the Covenant God and by hope of a glorious national future marked by a return to Zion.

Judaism survived as a racial cult group with unlimited nationalistic hopes. Ethically it was justified because its future was to be a vindication of the righteousness of God in the establishment of a reign of justice as well as material well-being. In a remarkable feat of intellectual legerdemain, the schismatic Christian sect adopted the Old Testament Covenant and Chosen People complex and the synagogue. Jewish Christians regarded themselves as the true people of God and taught their gentile converts to use the same language. They appropriated to themselves all of the Old Testament promises. But race and nation could play no part in their thinking. Consequently they lost the outstanding value of the prophetic social message that had been basic also in Jesus' preaching, and the apostolic *kerygma* (preaching) degenerated into an individualistic otherworldliness that promised a salvation in heaven, not a reign of righteousness on earth. The cult of individualistic salvation, with no economic or social implications, especially in its combination with Johannine mysticism, served to keep Christianity alive during long centuries of Roman tyranny and medieval barbarism. Strangely, real values can inhere in half-truths.

CHAPTER XII

What the Hebrews Learned

1. *The Components of Hebrew Culture* The "Hand of God in History," with its numerous corollaries, represents what the Hebrews thought, confusedly and uncertainly, that they had learned from their historical experience. The sketch in the previous chapters of the living process through which Hebrew culture arose must serve as a skeleton upon which to place the flesh and blood of cultural experience. The discussion of the "education of the Hebrew race" is intended to suggest the process, the means by which they learned. Now the question is, What had they actually learned? What was the spiritual content of their culture, "spirit" being taken in the largest possible sense?

A cross section of a culture at a particular moment amounts to a post-mortem. Vivisection of culture is difficult. Culture is dead when it is dissected. An attempt at analysis is made in these chapters and the ones following without, it is hoped, lessening the sense of history as a living process.

The material is extensive and can more easily be presented by dividing it. The present chapter will discuss the limitations and then the proficiencies of the Hebrews as a social unit, seen more or less externally. The next chapter will call attention rather to internal content, intellectual, moral, and religious.

In an attempt to analyze and summarize the conceptual and emotional content of Hebrew culture, many factors must be considered. Surely no one, however deeply convinced of the independence and originality of Hebrew religious conceptions and ideals, would assume that, after a leading group in the nation had lived for generations in

Egypt and then entered Canaan after a few years in the steppe, they could have developed their culture in entire disregard of that great civilization. It is equally impossible that a nation in an open corridor of commerce and conquest could escape influences from the other great cultures about it. On the contrary, the content of Hebrew culture is peculiarly rich and varied just because of the nation's wide contacts with Near Eastern civilization in all its phases. Just as, at one time or another, nearly every Near Eastern culture is represented in the artifacts that the archaeologist unearths in Palestinian tells (mounds), so also the conceptual content of Hebrew culture reveals traces of wide acquaintance with the mythologies, law, ethics, and religions of other nations.

Volumes would be necessary to catalogue and document either the artifactual importations or the conceptual contacts of Palestine with other lands and peoples. Much in Hebrew life and thought was common to all of the Near East. For example, in the thirteenth-century Canaanite temples of Lachish (Tell ed-Duweir) there were many bones from sacrificed animals, all from the right foreleg, just as required in Hebrew and also in Assyrian and Babylonian ritual.[1] In other cases, official Hebrew reaction against practices common in neighboring nations was strong—for example, against the sacrifice of swine, seething a kid in its mother's milk, and temple prostitution, a practice especially prominent in Canaanite worship. In their literature and practices the Hebrews reveal their close relationships with the cultures of other peoples, but unmistakably their unfettered originality. Their historical and cultural perspective had both depth and breadth.

In a further discussion of the components of Hebrew literature and religious thought, one caveat must be repeated. To say that certain influences from without were at work or that materials were "borrowed" does not imply any derogation of Hebrew independence and originality. An idea, an artifact, an institution, or a myth from another culture may make a suggestion or provide a stimulus, either positive or negative, without being slavishly followed. It may lead to a better product than in the primary culture, or a worse. The anthropologist regards "stimulus diffusion" as a most significant and usually beneficial social process.

To illustrate: Both cuneiform syllabaries and Egyptian hieroglyphs included signs for syllables and ideas that in pronunciation were hardly more than simple phonemes for which we would use a single letter. Some Palestinian or Syrian discovered that putting three of these together would produce the triliteral roots of words of his own language, and so, unintentionally, an alphabet was produced by adding character to character. Not by borrowing or imitating, but by stimulation, one of the most useful inventions ever applied to language was achieved.[2] By an analogous process a Hebrew, or rather many Hebrews, combined the Babylonian idea of creation with that of word magic, the spoken command of an all-powerful deity, into the notion of creation by God's *yehi,* his *fiat.* When God spoke, it was no longer mere magic. It is not the source of an idea, but the use made of it, that counts. Combinations and alterations of ideas, intellectual "hybridization," are among the chief agencies of progress. Hybrid ideas, unlike hybrid corn seed, are fruitful, but also fertile.

Societal hybridization, however, has its dangers. When cultures meet and interpenetrate, numerous problems result. In Egypt and Palestine and throughout their history, these problems harassed the Jewish race. The materially richer and more imposing culture is not necessarily the healthier or morally the more vigorous. The simple and sturdy cultural patterns brought from the steppe were inevitably in danger of distortion and destruction by contact with the more glamorous pagan cultures of the Canaanite nations engaged in agricultural, commercial, political, and especially military competition with one another. The almost impossible problem for the Hebrews was how to use the good in other cultures without losing what was best in their own.

In cultural fusion, the uneducated, the thoughtless, those completely preoccupied with making a living, and those equally preoccupied with a mad race for wealth, position, and power, that is, those at the lowest and highest economic and cultural levels, are certain to be mentally too dull or spiritually too insensible to make sound choices. Whatever may have been true of the aristocracy at the top and the mass of the people at the bottom of the economic and social ladder, throughout Hebrew history, from the earliest prophets to the close of the biblical

canon, the writers and the scribes and rabbis who were the final editors
of the twenty-four books and excluded the Apocrypha and Pseudepigrapha exhibited unusual perspicacity and critical judgment, both in
what they retained and in what they omitted. The Old Testament is
the authoritative exposition of their culture. There is little in the excluded books that contributes to their fame, although much that assists
in understanding their later history. It must be said that they succeeded
admirably in preserving in the Old Testament the unique and authentic
values of Hebrew culture.

2. *Hebrew Advantages* The conditions that limited Hebrew cultural achievements in some areas worked to their advantage in others.
The central position of the Promised Land and the amplitude of the
surrounding cultures have been sufficiently emphasized. The long aeons
of prehistory, savagery, barbarism, and city civilization did not leave
Palestine untouched. At the moment archaeologists are crediting that
little country with one of the oldest known villages and the oldest
known walled city, Jericho, where an extremely early agriculture was
based on rudimentary irrigation. The many races, languages, and
peoples who crossed and recrossed and occupied Palestine marked it
with their place names, their artifacts, and traces of their physiogno-
mies and cultures. All the millennia of unwritten history had left a
precipitate in the Canaan that the Hebrews conquered.

Man achieves his best, says André Malraux's spokesman in *Man's
Hope,* "by converting as wide a range of experience as possible into
conscious thought." [3] The Hebrews' position at the center of ancient
civilizations, as the inheritors of two millennia of civilization and
written history, made it possible for their priests and prophets to become familiar with a length and breadth of experience such as few
peoples have known. The fact that alphabetic writing had recently
been perfected—and that in the very Canaan where they settled—gave
them an immense advantage over any previous culture. Just as the
great burst of intellectual activity among the Greeks followed, by three
or four centuries, their adoption of the Phoenician alphabet, so also
it was among the Hebrews.

Their semi-isolation among the mountains, the enforced abstention
from all-consuming efforts (they had the lust) for wealth, power, and

military conquest, and the ethos of austerity derived from their nomadic inheritance and demanded by their geographic conditions lent
them an economic objectivity that resulted in unusual clarity of social
vision. Above all, perhaps, the prophetic attempt to see all human
activity from the point of view of a just, impartial, and august deity
prepared them for the task of converting the long historical experience
of their wide world into conscious thought at a remarkably high level.
History's mills grind slowly. The final grist of Hebrew history, ground
actually through many millennia, is the finest and the richest in moral
vitamins that the world has yet produced.

Exposure to a multitudinous variety of climatic and geographic
influences and of cultural concepts and forms, such as could scarcely
be found together anywhere else in space and time, contributed might-
ily to the richness of Hebrew thought and language and to the con-
creteness, simplicity, and universality of its ideas. Its metaphors, allusions, and other rhetorical forms have given the Old Testament remarkable intelligibility and emotional appeal to people all over the
world, even when translated into the most diverse languages. The Hebrews' literature could give adequate expression to the wealth and
abundance of the content of their cup of life.

Conservatives, both Jews and Christians, have emphasized the isolation of the ancient Hebrews in order to make it appear that their
inspiration came from God alone. A certain type of intellectual arro-
gance has argued from this mistakenly assumed isolation, from the
prescientific framework of Hebrew thought, and from the admitted
inconsistencies and contradictions found in the Bible, that such a book
can have little value for modern life. So the literati of Athens and
Rome felt toward the little nation that spoke a barbarous language
on the outskirts of their world. For many moderns the belief in miracle
that pervades the Bible is enough to condemn it. Both views, from
right and left, are proved erroneous by the facts of the situation as it
has been presented here. A fuller and more systematic discussion of
what the Hebrews actually accomplished will establish their right to
attention and, critically made, by claiming neither too much nor too
little, will indicate what values they contributed.

3. *The Long Perspective* Of the three peoples to whom the West-

ern world looks back as chief direct contributors to its cultural history, only the Hebrews had historical perspective. Although the Greeks had their Linear A and B scripts in the second millennium, Homer and Hesiod, contemporaries of Elijah and Amos, and Herodotus and Thucydides, contemporaries of Ezra and Nehemiah, represent the earliest Greek literary remains and the first Greek historians. The last Old Testament Hebrews to write firsthand historical documents were contemporary with the first Greek historians. Josephus was right when he said that to record the events of the past was an Oriental rather than a Hellenic tradition.[4] The Hebrews had been writing history more than half a millennium when the Greek "father of history" was born.

The Greek historians had no comparable historical theory, the Romans much less. History was "the sovereign corrective of human nature," said Polybius. Clio was pragmatic; she denounced evil, eulogized the good, and endowed her votaries with wisdom. The only Greek philosophy of history was that of the *Persians* of Aeschylus: pride earned the envy of the gods and doom.[5] Fate and the dastardly tricks it played on men were a standing theme in the folklore, epic, and drama of all ancient nations, and in Greek history. History assured men who revered the gods and lived noble lives the reward of a historical immortality in men's memories.

When Herodotus and Thucydides began to write, the Hebrews already had in their hands the five books of tradition and law that carried them from Creation to the birth of their nation in the Exodus and conquest of Canaan, with the four books of history, the "Former Prophets," Joshua, Judges, Samuel, and Kings, that continued the story to the Exile. They had scattered records of the Restoration, besides a mass of prophetic and other writings that were being gradually assembled and edited for incorporation in the nation's educational system.

In addition to their own records they had access, as their literature demonstrates, to the traditions and written literatures of the great nations that originated and developed Near Eastern civilization. Back of the great rabbis, Hillel and Shammai, and of Jesus stretched 3000 years of literacy in the Near East on both sides of Palestine, in Egypt and in the Tigris-Euphrates Valley. Both the early Sojourn and the later Diaspora, with the help perhaps of the Aramaic language, partly overcame the difficulty of Egyptian hieroglyphics.

On the other side, the Ras esh-Shamrah discoveries reveal the riches of Canaanite literature written in a near relative of their own language. The Assyrian conquest and the Exile put all Mesopotamian culture into their hands. For the centuries of Persian and Macedonian (Seleucid and Ptolemaic) rule they were exposed to all the cultural winds that blew, with almost no barriers, political or linguistic. Jews who were curious—doubtless many were—could easily become acquainted with the mythology, including of course the cosmological and religious notions, of all the Near Eastern and then the Hellenistic peoples. Some studied astronomy and the calendric theories of the Babylonians and the Greeks, as Ethiopic Enoch shows.

Because the peoples of Egypt and Mesopotamia had been publicly and historically minded, the scribes whom Jesus criticized could look back on thirty centuries of written history and literature, ten of the centuries their own. No other part of the world had such records as the Egyptians, the Mesopotamians, and the Jews. No one could become familiar with the Book of Genesis without being impressed with the antiquity of the human race and the Hebrew race. Even a rough computation of biblical data would put Abraham nearly two thousand years before Herod the Great and Methuselah a thousand years earlier. The Hebrews looked back upon a long schooling.

The modern historian knows far more about the events and the ideas of ancient times than any Jewish scribe could know—vastly more, indeed, than anyone knew even fifty years ago. But the Jewish apologists made much of the antiquity of Moses. The Greeks were deeply impressed with the ancient wisdom of Egypt. Historical perspective meant something even though the scene was filled with half-mythical figures and fabulous stories and was blurred by a multitude of misconceptions. There had been an abundant content handed down that was not immediately apparent to the onlooker then, and it is often overlooked now. Mores, institutions, and ideas (see above) inform and instruct as a major part of cultural content.

4. *Cultural Contributions* Both the limitations and the fruitfulness of Hebrew culture must be noted. To certain features, that ancient people in their homeland made no contributions. As a nation they were lacking in some cultural activities. Only their prophets developed world horizons. Great statesmanship and military ability, notable political organization (except for collecting taxes and making corvées, borrowed from Egypt), and democratic political institutions were lacking. In matters of physical training, scientific medicine, sanitation, and hygiene they were behind their contemporaries (notwithstanding their dietetic tabus), as they were in physical science, biology, and general scientific interest. In formal education, general literature, libraries, and inscriptions for the information of the public and posterity they were wanting. That synagogue schools for the popular study even of the Old Testament antedate the Christian era is questionable. They had no *gymnasia*. Children learned to read and write, if they did learn, at home. In some of these items, even the Greeks had made little progress from a modern point of view, but the Jews had made less.

In architecture, painting, sculpture, music, and drama, even in pottery making, metalwork, and ivory carving, that is, in everything connected with art and artistic skills, they were lacking in notable achievement. What they were able to do in textiles is beyond our knowledge. By comparison with their neighbors they were overorganized and overzealous as to religion. But they made no contribution to science, speculative philosophy, and systematic or speculative theology, on the one hand, nor, on the other, to the development of industrial arts and economic organization.

This is not to imply that as a people they wanted ability, but rather chiefly that they lacked opportunity. A people that had to wrest a mere living from marginal land, half of it rock and steppe, that was limited also by sea, mountain, and steppe from easy expansion in any direction, could never amass the wealth and man power necessary for great military operations. A land lacking in any kind of resources in raw materials such as mineral wealth and without a rich hinterland such as Phoenicia had could never produce riches by extensive industry or commerce.

As a buffer state, a military parade ground and battlefield for all the great nations of antiquity, the Jews rarely had peace long enough to develop the arts. Their marginal climate also came upon them with its hosts of locusts, with its droughts, and siroccos, and mildews, to destroy accumulations of wealth. When they were thus weakened, hungry hordes of nomads from the steppe were always ready to fall upon them. A life lived so near the margin of existence was not conducive to any literature of amusement; it provided no philosophic leisure. There was no time or incentive even to add ornament to pottery, although often an artistic eye unconsciously gave it shapes of beauty. Life was a series of concrete problems. Even the language never developed an easy philosophic or theological vocabulary. It dealt with life as seen and felt, not with abstractions. Life was a series of conflicts with nature and with man.

The conditions of existence in Palestine favored contributions to world culture in other than material or philosophical areas. The Hebrews' greatest achievements, aside from the literature that embodies them, are to be found in concepts of economic, social, and intellectual democracy. They present unusual practical rather than theoretical accomplishments in morals and religion and in the literature of morals and religion. Theirs were heroes, not of commerce, industry, or arms, but of personal moral character and of prophetic ethical and religious vision.

From their rugged limestone mountains between the sea and the steppe, they watched the pageant of history, with its military pomp and frightfulness, its commercial bickerings and dishonesty, its long caravans of disdainful striding camels led by diminutive trotting asses, its ships of Tarshish raising their billowing sails for long and adventurous journeys. Close at hand was the shepherd leading his flock, the solitary sower broadcasting his seed, the plowman with his little oxen and his wooden plow scratching the surface of the rock-strewn ground. They journeyed to see the great temples and palaces of Egypt and Byblos, of Assyria and Babylon, and they pondered over the ruins of towers men had built to reach the skies.

What is even more important was their literature. They had their own oral traditions and they had records of their racial history in an easily learned phonetic alphabet. Not infrequently, as the centuries passed, they were drawn into the vast and tragic drama of Near Eastern social, political, and cultural history. But their priests and scribes and prophets had developed their own political, social, ethical, and religious notions to an integrated consistency sufficient to build them a steady platform from which to gaze on the world pageant. Their kings and princes might lose themselves in political intrigue. The mass of the people might flounder in ignorance and want. Their great religious leaders stood somewhat outside the conflict and looked at the world, or at least tried to look at it, from the point of view of their unique deity. They seemed to have all that was necessary to achieve a solid and well-integrated *Lebensanschauung;* yet it failed to satisfy.

5. *Varied Currents of Thought* The Hebrews' distinctive cultural heritage, it is unnecessary to say, came to them as it comes to us, through their literature. All their artistic capacities were channeled through the one outlet. For them life was real, life was earnest—and the grave *was* its goal. Their literature was darkened by the shadows of the conflict between good and evil, and much of it was written under the eye of an exigent Deity. It was shadowed also by the frustrations of nationalistic and racialistic ambitions. However, it cannot be assumed that they lived continually in this atmosphere. They were assailed by varied and contradictory currents of thought.

In descriptions of life in its naked reality they exhibited their artistic and constructive abilities, and the reality was not all gloom. No doubt there was a very considerable literature of amusement. The storyteller could not have been absent from their homes and their festal occasions. The Books of Psalms and Job exhibit their ability to observe and describe nature. Ruth and Jonah, Judith and Tobit show no little novelistic talent. The Song of Songs and the tales of Samson, Elijah, and Elisha illustrate what they could do in their lighter hours. The Book of Proverbs, as well as their folk tales, suggest their keenness in observing and their skill in characterizing human weaknesses and foibles. Their dry humor and homely wisdom are still admirable and pertinent.

Being a people given to plastic thinking and to history, their forte was narrative, whether in the ballad, such as Deborah's paean, the folk tale as in the stories of the Patriarchs and of David's exploits, or the terse, spare language of the chronicles in the Books of Samuel and Kings. But, as befitted a deeply moral and religious people, the Psalms and the sermons and addresses of the prophets exhibit a beauty, an emotional intensity, and a shattering vigor and power of expression that are without superior. Their literature is their enduring monument.

The dozen books that embody Hebrew law and history constitute a fascinating field of study for the folklorist, the historian, and the student of religion. As the Western world has classified them, they are history. The Pentateuch, Joshua, Judges, Samuel, Kings, and Chronicles, with Ezra-Nehemiah, center around a very few legal, cultic, and nationalistic ideas. They give the long perspective, but, aside from the legal codes, they are like a railroad track through the desert, with only an occasional semaphore showing.

The editors who made the Pentateuch out of two regional groups of narratives (from Judean and Ephraimite, and possible Edomite, tradition) and added the Deuteronomic and Priestly codes had in mind the nation as the Chosen People with its God, its laws, and its cult practices. The editors who prepared the national traditions and royal records for public use in the Books of Joshua, Judges, Samuel, and Kings read into them the Deuteronomic theory of material blessings for an obedient and curses for a disobedient people. The books thus became, not histories, but, as Jewish scholars appropriately named them, the "Former Prophets," books of religion. Bible history would be bare indeed and false but for the pre-exilic and some of the postexilic prophets, who saw their situations as they were, not according to materialistic and nationalistic presuppositions. The work of the Chronicler betrays an even greater preponderance of dogmatic assumptions. The modern student must not forget the Torah, but the religious and moral values of Hebrew culture are to be found chiefly in what were called the "four prophets," Isaiah, Jeremiah, Ezekiel, and the Book of the Twelve, the "minor prophets," along with Job and the Psalter.

In the exilic period Hebrew literature began to exhibit a wider variety of form and content. New forms of expression, new literary types, new social problems, and new ideas emerged, of which the historical books and even the earlier prophets show no signs, except in what many Old Testament scholars regard as later interpolations. The Torah and the "Former Prophets" were edited in the exilic or early postexilic period before these novelties entered deeply into the Hebrew consciousness, or, quite possibly, by men who either rejected the new or were historically minded enough to recognize their incongruity in the pre-exilic setting. But these new types of literature, which appear to have originated after Nehemiah's time, became an essential element in the thought world of educated Jews, and their ideas dominate that of the illiterate in the first century of our era. Reckoning of them must be taken in order to understand what happened when Judaism and Christianity came to the parting of their ways. The history of Hebrew education is the account of the cultural conflicts through which the nation passed.

A. N. Whitehead described "civilization" (that is, culture) as discoverable in a society that exhibits "truth, beauty, adventure, art, and peace." Hebrew society, even at its best, can hardly be said to embody a combination of such qualities. With respect to art and beauty only the Hebrews' literature would qualify, while as to truth the moral and religious notions of their best prophets and psalmists deserve the highest praise. Peace, which involves, not anesthesia or self-satisfaction, but self-control, a harmony of life and motion, a wide sweep of conscious interest, and the love of mankind as such, can hardly be said to characterize ancient Israel. Progressive religion cannot escape conflict. But, among the qualities in which the best of them excelled, adventure certainly is an outstanding trait.[6] Neither socialization nor oppression killed their originality, initiative, and adventurous spirit. Before Judaism could become a world-wide influence, elements wanting in pre-exilic Hebrew culture had to be supplied from Iran and Hellenism through the Diasporas. The new was not rejected.

CHAPTER XIII

What the Hebrews Created

1. *Relations with Other Literatures* The discussion of the limitations and values of the Hebrews' culture in its more external aspects leads to the consideration of the ideational content of their cup of life and their adventurous contributions, as seen—where they chiefly can be found—in their literature. This and the succeeding chapters attempt to distinguish what they learned from what they created, what they received from what they contributed of original thought. From tradition and observation they knew the history of other peoples; they reacted vitally and vigorously to history as they experienced it. It is their creative adaptations of the traditions, the literatures, and the thought of their neighbors, but still more their unique interpretations of the complicated social-historical experience of the long past, that have given their literature, not a merely antiquarian interest, but an undeniable appeal to modern thought and an inescapable pertinence to modern life.

Other cultures made many contributions to Hebrew society, creating or exacerbating its conflicts, but also assisting in the solution of some of its problems. A long-accepted assumption, held on very slender evidence, has been that the Hebrews derived a large part of their intellectual, as well as material, culture from the peoples of Canaan. Settled among them, absorbing them, and speaking their language, they must have acquired a close acquaintance with Syro-Canaanite literature, mythology, and religion.[1] Now a mass of that literature is slowly becoming known, and the evidence for the assumption is incontestable.

One of the most remarkable groups of documents to throw light upon the original character of Hebrew culture is the collection of fourteenth-century tablets in a cuneiform alphabet that, beginning in 1929, the French archaeologist, Claude Schaeffer, discovered at Ras esh-Shamrah, the ancient Ugarit.[2] Although with every succeeding expedition more are found, they cannot compare in bulk with the Sumerian, Akkadian, and Assyrian tablets that have contributed so abundantly to the interpretation of ancient Near Eastern and Hebrew history and culture. But they have the great advantage that they are original documents in a Semitic tongue and both linguistically and historically are very close to Israelite culture. They disclose something of the mythology of the western part of the Semitic world, in which the Hebrews lived, with a fullness and precision quite unattainable through the third-hand Greek report of Philo of Byblos taken from the Phoenician of Sanchuniathon.

Parallels to Canaanite literature are to be found in the Song of Deborah and in David's lament over Saul and Jonathan. Therefore W. F. Albright places these songs and certain "Canaanizing" Psalms in the twelfth to the tenth century.[3] For the next four centuries less evidence of Canaanite influence has been found, but other Psalms, belonging to the sixth to fourth centuries are "saturated with Canaanite stylistic and verbal reminiscences and even with direct quotations from passages found in Ugaritic sources already known to us." In Hebrew literature from the seventh to the third century Albright finds "a veritable flood of allusions to Canaanite literature."[4] Some of the allusions and reminiscences will be noted later. It is understandable that the beginnings of Hebrew literature should show dependence and that in its virile prime Israel should be as independent in its literature as it was in politics, but that, in a time of national decadence and international archaism, it should follow the fashions of its neighbors.[5]

Ever since December 3, 1872, when George Smith of the British Museum read his paper on "The Chaldean Account of the Flood," the nature and extent of Sumero-Babylonian influence on the Old Testament has been a matter of constant dispute.[6] The times when borrowing from Babylon on the part of the Hebrews was possible are fairly clear. Some traditions might have come down among the descendants of Abraham from the age of the patriarchal journeys from Ur of the Chaldees. Or, to put it more generally, the mythology of Babylonia might have been vaguely known throughout the Fertile Crescent.

The time of Hezekiah and his son, Manasseh, is not only possible but more probable. But easily observable data point to the time of the Exile and Restoration, when the Jews in the eastern Diaspora were continually in contact with the life and thought of Babylonia, and communication between that area and the Mediterranean coast was constant. It was the critical period when much of the Old Testament was receiving its permanent form. With a consistent and well-integrated doctrine of monotheism, the priestly editor (P) of the traditions in Genesis could rework (even demythologize) Babylonian myth and assimilate it to a conception of God that cannot be discovered in those far-off times in any other people except the Greeks (Aristotle a little later) and the Persians. In an ancient culture that knew only animist-personalist causes, the first chapter of Genesis is an achievement of the first order.

The next ten chapters reveal a much more primitive mentality. Naïve stories of the "just so" type were intended at least originally to explain the farmer's hard labor and woman's suffering in childbirth, the serpent's lack of feet, and the multiplicity of men's languages. Instead of a creation out of the watery abyss of the sea *(tehom),* a waterless steppe like the Negeb waits for God to send rain upon it. God is a potter who molds men out of clay; he is a sculptor who carves woman out of a bone. The story of Cain and Abel embodies the peasant-nomad conflict. However, Cain, the branded murderer, outcaste, and vagabond, becomes the founder of the first city and the ancestor of those who dwell in tents and have cattle, of those who play the lyre and pipe, and of those who forge bronze and iron. In other words, from Cain, the first unhappy farmer, came the city dweller, a type of pastoral nomad, and the refinements of life.[7]

From Seth came ten generations of long-lived Patriarchs, who form a striking parallel to the ten antediluvian Mesopotamian kings of the Greek writer, Berossos, and of cuneiform tablets found at Nippur and Larsa. The Hebrew narrative is modest as to their ages, 8575 years all told. The reigns in one Larsa list and in Berossos reach an aggregate of over 400,000 years.[8] In Genesis 1–11 the rich culture of the irrigated river valley and the austere primitivity of the steppe are inextricably combined. That some of the Babylonian material was added by the priestly writer during the Exile has been widely assumed. Albright insists that much of it (the second Creation account, the stories of Eden, the Flood, and the Tower of Babel, and the list of the ten Patriarchs) goes back to pre-Israelite times, even to the first half of the second millennium, and was brought from northwestern Mesopotamia. Sigmund Mowinckel, on the other hand, regards such material as adopted in the "Assyrian epoch."[9]

Widely told flood stories have made the biblical legend seem an unsolvable puzzle. But devastating floods occur in all parts of the world and in a time of minute tribalism could easily seem universal. Varied details in the legends demonstrate that no single occurrence and no one story can be assumed. On the other hand it can hardly be denied that the biblical story is related to that handed down in Babylonian tablets. Palestine could never have produced it. There were repeated floods in the Babylonian area, as excavation has demonstrated (if demonstration were necessary in such a terrain). Vivid imagination and repeated rehearsals dealing with some incident of miraculous escape provided the details.[10] The Hebrews naturally used the story to expound the course of history, their reasons for believing in Providence, and the righteous purposes of God.

It is not possible at present to assign to various ethnic groups the many literary and intellectual stimuli that came from the composite racial inheritance of the southwestern end of the Fertile Crescent. It is difficult to discriminate between what is peculiar to Canaan and Syria and what to Mesopotamia, except in material actually present in the Ugaritic tablets. However, the immense mass of written materials on tomb walls and papyrus in the Nile Valley gives the Egyptologist a decided advantage. The history of Egypt's life, literature, and thought is better documented for a longer period than that of any other ancient nation.

There was always constant interchange of material and cultural goods between Palestine and Egypt. The times when contacts were especially close are well known: the period from the Hyksos to the Philistines, roughly from 1700 to 1100; the periods of the Assyrian and Persian empires; and the Ptolemaic era, followed by that of the Romans. The time of the Sojourn might seem to demand special reckoning. References to Egypt in Solomon's time and to Egyptian intrigues in the period of Assyrian dominance in Palestine suggest much that cannot be estimated. When search is made for specific literary evidence of Egyptian influence on Hebrew thought, the data are far from abundant. But there is more than has usually been recognized, and it makes its appearance, not in connection with tales of the Patriarchs, the Sojourn, or the Exodus, but in exilic and postexilic times.

Evidence which is completely unassailable is found in the Book of Proverbs. The author of the book borrowed a whole section from Amen-em-ope, the Egyptian scribe who compiled a book of proverbs borrowed in part from the "Maxims of Ptah-hotep," of the Old Kingdom, 1000 or 1500 years earlier. The item that clinches the evidence comes from a clause that had a meaning in the complete work of Amen-em-ope but not in Proverbs: "Consider for thyself these thirty chapters, that they are satisfaction and instruction" (27:7–8). In Proverbs one reads (22:20), "Have I not written for you thirty [sayings] of admonition and knowledge?" Thirty parts can be counted in the "Words of the Wise" (Prov. 22:17–24:22), but they are far from self-evident, and, since the word "thirty" seemed to make no sense, a Hebrew scribe copied it incorrectly by adding a letter, with sad results for interpreters and translators. The discovery of the parallelism between the proverbs in Amen-em-ope and this section of the Book of Proverbs solved the puzzle.[11]

Other parallels to the Book of Proverbs are found in the "Maxims of Ptah-hotep," in the story of Akhiqar, and in Mesopotamian literature also. Part of the material is merely floating ideas common to all the

Near East; part may be literary borrowing. There developed a large body of "Wisdom Literature" in the Near East, partly good common sense, partly philosophical, partly Gnostic in character. While philosophical and Gnostic trends left pre-Christian Judaism largely untouched, the appearance of "Wisdom" (*Hokhmah*) as a hypostatization in Proverbs and Ecclesiasticus is paralleled in the Ugaritic epic of Baal (*c.* fifteenth century) and the Aramaic proverbs of Akhiqar (*c.* sixth century). The discovery of a papyrus copy of Akhiqar in the Jewish colony at Elephantine is indicative of Jewish receptivity to contemporary currents of thought.[12]

The compiler of the Book of Proverbs made it perfectly clear that he was preparing an anthology, to use a modern term. Not only is more than one Hebrew collection marked by a title, but the last two chapters are assigned to a certain Agur and to Lemuel, a king, both of Massa, presumably in Edomite territory.[13] But the only considerable direct quotation at present traceable is from Amen-em-ope.

Evidence of Egyptian influence has also been found elsewhere in the Old Testament. How deeply and how extensively Jewish thought was affected by Egypt is a difficult problem. Various questions arise. Was Job's affirmation of innocence suggested by the "negative confessions" on the walls of Egyptian tombs? Again, in Egyptian literature of the First Intermediate period in the "prophecies" of Ipu-wer and Nefer-rohu describing a "time of troubles" in Egypt, there is language that resembles very closely the accounts of the woes of the "last days" in Jewish apocalypses. In both there follows a prediction of a sudden return to law and order. "Right shall come to its place and iniquity be cast [?] forth." A new prince will arise to restore justice, peace, and prosperity. The "messianism" of these passages—and others—has been much discussed. The conclusion as to both Job and the Jewish apocalypses—especially in view of the difference in time of the latter, well toward 2000 years—is that congruence rather than diffusion is to be assumed. Similar conditions called forth similar responses in the two societies. Yet there is a probability that, either directly or through Phoenicia, as James Henry Breasted thought, this type of Egyptian thinking was known to late Judaism.[14]

Three passages in the Old Testament are regarded by many scholars as written under Egyptian suggestion. Since Breasted called attention to the similarity between verses in Psalm 104 (20–26) and a portion of the beautiful hymn to Aton written nearly a thousand years earlier in the heyday of the religious revolt in the reign of Akh-en-Aton, there has been much debate as to a possible connection between these two noble descriptions of God and his activities in the world, especially of his care for animals as well as man. Similarities of content and order of thought make a connection probable.[15]

Two other passages, both belonging to the category "be good and you will be happy," seem to reflect Egyptian thought. In Jeremiah (17:5–8) and the first Psalm a righteous man is likened to a tree planted by streams of water, while a wicked man is like a tree in a salty desert. The "Wisdom of Amen-em-ope" contrasts a hothead and a prudent man, the one a tree in a forest, the other in a garden. The Old Testament parables suit the arid climate of Palestine; the other, conditions in Egypt. Otherwise, similarity of total concept as well as of details of language may seem to make a connection plausible, at least by way of stimulus. Yet a Dungi hymn runs: "Dungi the king, the gracious lord, is a date-palm beside a watercourse. Thou art a cedar rooted by abundant waters (giving pleasant shade)." An Egyptian scribe addresses his god thus: "O thou great dom-palm, sixty cubits high." Perhaps arid lands, long deforested, where large trees were few, gave special point to so pleasing a metaphor. In any case, such resemblances show that Hebrew culture was one with that of its neighbors.[16]

2. *Archaizing Revivals* Without discounting other possibilities, there is one period when there was every opportunity for Hebrews to become acquainted with Babylonian, Ugaritic, and Egyptian literatures. Three features of exilic and postexilic times make borrowing possible and probable. Two of them, "universal" empire and a "universal" language, Aramaic, are obvious as to fact and effect. The other, once it is recognized, is equally pertinent. About the seventh century a less familiar pattern of culture appears in Babylonia, Syria, Egypt, and among the Jews themselves. There was an archaizing revival of interest

in ancient myths and literary remains. Without any denial of the survival of ancient myths and traditions among the Jews themselves, the unexpected resurgence of mythical materials in postexilic times suggests community of interest.

Psalms that reveal Ugaritic influence may come from the period of the Judges and the early monarchy. If Genesis 2–11 is assigned to J and E, their Babylonian reminiscences must be patriarchal material. But what of the "veritable flood of allusions" to Babylonian and Canaanite myths, to Leviathan, Rahab, and the dragon of the sea in Assyrian, exilic, and postexilic times? What of Canaanite stylistic and verbal reminiscences and direct quotations from Ugaritic sources that multiply in Jewish literature in this period?

Albright would place Sanchuniathon, whom Philo of Byblos credits with being the source of the mythology that he collected, in the seventh century and thus makes him contemporary with a general revival of literary interest in his own land. An exact contemporary would be Assurbanipal, who collected the greatest library known in antiquity.[17] A little later Nebuchadnezzar and Nabonidus show a similar zeal. Interest in the past and desire to follow ancient models led to the republishing of ancient classics in Egypt during the seventh and sixth centuries.[18]

It is worth noting that a similar interest marks the sixth to the second century as the period when the Old Testament was made what it is today. It is the period also of great religious leaders, but not in Babylonia, Syria, or Egypt. These cultures had run their course and turned to look backward. It is the period of allusions to ancient myths in the later Psalms, Job, Ezekiel, and in exilic and postexilic portions of other Hebrew writings. But much of the vigor of the great original works of the eighth to the sixth centuries carries over into some of the later writings.

Thus at a time when they were part of world-wide empires, the Hebrews made full use of their opportunity to become acquainted with the literatures, religions, and mythologies of their various neighbors and overlords. Stimulated both negatively and positively by these contacts and by the threat of national and religious annihilation, they both conserved and created. They edited their own ancient traditions and writings and added original contributions in order to glorify their past, preserve their history, and encourage hope for the future. In editing they doubtless both "compiled and revised" as Assurbanipal's scribes had done, how thoroughly we shall never know.

How literally did they accept the myths of their own traditions and of the peoples all about them? That is a difficult question. The distinction between literal and figurative was then unknown, and it will not do to say blithely that such allusions were mere figures of speech. To the modern theist, with his more or less scientific background and his familiarity with the rhetorical personification of abstract ideas, it seems impossible that they could have believed in the actual existence of such monsters as Rahab and Leviathan if they had already become believers in one universal deity. Yet, as becomes perfectly clear in the apocryphal writings and the apocalypses, in that prescientific age they could deny that the gods of the heathen were gods, but did believe in the actuality of Satan and his demonic hosts.

The images that the heathen worshiped were, of course, mere wood and stone for exilic and postexilic writers, although real deities for the mass of the people.[19] But the Hebrew deity was himself imageless, and there were no reasons in the whole warp and woof of their thinking for the Jews, even the most violently monotheistic, to deny the existence of either friendly or hostile "spirit" beings. Ethiopic Enoch 1–36 illustrates how freely they accepted angelology and demonology when censorship was absent. The lapses into idolatry and magic infrequently mentioned in the Old Testament emphasize the remarkable achievement of the Old Testament editors in eliminating references to what the people all along must have believed.[20]

In Hellenistic and Roman times all the world became hagridden. Demonism became an obsession everywhere as it always had been in Babylonia. It was a step in advance when Judaism and Christianity learned to regard the heathen gods as demons, as Paul, for example, did ("What the heathen sacrifice they offer to demons." 1 Cor. 10:20). As potent remedies against mind- and soul-destroying fears, the Ineffable Name and the word "Christ" and the sign of the Cross appeared as invincible charms against demons and magic, when "Chaldean" and "Jew" were titles of priests of an immensely profitable cult of magic, demonology, and astrology.[21] The recrudescence of primitive superstitions signalized the breakdown of nerve and intelligence in the Roman imperial period as it does in our modern "time of troubles."

Belief in an all-powerful God made it possible for the Jews to accept without any feeling of "heresy" the existence of Rahab, Leviathan, and the whole host of one-time gods and mythical monsters as existing and fighting against God, but as destined in the end to annihilation or eternal punishment. Fortunately for biblical theology, the author of the first chapter of Genesis did not incorporate any such beings in his cosmography, and the later writers and final editors of the Old Testament were remarkably circumspect in ignoring or omitting the cruder demonology with which they must have been familiar.

Thus, at the time when the priestly editors of the Torah and their successors, Ezra and Nehemiah, were building a legal wall about the nation to keep it physically pure in order to save it from spiritual infection, their very progress toward a higher conception of deity began to open a wide door, as the literary evidence proves, to debasing primitive magic and myths and demonological superstitions. Similarly, in defiance of authority, only a little later infiltration began to come from another direction, as E. R. Goodenough has shown with super-abundant archaeological documentation.

While the Pharisees and rabbis were making every effort to enforce legalism and a clarified, rational concept of the father-son relationship between the nation and its God, a similar revival, or recrudescence, occurred of sublimated fertility-cult patterns of thought. They proposed, not filial obedience to God, but union, or at least communion, with him now and to all eternity. Magic angel names and amulets gave men security from haunting demons. Eternal life was promised by magical symbols of divine vitality and inspiration: the baetyl, the vine and wine cup, and perhaps above all the *menorah,* emblem of divine life and light and of the All-seeing Eye, or possibly of the seven planets. All these and many more begin to appear on the façades of the large rock-cut Jewish tombs of the last century B.C. In both

Jewish and Christian tombs, synagogues, and churches they multiply in number rapidly in the early Christian centuries.[22] Rabbinic orthodoxy saw to it that literary evidence as to their meaning for Jews is wanting. But they can hardly have sunk to the level of mere ornamentation, like the lights on a Christmas tree. They testify, rather, to the spread among Jews and Christians of the same longing for divine assurance of security and immortality and the same faith in magic that flooded the heathen world with the same symbols.

3. *Ritual, Civil, and Moral Law* In one regard the Hebrews were always much like their neighbors. They believed in tabus of various kinds. Indeed, the word *qodesh,* "holy," really meant "belonging to God," and therefore forbidden to man, or only "magic, mana, danger." Yahweh demanded sacrifices and offerings as symbols of his right to demand, or as payments for his favors. The Sabbath was holy; it belonged to God, not to man. It is quite generally agreed that the tribes came into Palestine with the simple ritual practices of the nomad. The cultus shows little evidence of Egyptian influence, but many Canaanite traits.

Strict Yahwism fought always, but not always successfully, the introduction of the seductive Canaanite fertility rites that were supposed necessary to the fecundity of man, beast, and plant. The prophets repeatedly protested the continuance of the partly borrowed cultus of sacrifices, offerings, tabus, and ritual cleansings, but the practices persisted and, in sublimated, allegorical fashion, became so much a part of New Testament mores and theology that they have formed, or deformed, modern creeds. The Temple had become a symbol, a fetish, and an incubus. Judaism escaped from the incubus in part, but retained the externalism in many of its rites and ceremonies. Even Paul could not use language that made clear the distinction between moral and ceremonial requirements. In Sabbatarianism, immersionism, soteriology, and the Mass, for example, this intellectual failure still remains to plague modern Christianity.

As to the Torah, ever since Jacques de Morgan found the Hammurabi stela at Susa (in 1901–1902), it has been customary to speak of the influence of that ancient code on Hebrew legal practice for there are numerous close resemblances. Since that time various other codes, Assyrian, Hittite, Akkadian, and Sumerian, have come to light, and more may be expected. The relation of Hebrew laws to those of Babylonia is now regarded as indirect. A more or less common body of law evidently was accepted throughout the Fertile Crescent. The Hebrews received the Canaanite version of it after they entered Palestine and reworked it with limited additions of Bedouin customs, the *lex talionis,* for example.

The various compilations in Exodus, Deuteronomy, and Leviticus are revisions, with more or less of new material, especially in the civil code and in ritual. There were many modifications, occasionally with added severity ("Your eye shall not pity"), more often with suggestions of progress in moral and social thinking.[23] For example, the Deuteronomic Decalogue urges consideration for slaves because the Israelites had been slaves in Egypt. None of the codes overlooks the widow, the orphan, the alien, the poor, the weak, the oppressed. But the unbridled savagery of the attitude assumed toward idolaters reflects unlovely theological heat (Deut. 7:2, 16; 13:8). Priestly legislation (P) was introduced throughout the Pentateuch when it was compiled and edited (sixth-fifth centuries). Its unified law, the Holiness Code (Lev. 17-26), is a strange mixture of high morality (especially "love your neighbor," and "love the resident alien, as yourself") and fierce and brutal penalties.[24]

Without going farther into legal history, it is enough to say, with J. M. P. Smith, that here is a record of progress, deeply influenced by the course of history.[25] Except in the manumission of slaves and the *lex talionis* and in the area of heresy, which was also treason,[26] the Hebrew codes made advances in nearly all particulars over those of other nations. But it must be remembered also that, with an occasional exception such as the appeal to history and gratitude in the Deuteronomic fourth commandment, the sanctions invoked, the motives to which appeal was made, are purely external and nonmoral. The intention of the Deuteronomist in centralizing worship in Jerusalem was to root out Baalism and other idolatrous and immoral practices at the high places. The Ritual Code and the Priestly Code were intended to make worship more orderly and keep it uncontaminated and so, no doubt, render it more effective in pleasing God. Yet, although prophetic morality, justice, and kindness to the poor and helpless were by no means overlooked, the total effect was to promote legalism and ritualism as in the other nations.

4. *The Psalms: Lyrical Ideology* The Book of Psalms is a most remarkable outpouring of the Hebrew soul. It constitutes a lyrical summary of Hebrew ideologies. Written largely in the obscure postexilic period, more than any other book in the Old Testament it gives unrestrained expression to the results of the race's education through its long history. In effect the Psalms complete and summarize the cultural experience of the nation up to the time of the Maccabees and present it almost as it existed at the beginning of the Christian era. As an anthology of personal piety the book expresses not so much ideas as emotions; it reflects strange types of piety and an extraordinary range of feeling. It is anything but the product of a single mind, and, for that reason, the collection is so much the more truly representative of total Hebrew culture as it reached a certain consistency and unity during the Maccabean persecutions and wars.

As a summary of Hebrew ideologies it exhibits the characteristic free and original manner in which the Hebrews thought of life and met its problems. It is characteristic in the very fact that it is lyrical, emotional, and religious, not logical and philosophical or theological. It is characteristic in its emotional intensity and in its wide diversity. It is characteristic in its preoccupation with God and righteousness.

As a unique and typical product of Hebrew genius, it is the last place in which foreign influence would be expected. Yet that would surely be a mistaken judgment, for the Hebrews had a remarkable ability to respond to stimulation of the most varied kinds and to mold what they received in accord with their own culture. The foreign influence is patent, not only in expressions and figures of speech, but in the structure of entire poems. The Psalms as a whole are not naïve outpourings of simple souls but products of high artistry and calculated rhetoric. Therefore it is not surprising that mythological allusions are numerous.

Various Psalms have been regarded as belonging to festival liturgies similar to Babylonian and other rituals for seasonal celebrations. Some are said to be enthronement Psalms celebrating Yahweh's entrance into the Temple at New Year (Mowinckel). T. H. Gaster finds a series that reflects the rituals of seasonal rites. According to some scholars nearly all were written for use in the Temple; others think of them as representing individual piety. Without attempting to settle such questions, it is important to recognize the various possibilities.[27]

Actually, judged from its contents, the Psalter is neither a real book of songs nor "the hymn book of the Second Temple." It is impossible to describe it or summarize it briefly and adequately. Some of the Psalms are prose or prosaic. One (45) is a royal marriage song for a Hebrew king and possibly a Tyrian princess (vv. 10, 12). Some are similar to the wisdom poems of the Book of Proverbs.[28] Some are lyrical history, even historical litanies (78; 106; 136). Others are purely didactic poems, lacking all lyrical quality (19:7–14). Psalm 119 remains "the most dreadful example of uninspired versification" (Pfeiffer).

Some are inspiring nature poems. The Hebrews rejoiced in the visible world as the work of God, and, as such, it revealed his character: his might and majesty and sternness in its more terrible spectacles of storm and earthquake and volcano; his bountiful goodness and loving-kindness in its kindlier aspects.[29] The grass of the field, which springs up in the morning and fades and withers under the hot Syrian sun before evening, is a fitting symbol alike of human weakness and impermanence (90:5–7) and of God's wrath at man's sinfulness. Nature was a revelation of God's activities and of his moods, his attitudes toward men.

Many beautiful passages express trust in God, joy in a sense of fellowship with him, and thankfulness for his goodness, especially his *hesedh,* his "loving-kindness" (AV), or his "steadfast love" (RSV), toward his worshipers.[30] Such Psalms must be mentioned, as many more might be (some greatly improved in the RSV). They express the confident spirit that, as one must believe, lay behind the *Sayings of the Fathers* (*Pirke Aboth*), while, on the contrary, the didactic poems are poor representatives of the love of the Law and of the sound, but prosaic, common sense of many rabbis, or scribes, who were like Jesus the son of Sirach.

There are other Psalms that may be thought of as coming from the "quiet in the land" (35:20), simple trusting souls such as are pictured —and idealized—by Luke in his account of Simeon and Anna. Somewhere Luke found the psalms or models for the psalms that glorify his first two chapters. For the Magnificat Hannah's song in 1 Samuel served as a model and a mine. Many of his best phrases are found in the Psalter. Isaiah's heartening message to Hezekiah (30:15), "In quietness and confidence shall be your strength," is echoed in the magnificent Psalm (46—"God is our refuge and strength. . . . Be still and know that I am God") that was the inspiration of Luther's *Ein' feste Burg ist unser Gott.*

Yet the Book of Psalms as a whole makes a totally different impression. A large proportion of the collection seems to have been written by torn and tortured souls who stood frustrated and helpless in the face of triumphant evil and wrongdoing. "Fret not because of evildoers" is a constant theme. Like the modern phrase "confident living," it proves that a vast number of people were not confident but were constantly fretting. Their *malaise* resulted in three recurrent themes: hatred of enemies and workers of iniquity, complaints of personal illness and (also national) misfortune, and protests against mistreatment and injustice.

There are many references in the Psalms to God's "steadfast love" for his Chosen People. There is very little about man's love and kindness toward man. For that theme one must go to Job and the Torah, to Leviticus (19:18, 34), where one would least expect to find it. Quite in contrast, the Psalter is a book of hates. There were precedents enough in earlier writings, even in the greatest of the prophets. Some of the "oracles" against the nations that were hostile to Israel are among the most powerful pieces of literature in the Old Testament. But the dominant note in the prophets is not whining or frustration or vindictiveness, but assurance that evil will be punished. Not so in the Psalter.

Thirty-nine or forty Psalms may be listed as imprecatory. Psalm 74 whines, "O God, why dost thou cast us off forever?" and attempts to arouse God's pride: "Arise, O God, plead thy cause, do not forget the clamor of thy foes!" So also Psalm 79: "O God, the heathen have come into thy inheritance, they have defiled thy holy Temple." Another (44), which protests that the Chosen People is innocent of any neglect of God, actually shouts, like the priests of Baal on Mount Carmel, "Rouse thyself! Why sleepest thou, O Lord?" Where one Psalm urges, "Refrain from anger and forsake wrath!" another, which carries the beautiful hymn on God's omnipresence—"Whither shall I flee from thy Spirit? . . . How precious to me are thy thoughts, O God!" —ends with, "O that thou wouldst slay the wicked, O God! . . . Do I not hate them that hate thee, O Lord? . . . I hate them with a perfect hatred." [31]

Such Psalms must make sweet music for the Old Testament "Christians" of the Transvaal. Once they were loved by persecuted Protestants. Later history, in recent World Wars, makes them at least understandable. Surely such hymns of hate make strange music in a Christian church.

Many a psalmist seems to delight in portraying the wickedness of the wicked as a background against which to glorify his own righteousness. But the often-impassioned penitential Psalms have served to express men's deepest feelings of remorse and abasement from their day to ours. As has often been pointed out, the penitential psalms of Babylon are of a different sort. They express the singer's chagrin and dejection at the deity's infliction of some illness or misfortune. It is not the deity's favor but his favors that are sought. Certain Hebrew Psalms, particularly some that record the community's abasement, represent a similar attitude. But, on the whole, the penitential prayers of the Psalter are real cries *de profundis,* not merely appeals for benefactions. They come from spirits clouded by a sense of estrangement from a revered deity. "Blessed is he whose transgression is forgiven, whose sin is pardoned," comes from one who had suffered spiritual deprivation due to unacknowledged sin and who knew the relief that came from confession (Ps. 32, Augustine's favorite Psalm).

It is to be noted that there is no doctrine of the resurrection running through the Book of Psalms. Indeed, it is taken for granted that Sheol is beyond the reach of God's interest or care.

"In death there is no remembrance of thee [God]; in Sheol who can give thee praise?" (6:5) Life is short and vain. No man can escape death and Sheol. God should remember this and not allow his servants to suffer too long. "Man is like the beasts that perish." [32] There is never a suggestion of heavenly mansions for the righteous.

Since there can be no reward for the righteous and no punishment for the wicked except on earth, it is taken for granted that health and wealth are tokens of God's favor and must come to those who serve him, disease and disaster to sinners. Both the individual and the nation suffer material punishment for sin. Humility, contrition, and repentance should restore both the one and the other to God's favor and put an end to their humiliation and suffering. The prosperity of the wicked and the poverty of the righteous are the greatest trials of faith, the chief causes of frustration and despair. The only answer to this problem is that God must intervene to establish righteousness on earth.

5. *The Hebrews' God* It would misrepresent Hebrew piety and intelligence to leave the subject with this obscured picture of the religious conceptions presented in endless variety in the Psalms. The impressive picture drawn by the Psalms of God's goodness, his majesty, and his power as revealed in the bountiful earth, in the heavens, the mountains, the sea, and storms over sea and land is brilliantly illuminated by Job and Second Isaiah. Both equal, if they do not surpass, the Psalms in eloquent and moving tributes to God's overwhelming glory and the magnificence of his works.

Job's pessimism, which often seems to pre-empt the chief claim to modern interest, is offset by another distinction, its remarkable descriptions of God as Creator and Master of all nature. After Elihu's last ponderous chapter (37), there follow, in God's "answer to Job from the whirlwind," successive passages of the most beautiful, imaginative, and intelligent poetry in the Bible. Small wonder that Job despises himself and "repents in dust and ashes" (42:6) before such a God. The author exhibits remarkable learning and skill in selecting natural phenomena that are recondite, mysterious, and astonishing as illustrative of God's unlimited superiority over man. It is even more

surprising that, while the basis of the writer's thinking is anthropomorphic and creationist and some of his science doubtful, there is no
appeal to myth or miracle in order to glorify God. Of Jewish nationalism, the Patriarchs, the Covenant, Moses and the Law, there is never
a hint.

In Second Isaiah, which may have been written under the inspiration of Job (so Pfeiffer), there are similar and equally eloquent, but
much briefer, glorifications of God as Creator and Master of the universe. To such passages there are no comparable foreign parallels. It is
to be noted, however, that the motivation and purpose of the enthusiastic prophet are very different from those of Job. Each writer is dealing
with suffering, Job with that of the individual, the great Prophet of the
Exile with that of the nation. Job exalts God to humble man and teach
him to accept suffering as in some way justified by the will of the all-
powerful and all-wise deity. Second Isaiah glorifies God as one who,
in his might and goodness, will turn sorrow into joy and suffering
into triumph. Hope is the greater because of present despair.

The Psalms that concern themselves with the problems of suffering
and injustice, with their loud complaints and inhuman vindictiveness,
are almost entirely motivated by the failure of divine justice, as the
poets see life. God has failed to honor his covenant with Israel and to
protect his people from the oppression of the *goyim*. The attitude is
purely selfish and nationalistic. The righteous remnant, as they believed themselves to be, indict, not only outsiders, but also members
of the Jewish community. The sins are those typical of landlord-
peasant-tenant agricultural communities, such as Amos, Isaiah, Micah,
and Nehemiah criticized. The oppressed appeal to the might and justice of God. Nearly all phases of the social-economic problem appear.
These Psalms, therefore, offer one of the best Old Testament sum-
maries of a main theme of the two following chapters, which is the
plebeian-patrician conflict. The "Hebrew hope" was based upon the
Hebrew conception of God as a God of justice.

PART 4

IDEALS — ACHIEVEMENTS — HOPE:

THE OUTCOME

Wherever I found a living thing, there found I Will to Power, . . . that to the stronger the weaker shall serve. . . . And this secret spake Life herself unto me. "Behold," said she, "I am that which must ever surpass itself."

NIETZSCHE, *Thus Spake Zarathustra*

"Right, as the world goes, is only a question between equals in power, while the stronger does what he can and the weak suffer what they must."

THE ATHENIANS TO THE MELIANS—
THUCYDIDES V (18) 90

From the death of the old the new proceeds
And the life of truth from the rot of creeds.

WHITTIER

"I say that man was made to grow, not stop."

"JOHN" IN BROWNING,
"A DEATH IN A DESERT"

"The primary function of government is the protection of the weak."

QUOTED BY HAROLD L.
ICKES, *Secret Diary II*

Happy are you who are poor, for the reign of God is yours.

JESUS (LUKE 6:20)

JEWISH HISTORY AND LITERATURE	NON-JEWISH HISTORY	POLITICAL SYRIA
170 B.C. Damascus Covenanters and	c. 175 Hyrcanus' suicide	175 Antiochus IV Epiphanes
70 A.D. Qumran community and rolls	170 Onias' temple in Egypt	MACCABEES
B.C. 170 Temple plundered	2C Astrologers, Nechepso Petosiris	166–161 Judas Maccabeus
168 Temple desecrated		
163–63 Apoc. of Enoch	163–121 The Gracchi	162 Demetrius (Syria)
	2C Boethus of Sidon	
150 Judith		161 Jonathan Maccabeus
150–130 Final ed. of Chron., Ezra, Nehemiah Isa. 24–27; 33; 34–35; Zech. 9–14; Macc. Pss. 44; 74; 79; 83; et al.	Antipater of Tarsus, Stoic Philodemus of Gezer, Epicurean	
	2–1C Posidonius of Apamea	
c. 140 Sibylline Oracles iii. 97–829	144 Corinth destroyed	143 Simon Maccabeus
130–100 Letter of Aristeas	2–1C Antiochus of Ashkelon, Platonist	135 John Hyrcanus
c. 125 Esther		
L2C Testament XII Patriarchs	106–48 Pompey	105 Aristobulus I
	106–43 Cicero	
100–50 Wisdom of Solomon	Zeno of Sidon, Epicurean	104 Alexander Janneus
c. 100 1 Baruch, 1 Maccabees, Jason of Cyrene, 2 Macc.	100–44 Caesar	78 Alexandra
63 Apoc. of Enoch completed		69–63 Hyrcanus vs. Aristobulus II
	70–19 Vergil	
L1C Pss. of Solomon, after 48	69–30 Cleopatra	63 Pompey takes Jerusalem
3 and 4 Maccabees	65–8 Horace	63–40 Hyrcanus and Antipater
36 B.C.–6 A.D. Hillel, Shammai	44 B.C. Corinth rebuilt	
	43 B.C.–17 A.D. Ovid	40 Parthian inroad
	30 Battle of Actium	ROME
		37–4 Herod the Great

8–5 B.C. Birth of Jesus		30 Augustus princeps
4 B.C. –6 A.D. Assumption of Moses		4 Revolts in Palestine Accession of tetrarchs
A.D.	**A.D.**	**A.D.**
1–100 Shemoneh Esreh		6 Archelaus deposed
18–36 Caiaphas high priest		Judah and Samaria a Roman province
26–28 Prophecies of John the Baptist		Revolts
28–30 Ministry of Jesus		14 Tiberius
1C Rabban Gamaliel I	37–100 Josephus	26–37 Pontius Pilate
40–60 Collection of Sayings of Jesus	40 Philo in Rome	37 Caligula
		41 Claudius
40, or 63 Markan "Flysheets"	c. 40–102 Martial	41–44 Herod Agrippa I
50–58 Letters of Paul	c. 45–96 Statius	44 Revolt of Theudas
	c. 60–140 Juvenal	
65–90 RR. Johanan b. Zakai, Hanina b. Dosa	64 Burning of Rome	44 Nero
		50–100 Herod Agrippa II
	Persecution of Christians	52–66 Many outbreaks in Palestine
66–71 Jewish-Roman War		
69–75? 2 Baruch, 2 Esdras– 4 Ezra, final ed.		69 Vespasian
70 Destruction of Jerusalem		
c. 70 Gospel of Mark	75–79 Josephus, *Jewish War*	
c. 80 Sibylline Oracles iv		79 Titus
	89 Epictetus in Rome	
80–100 Luke, Acts, Matthew, James, 1 Peter, Hebrews		81 Domitian
90 Council of Jamnia		
90–100 Revelation, 1 Clement, Gospel to Hebrews (?)	93–100 Josephus, *Antiquities*	93 Persecution of Christians
		96 Nerva
		98 Trajan
100–125 Gospel, Epp. of John, Pastorals, Jude, 2 Peter		

CHAPTER XIV

Ancient Hopes and Social Ideals

1. *Beginnings of the Social Conscience* Hebrew experience, emotion, and thought have been pictured with something, I hope, of "atmosphere" and empathy. Against that background, the ancient Hebrews' final desperate attempt to solve the problems of social justice and the "morality of the universe," to "justify the ways of God with men," remains to be considered. The attempt, its success or failure quite apart, was one of their greatest contributions to culture. The problems and their unsatisfactory solutions must be studied in the light of conventional language and patterns of thought current in the Near East, as well as in the light of the Jews' own historical and cultural experience. They were not alone in hoping for a better world. They were not alone in believing in divine justice. The fundamental character and the manifest superiority of their social ideals over those of their neighbors have given their contribution survival value, permanent value, indeed, that can be appreciated only by comparison with those of the cultures around them. This chapter is a necessary historical preface to one on "The Hebrew Hope."

The problem of evil and injustice arises from a belief that genuine righteousness and justice are normal characteristics of human society. In one of his works, Aldous Huxley referred with scorn to the "mere conjuring trick . . . that deduces justice from our inequalities." Without the scorn, his dictum may be accepted as a partial truth. Expressed more reasonably, belief in justice may be said to be the product of a social experience that discovered the indispensability of justice and order in a stable and livable society. What-

217

ever the ultimate source of humanity's belief that goodness and justice are normal and that evil and wrongdoing are abnormal, the fact remains that men so believe, and the experience of inequity and ill-treatment deepens the appreciation of virtue and beneficence and heightens aversion to vice and maleficence. The belief in the fundamental justice and trustworthiness of God in all his ways was the basis of the Hebrew hope.

The belief that "God made men upright and they have sought out many devices" (Eccles. 7:29) appears at the beginning of recorded history. Back of the invention of writing there is, of course, no way of proving directly that men believed in the righteousness of the gods, but it can be inferred with a high degree of certainty. From the less complicated societies of the preliterate period in both Egypt and Babylonia, as well as from the tribal, nomadic age of Israel, a "democratic tradition of equality and impartial justice" seems to have been handed down.[1] In Sumerian myths of the gods and in Hebrew legends that arose in preliterate times there is convincing, though inferential, evidence of a belief in democratic and orderly procedures among both men and gods. The earlier social organizations that can be clearly descried and accurately described presuppose law and order and respect for individual rights. Not only so, but there was a large measure of practical democracy and equality.

There are various ethical motifs in royal pronouncements and other ancient records. From the beginning there seems to be a recognition of the duty of a ruler to take the part of the poor and the weak against the rich and the strong. All of the early law codes of the Near East recognize and penalize crimes of murder and theft, of fraud and violence. But the duties of a ruler, whether king or noble, went much farther than the maintenance of common mores, of law and order, and the punishment of antisocial crimes of violence and dishonesty. The ruler was the shepherd of his people. It was his duty to dispense equal justice to all and, therefore, to protect and help the weak and the poor.

2. *The Social Conscience in Egypt*   In Egypt the conception of
ma'at, "truth, order, justice, right relations," had been developed
before written history began. The goddess Ma'at was the daughter
of Re. He had created justice as part of the divine order.² The concept played no small part in the development of society during the
earlier dynasties. The remarkable "social literature" of Egypt begins
in the First Intermediate period, when the apparently solid foundations of society had been swept away. It reaches its noblest expression
before 2000 in one of the most eloquent documents of ancient Egypt
and, indeed, of the whole ancient East. The plea of the "Eloquent
Peasant" is that justice be administered impartially by all officials,
even up to the Pharaoh himself. Then and in subsequent centuries,
in papyrus after papyrus, in tomb after tomb, the idea is repeated
that there must be no bribery, no partiality in the administration of
laws and customs, but that the poor man's rights must be respected.
Amon, as god of justice, "comes at the cry of the poor." He is the
poor man's friend, and, in one document, he appears in court as
vizier to see to it that the poor just man overcomes the unjust rich
man. So Yahweh will plead the cause of the poor and afflicted and
despoil their despoilers (Prov. 22:22–23).³

John A. Wilson points out the decline of Egyptian culture from
the freedom, vigor, and discerning social ethics of the First Interregnum and the Middle Kingdom to the post-Ramesside age. The
"social conscience" of the empire is a poor echo of the time of the
Eloquent Peasant. Nevertheless, the phrases that expressed the ideal
remained, and, indeed, there arose under the empire a "religion of
the poor" that testifies to the ideal, if not the actuality, of justice for
the weak and weary. The poor, the widow, the fatherless and mother-
less, the forsaken must be protected.⁴

If the "Maxims of Amen-em-ope" are as late as the sixth, or only
the tenth, century, then the concept of social justice had not been
entirely forgotten, even in the nadir of the decline of Egyptian culture. From the passage of the "thirty instructions," which are partly
quoted in the Book of Proverbs, comes the significant saying, "Re-

move not the landmark on the boundary of the fields. . . . Be not greedy for a cubit of land, and do not trespass on the boundary of the widow." Proverbs 23:10 should, therefore, read,

> Remove not the widow's landmark,
> And enter not the fields of the fatherless.[5]

The Hebrew editor introduced a characteristic parallelism and vigorous brevity lacking in the Egyptian original.

3. *The Social Conscience in Babylonia* During the Early Dynastic, or Sumerian, period in Babylonia, wars between the little cities over disputed boundaries eventually saddled them with temporary military rulers who became permanent. Gradually democracy gave way to autocracy, and the rights of the common people were flouted by "strong men." Very early evidence comes in so many words from inscribed cones of Uru-kagina, Sumerian king of Lagash (*c.* 2450). He claims to have restored ancient freedoms and ended usurpations of the rights of the people by a horde of minor officials, especially the priesthood. He had sworn to the city god, Ningirsu, not to deliver the widow and the orphan to the powerful man. It is, I believe, the earliest occurrence of the phrase "widow and orphan," which became a standing symbol and test of justice and injustice in Semitic speech. He prevented the high priest from making requisitions from the poor widow; he was champion of the weak against the strong (another historic phrase) and established liberty in place of slavery. Unhappily defeat in war cut short Uru-kagina's reform movement, as war, whether ending in defeat or victory, so often has stopped or postponed progress.[6]

Three centuries and a half later Gudea, another Sumerian ruler of Lagash, constantly repeated the assertion that he was a faithful shepherd of the people and that, as such, he would put the laws of Nanshe and Ningirsu, the city's goddess and god, into effect. What this meant ideally may be discovered in his descriptions of conditions during certain religious festivals. The maid and her mistress, the servant and his lord, the mighty man and his underlings, all were equal. The scantily clad were not disturbed by the well clothed. No orphan was abandoned to the rich man's mercy; no widow was left in the power of the strong. It must be added that, as a feature of paradise, all work ceased.[7]

Recently new law codes of Sumer and Akkad have come to light. The oldest yet known, found on an eight-by-four-inch tablet, was issued by Ur-Nammu (Ur-Engur), the Sumerian king who founded the Third Dynasty of Ur (*c.* 2060). Since it repeats some of the ideas of Uru-kagina and Gudea, it may well be a revival or revision of a code that had long been known. In the prologue Ur-Nammu tells the same story of reform as Uru-kagina 400 years earlier, and he adds, in Gudea's words, that "the orphan did not fall a prey to the wealthy, nor the widow to the powerful, nor [he adds] the man of one shekel to the man of a mina" (sixty shekels).[8] The last piquant clause is Ur-Nammu's unique contribution to the phraseology of social reform.

Shulgi (Dungi), Ur-Nammu's energetic son and successor, was greeted by Enlil, god of the religious capital, Nippur, as "my shepherd" and was commissioned to enforce even-handed justice for the poor and oppressed. Similarly, Ishme-Dagan, fourth Semitic ruler of Isin, instituted justice in order to restrain the rich man. A hymn to Lipit-Ishtar, fifth king of Isin, hailed him as one who saves people from violent men. "The powerful man [it runs] commits no robbery; the strong man does no injustice to the weak. You have established law and righteousness for Sumer and Akkad; you have caused the land to prosper."[9] The last two lines doubtless refer to the recently discovered code of laws that Lipit-Ishtar promulgated. The royal hymns of Sumer and Akkad tend more and more to praise monarchs as sources of prosperity, as givers even of rain, rather than guardians of justice. But the line of descent of the ideal of justice from Uru-kagina (and probably earlier monarchs) is clear down through Gudea, Ur-Nammu, and Lipit-Ishtar to Hammurabi.

Hymns of various dates praise Shamash, the sun-god, whose all-seeing eye marks every evil deed. He was "supreme judge of heaven and earth," the "merciful god, who lifts up the lowly and protects the weak." His eye rested especially on judges who accepted bribes and dispensed injustice and upon persons who altered boundaries. The light of the sun symbolized justice and righteousness.[10]

It was from Shamash that Hammurabi received his famous code (or divine sanction for it), as Moses received the Decalogue from Yahweh. It is notable that neither the Decalogue nor the Babylonian code mentions justice for the poor. Yet the Hebrew codes and both prologue and epilogue to Hammurabi's code make much of the idea.

> Anu and Bel called me [says Hammurabi] to cause justice to prevail in the land, . . . to prevent the strong from oppressing the weak. . . . The perfect king am I. . . . In my bosom I carried the people of Sumer and Akkad. . . . In my wisdom I hid them, that the strong might not oppress the weak, and that they should give justice to the orphan and widow in Babylon . . . , to give justice to the oppressed. . . . Hammurabi is a ruler who is a real father to his people.[11]

The tenacity of the ancient tradition is demonstrated by the archaizing Assyrian revival of humanitarian phrases. The Assyrians are the last people whom one would accuse of respect for the rights of poor. They were long in coming to such moral concern. Beginning with Shalmaneser I (*c.* 1280–1250), their monarchs rejoiced in the title of "shepherd." They were shepherds of their own people. They humbled the mighty, overthrew the proud, and shattered the power of the strong, that is, their various enemies. It is not until Sargon II (722–705) that genuine moral ideas appear.

Then, just in the period of Amos and Isaiah, Sargon, the "mighty hero clothed with terror," was also a "sagacious king full of kindness." He was a "helper of the poor, who made good their losses," for the great gods had "given him a name to maintain justice and right, to give guidance to those who are not strong, not to injure the weak." Sennacherib also was a "wise and prayerful shepherd," a "guardian of right, a lover of justice, . . . who comes to the aid of the needy." Even the brutal Esarhaddon claimed to be a "liberal king who holds a "righteous scepter" and prays "that he may rule in justice and righteousness." Assurbanipal gave his attention chiefly to the restoration of temples and offerings and to his antiquarian and literary interests. Three times he records, "The feudal protection of Babylon I maintained, that the strong might not injure the weak." [12]

It is a striking coincidence that, exactly at the time when the Hebrew prophets were harking back to older ethical standards and bitterly criticizing their monarchs and nobility for preying upon the poor and the weak, the inscriptions of the great Assyrian military conquerors should have revived the phrases that demand justice for the poor and the protection of the weak. But the inscriptions are full of linguistic archaisms and reminiscences of ancient epics. Assurbanipal's allusions to the monarch's duties seem to have been suggested by his studies of the "dark Akkadian" (which he found a most exasperating language) and are connected with Babylon. It would appear that the closer relations of the Assyrian monarchs with Babylon, which began in the ninth century, may have been responsible for the use of the old phrases. The scribes in the chancellery, familiar with the ancient records, were the real authors of the inscriptions we read. The kings could hardly have been interested in the poor and the weak. Possibly the scribes were; more probably the language was regarded as pleasing to the gods and soothing to the people.

These few selections illustrate how, in Babylonia, the "social-ethical tradition," first mentioned by Uru-kagina, persisted for 2000 years. Darius the Great weakly echoes it. Once he says that he has done no wrong to either the weak or the strong; once that he does not wish either weak or strong to injure the other; and once that his law is to be feared "so that the stronger may not injure or destroy the weak." [13] Between the two limits, Sumer and Persia, the tradition in Babylonia, very much awake for centuries, sleeps during the Kassite period (because records are scant?) but comes to life, *mirabile dictu,* in Assyrian times, when it appears in another form in Israel. However, the tradition was not peculiar to Egypt and Babylonia. Israel had another source nearer home.

4. *The Social Conscience in Ugarit* Evidence of the presence of the humanitarian tradition has long been clear in Egypt, Babylonia, and Israel. It has been uncertain or lacking in Syria and among the neighbors of Israel. A trace had been discovered in Samal, or Ya'di, but it was

slight and dubious and probably is merely an echo of Assyrian court style. However, as in so many other problems, the Ugaritic alphabetic texts have thrown light into the darkness.

In the legend of Keret is an interesting series of most explicit parallels to the phrases that occur so frequently in both Babylonian and Hebrew, as well as Egyptian, texts, alluding to the problem of social justice. One of King Keret's sons accuses his sick father of neglecting his duties as judge. He says,

> Listen and incline your ear,
> Do you command like the strongest of the strong[?]
> And govern [like] the Mountain [i.e., the great god?]?
> You have let your hand fall into mischief[?].
> You do not judge the cause of the widow
> Nor adjudicate the case of the wretched
> Nor drive away those who prey upon the poor.
> You do not feed the fatherless before you
> [Nor] the widow behind you.[14]

By no means all of the expressions in these lines are clear, but the general tenor is unmistakable, and the roots of the familiar Hebrew words for widow, fatherless, and poor are unquestionably present. Lines two and three are most uncertain, but there is no uncertainty as to lines five to nine. The words translated "case" and "adjudicate" are the Ugarit equivalent (*th-p-t*) of Hebrew *shaphat* and are exactly paralleled in Lamentations (3:59), "Judge my cause" (*shaphtah mishpati*). The second line of the triplet is notable. The word "wretched," for *q-s-r n-ph-sh,* "short of soul," may be close to what Matthew probably meant by "poor in spirit."

That the passage in the Keret legend as a whole is no *hapax legomenon* is clear from a couple of lines in the story of Aqhat. The great king, Dan'el ("God is judge"), true to his royal vocation, as Keret was not,

> . . . sits at the entrance of the gate
> Among the mighty [?] who are on the threshing floor,
> Judging the cause of the widow
> Adjudicating the case of the fatherless.[15]

The passage is the more remarkable because not only are the last two lines almost word for word identical with those of the Keret legend (using the same two verbal stems, *d-n* and *th-p-t*), but the setting of the "judgment" is closely paralleled, in part word for word, in 1 Kings (22:10), where King Ahab and King Jehoshaphat "sit at the threshing floor at the entrance of the gate of Samaria." Moreover "Jehoshaphat" ("Yah is judge") is the semantic equivalent of "Dan'el." Evidently "gate" had been synonymous with "court of justice" long before the Hebrews entered Palestine.[16] Three times Jeremiah has the exact parallel, once with both roots and "orphan" and "afflicted," once with *dan din* and "poor" and "needy."[17] Must one not assume that Canaanite and Israelite popular tradition handed down these ideals from the fourteenth to the sixth century?

5. *The Return of Paradise* Another literary pattern found in Babylonian and Assyrian documents is also used by Hebrew writers to portray the glorious future after the divine judgment has purified Israel. It is so closely connected with the idea of justice for the poor that it has of necessity been already mentioned. Beginning with Gudea's description of a brief Golden Age of utopian righteousness, peace, plenty, and happiness when the laws of the gods are fully observed, the same language recurs from time to time to portray the excellence of the rule of various kings. Hammurabi claimed to establish all the good that the rule of Shamash the sun-god promises.

On his enthronement, so Assurbanipal said, a period of divine peace, order, and justice ensued. War stopped. "The on-coming javelins of the enemy fell to the ground . . . no gentleman did any evil. The traveler on the farthest road was safe. . . . " Another inscription (of which there are three copies) claims that, after his enthronement, "Adad sent his rains, Ea opened his fountains, the grain grew seven feet tall, the ear was fifteen inches long. . . . In my reign there was fullness to overflowing. . . . " An address to the king from a courtier contains the most exuberant account of the blessings that Shamash and Marduk showered upon his reign: "Days of justice, years of righteousness, abundance of showers, mighty floods, favorable prices. The gods are pleased: the fear of the gods is great; the temples teem [with people], . . . old men dance; young men shout for joy. . . . "[18] (It sounds very modern.)

Such court style, as Hugo Gressmann suggested, was not a claim that Paradise had returned.[19] It was rather like the boasts of modern politicians and the "tall stories" from Kansas and Texas. For the Assyrians and Babylonians such language became commonplace but, nevertheless, as much a part of the documents describing the kings' reigns as excess verbiage in legal documents. It was merely a matter of good form for the courtier, and the king liked to hear it. Whether the mass of the people were sufficiently naïve to take such patter seriously may be questioned. Yet, when people in a highly literate nation are influenced by the language of advertising and political campaigns, it is not safe to discount ancient gullibility.

Similar claims appear in ninth-century inscriptions of Kilamu, Panammu, and Hadad, found at Senjirli, or Samal. The language is quite matter of fact. King Kilamu says that to the "prostrated" common people (?) he had been a father, a mother, a brother. He had clothed the naked in linen, he had made the poverty-stricken the owners of flocks and herds, of silver and gold. Since all of these kings were vassals of Assyria and doubtless were copying their masters, they serve to confirm the Syrian acceptance also of the language of boasting kings and flattering subjects. This "oriental hyperbole" must be borne in mind in the discussion of biblical "hyperbole."[20]

6. *A Divinely Chosen Ruler*   A closely allied motif is the fiction that appears all over the ancient Orient according to which the king was specially chosen by deity to bring to the people the blessings of the divine righteousness and beneficence. Early Assyrian monarchs called themselves "viceroys of the God Assur." Not only in Egypt, but also in Asiatic lands, the ruler was often represented as of divine birth, or as adopted by the deity, especially if he were a usurper. According to his legend, Sargon of Akkad was of lowly birth, but, when he was a gardener, the goddess Ishtar loved him and made him ruler.[21] Some kings, down to the nameless adventurer who became the great Sargon II, conqueror of Samaria, made much of their lowly origin, changed by the gods to a lordly birth. They were all chosen by the gods, chosen in the womb, called in youth, called by name, named for great deeds,

given a mighty scepter and entrusted with an unrivaled kingship by the gods.[22]

The extravagance of the royal titulary is almost unbelievable. Sennacherib was

the great king, the mighy king, king of the universe, king of Assyria, king of the four quarters; the wise shepherd, favorite of the great gods, guardian of the right, lover of justice; who lends support, who comes to the aid of the needy, who turns to pious deeds; perfect hero, mighty man; first among all princes, the flame that consumes the unsubmissive, who strikes the wicked with the thunderbolt; the god Assur, the great mountain, has entrusted to me unrivaled kingship. . . .[23]

The mentality of the ancient scribe who prepared royal inscriptions may be illustrated by a young Arab meteorologist. He had to send a weather report to guide a royal airplane. While a dust storm blacked out all visibility, he wrote, "Visibility excellent, ceiling unlimited." When his superior caught the message just in time, he explained, "I have no right to say that his Majesty's country is not perfect." [24]

The long, fulsome list of titles is still applied to the unhappy Sin-shar-ishkun, last Assyrian king to rule at Nineveh.[25] Babylon had long followed the custom. Marduk surveyed all peoples and assembled all mankind and from among them chose Hezekiah's contemporary and would-be ally, Merodach-baladan, as he who should restore Babylon and "gather the scattered together." [26] Less than two centuries later Babylonian scribes were applying the same language to Cyrus, the alien "liberator" of Babylon.[27] Second Isaiah (45:1-4) echoes the ideas and in part the words of the cuneiform text.

7. *Pride, Catastrophe, and Humility*   In Egyptian and West Asian literature a group of complementary motifs is found that eventually appears among the Hebrews also, often in altered form. Some of the mighty Assyrian and Babylonian conquerors thought well of combining the fiction of lowly birth with the motif of humility, but also with the claim to a noble birth or to great might. Assur-nasir-pal I, in an invocation of Urta, "chief of the gods," calls himself "the submissive

one dear to thy heart." In a prayer to Ishtar, "the Lady of the land," he is, somewhat equivocally, "the mighty one of the gods, the humble one dear to thy heart." Sargon II is "the humble and unceasing worshiper of Nabu and Marduk." Esarhaddon writes himself down as "the abject suppliant and slave, the submissive, groveling worshiper" of the exalted gods. The Neo-Babylonian monarchs of the sixth century often put at the end of their extravagant titularies, "the meek and humble one." [28] According to Albright, Zakir, king of Hamath (*c.* 800) begins an inscription, "I am a humble (*'anah*) man."

Beginning in the Nineteenth Dynasty a chastened mood came over Egypt, possibly as a result of comparing current conditions with the more glorious past. It was an "age of personal piety" (Breasted), the period of "the religion of the poor" (B. Gunn), when Amon was praised as "the Lord of the silent man," the "rescuer" of the poor, the weak, the distressed, the prisoner. Confession replaced the "affirmation of innocence." God was merciful to those who confessed their sins. Patience, humility, obedience, and resignation were the recommended virtues. The classic illustration is the poem that, like the first Psalm, contrasts the "heated man in the temple" with the "truly silent man," who holds himself apart. Amen-em-ope urges silence and withdrawal in the face of him who speaks evil. "God will know how to answer him." [29]

This formal, ritual humility should not be hastily discounted. It may be real, not merely conventional, but due to a loss of nerve such as John Wilson believes came upon Egypt after the Eighteenth Dynasty. It may be due to the almost universal belief of the ancient, not to say the modern, world, that pride and boasting arouse the envy of the gods, or of Fate. The proud monarchs of the ancient world were "knocking on wood." Like many modern religionists and pious politicians such as Gladstone, they made elaborate protestations of trust in their deities and credited their gods and not themselves with their valiant deeds and glorious successes.

The concept of a reversal of fortune, *peripetia* in Aristotle's discussion of tragedy, the sudden, calamitous, and catastrophic fall of the great, was as common as the success story. However, the divine re-

versal of the poor and unfortunate man's lot and his elevation to fame
and fortune were not the complement of the fall of the mighty. The
constant boast of ancient monarchs was their ability to overthrow the
wicked at the command of their gods. Of course the wicked were
kings whom they wished to conquer, rebels whom they wished to
chasten. They shattered the might of the haughty, the hosts of the
proud, the power of the strong. They humbled the wicked, trampled
on the mighty, and smashed all lands like a pot. But, spreading disaster themselves, they had to reckon with its return upon their own
heads. Therefore it was well to praise the gods, credit them with all
their own successes, and profess themselves loyal and humble worshipers of deities who, as Assur-nirari said of Nabu, were merciful,
compassionate, kindly, and forgiving.[30] Such competing and complementary motifs enter into all literature and history.

8. *Pessimism and Life's Problems*   The blatant boasting and pious
professions of humility in the royal inscriptions of Assyria and Babylon
almost drown out the voice of genuine pessimism and complaint. But
open-eyed sophistication and keen sensitivity to the discrepancies between what the kings promised in the name of the gods and what
they did could not fail to appear. The belief that the gods decreed
justice, justice as right and not as favor, which appears in the latter
part of the third millennium, seems, as Thorkild Jacobsen says, to have
become the general conception in the second.[31] But along with this
ideal progress, arose inevitably the problems of unjust suffering and
death, for fact contradicted faith.

The Epic of Gilgamesh comes from Sumerian sources that are at
least as early as the third millennium. Its story of the search of the
mighty, semidivine Gilgamesh for immortality, one of the great literary
compositions of antiquity, ends with no solution to the problem. Until
death takes his boon companion and alter ego, Enkidu, the Herculean
hero rejoices in youthful adventures that prove him invincible. Then
the meaning of death comes home to him, and he travels to the ends
of the earth through countless dangers in a vain search for endless
life. From Ut-napishtim he learns of the plant at the bottom of the
sea that renews man's failing youth. Almost back in his own land

through further adventures, he leaves the precious plant unguarded for a moment, and a snake finds it and eats it. So snakes never die, but merely slough off the old body in exchange for a new. But man is helpless before death. In bitter irony he asks,

> For whose sake has my heart's blood been spent?
> I brought no blessing on myself—
> I did the serpent underground good service.

Jacobsen calls it "a jeering, unhappy, unsatisfactory ending," a tragedy without a catharsis.[32] It is a shrill, irrational cry of protest to unanswering heavens. The ghosts in dark Sheol still await all men. While the Egyptians were building their pyramids, affirming their innocence, and repeating their incantations to insure themselves a happy semimaterial life after death, nearly two millennia passed before the Semitic world began to consider the idea possible; and then they learned hope from their Persian conquerors.

However, Egyptians had long before begun to complain of social injustice, to question the value of life, and even to cast suspicion on the common faith in a life to come. In the "Song of the Harper," as Breasted suggested, the singer (*c.* 2100) looked out upon the Old Kingdom pyramids and concluded that all the glory of the ancients in life and in death had departed leaving no value or hope behind. Plundered tombs promised no future life. Man should consider neither the past nor the future but, with Koheleth and FitzGerald's Omar, "enjoy the glad day," for no one can take his goods with him and no one returns who has gone thither.[33]

In the highly original and effective "Dialogue of a Misanthrope with His Own Soul" (as Breasted named it), the writer first viewed life much as did the Harper: "Follow the glad day and forget care." But, apparently, he recoiled from an existence devoted to mere pleasure and, after debating the matter at length, reached the conclusion that death is better than life. It is not merely that, like the biblical Job, he had been overtaken by searing misfortune, by illness, by the loss of friends, and by false accusations until his name was justly abhorred. (A poem of four tristich stanzas describes the stench that his name arouses.) Worse even than that was the breakdown of the social order, over which Egyptians were deeply concerned. All law and justice were disregarded. Evil men throve while the good, the peaceful, were wretched. "The land is left to those who do iniquity." Therefore death is a glad release. For "he who is yonder" will be accepted as a wise man and will not be repelled when he prays to Re.[34]

Khe-khepere-soneb, a priest of Heliopolis, draws the same gloomy picture of the ills of the First Interregnum. There had been a complete collapse of society. He is in misery himself, but he is equally concerned for society. The social classes, fixed by the gods, no longer are maintained. "Righteousness is cast out; evil dominates the council hall. . . . The poor man has no strength to save himself from a stronger man." Worse still, all men are silent concerning the evil situation. None is wise enough to perceive it, none angry enough to speak.[35]

The Babylonian "Dialogue of Pessimism" is wholly cynical and accordingly less effective. A master, talking with his slave, makes statement after statement regarding various phases of life. When the slave agrees with him and adds various arguments in support, the master turns about and proves him wrong. It is an irresponsible devaluation of all values by a satiric, cynical Koheleth, the work of a sardonic sophist. The conclusion the master reaches is, "To break my neck and thy neck, to fall into the river, that is good." When the slave stoically agrees, the master changes his mind once more. He will kill the slave only and let him go on before. But the slave retorts, "And would my lord want to live three days after me?"

A later Babylonian dialogue, somewhat after the manner of Job, has as one speaker a wretched sufferer who is completely skeptical and enforces his views with many examples of the injustice of the gods. The other, a pious man, urges complete submission to the will of the gods on the ground that man cannot understand divine justice and can only submit in humble devotion.[36]

9. *The Righteous Sufferer* Far more vigorous and original is the earlier so-called "Lament of a Babylonian Job," which begins "I will praise the lord of wisdom." However, it is still an inferior counterpart of the later biblical Job, inferior also to the much earlier Egyptian

"complaints." A man who had been rich and powerful, evidently a noble, possibly a king, and who had consistently worshiped the gods, fell a prey to a disease that completely prostrated him and consequently he lost everything of value, health, friends, reputation. He described his piety in terms that resemble some of the Hebrew Psalms. His only thought had been of prayer and supplication and sacrifice. He delighted in days of worship, "when he followed the procession [of the goddesses]." He taught his people to observe the ritual of the gods and to revere the names of the goddesses. Now he wonders whether these acts are pleasing to the gods. He concludes that man cannot "comprehend the mind of the gods in heaven's depth." Man, "who came to life yesterday and dies today" cannot pit his judgment against that of the gods. It is the usual hopeless conclusion. But suddenly there is a reversal of his fate. Marduk appears to him in dreams, cures his disease, and restores to him all that he had lost, even as Yahweh does to the biblical Job. But the problem of unmerited suffering is not solved.[37]

To these anonymous literary works there are remarkable parallels in royal inscriptions. In a long lament addressed to Ishtar, Assur-nasir-pal I (1049–1031) tells of the favors the goddess had formerly shown him, of the statues of the gods he had erected, of the temples he had repaired, of the offerings he had established, and of a costly throne of boxwood set up and adorned with gold and precious stones. He continues, "In what have I done wrong? Why hast thou allotted me disease, boils, and pestilence? If I have not incurred sin or evil, why am I afflicted? . . . Look on me with compassion. . . . Intercede for me with thy Beloved, the father of the gods. Then, till the end of time, I will exalt thy Ladyship."[38]

By coincidence or imitation of "I will praise the lord of wisdom," a clay tablet, which gives a fulsome account of Assurbanipal's pious foundations, carried on the reverse a bitter and, for a great monarch and conqueror and scholar, most unseemly complaint over his fate. He had restored ruined temples and revived neglected offerings to the gods and forgotten rites for dead kings, and so had "done good to god and man, to the dead and the living." Why then had disease, heartache, distress, and destruction clung to him? Enmity, strife, disturbance, and evil words were continually assailing him. He spends his days sighing and lamenting; death is making an end of him. He moans, "O God, let me see the light. How long, O God, wilt thou do this to me? As one who does not fear god or goddess I am treated." [39] There is no need to dwell upon the numerous parallels in this literature to various Psalms and to Job.

Assyrian records are few after 640, but the last years of Assurbanipal's reign must have been extremely difficult and disturbed. For a century there was a "time of troubles." The whole of the Near East was in commotion because of the rising power of the Medes and the Persians. Nineveh was destroyed only fourteen years after the king's death. Josiah, another king who tried to restore the cult and establish the laws of his God, died three years later, and it was but a couple of decades until his capital was destroyed and thousands of his subjects were miserably exiled. Jeremiah and Ezekiel struggled with the problem, and a little later a great Unknown, debating his own sufferings with himself amid the mountains of Edom, draped his emotions about the figure of Job. Woes unmerited and unexplained came upon myriads all over the Near East.

The flamboyant promises of monarchs to bring peace, prosperity, and some mitigation of the lot of the lowly were only resounding brass. (They never were mere tinkling cymbals.) Laments and penitential psalms reflected only personal and individual fears, wounded feelings, and physical sufferings. Concern for social wrongs, for the man-inflicted woes of the poor and humble, was swallowed up in a sea of self-centered troubles.

Only "that so strange and passionate Jewish people," to use Santayana's phrase,[40] who had endured more than they all, found strength in their weakness and hope in their despair, as did the Suffering Servant of their great Prophet of the Exile and their apostate Apostle to the Gentiles (2 Cor. 12:9-10). Equally paradoxical was the reaction of the humble band of Galilean Jews who had gathered about Jesus

234 Man, Morals and History

and had fled incontinently before his captors. They discovered in the neglected Suffering Servant of Isaiah the prototype of their Master and, in the anomaly of his fate, the divine promise of the Great Reversal, which was to overthrow the mighty and raise up the lowly and the weak.

CHAPTER XV

The Hebrew Hope

1. *The Problem of Justice* Except, ironically, for their brief periods of commercial prosperity or foreign conquest, the hope of the Hebrews for the future could never have been based upon any promise of external circumstances. Quite the contrary! It rested solely upon an indefeasible confidence in the righteousness and justice of God. But what did "righteousness" and "justice" mean?

The question has been much discussed and too often neglected—neglected by theologians and overemphasized by the socially minded. The actual usage of the words in the Old Testament exhibits manifold denotations and connotations, as invariably happens with much-used abstract terms.

The root (*shaphat*) of the word for "justice" (*mishpat*) meant "establish, decide, judge," and the noun stood for something "established," or "decided." Therefore it includes "custom, right, due, law," and so "justice, judgment," either acquittal or condemnation; also a "case," to be judged, a "cause" to be pleaded, a "suit" to be pressed. To "do justice," then, meant to do what was right, to see that the right was upheld. But "right" must always be defined. Its actual content is determined by law, precedent, custom, and public opinion. To the priest to "do right" might mean merely to offer sacrifices and observe the ritual tabus.

So also as to "righteousness." The root, *tsadhak,* meant to be "straight," or "right." The noun, *tsedhek,* meant either physical straightness or moral rectitude; *tsedhekah,* used only in a moral sense, meant "justness, integrity, righteousness." There were "right sacrifices" (Deut. 33:19) and "right social action," all to be defined according to some recognized standard. The pre-exilic prophets (with minor exceptions) accepted the task of defining both words in social terms.

For the Hebrews the problem of justice had two facets, national and individual. On the one hand, the justice and righteousness of God were at stake in the fate of his chosen nation. This aspect was dominant in pre-exilic times. After the Exile emphasis shifted toward the individual. Both the righteous person and the righteous nation must receive the rewards of obedience to God's laws, and the wicked, whether nation or individual, must be punished, all of course in this life.

The ecological situation being what it was, neither nation nor individual could receive what Hebrew tradition promised. In a little area that was climatically, agriculturally, and politically marginal, peace and security, not to mention an economy of abundance, were completely out of the range of possibility. Disasters such as Job suffered were always impending. Poverty and want were endemic and inescapable. Even the king could not escape drought and famine.[1] Debt, mortgage, usury, measures, and prices, always plagued the man who was not strong enough to protect himself.

If it is difficult for the poor man to get justice and the rich culprit to be given his deserts today, how much more so in ancient times. The judicial system was local and informal. There was no organization. Local elders, chosen by informal public consent, gathered at the city gate to hear any complaint brought before them. In this social center, place of business and gossip, a litigant could summon to his support all his friends and relatives. One of the elders might be involved, in which case his colleagues could hardly be expected to be objective. Appeal to the king was theoretically possible, but usually impracticable. The difficulties that petitioners experienced when David became preoccupied with affairs of state and harem (2 Sam. 15:1-4) illustrate the situation. It was not a world made for the man who had neither money, friends, nor influence.

As has already been shown, the Hebrews lived in much the same intellectual and literary atmosphere as their neighbors. They also enjoyed much the same social atmosphere: the king, the court, the patricians, and the rich on one side, and, on the other, the middle class (lower middle) of small landowners, artisans, and merchants, with the depressed groups of landless laborers and slaves below them. But they differed from other Near Eastern peoples in that the middle class, Finkelstein's "plebeians," included many literates. Perhaps they were found chiefly among the priests. Often, doubtless, they were better educated than the patricians, as was true of the "clerks" of the Middle Ages.

In Egypt there had been a vocal "religion of the poor" because the scribal artists who copied biographical records and funerary texts on tomb walls and papyrus rolls had to be educated and thus learned to speak for themselves. But among the Egyptians, the enormous weight of ancestral tradition and the social hierarchy crushed this religion of the poor in its beginnings.[2]

Among the Hebrews, however, numerous social factors already mentioned worked to preserve a strain of thought that was obliterated by militarism and wealth in other lands. The tradition of nomadic democracy; the late development of the monarchy; the theoretical equality of all priests as (supposed) descendants of Aaron and of all Israelites as children of Abraham; the very simplicity of the alphabet as compared with cuneiform and hieroglyphic—these and other factors combined to produce, from among both laity and priesthood, prophets and scribes who preserved the good (as well as some of the bad) from their historical experience. Their education resulted in conclusions along lines far in advance of their neighbors.

2. *The Hebrew Social Conscience* The prophets used the same clichés to express social ideals as did their neighbors. But their language did not reflect either archaism or convention, and its application was both more specific and more comprehensive. They took the immemorial Near Eastern belief in divine justice seriously. God was against the amassing of wealth by the few at the expense of the many; power of position and wealth should not be used for selfish purposes. They announced in no uncertain terms the ancient Oriental maxim

that, to use a modern expression, "the primary function of government is the protection of the weak." [3] The poor, the weak, unprotected widows and orphans, and (notably among the Hebrews) the resident alien *(ger)*, those who had no natural guardians, were especially under divine protection.

In the prophets the Hebrews had an institution that was without parallel in other nations. They were the nation's conscience. Their application of national and international ideals to current conditions forms one of the great dramas of history. When Nathan stood before David and said, "You are the man"; when Elijah found Ahab in Naboth's vineyard and asked him, "Have you killed and already taken possession?" something new entered into recorded history. Strange to say, the "Former Prophets," the historical books, and Chronicles do not refer directly to the rights of the poor or the protection of the widow, the orphan, the weak, the alien.

However, even if the historians judge the monarchs by their attention to the Yahweh cult and not to Israel's social morality, the other types of Old Testament literature more than compensate for their blindness. The obligation to protect the unprotected is enjoined again and again in the various law codes and not merely acknowledged by pious phrases in prologue and epilogue as in Hammurabi's code. The Psalms and Proverbs allude to it as taken for granted. It forms one of the chief refrains in Job and the greatest of the prophets.

The earlier prophets do not assail any king directly or by name, but their criticisms are clearly implied and are recognized as such. Amos attacked the "people of Israel, the whole family" that God had brought out of the land of Egypt, but he was accused of plotting against Jeroboam. Micah, like Amos, was an enemy of the city and city luxury, and he attacked the whole people. But he specified "the heads of Jacob, the rulers of the house of Israel," as the chief sinners. The injustices that the prophets define and reprobate are those of rich landlords and moneylenders, who "sell the righteous for silver and the needy for a pair of sandals, who trample the poor in the dust and abuse the afflicted." [4]

It is hardly necessary to quote at length the familiar denunciations.

The rulers eat the flesh of God's people and flay their skin off them; Zion's heads give judgment for a bribe; its priests teach for hire; its prophets divine for money; Israel's princes are rebels and companions of thieves; they love bribes and run after gifts; they do not defend the fatherless and the widow. The "rulers of Sodom" and the "people of Gomorrah" decree iniquitous decrees and the writers write oppression to turn aside the needy from justice. All these expressions of the social conscience in Amos, Micah, and Isaiah are clear and explicit.[5]

Jeremiah speaks more specifically. God had set him as "a fortified city, an iron pillar, and bronze walls" against the king of Judah, its princes, its priests, and the "people of the land," the landed gentry. Both he and Isaiah were opposed to intrigues with Egypt or Assyria or Babylon. They were isolationist and neutralist, as suited a helpless buffer nation. But with regard to internal politics they had a positive policy. They were against the nobility and for the commonalty, against the rich and for the poor. Repeatedly Jeremiah names, as those responsible for the people's evils, "their kings, their princes, their priests, their prophets, the inhabitants of Jerusalem, and the men of Judah"—in other words, all the upper classes.[6]

In a series of oracles on "the house of the king of Judah," the sons of Josiah, he demands justice, righteousness, deliverance of the oppressed, that no wrong be done to the alien, the fatherless, and the widow, and no shedding of innocent blood. Attacking Jehoahaz (Shallum), he condemns the corvée: "Woe to him who builds his house by unrighteousness, . . . and makes his neighbor serve him for nothing and does not give him his wages." Josiah had "done justice and righteousness; then it had been well with him." (Note that Kings and Chronicles never mention this.) He had "judged the case of the poor and needy; then it was well. 'Is not this to know me?' says the Lord." The theoretical democracy of Israel is lighted up by Jeremiah's reference to the monarch's misuse of his "neighbor," not his "subject," in the matter of forced labor. The same demands are made of "all of Judah." [7]

Ezekiel is not usually regarded as a social prophet, yet his moral demands in social relations are more comprehensive and specific than those of any other prophet. It is true that his chief emphasis, like that of Hosea, is on cult. It is the avoidance of the worship of other deities and of the abominations connected with pagan cults in which he is especially interested. He deplores the people's more or less orgiastic rites, including sexual license. Yet he specifies a longer list of economic sins than the other prophets. They are pride; surfeit of food and prosperous ease combined with failure to provide for the poor and needy; oppression of the poor and needy; robbery; failure to restore the pledge, taking "interest and increase" (the profit motive); practicing extortion, especially on the sojourner, the alien.[8]

Clearly Ezekiel had familiarity with a collected Torah, which is lacking in other prophets. This made it possible for him to base every item in his indictment on its enactments; and there is a touch of legalism in his demands. He appealed to the tradition that was known to all Israel, to God's written will. What were mere pious phrases, traditional, conventional, and high sounding, in the proclamations of Babylonian and Assyrian monarchs were God's specific decrees and ordinances. The contrast between Israel and her neighbors in this regard is striking.

In two directions, then, Hebrew tradition departed radically from that of Babylonia and Assyria. The prophets of Israel, like the Egyptian Eloquent Peasant, complained bitterly of the failure of the "rulers of God's people" to carry out their divinely appointed role as protectors of the poor. And the Hebrew codes, in sharp contrast to those of other Oriental peoples, are notable for repeated explicit injunctions regarding justice and protection for the poor and needy and all the depressed and unprotected classes. This is particularly true of Deuteronomy, which clearly reflects the influence of the prophets of the eighth century. Among the Assyrians, the strident claims of the royal chancelleries in reign after reign that justice prevails witness only to their failure.

3. *The Ethical Ideals of Job*   There is an even more fundamental contrast between the biblical Job and the laments and boasts of the "Jobs" of other nations. A large proportion of the motifs and, indeed, of the very turns of expression in the literatures of pessimism and complaint of social ills and the injustices of man's lot appears also in

the Book of Job. If its writer were not so vigorous, vital, and masterful in his language and thought, one could imagine him sitting down with Babylonian and Egyptian documents before him and weaving their ideas into his bitter denunciations of life's insufferable inequities and the insoluble mysteries of evil. But he differs from the Egyptian pessimists in that his sufferings are personal and in no way caused by social disintegration. He is unlike the Babylonian Jobs in that his righteousness consists in obedience to moral, not ritual, law. He does not try to please God by sacrifices and pious works. Indeed, he does not speak of pleasing God but of doing what is right, without any ulterior motive. His morality is wholly within the prophetic orbit. He does not quote the Torah, but a law written on the heart.

It would be difficult to find a more comprehensive list of social sins than those enumerated in Job's great protestation of innocence (chap. 31). Falsehood and deceit; lasciviousness, not only in act, but also in thought ("a covenant with his eyes"); mistreatment of servants; neglect of the poor, the widow, the fatherless, the naked; trust in wealth; use of influence in the courts; haughty pride and self-confidence; neglect of the alien and the wayfarer; secret evil-doing—to these may be added his briefer positive statement of virtues (29:11-17), which repeats his claim to have cared for all the needy, the depressed, the distressed, and adds, "I was eyes to the blind, feet to the lame, a father to the poor." He investigated the cause of the stranger; he saved those who were attacked by the wicked. He barely mentions the robber and the adulterer who work under cover of the darkness, but describes at length in vivid language the sufferings of the poor and helpless whom the prosperous wicked exploit and wrong (24:1-17).

How far the ethical and religious outlook of the author of Job and his conception of the character of deity surpass those of Assurbanipal needs no emphasis. Job never thinks of placating God with sacrifices, offerings, festival rituals, and the building of temples but carries out what he believes to be his moral obligations in society by positive acts of social helpfulness. There is no disparagement of ritual "services." Apparently it never entered the author's mind that they were worthy of mention, except in the (editorial?) prose prologue and epilogue.

Job's complaint is of the unjust suffering of an individual, but of an individual whose whole conception of righteousness is thoroughly social, and anything but formal and legalistic.

If it may be said that Job's morality is within the prophetic orbit, in another sense he ranges far outside the somewhat narrow circumference of prophetic and Israelite thought. All of the prophets were concerned with their own national future. They were dismayed by the sufferings of "God's people." Their consciences were deeply troubled by flagrant wrongs inflicted upon the helpless. But the special motivation of their bitter criticisms of the ruling classes was fear that God's punishment would entail the destruction of the nation. Job's concern was the much larger and more inclusive problem of evil as such.

4. *Postexilic Problems and Ideals* Job's equally magnificent counterpart, Second Isaiah, whether predecessor or successor, returns to the sufferings of the nation, and, if the Suffering Servant is at times an individual, he is only a vivid figurative representative of the nation and its sufferings and vindication. Second Isaiah's paean of encouragement made place for little reference to social evils, although it might easily have done so. Third Isaiah (56–66) makes sufficient allusion to the stock phrases of prophetic social criticism to establish at least a nominal, or formal, interest in practical social righteousness. The picture of the glorious future in both includes justice, with sufficient specification to indicate its social and moral character, even if it lacks the vivid personal participation in the wrongs of the oppressed and the sense of personal obligation of the strong that appear in Job.[9]

Second Isaiah thus records and furthers a new trend in Hebrew thinking. The problem is the restoration and preservation of the nation, not its repentance and regeneration. The emphasis on social justice falls lightly on the consciences of nearly all of the postexilic prophets, but it is not forgotten. The social passion of the First Isaiah (or is it the social concern of the apocalyptist?) seems to have infected his interpolators, for, in passage after passage that is critically doubtful, the conventional terms that belong to the ancient "social creed" are at least quoted.[10] Similarly Zechariah (7:8–10) quotes from the pre-exilic prophets (and Deuteronomy?) the Lord's demands for justice, kindness, and mercy for the four conventional representatives of the oppressed.

Nehemiah's chief concern was ritual requirements and other externalities, but he dealt with a significant crisis in the spirit of the prophets. The invasion of the rights of the poor, the evils of landlordism, moneylending, mortagages and distraint, even enslavement of Jews, including the selling of Jewish children into slavery, were among the complaints of "the people and their wives against their Jewish brethren." He took energetic measures to remedy the situation and secured promises, especially from the priests, that such evils would come to an end. But how long would his measures be enforced?[11]

How the patrician-plebeian conflict runs through all Jewish history has been shown by Louis Finkelstein—just as it runs through the history of other nations. It comes to the fore in the later apocalypses and again in the second century of our era. Then, in Roman times, the term "people of the land" (*'Am ha-'arets*) takes on a new meaning, different from that in the Old Testament. They are no longer the landowners, but Jews who will not or cannot keep the Law as the rabbis demand.[12] But the conflict is still between the well-to-do and the poor. The rabbis were against the poor, not for purposes of exploitation, but because they did not know the Law or keep it. They still maintain, at least in words, the prophetic moral standards.

The two conflicts, ritual vs. ethics and plebeian vs. patrician, haunted Jewish society through all of its history. They were uppermost in the attack of Jesus on Jewish morals and religion. Indeed, the conflict is never-ending and is very much to the fore in modern Protestantism and Catholicism, because it is so much easier to meet external obligations than to measure up to high standards of ethical principles and corresponding moral action. It is safer to attack individual sin than social wrongdoing. Ritual may be boring or delightful depending on the worshiper's temperament and training. It will be undergone gladly if it satisfies the conscience. It makes no demands upon either the individual or the social conscience; it affects neither individual conduct nor business methods.

It is sometimes urged that the earlier prophets did not mean to do away with sacrifices and offerings, but only insisted that they be accompanied by the right inner attitudes and outward actions. It is difficult to square this claim with the words of the greatest of the prophets. If God had had enough of burnt offerings and the blood of bulls and goats, if he regarded incense as an abomination and hated new moons and appointed festivals, does Isaiah (1:11–20) mean merely that, without morality, these observances are vain, that God cannot accept them along with iniquity? Of course this would be true, but it is hardly what Isaiah says. Amos insists that God abominates the festivals, the solemn assemblies, and the offerings. Third Isaiah (66:3) likens his people's sacrifices to killing a man, breaking a dog's neck, and pouring out swine's blood. In the Psalms God does not desire sacrifices and offerings. Does God eat the flesh of bulls and drink the blood of goats? No! He desires a sacrifice of thanksgiving. The sacrifice acceptable to God is a broken spirit.[13] The language is explicit.

Whatever the date of Micah's various chapters, the book contains what Fleming James has called the most telling denunciations of the oppressing rich to be found in the Bible. The famous verses 6:6–8 (which may be postexilic) can be legitimately interpreted only as carrying on the anti-cult attitude of Amos and Isaiah. Burnt offerings, thousands of rams, and rivers of oil, even the utmost sacrifice of the ancient pagan, his own children, cannot atone for sin. The following summary of true religion goes beyond anything found elsewhere in Micah or in any other Old Testament book. To do justice and love kindness is genuine prophetic doctrine and is clearly so interpreted in the later denunciation (vv. 10–12) of scant measures, wicked scales, deceitful weights, and the violence of rich men. To "walk humbly with God" adds a touch that is reminiscent of sixth-century Assyria and Egypt and of many Hebrew Psalms. But the combination of the three Hebrew phrases, "do justice, love mercy, walk humbly with God," has a fullness of meaning that raises the passage far above any parallel. Micah's ethical summary of God's requirements is not quoted in any later Hebrew writing or in the New Testament. Yet it is now universally recognized as one of the greatest descriptions of true religion and one that most closely resembles the Christianity of Jesus.[14]

5. *Mythological Motifs* The varieties of motifs of mythology and court language that appear in Babylonia and Egypt are familiar to everyone who reads the Bible. The return of paradisiacal peace and plenty, the divinely chosen leader and ruler, the sudden reversals of fate, and the becoming humility and penitence that should save the wise man from catastrophe and the nation from destruction—all appear in the later books of the Old Testament and in the apocalypses. The Hebrews added the significant feature that played the dominant role in their expectation of the future: the anticipation of the Day of Yahweh, when all wrongs should be righted and justice enthroned on earth. It was a motif that included all others, a comprehensive idea that characterized and transformed all others, for it pointed to a glorious future and, in answering all doubts as to the justice of God, it promised to make possible the realization of the Hebrew hope.

The Day of Glory anticipated by the naïve, optimistic, and headstrong nationalists of Amos' time, the Day of Doom threatened by Amos and all the other pre-exilic prophets, had been reinterpreted by Second Isaiah. The Day of Doom had passed, the Day of Glory was just on the eastern horizon. The punishment had fallen, the purification had been wrought; restoration must ensue. This was the pattern of thought that created a mosaic of irrelevancies, of inconsistent threat and promise in passages such as Isaiah 28–29. The chapters as a whole fit the situation in the late eighth century and continue the "woes" of earlier chapters. But the editor, taking 28:2–4 as a description of the Day of Doom added vv. 5–6, as a description of the glory that should follow to bless the saved remnant of the Chosen People. The various prophetic "doom songs," directed against the enemies of Israel, are echoes of the popular view that Amos rejected. Those, within and without the nation, whom the poet and his remnant hated would be put down; those whom they favored would be raised up.

Without any attempt at an inventory of these various fragments and fugitive poems, the nature of this type of literature may be in part discovered by noting their characteristic ideas. The Day of Yahweh, described in terrifying, but vague and mythological, detail, includes the destruction of hostile nations and their rulers. The punishment of Israel, or of the wicked in Israel, leaves a repentant remnant to be saved and returned to their own land, a restoration that may be described as the creation of a new heaven and earth. God will reign over a kingdom, perhaps universal in its scope, and marked by undisturbed peace and unlimited abundance.

Whether the writers actually believed what they wrote is a question that raises its head once more. Would God in the new day actually make the desert blossom like the rose? Why not? They had seen portions of the desert blossom under an unexpected shower, and God was Lord of the storm. Why should he not work such a miracle? Anything was possible in their prescientific world, where there was no "natural law." It is wrong, however, to freeze their glowing fancy into icy fact. They believed in the power and righteousness of God and, therefore, in the triumph of peace, goodness, and justice, with material abundance and universal happiness, under the beneficent reign of God. Their Oriental conventions of style must not be allowed to obscure their moral passion, nor their unscientific primitivity suffered to cast a cloud upon their sensitivity in ethical matters or upon their penetrating understanding of human character. Their moral discriminations created for them problems that the rest of their world never suspected of existing.

Among the historically and theologically most important of these ideas was that of the future messianic king. What the Hebrews expected of an ideal king is not difficult to discover. No formal decrees or records of achievement like those of Assyrian monarchs have come down from any Hebrew ruler. The Bible has preserved no elaborate titulary of any of them. Foreign secretaries employed by Hebrew kings might have imported alien forms of speech for royal documents. But it is not necessary to assume that the Hebrews consciously borrowed foreign language or customs. The total outlook of the ancient Orient was so much the same that the use of high-flown compliment and exaggerated courtesy was universal. The important point is that the Hebrews also had their court style. The Psalms again offer a convenient conspectus of Hebrew ideals and practice.

If there are no boastful royal inscriptions in Hebrew, there are the "royal Psalms." In them the various motifs of Assyrian royal inscriptions, substantially repeated, are more modestly applied to the Hebrew monarchs in the third person: the king chosen and established on his throne by Yahweh, called son of the deity and given dominion "from sea to sea and from the river [Euphrates] to the ends of the earth." He is endowed with power to dash his enemies in pieces like a pottery vessel. Yahweh will seat him on his right hand and make his enemies the footstool of his feet. Yahweh will give him length of days for ever and ever; his throne endures forever. Yahweh trains his hands for war and his feet for battle. Many of these phrases are paralleled in the inscriptions of Assyrian monarchs. Therefore some scholars believe that Psalms like the Seventy-second were written in the seventh century under Assyrian domination.[15] It may well be, however, that the mythological atmosphere of Semitic thinking accounts for the resemblances.

One historically important combination of ideas appears in Psalm 110. The Hebrew king sits with his scepter as a mighty ruler and ruthless judge on a throne beside Yahweh himself. Uzziah was believed to have been stricken with leprosy for aspiring to priestly functions, and Hebrew kings never served as priests before the time of the Maccabees, when priests became kings. Yet, by Yahweh's decree this king is made "a priest forever after the order of Melchizedek," the shadowy priest-king to whom Abraham paid tithes. The New Testament and Christian theological echoes of the Psalm are still reverberating.

In Psalm 110 the scepter stands for the bloody slaughter of enemies. In Psalm 72 it is a scepter of equity;

> For he delivers the needy when he calls,
> The poor, and him who has no helper.
> From oppression and violence he delivers their life,
> And precious is their blood in his sight.

The Psalms include practically all of the often contradictory motifs that go to make up the variegated picture of past, present, and future. They repeatedly contrast the fortunes of the wicked and the righteous. Too often the rich, the proud, the lofty, the mighty were remarkably prosperous and oppressed the meek, the poor, the weak, and the humble, both the nation and individuals within it. But the writers were confident that God was just and would eventually reverse the roles to vindicate the righteous. "The needy will not always be forgotten, and the hope of the poor will not perish forever. . . . The humble will possess the land." On the contrary, one writer could shut his eyes (he must have been rich) and aver, "I have not seen the righteous forsaken or his seed begging bread." That involves a condemnation of all the suffering Jobs and a denial of all expectation or need of a future reign of God.[16]

Nearly all of the Psalm writers take the contrary view. But they are full of confidence as to the eventual outcome. In fact, they are so convinced that the poor must receive their deserts that the phrase "I am poor and needy" seems to establish an inalienable right to God's attention. One says, "I am poor and needy; hasten to help me, O God!" Another, "Incline thine ear, O Lord, and answer me, for I am poor and needy." He adds, "Preserve my life, for I am godly." By poetic parallelism, piety and poverty are thus practically equivalent.[17] But commonly no such added assurance is given for it is taken for granted that the righteous will be poor and needy, while the wicked will be prosperous, and that the converse also is true. Yet God was just and faithful. He must redress the balance. Justice and righteousness must triumph.

This raises the question of the "prophetic dilemma." It was *the* Jewish dilemma, a dilemma for the individual and also for the nation. Often one cannot feel certain that the Psalmist is not speaking for the whole people, using a collective "I." In either case, the trustworthiness and power of God were in question. Could one believe in the righteousness and justice of an omnipotent and universal deity, ruler of heaven and earth, when wickedness flourished and righteousness was doomed, so it seemed, to perpetual powerlessness and oppression? Where were God's promises to Abraham and his seed, to David and his dynasty? If the nation had suffered double for all its sins, where was now its consolation? The question became a perpetual dilemma for both Jew and Christian, and differences over its answer led to a new type of literature and doctrine and to the "great schism" and the destruction of the Temple.

CHAPTER XVI

The Neoprophetic Hope

1. *The Apocalypse a New Type of Prophecy* Some time in the
second century the scribes and rabbis virtually ended the Hebrew
record of "the mighty acts of God" and closed the door to prophecy.[1]
Not that God was to abandon his control of history or his purpose
to vindicate his Chosen People and his own power and righteousness.
Quite the contrary! Perhaps, like the author of the Apocalypse of
Daniel, the latest book admitted to the canon, they believed that the
end of history was not far distant. They were correct, in any case, in
seeing that the fountain of inspiration was running dry.

The author of Daniel expressed his conception of the end and of
God's method of revelation in his own way, which reflected ideas new
to prophecy. He used strange figures of speech and inartistic symbols.
The book was not prophecy in the old sense, but was pseudoprophetic
as well as pseudepigraphic; and, as should be remembered, it was
admitted to the canon, not among the prophets, where modern Bibles
place it, but merely in the catchall appendix, the "Hagiographa," called
merely "The Writings" by the Jews. The Book of Daniel had numerous
pseudepigraphic contemporaries like it but even more extravagant;
and the close of the canon may have been intended to shut them out.
For that both Jews and Christians may be grateful.

The new literature expressed a novel kind of future hope. While it
was Jewish, passionately and often narrowly Jewish and based upon
Jewish hopes expressed in the Old Testament, it was not *the* Jewish
hope, just as modern Neo-orthodoxy is not *the* Christian theology. It
was rather *a* Jewish hope, a hope created by unusual circumstances

and a special type of mind that reflected a strange attitude toward history.

The pseudepigraphic apocalypses, all dating roughly between 200 B.C. and 100 A.D., differed greatly in detail and style, but they all had an essentially common solution of the prophetic dilemma and a basically similar conception of the past and future history of the world and of Israel. Their ideas were sufficiently vague to allow much difference of opinion among those who accepted them as divine revelation and they promoted the most fantastic and exuberant hopes. They were also expressed in fantastically exaggerated language. How this apocalyptic ideology and its uncouth expression came to be, can be understood only in the light of the ancient, Oriental world in which the Hebrews lived.

Various influences and conditions combined to produce this new type of writing. It was pseudonymous or anonymous because prophets were no longer acceptable. The documents were explicitly or implicitly placed in an ancient historical context, from which the assumed ancient authors predicted what would happen in the future. From the asserted earlier temporal locus the documents successfully "foretold" events of history down to their own actual time. Consequently they appeared to establish their competence to reveal what was still in the future, which they clothed usually in cryptic figures of speech.

They were thus pseudoprophetic. But in one respect they were true successors of the ancient prophets. In language, at least, they continued the tradition of social morality that the great prophets had established and maintained. They were vigorous, indeed bitter, champions of the poor and oppressed against the rich and the mighty who abused them. It is this service, above all, for which they deserve to be gratefully remembered.

They may properly be called "neoprophetic" for they used the reputation of their famous predecessors to establish doctrines and to arouse hopes that were quite foreign to ancient prophecy. With only a modicum of the prophetic spirit—an important modicum indeed— they altered the Israelite national hope in the direction of myth, magic, and miracle, with a strong infusion of demonology and ethical dualism.

Whereas the pre-exilic prophets had emphasized God's activity in history, the new prophets saw their times as the Last Days before God would end history. History, for them as for many moderns, had turned out to be hopelessly evil. God was not in it. But he would shortly step in to end "the present (evil) age," which was under the domination of Satan and his hosts, and to introduce a "new (and perfect) age," in which his will would rule both nature and man.

Perhaps the dominant color in their picture of the future was their narrow nationalism. A just God must keep his Covenant with his Chosen People. Therefore, Israel must rule the world, for the world's good, of course, but with a large net profit to the Chosen People. In his Day, Yahweh was to visit deserved punishment upon those who did not serve him. Since Israel had already suffered for its sins, at least a righteous remnant would survive the woes of the Last Days. Jerusalem would become the world capital, and all nations would come to it to worship Yahweh in his holy city and Temple, bringing gifts with them.

Certain facts disturbed this hopeful vision. Many Jews did not obey God's laws, either ritual or moral. Worse still, these same Jews were usually rich and powerful. They persecuted and oppressed their fellow Israelites, especially the pious poor. In assessing the ethics of the apocalyptists, it is necessary to admit that, for them, their group was the only true Israel and, therefore, "the poor and needy," who were to be vindicated. Unfortunately the phrase seems to have lost its clear ethical and social significance and to have been turned into a mere party slogan.[2] As in the Psalms, it represented the "plebeians," to use Finkelstein's terminology, in contrast to the godless "patricians."

The idea of a righteous remnant was a standard motif in the prophetic and apocalyptic writings, used to steady the faithful when evil became unbearable and deliverance seemed impossible. Similar encouragement had appeared in the prophetic version of the legend of Elijah. There were still "seven thousand" who had not bowed the knee to Baal, and Elijah need not lose hope of the nation and of his mission. Isaiah's son, Shear jashub, "a remnant shall return," was a symbol of hope. The new age was for the pious remnant.

The long disappointment of Israel's hope and the dominance of evil, the present impotence and sufferings of God's people, in such strange contrast to their ancestors' supposed miraculous escape from Egypt and glorious conquest of Canaan and to the might and magnificence of the reigns of David and Solomon—all this demanded explanation. Had not Moses promised, "The Lord will make you the head and not the tail, and you shall tend upward only and not downward"? One apocalyptist takes God to task: "We had hoped to be the head and have become the tail." [3] God's reputation for might and trustworthiness was rescued by the theory that he had allowed Satan and his demons temporary power over this evil earth (or during these evil days) in order to try the faithful as Job was tried and to discover the faithless. By the steadfastness of the righteous and by the eventual overthrow of all evil, he would demonstrate all the more emphatically his own sole rulership of earth and heaven.

All of these motifs, the conflict between rich and wicked patricians and poor and pious common people, the salvage of the righteous remnant, the reward of oppressed goodness and the punishment of oppressive wickedness, the restoration and glorification of the long-suffering Chosen People, combined into an entirely new kind of *peripetia,* a "reversal" that put down the rich but raised up the poor to become the rich and the powerful. The great fell, not because of some flaw or weakness of character, but for their downright wickedness. The reversals were not mere irrational fluctuations of fate. "God executes judgment in putting down one and lifting up another" (Ps. 75:7). The apocalyptic view makes the motif of moral judgment central.

There is such close superficial resemblance between Egyptian and Hebrew sayings regarding the rights and the protection of the poor that it comes as a surprise to discover that the Egyptians, like the Greeks, thought of the fall of the rich, the overturn of the upper classes, as a great disaster and never spoke of the rise of the poor, the restoration of their rights to a full cultural heritage, as the establishment of justice. They accepted the view that the poor would always be with them. The poor were to be protected as poor people by showing them kindness and charity. The rise of the poor to positions of affluence was never anticipated by any ancient nation except the Hebrews. Even the Hebrews, as a rule, extended God's protection only to Hebrews and the resident alien who had become one of them.

The late entry of the Hebrews upon the level of civilized culture and the very limitations of their Promised Land allowed, even forced, them to retain the nomadic ideal of equality for all of them; and the fact that the rich among them exhibited infidelity to Yahweh, while the faithful remained poor and oppressed, gave the concept of God's reign its "proletarian" color. Amos' reinterpretation of the popular concept of the Day of Yahweh made the apocalyptic view possible. Reversal would come to the very people who trusted in the Day. The rich, the proud, the powerful would be brought down; the poor, the needy, the sad would be raised up from misery to wealth and happiness. The last would be first, the first last. The reign of God belonged to the poor; the rich had already had their day in the sun.

In his own good time, the time he had ordained from the beginning, God would set everything right. He would reach down from his throne in the heavens, overthrow the demons who peopled the air, the earth, and the sea, judge and punish or reward men according to their deeds, and establish his reign over all creation. Then a more-than-Edenic peace and abundance would take the place of present strife, want, and suffering. The apocalypses are flaming war pamphlets. They attempt no reconciliation of the many contradictions and inconsistencies that fill their pages. The fate of the individual and the nation, the relation between future rewards and punishments in heaven and hell and the establishment of God's reign on earth—these and other dilemmas were left unresolved. The many strange elements in these peculiar documents also demand explanation.

2. *Evolutionary Stimuli*   During the historically unilluminated post-exilic period, the apocalypses begin to develop various completely novel conceptions, such as belief in a resurrection, a final Judgment, future punishments and rewards in hell and heaven, and, indeed, a Satanic reign on earth and in history. Pre-exilic Israel had never dreamed of such ideas. They came to be acepted by the majority of the

nation sometime during the Persian and Greek periods. Clearly, Jewish thought had gone through a remarkable evolution. Stimuli from some source excited Jewish thought and speculation to seek new solutions for the insistent problems that plagued the Jews as a nation and as individuals. Stirred by their contacts with the thought and aspirations of other peoples with whom their exile and their membership in the great empires of the period made them acquainted, they entered upon a new era of cultural creativity.

Since the greater part of the postexilic literature cannot be precisely dated, the course, time, and manner of this doubtless long and slow process cannot be definitely followed, although some of its stages can be inferred from the Psalms, Apocrypha, and Pseudepigrapha. Its eventual results appear in the New Testament and the rabbinic literature, as well as in Josephus. It is to be remembered that only the Sadducees, who regarded the Pentateuch alone as the word of God, rejected these new beliefs along with the Prophets and the Writings.

It usually comes as a shock to the pious student of the Bible to discover that, before the Exile and for some time after it, the Hebrews had no conception of a resurrection or of future rewards and punishments, but looked for the reward of the righteous and punishment of the wicked solely in this life.[4] Such surprise is natural. The lack of a belief in a future life, either resurrection or immortality, is all the more astonishing since the Hebrews must have had some acquaintance with Egyptian conceptions of a continuation of life after death. Actually, the Hebrews shared the common Semitic and earlier Greek view of Sheol or Hades as a dark and dismal abode of disembodied spirits, who merely existed, neither alive nor dead. Whence, then, this new conception?

No elements in Egyptian, Mesopotamian, or Jewish culture could naturally develop into such a belief. But both Hellenism and Mazdaism had produced close parallels to the conceptions that appear in Daniel and later writings. Hellenism had borrowed from the Semitic Near East, and it developed its resulting threefold fund of tradition ("Pelasgic," Indo-European, and Semitic) in its own unique fashion. As early as the sixth century Orphism had introduced punishments into Hades and had begun to portray the joys of the Elysian Fields. The transformation of Hades into Tartarus is paralleled by the later Jewish evolution of Sheol into Gehenna. The Greeks never dreamed of a bodily resurrection. Their idea of immortality came to color the idea of the resurrection, as when Paul talked of a spiritual body, and, for many, supplanted the concept of a physical resurrection. Thus Hellenism may have contributed to the conception of Gehenna and of immortality. Bodily resurrection came from another direction, Mazdaism.[5]

One of the remarkable virtues of the Old Testament in its demon-haunted world was the rarity of references to magic and demonological superstitions. Magic plays only a small part in later Jewish Palestinian literature, even though Jews became famous as magicians and sorcerers. Such superstitions, rife as they were everywhere in the ancient world, cannot have been absent from Jewish folklore and popular beliefs.[6] When Paul (1 Cor. 10:19–21) insisted that idols were nothing, but that the heathen worshiped demons, not gods, he was following a Zoro-astrian practice that had turned Mithra, Anahita, and other Aryan deities into *daiva,* "demons," but also a similar Jewish device that made over Ugaritic Aleyan Ba'al, Zebul Ba'al *ars,* ("Victorious Baal, Exalted Lord of the Earth") into Beelzebul, prince of demons and ruler of this age.[7] One can appreciate the Jewish pun which made him Baalzebub, "lord of flies." The device preserved monotheism but threw the door open to all the fears and superstitions that swarmed in the ancient mind.

Greek popular thinking was obsessed with demons. The *keres,* "diseases," were everywhere, as were the *daimones,* good and bad. But demonology had its rankest growth in Babylonia. Few ancient cultures were so demon ridden. Popular superstitions must have been similar throughout the Semitic world. It is small wonder, under the circumstances, that, after the Exile, Judaism shows an unhappy recrudescence of these primitive irrationalities. In the apocalyptic literature, which escaped the editorial censorship of the rabbis, demonology, along with angelology, luxuriates like a tropical forest.

As Lord of hosts, Yahweh had a court of "messengers" (*mal'akhim, angeloi*), the hosts that did his will. As time passed and the Chosen People's sufferings increased, it was not an unnatural process of thought to conclude that this was an evil age, ruled by the demons, who warred against men and angels. But they clung to their faith that the machinations of Satan and his hosts must soon come to a catastrophic end. God's promises guaranteed a glorious victory in the end for righteousness and a righteous people.

Note, however: the idea of a Satanic kingdom never occurred to either Greeks or Babylonians. The Jewish idea of war between good and evil had no parallel—except in Mazdaism. The Hebrews came within the area of Zarathushtrism just at the moment when they needed stimulation. Dualistic and eschatological doctrines appear in their literature in the centuries just after they had made that contact.

3. *Stimuli from Mazdaism* By all odds, Mazdaism is the most obviously fertile source of the strange new ideas that sprang up in Judaism during the last two or three centuries of the Second Temple. With that religion the Jews had been in contact during the two centuries of Persian rule in the period when Zarathushtrism (the religion of Zarathushtra in the genuine Gathas) had been purest and strongest, especially in the reigns of Darius I and his three immediate successors (522–404). Zoroastrism in its developed form, as it appears in Sassanian times and later, cannot be assumed to represent the religion which the Jews met in the Persian Empire, for Magianism had debased it. But there is evidence enough in the authentic Gathas of Zarathushtra, the Achaemenian royal inscriptions, and Greek writers of the fourth century to outline the chief features of the Iranian religion as it must have appeared to outsiders.

That Jews in the Persian Empire would have had abundant opportunity to become acquainted with Zarathushtrian religion can hardly be doubted. Many like Nehemiah, Mordecai, and Esther must have maintained their faith and loyalty while entering into the social and intellectual, as well as the commercial and administrative, life of the empire.

The Behistun inscription was written in four languages: in "Aryan" (Old Persian), Elamite, and Akkadian on the Rock and "on clay tablets and on parchment," to quote Darius, some of the parchment copies doubtless in Aramaic. Darius also states that "this inscription was sent by me everywhere among the provinces." [8] At Elephantine the Jewish colony had an Aramaic copy on papyrus, parts of which have been preserved to this day. A verse in Esther (8:9) seemingly records as common practice the dispatching of decrees "to every province in its own script and in its own language." It seems reasonable, therefore, to conclude that Jews everywhere would become familiar with at least the most important tenets of the religion that was taking shape as the result of Zarathushtra's labors, whether he lived in the late sixth century or earlier.[9]

The exact form of that religion cannot be determined for, aside from the royal inscriptions, there is no definitely datable body of documentary evidence. However, the ancient Jew of Susa or Persepolis or Babylon would hardly be troubled by modern critical distinctions. He would be impressed by religious ideas similar to his own and would be attracted to related notions that seemed to solve his practical and intellectual problems. The kind of Jew who was editing the Old Testament evidently was sufficiently sophisticated to select the better elements (as they still seem to us) in Iranian religion. That, along with the good, they took items which modern criticism would discard is hardly surprising, for both religions shared the common prescientific culture.

In Zarathushtrism there is a remarkable complex of attractive ideas. Hugo Gressmann named three elements as characteristic of Zarathushtra's religion: its peasant origin, its dualism, and its eschatology.[10] To these must be added, from the ancient point of view, its monotheism. Zarathushtra and his followers were not members of a world-conquering group, and the Persian monarchs never were seized with missionary zeal. The peasant origin of the religion, however, would appeal to the Jews, who for half a millennium had been farmers. Zarathushtrian dualism involved angelology and demonology, not so much as connected with physical ills and their cure as with a cosmic conflict between moral good and evil. The concepts of an evil spirit as ruler of this world and of a perpetual conflict between Ahuramazda, the "Wise

Lord," and Angra Mainyu, the "Hostile Spirit," or, more frequently, Druj, the "Lie," would exactly suit the mood of the exiled Hebrew thinkers. Zarathushtrian eschatology included a divine Savior, the eventual overthrow of the kingdom of evil, a final Judgment, future rewards and punishments in heaven and hell, a bodily resurrection of the righteous, and a benign reign of the "Wise Lord." It thus offered a resolution of the conflict between good and evil and a solution of the problem of God's justice. To these attractive notions must be added the impressive monotheism of the Achaemenian creed.

The fact that some of these beliefs, for example, demonology and future rewards and punishments, were already found among other neighbors of the Jews must be given due weight. Yet the presence of the whole internally consistent complex of eschatological ideas in a religion with which the Jews were familiar for centuries, just the centuries when the same complex finds its way into Judaism and thence eventually into Christianity, indicates the chief source of the stimuli. Strange and revolutionary as these new concepts were, they could appeal to the Jews for several reasons. They involved similar moral and religious assumptions. They came from an agricultural society with similar experiences of social struggle and frustration and similar insistent and tormenting moral problems.

Like the Jews, Darius and his successors worshiped one great God. Whether they were genuine and consistent Zarathushtrians is, for the present argument, immaterial. Monotheism is as clearly expressed in the earlier Achaemenian inscriptions as in the Avesta and the Old Testament. The inscriptions are especially valuable since they are the only definitely dated evidence now known. There is no information as to the religion of Cyrus. But that Darius I, Xerxes, Artaxerxes I ("reign of justice"), and Darius II were nominal Zarathushtrians is at least probable. Second Isaiah and Ezra-Nehemiah illustrate the favorable light in which the Jews viewed them. The "Achaemenian profession of faith" in the initial lines of inscription after inscription is thoroughly monotheistic and optimistic. It could not but arrest attention among monotheists.

A great god is Ahuramazda, who created this earth, who created yonder sky, who created man, who created happiness [or "well-being," *shiyatish*] for man, who made Darius king. . . .[11]

Xerxes' *"daiva* inscription," found in 1936 at Persepolis by Ernest Herzfeld in two Old Persian, one Elamite, and one Akkadian copy, is hardly more positive evidence. It is notable for its prohibition of *daiva* (i.e., "demon") worship and for its references to a happy future life. Xerxes proclaims that he destroyed a sanctuary of the demons (*daiva-dana*), probably at Babylon, and decreed, "The demons shall not be worshiped." The last paragraph but one twice promises that "he who has respect for the law that Ahuramazda has established and worships Ahuramazda and Arta ['Law, Justice'] reverently, he becomes both happy [*shiyata*] while living and blessed [*artava,* 'righteous, justified'?] when dead." [12] Even if motivated more by politics than religion, the inscription has a decidedly monotheistic ring.

As to the future life, a similar promise appears twice in the Behistun inscription (V. 19–20, 35–36). Darius says, "Whoso shall worship Ahuramazda, divine blessing will be upon him both while living and when dead." So also the Gatha Vahishto-ishti (Ys. 53:1) says that Mazda Ahura will give "the best possession," that is "blessedness for all time" (or "eternal blessedness") to Zarathushtra Spitama and "likewise to those who practice and learn the words and actions of his good religion." Complementary to this is the saying in the Gatha Ushtavaiti (46:11) that the wicked will be tormented forever as dwellers in the house of the Lie. Such expressions take for granted a well-established belief in a hereafter that is very different from either Sheol or Hades.[13]

Aside from some debatable references (in prayers) to "other gods," for over a hundred years (522–405) no god but Ahuramazda was named in the royal inscriptions. When, under Magian influence, Artaxerxes II introduced Mithra and Anahita along with Ahuramazda, it is to be assumed that the corruption of the Zarathushtrian faith was under way. However, the positive features that appealed to the Jewish mind were not lost. The emphasis on truth, justice, self-control, seen in Darius' portrayal of the ideal Achaemenid and, of course, found throughout the Avesta, would certainly attract the followers of the Old Testament prophets and the "Mosaic" Law.[14]

For Zarathushtra and the Achaemenian monarchs, Ahuramazda, like the Jewish Yahweh, was anything but a *deus otiosus;* he was actively engaged in the war against evil and far from indifferent to the struggles and sufferings of his followers. Yet, unlike the primitive tribal Yahweh, he was not fierce and terrible, but stern and just, like the Yahweh of the prophets, dispensing rewards and punishments fairly. He was jealous and demanding because of his vigorous engagement in the conflict with evil.

However, both Zarathushtrism and Judaism, when they met, were progressing from naïve anthropomorphism toward divine transcendence; hence the multiplication of intermediate beings. They threatened to form a barrier between God and man, even while they served to maintain monotheism in a polytheistic world and to balance demonism. The six Amesha Spenta, with whom Zarathushtra surrounded Ahuramazda, almost became subordinate deities. As hypostatized aspects, or attributes, of Ahura, along with Mazda, "Wisdom," they certainly are superior to the less meaningful archangels of Jewish angelology. It is interesting as a comment on the moral element in Persian religion that Asha (Arta in Old Persian), "Justice, Right, Law," is often named with Ahura as a consort, or equal.[15] Mazda, "Wisdom," is Ahura's alter ego, as in the Book of Proverbs and Jewish Wisdom literature.

As time went on, even perhaps in Zarathushtra's lifetime, to the Amesha Spenta, the "Immortal Beneficent Ones," were added various nature deities, as *Yazata,* "Adored Ones." They were to be worshiped, just as Greek, Roman, and Mexican gods became Catholic saints and as ancient heathen deities in the Near East and India became Moslem holy men. Parallel to the popular deities on the higher level of the Amesha Spenta were the various Jewish hypostatizations, the Shekinah, the Spirit (of God), the Name (of God), and the Logos.[16]

The Fravashis in Mazdaism correspond to the guardian angels, or spiritual doubles, in which Judaism and Christianity believed. The Egyptian had his *ka,* the Roman his *genius,* the Greek his *agathos daimon,* and there are numerous other parallels. In Acts (12:15) Peter's double was supposed to have appeared, when it was Peter himself. In the most Jewish of Gospels, Matthew (18:10), "little people" have their angelic doubles "in heaven, constantly watching the face of the Father in heaven." In the Old Testament, the belief appears in Daniel where Michael is the "great prince who has charge of" the Jewish people, while the "prince of the kingdom of Persia" strives with Michael and Gabriel.[17] The same hypostatization of collective groups appears in the angels of the churches in the New Testament Apocalypse.

In the history of Christian thought, the most puzzling and also theologically the most influential of all these group hypostatizations is the "One like a human being" ("son of man") of Daniel (7:13–14, 27). There, be it noted, he is a mere lay figure, a symbol of the "people of the saints of the Most High," as the various beasts are symbols of the nations that are enemies of God. He is hardly regarded as the Fravashi of the nation. In Ethiopic Enoch, however, "this Son of man" of one source is equated with the "Elect One" of another and becomes the representative, or vicegerent, of God, a being in his own right. He has a "face full of graciousness like one of the holy angels." He is "the Anointed," who sits on the right hand of God, just as, in the Persepolis reliefs, Xerxes in royal regalia comes to the right hand of the aged Darius. Enthroned by God, "this Elect One" becomes the final Judge, who condemns the wicked and to the righteous brings salvation from all their woes. In Enoch as in the Gospels, the "Son of man" takes the place of the anointed Davidic prince.[18]

That the "Son of man" in Daniel was nothing more than a symbol can be disputed. At most he was merely a Fravashi. In early Christian times the figure was drawn into speculation on the complex of Iranian ideas regarding Yima, Gayomart, Sraosha ("piety, obedience"), and the Savior, Saoshyant. Later speculation may have been influenced by the idea of Zarathushtra himself as the first man and final Saoshyant. As Gressmann believed, Egyptian myths of Re as the "Shining One" and of Thoth as the "Book Keeper" and Judge may have affected later Jewish and early Christian speculation. But all of this hardly appears until the second and third centuries of our era.[19] As to the meaning of the term "Son of man" in the Gospels, the decision depends on whether the figure is merely the symbol of the Book of Daniel or the Amesha Spenta of Ethiopic Enoch.

4. *Judaism and Mazdaism Contrasted*　In their emphasis on fundamental features, Judaism and Mazdaism differed. That the latter had been a peasant religion whose symbol was the cow and the former originally nomadic with the lamb as its favorite animal hardly mattered in the fifth century. There are, however, sharp contrasts. Zarathushtra's religion was neither tribal nor national, but rather individual, without being individualistic. His thought was dominated by a cosmic conflict between right and wrong, between Truth and the Lie. It was love of the Right and hatred of the Lie that gave his eschatology its characteristic qualities. His prayers to Ahuramazda and his exhortations to men continually voice his longing for the victory of Truth, Good Thought, Piety, and the goodly, desired Dominion (of Ahuramazda) over the Lie, Violence, the Worst Existence, Bad Thought, and Bad Word. (Thus, the Amesha Spenta are set over against the daiva.) He was deeply concerned with moral conduct and continually urged his hearers to be "in spirit and in actions . . . friends of Ahuramazda." By promoting the Right, he says, "We may be of those who prepare this world" for the *akereti,* its "good renewal" (regeneration), when the goodly, desired Dominion overthrows all evil.[20] This Renewal is the Jewish Great Reversal.

In its fundamental aspects the problem that threatened the faith of both the Judean prophets and the Mazdian reformer was the preponderance of evil in the world and the sufferings of the righteous at the hands of the wicked. Zarathushtra and the Jewish apocalyptists were at one in believing that God could not allow the cry for justice to remain unheard. The new age was at hand. Zarathushtra hoped to see it and thought of himself as the Saoshyant who was to prepare for it and (as some believe) was already in it. But the nationalism, the Chosen People complex, of Judaism gave its faith a very different aspect. Another striking difference was the Jews' lack of faith in their ability to affect the world's future. By obeying God's commands they could save themselves and their people, at least as a remnant, from annihilation. But the coming of his reign was his act alone at a time he had chosen, although for apocalyptists ever close at hand.

Even more fundamental was the "proletarian" aspect of the Jewish hope. Darius, or his scribes, still echoed the ancient tradition. He himself had wronged neither the weak nor the powerful; the strong should not wrong the weak nor the weak the strong (as if they could); there must be even-handed justice. He even says that the strong should not smite or destroy the weak,[21] a far from extravagant ideal.

Avestan references to the poor (both possibly later than Zarathushtra) carry on the correct attitude of the Achaemenian monarch. The Gatha Vahishto-ishti (Ys. 53:8–9) prays that bloodshed and death may come upon the workers of evil, but peace from their assaults may come to rejoicing villagers; that the Just Lord may take freedom and life from misbelievers, but give the "better portion" to the "right-living weakling," or "poor man." In the Ahuna Vairya (Ys. 27:13), the "Lord's Prayer" of Zoroastrianism, which may be only a little later than the founder, Zarathushtra (or Ahuramazda?) is "the shepherd of the poor." Once Zarathushtra calls himself Ahura's "poor man" (*dregum,* Ys. 34:5). The word in Old Persian, *skauthish,* translated "weak, poor, lowly," probably is replaced by Avestan *drigu,* which may mean no more than Arabic *faqir,* "mendicant." At best its force is given in the Gatha Vahishto-ishti, just quoted: they are the poor farmers who suffer from nomadic depredations or from exploitation by the rich and powerful of their own clans, who shall be punished.[22]

If this last definition is taken, Mazdian society and Zarathushtrian ethics move in the same general situation as the Prophets. But how different the emphasis! In the Old Testament and the apocalypses there are continual protests against the deprivations and oppression of the poor and the wickedness of the rich, the haughty, and the powerful who maltreat and exploit them. The complaints of the Psalmists and the anathemas of the Prophets are echoed again and again, particularly in the so-called Similitudes of Enoch (37–71). At the end "the kings and the mighty and all who possess the earth" will fall down and worship and vainly beg for forgiveness. They will be handed over to the angels for punishment and even the archangels will be astonished at the severity of the judgment pronounced upon them.

But "in those days a change shall take place for the holy and the elect, and the light of days shall abide upon them, and glory and honor shall turn to the holy." Then earth and hell and Sheol will give back what was entrusted to them, and the Elect One will choose the righteous and holy from among them. "And the earth will rejoice, and the righteous will dwell upon it, and the Elect will walk therein." [23]

The complete absence of any Hebrew belief in a future life, either immortality or resurrection, until after the centuries of contact with Persia can hardly be a mere coincidence. Of the mass of peculiar and often grotesque details of later Zoroastrian eschatology, Judaism knows little or nothing. Distinctive items, such as the Bridge of the Separator and the flood of Molten Metal, do not appear. Although the Gathas do not speak clearly on the nature of the resurrection, it is made abundantly evident that the dead would be allowed to enjoy the divine Sovereignty, for they are represented as sharing in all of the glories of the renewed earth.[24]

The future reign of God, "the goodly, desired Dominion" of Ahuramazda, was one idea on which Judaism and Zarathushtrism were most completely in accord, and it shaped the eschatology of both. Its basic concept, the universal sovereignty of a just and omnipotent God, seems to have been common and original. For Zarathushtra, the apocalypses, and Jesus, its full establishment was "at hand." The critical imminence of its coming and its overshadowing importance were alike for all three. Zarathushtra and Jesus are far from clear as to the conditions of life in the reign of God. Only in the palpably spurious phrase, "in the regeneration" (Matt. 19:28), does any allusion to a Stoic cosmic rebirth or a Zoroastrian "renewal" appear in the Gospels. Some of the apocalypses are more definite, but their testimony does not agree. The one point of general agreement is moral: the punishment of sin, the reward of righteousness, and the reign of justice and well-being; these are the marks of the reign of God.

5. *Christian Hopes* The great schism in Judaism, which produced rabbinic Judaism on the one hand and Christianity on the other, arose

chiefly over differences of attitude toward the future hope (technically, "eschatology"). All apocalyptists must have been essentially Pharisees. But the Pharisees, including the leading scribes and rabbis, emphasized the Law, the rabbinic traditions, and a middle-class (plebeian) ethics, while Christianity, as seen in Jesus and his earliest Jewish disciples, turned to the prophets and the proletarian doctrine of the apocalypses, which they interpreted as applying to the really "poor," the laborers and village farmers, the ignorant and "lawless" *'Am ha-'arets* of the rabbis.

The Qumran documents, recently discovered in the "Wilderness" just above the shore of the Dead Sea, are throwing welcome light on the Essenes and other separatist groups and possibly on the origins of Christianity.[25] What has so far appeared does not affect the larger aspects of the total situation, except to emphasize the significance of the apocalyptic hope and a common inheritance from Mazdaism. Both Mazdaism and Christianity shared the concept of a cosmic conflict between evil and good, as did the Qumran stalwarts and Jewish apocalyptists. The Gospel of John and the Covenanters borrow from Mazdaism the figure of conflict between light and darkness. It is clear that economic problems bulked large in the dissatisfactions of the early Jewish Christians and of the Covenanters, or Essenes, and that the want of social and economic justice was among the basic causes of these two sectarian divisions, as it was, perhaps even still more, the driving force behind the revolutionary group that brought on the Roman War.

Jesus and his disciples were from the *'Am ha-'arets*. It is difficult to surmise what they and the people who followed him in Galilee regarded as their most severe and pertinent criticism of the "scribes and Pharisees" and the conventional religiosity of the rulers of the synagogues. As it looks today and evidently as Matthew saw it (23:23–26), the chief evil was emphasis on the observance of cult rules and traditions to the neglect of the "weightier matters of the Law, justice, mercy, and fidelity." Certainly Jesus made it his business to criticize most bitterly all literal obedience to the Law in contrast to an overflowing spirit of good will coupled with actions that demonstrated wholehearted loving-kindness and self-sacrificing purpose.

Along with this, the beginning, middle, and end of Jesus' work was preaching the great good news, saying that the reign of God was at hand. From early in its history, Christianity missed the meaning of the Greek word *basileia—malkhutha* in Jesus' Aramaic. Like Zarathushtra, who had no Canaan, Jesus was concerned, not with an area or country or future Jewish kingdom centered at Jerusalem, not even with heaven, but with God's sovereignty, his lordship, his dominion, his reign over men. The reign of God over men's hearts and lives was "the one thing needful," the one thing that would bring heaven to earth. That was the one pearl of value, worth all of a man's possessions, because it was the door to all other values. The sovereignty of God, so long awaited, would bring all other good things with it.

Among the most significant of those values was the righting of economic and social wrongs. Like Amos, Micah, and Isaiah, Jesus was a prophet of the poor and needy. When God ruled, the poor and hungry would have food, clothing, and shelter; the sad would be comforted. But the rich, who had had their fill of comfort, the well-fed, the play-boys who had had more than their share of fun, would suffer that complete turn of the wheel of fortune that the ancients believed they deserved. Under the dominion of God there was scant room for the rich, the proud, the self-righteous, the self-satisfied. But for those who approached God in sincere humility and penitence and obedience, like Zaccheus and the other tax farmer of the Lucan parable, the windows of heaven and the gate of the kingdom were open wide.[26]

Jesus followed the apocalyptists in the vividness and urgency of their demand for judgment, for present, immediate vindication of God's justice. But he did not believe that the world and mankind were ruled by Satan and his demons. Like the Old Testament prophets and official Judaism, he was not a dualist. Many of the apocalyptic writers believed in the two realms of good and evil, of God and Satan. They practically took over the dualism of Zoroastrianism. Jesus' basic message had a deeper foundation, in the immemorial faith of the Near East, both Semitic and Iranian, in the thoroughly moral character of the divine oversight of the ethical and spiritual interests of the world of gods and men. God ruled the world.

Jesus' sense of the injustices of life, his recognition of the futility of revolt against Rome and of any efforts of the people to better society, along with his acceptance of the personalistic theory of nature and history as directly subject to divine direction and miraculous interference, led him to his major error. Men could do nothing to hasten the coming of God's reign. The end was at hand. But only God himself could conquer evil and "make the world excellent." Long generations of frustration and helplessness on the part of God's people made the common fatalistic view plausible. In this he and his age fell below the prophets, for the prophets had believed that God worked in history through human agency.

Because of its political and nationalistic connotations, Jesus never called himself the Anointed, the Messiah, and he forbade his disciples to use that title of him. Instead he tried to teach them to accept the designation, "Son of man." As a "man," he must suffer and possibly die before the reign of God could arrive in all its glory and power. As the Elect One, the "man" chosen to proclaim the good news of the coming reign of God, he would also reign.

He never called himself the Savior of the world, never hinted that he was a sacrifice for the sins of the world, or was placating the wrath of his loving heavenly Father, or dying an innocent victim to save others from punishment. He saw his duty to preach the good news, even in that most wicked of cities, Jerusalem. He died there, and his confidence that God would at once bring in the new age proved false. The apocalyptists' dream was a brilliant but unhappy illusion. Yet, by the "greater things" that Jesus' disciples were able to do after and because of his death,[27] his confidence in God's goodness and justice, his moral and social convictions, and his hope for mankind were proved to be, not false, but grounded in the nature of society and of the individual.

The unforeseen and unaccountable history of Christianity has strangely vindicated Jesus' confidence—not by blazing catastrophe or miraculous transformation. No Holy City has come down out of heaven upon an earth cleansed by the fires of divine wrath. As in all the story of the earth and the history of mankind, no gradual and steady increase of goodness and greatness has been recorded, even since

Jesus lived and died. Yet his influence, as divine Counselor, has never perished from the earth.

However, almost immediately his teachings were sadly perverted by his most devoted and brilliant followers. For Paul he was waging victorious war against demonic hosts of wickedness in the heavenly regions and would soon return on the clouds of heaven.[28] For John the victory had already been won when he was "lifted" up, and the Pentecostal coming of the Spirit had been the Second Coming.[29] His Jewish disciples could find in "Messiah" and "son of David" titles fitting to interpret him to their Jewish world, thus practically pleading guilty to the charge which he had vigorously repudiated but on which he had been crucified. When they carried the good news of God abroad, they called him Savior, Son of God, and *Kyrios,* Lord, thus putting him beside the deified emperors and the many deities of the pagan world. His crucifixion had to be explained as a temporary victory won by the demonic world, turned into a magical catharsis that destroyed the Satanic kingdom, or as an appeasement of the wrath of an offended and vengeful deity and a satisfaction of the demands of his inexorable laws—this in the name of Jesus' just and loving heavenly Father.

Under the glow of the "immense majesty of the Roman peace," the Hellenistic world recalled its own deep longings for the restraint of ruthless power and the protection of the common man from an economic order of heartless competition for wealth and luxury. Hesiod's complaints (in the very century of Amos, Hosea, and Micah) of the oppression of the poor farmer by the rich and powerful, Solon's attempted establishment of law and order, Aristotle's emphasis on justice had been forgotten. Aristocracies and oligarchies had ruled in their own interests. Democracy had degenerated into ochlocracy, mob rule, led by demagogues and selfish minorities. As Livy put it, "An accumulation of wealth had stimulated avarice; the superabundance of material goods an itch on the part of men to indulge in a passion that is ruinous to everything, including themselves."

In such a situation, the Roman world turned, on the one hand, to the benevolent justice of the Divine Augustus as their Savior, and, on the other, to proliferating religious sects that promised, not justice on earth, but peace and security in Elysian Fields through magico-mystical union with Mithra, or Attis, or Isis. The Christians, quite naturally, were hopeless of attacking and overthrowing the entrenched social and economic evils of Roman culture. Why should they attempt the impossible? The "reign of God was at hand." Christ must soon "put all his enemies under his feet." Even "death would be swallowed up in victory." Christianity succeeded because it was not a social-moral reform movement but promised what men most desired, escape from sin and an evil world.

Only the Epistle of James carried on the tradition of social justice for the poor as the prophets, the apocalyptists, and Jesus had voiced it. Along with vigorous exhortations to individual morality in action as well as in word, James emphasized God's opposition to the proud and his graciousness to the humble, the final humiliation of the haughty and the exaltation of the lowly. He overlooked the woes of the hordes of Roman slaves. But he is famous for his excoriation of the rich for their pride of place, their injustice to their workers, their luxurious ways, and their murder of the righteous—all of which draws a warning for them to weep and howl for the miseries that are coming upon them. Christians, therefore, should be patient "until the coming of the Lord."

Judaism retired within itself after the Bar-Kochba revolt, content to preserve itself as a religio-racial community. The social-ethical tradition slept until reawakened by modern liberals. A subject worth considering would be the trend to the city and to commerce on the part of the two originally rural and proletarian religious groups, the Hebrews and the Zoroastrians, which produced apocalyptic eschatology.

The many facets that primitive Christianity exhibited to the world, as Shirley Jackson Case showed, gave it a wide appeal and allowed its adaptation to all sorts and conditions of men, not without sad alterations. Judaism had rejected the high mission to which Second Isaiah summoned it, to convey to the world the values of its noble experience in history. Christianity was left to carry on, not always successfully. The persecutions it bravely suffered contributed to the respect in which it came to be held, and its inherent qualities won a large minority of the

Roman world. The disfigurement it suffered at the hands of its own leaders and of the untaught masses that followed fashion into its churches gave it temporary success at the expense of crippling weaknesses and even dismemberment.

The diverse and contradictory conceptions of society and history, of morals and religion, to be found in the Old and New Testaments proliferated into sharp divisions and bitter conflicts. The history of the evolution of Christianity is like that of plant and animal genera and of man himself. Progress has been slow, uncertain, often retrogressive, and yet it has been real. It does not promise perfection; there is no prospect of finality, no millennium even on the most distant horizon. Yet there has been movement, if never to the best, yet unquestionably toward the better.

Today the neoprophetic hope is as sadly splintered as Christendom itself. The apocalyptic element lives on in Second Coming and millenarian sects. The prophetic proletarian ethical tradition is maintained chiefly by liberals to whom apocalypticism is anathema. The majority of Christians care for neither, but divide their interests among ritual, theology, conventional individualistic morality, emotional salvation, and churchmanship of which Jesus knew nothing.

Yet the Beatitudes make sure that the immemorial faith in justice for the weak and helpless shall never be quite forgotten. Matthew may etherialize prophetic morality. But the fact remains that Jesus said, "Happy, you who are poor, for the reign of God is yours! . . . Woe to you who are rich!"

CHAPTER XVII

Hope in History

1. *History as Adventure* The foregoing survey of a portion of the ancient past closes on a pessimistic note. Is the conclusion, nevertheless, justified that hope for the world is to be found in history? It is, and that for two reasons. First, broadly conceived and rightly understood, history, even in this brief survey, demonstrates the potentialities of human nature and human culture. A survey of recent history would strongly reinforce the conclusion. Second, from history as from no other source illumination falls upon the uncertain path into the future.

As Alfred North Whitehead has said, history presents summits of attainment far beyond our own immediate experience.[1] Appeal to its authority is an appeal to reason, the judge that is over all authority, for history has authority only so far as it is rationally interpreted. In history as such human culture and the human race have become what they are. Written history, with all the rest of society's cultural heritage, distinguishes the human race from all other animals. As the collective and collected memory of mankind, it places man on the higher level where cultural achievement is cumulative. No individual has to start from the beginning. Consequently history, rightly viewed, offers good reason to hope for man's further advance and for the progress of religion. What, then, is a rational interpretation, a "right view," of history?

Whitehead himself does not discuss the philosophy of history, but, within his philosophy of organism, he illustrates a most adaquate interpretation. His philosophy puts special emphasis on interrelations, togetherness, as resulting in the emergence of the new, the higher, and the better. Objectively and comprehensively regarded, society is part of a total organism that provides both permanence and adventure. Every occasion, or event, is a product of the *eros* of the universe. It results from the concrescence or growing together, of previous occasions and constantly produces new occasions without limit.

"The religious impulse in the world," according to Whitehead, "transforms the dead facts of science into the living drama of history" and creates perpetual novelty. A "Deistic impulse of energy . . . implants in the historic process new aims at other ideals." The organismic process is a constant series of high adventures into the unknown. The same terms that describe the actions of the neutrons and protons and mesons in creating an atom, the combinations of atoms to make a molecule, and the coming together of a multitude of atoms to make a star can be used to describe the growth of a tribe, a state, a culture. History is a process of "concrescence" that records progress. And progress, according to Whitehead, "consists in modifying the laws of nature so that the Republic on Earth may conform to that Society to be discerned ideally by the divination of Wisdom." Tennyson had beautifully expressed two of Whitehead's characteristic ideas in Ulysses' words,

> I am a part of all that I have met;
> Yet all experience is an arch wherethro'
> Gleams that untravell'd world whose margin fades
> For ever and for ever when I move.

What Whitehead is saying Paul had said: "In everything God works for good" (Rom. 8:28, RSV). Whitehead, like Paul, by no means overlooks the existence of evil. Beauty and harmony are two terms often used by Whitehead to describe the Good. Their opposites and whatever destroys them are evil. But values are relative. There are many levels of ideals. Imperfection striving for higher perfection is better than a lower perfection, a lower ideal achieved. Stability, perfect peace, perfect security at any level are evil. "Discord—in itself destructive and evil"—can contribute to harmony and beauty by shifting the aim "from the tameness of outworn perfection" to a new and vital ideal.

In its way the Byzantine Empire represents the beauty of classical Greece preserved unchanged for a thousand years to wither under "the tedium of indefinite repetition." The destruction of the old Greece and Rome by the rise of two new religions, Christianity and Islam, and the barbarian invasions—evil as they seemed—enforced new adventures, "the search for new perfections." Tame, vague, low, static, all are terms to describe evil. Evil is not merely negative or privative; it is positive and destructive. But, fortunately, it is not stable or cumulative, while good is positive, creative, and cumulative. Civilization is preserved by the zest of adventure on the upward path toward new ideals. "Morals and religion arise as aspects of this human impetus towards the best in each occasion." "New occasions teach new duties."

History as such, then, is man's great adventure in search of ever new perfections. Aristotle remarked that "when we are able to give an account conformable to experience" regarding any matter, we shall be able "to say something worth saying about its essential nature." [2] History's records of man's experience in this great adventure have been amassed, sifted, and interpreted with the aid of modern science in all of its forms to provide increasing volumes of accounts "conformable to experience." Here is information regarding the essential character of the human race and its cultural achievements.

Human nature, that is, human anatomy, physiology, and psychology, has not had time to evolve since written history began to record man's experience or, indeed, for thousands of previous years. It is society, not man, that has changed in the last 50,000 years. The actual experience of men of 5000 years ago, when writing began, is, therefore, still valuable today. A people like the Hebrews, who lived in the midst of great cultures, but who were not deeply corrupted by wealth, who were rarely bitten by military ambitions, and who had not suffered from an enervating climate and luxurious living or from intractable physical conditions or dire poverty, could make observations regarding individual conduct and social relations that have pertinence for today. The early and long literacy of the peoples of Egypt and the Near East and the modern historian's constantly increasing mastery of their histories give unsurpassed value to the records of their experience and observations of life.

2. *Ancient and Modern Misconceptions* Their interpretation of their experience is quite another matter. Whitehead has remarked that the profound suggestions of Plato's *Dialogues* are half-smothered by the archaic misconceptions of the age in which he lived.[3] It is illuminating to read Aristotle's keen and pertinent remarks on many matters of scientific interest and then turn to his pathetic attempts to explain light and sound on the basis of the theory of four elements, earth, air, fire, and water.[4] His observations are often remarkably keen and correct, if his lack of tools and of technical concepts and terms be considered. His interpretations are often laughable. The ancients' conceptions of God and the universe were inevitably naïve and gross in the predawn age of science and philosophy, as gross as their four elements. Their observations of astronomical phenomena were often correct and are still valuable. Their astrology, their conception of the heavenly bodies as divine, their myths of the gods, their demonology and magic, and their cults, above all their dying and rising savior-gods, have value only as revealing the stumbling and futile steps that infantile processes of thought were taking in an effort to understand the universe.

The same criticisms apply *a fortiori* to the cosmology and theology of the Hebrews. How simple, direct, and pertinent their conceptions of social morality as compared with their attempts to understand the divine and to interpret history! With all due respect for their monotheism and their ethics, it cannot be said that, as a group, they ever escaped from their primitive mythologies and the dubious religious conceptions inherited from their fierce nomadic ancestors. Monotheism and morality could not be expected to clarify their conceptions of natural, social, and psychological phenomena. Their prescientific notions of God and his ways were untouched by any suggestions of a reign of law. God could do whatever he would. Monstrous ideas and actions ascribed to him must be right. His will was law.

It should be unnecessary to waste space and time on the negative lessons of history. Yet hoary errors persist. What must be eliminated from our ancestral traditions may be summarized in a few general statements. First of all stands a basic principle. Anything handed down by ancient tradition in the Bible or Plato or anywhere else that contradicts the positive findings of modern science must be forgotten.

For example, that the earth is not the center of the universe is an important fact for theology. Even more important is the discovery that God works by law and not by miracle in either nature or history. Neither is the world a prey to irrationality, either demonic or divine. What appears to be irrational or miraculous is merely not yet, and perhaps never will be fully, understood.

Physical nature is still mysterious in spite of the almost miraculous progress of science in the last three centuries. Hardly a beginning has been made in understanding the laws of human nature and the springs of human behavior. The observations of human conduct by the ancients were keen and pertinent. But, in the area where the human impinges on the divine, their faulty cosmologies and myths and their anthropomorphic conceptions of God corrupted their conclusions. The Christian has the right on the basis of his experience to believe that he can have communication with God and that he profits immensely by the experience, although he cannot demonstrate the fact to others. But this gives him no basis for a belief in activities of demonic or angelic agencies or of divine forces aside from those embodied in physical nature and the human spirit. Such beliefs belong to a prescientific mentality. All notions, ancient and modern, must be judged by rational, scientific standards.

In the second place, a set of remarkably valuable ethical standards and religious concepts are to be found in the experiences of the Hebrew prophets and other ancients, and, above all, in Jesus' teachings and life. This is a generally accepted fact that needs no emphasis or argument. But all such materials are to be criticized and reinterpreted by their own and subsequent experience, including naturally our own. Nothing finite is perfect. Only a purely static conception of society and of God's ways of working can maintain that there has been no spirit of truth to lead men beyond the attainments of the first century, or that the Old and New Testaments hold the total revelation of the mind of God, even when they are disencumbered of all ancient misconceptions.

In the light of modern experience, conceptions of revelation and of methods of interpretation must be revised. Psychology has made enough progress to clarify the idea of revelation, even though parapsychology deals with seeming potentialities as yet unexplained. The late Archbishop William Temple emphasized a truth that must be continually reaffirmed. God does not reveal truths to men. All truth comes to human beings through their own and others' experience in the largest sense, often through hard and long labors of the mind and sufferings of the spirit. Communion with God tends to clarify and catalyze the mind and restrain selfish subjectivism, as Canon B. H. Streeter argued at length shortly before his death.[5] God inspires men. He works neither physical nor intellectual miracles for them.

Man makes his ethical and religious discoveries by individual and social experiment. Archaeology, biography, and history, indeed all written and unwritten records of man's past, are laboratory notebooks describing successful and unsuccessful experiments. The modern sciences, physical, biological, psychological, sociological, anthropological, cultural, and historical, along with philosophy, are attempts to understand God's ways of working in the world. For successful lives and successful societies, a knowledge of the laws that govern all of these areas is necessary. The theist can neglect none of them. Such knowledge is the reward of hard labor and critical thought. Errors of the atomic scientist, the physician, the sociologist, of any scientist, and of any teacher of ethics and religion can destroy human lives and sciences.

Errors of biblical interpretation are especially dangerous in view of the reverence in which the Bible is held. By strange mental twists very human interpretations are given the value of divine revelation. Insistence on a literal application of biblical texts and concepts to modern problems can lead only to absurdity because of the abysmal gulf between ancient and modern conditions. Allegorical, symbolical, and typological interpretations are equally unacceptable because they claim biblical authority for what the fervid imagination of some modern mind reads into the sacred text.

For the Christian a fundamental principle is that both the Old and the New Testament are to be interpreted in the light of Jesus' basic ethical demands and his equally basic symbolic concept of God as a just and loving heavenly Father—all as seen in the light of nineteen centuries of Christian experience of God, society, and the universe.

That involves modern historical method. Such a method forbids all a priori theological assumptions, whether drawn from the Bible or the creeds. The true historian makes every attempt to be thoroughly objective. The Bible must be interpreted on the same principles as Plato or Aristotle or Herodotus, with critical empathy, with religious feeling, but without prejudice. Before the bar of truth the Christian interpreter can demand no immunities or favors on the ground that his are religious beliefs. Ancient, Reformation, or modern creeds must not affect his judgment. Interpretation is not eisegesis but exegesis. It puts no meanings into the texts but only brings out what is already there.

Among particular notions to be discarded are belief in miracles, in a direct divine interference in history, in "special providences," in a semimiraculous fulfillment of Old Testament prophecy in the New Testament. Attempts to harmonize the Old Testament with the New, to discover the New in the Old, and to argue away the inconsistencies and contradictions within the Old and within the New Testament constitute a denial of progress and a confession of historical incompetence. There is no consistent "biblical theology," except for a blindly uncritical mind.

It goes without saying that adventism and millenarianism in all their forms are impossible. Connected with them, explicitly or implicitly, is a semidualistic belief in angels, in the rule of the earth by Satan and his demonic hosts, and in a miraculous end of history by divine intervention, with a final spectacular Judgment. These beliefs, reinterpreted and denied by the Gospel of John, can have no place in the modern mind. The neoprophetic cosmologies and theories of history, along with all kinds of messianic speculations, which flourished in the times of trouble in late Judaism and early Christianity, can furnish no consolation in our modern shaken world.

It is now generally agreed that evidence from proof texts, chosen at random from here and there in the Bible, has no value. It is equally true that biblical stories and concepts, taken out of their historical context, inevitably are falsely interpreted. Theories of man's sinfulness based upon the story of the Fall, the concept of the Covenant and the Chosen People, including foreordination and election, and also any

literal notion of a paradisiacal reign of God on earth are entirely outside of intelligent consideration. Any concept of man that is anthro-
pologically and historically false or that is based on prescientific concepts cannot be theologically acceptable. Concepts of material rewards
for right conduct contradict accepted modern ethical standards. The
values of Hebrew history and the biblical documents are to be found
in entirely different directions.

3. *Positive Conclusions* To turn from misinterpretations and ob-
scurations of the historical evidence, from the negative to the positive,
how can valid conclusions be summarized? What has been attempted
in the earlier chapters of this discussion is an objective historical sketch
of biblical society and cultural ideas within the frame of ancient Near
Eastern society. In contrast to theological constructions of history, it
is intended to illustrate a nondogmatic interpretation of the past in the
area from which the basic cultural elements and especially the moral
and religious ideas of Western civilization derive. In summary, what
were the essential features of the cultural developments in this highly
favored and richly productive part of the world? Does its history suggest hope or despair?

Two familiar notions, evolution and progress, have dominated the
discussion. They are not assumptions, or presuppositions, but hypotheses. They were chosen to guide the discussion because they are now
widely accepted as theories that satisfactorily interpret experience. The
question has been: Does this long stretch of history, the best known
that we have, substantiate the theory of evolution and progress? If
so, what is the nature of the progress that is discovered?

In Chapter II a summary answer was given as to geophysical and
biological matters. Hardly anyone who understands the evidence will
deny that the evolutionary hypothesis must be accepted as the best
explanation of the facts as now known. Man stands at the summit of
a long process of development and, as the crown of creation, he can
look back upon billions of years of progress. Man's peculiar physical
and mental constitution enables him to carry out the divine command
of Genesis (1:28) to fill the earth and subdue it and have dominion
over everything upon it.

It is difficult to see how anyone can follow with unprejudiced mind the story of human development from the Stone Age to modern times and not discern the remarkable progress that has been made. There are not a few persons who believe they could have planned a better world. They have definitions of progress that are not satisfied by what they discover in history and its product, modern society. Only he who can doggedly shut his eyes can blandly insist that this is the best of all possible worlds. It is equally ridiculous for cynical self-confident rationalism or theological dogmatism to refuse to accept the universe —and history.

In the gloom of two world wars and their even more terrible possible consequences, many persons scorn a theory of progress. Biologists are slow to tie evolution to progress; sociologists and anthropologists, as scientists, are wary of theories and hesitate to argue for human progress. Yet the facts, judged from a widely human point of view—the only view human beings are justified in adopting—can lead to but one conclusion. Geological, biological, and finally cultural progress has been an inescapable reality. From the amoeba to man evolution consumed uncounted aeons. From the first human beings to the twentieth century is a much briefer period. But even within historic times, from the caves and first rude huts of primitive man to the United Nations building, not only growth of culture but the enlargement of human capacity is almost beyond our comprehension.[6]

Evolution and human progress have been, not only slow, but halting and uncertain. Degeneration has often seemed irreversible. So the Egyptians of the first millennium thought as they looked at the pyramids of 2000 years before. So the members of each of the great empires and cultures of the Near East must have felt as they saw new, barbarous enemies overrun their countries and destroy the finest products of their hands and brains. History exhibits long periods when destruction was not visibly replaced by construction, when no future greatness was in sight. Yet there always has been recovery, and always, despite real losses, a step upward to higher levels.

Christianity has suffered its own waves of fortune and misfortune. Its very successes have all too often proved to be disasters, just as the size of the gigantosauria and titanotheras became a handicap. As cultures built on slave labor blossomed quickly and brilliantly and then slowly decayed because of the inherent defects of that type of social and economic organization, so also Christianity, spreading rapidly because of court influence and compromises with heathenism, shortly became, so it seemed, completely stabilized and immobilized under the rule of Pope and priesthood. Only a new growth in Irish, Anglo-Saxon, and Teutonic lands produced progress. Western society has constantly exhibited (and still exhibits) the weaknesses inherent in a half-christianized populace, ruled by an ecclesiastical leadership that has yielded to the corruptions of power and wealth. The highly romanticized Age of Faith produced a highly unsatisfactory culture. As Western civilization is threatened today by the products of the science that has produced its obesity of wealth and luxury, so Christianity is threatened again by the gigantism of swollen church rolls and by the corruption of power and wealth. Yet there has been progress.

4. *Social and Economic Morality* Along with evolution and progress, a third subject has served as a guiding thread throughout this discussion. The history of the development of ethics and religion, particularly in aspects of socio-economic justice, is not only a guiding thread but a standard measure of progress. Material and intellectual culture, biblical interpretation, theology, and ecclesiastical organization mean nothing unless men learn to live together in an ordered, democratic society, unless Christians try to do God's will as it is done in heaven. "Faith and order" have no value without "life and work," to use notable ecumenical phrases.

Social morality is not only the touchstone of cultural progress. Granted that there are many others, both material and spiritual, and that not all morality is concerned with social and economic justice; still, insofar as a society does not embody the ideal of regard for one's neighbor as for oneself and does not allow all men an equal opportunity to live useful and happy lives, the other values are tarnished or destroyed. But social ethics is useful to the historian for another reason. The history of the fluctuations of moral ideas through nearly all the recorded experience of mankind is peculiarly significant and instructive as setting forth in capital letters the nature of cultural progress as to the fact and as to its limitations.

The historical permutations of the proletarian ideal make a fascinating, not to say tragic, drama. How strange that, so early in history, the ideal ruler was a protector of the weak; and the poor, the humble, and the helpless were pre-eminently the clients of the gods, while the rich, the proud, and the powerful were enemies of divine justice and of the gods! Who would have expected to discover a proletarian revolutionary as a social reformer restraining the rich oppressors of the poor in the name of the gods of Sumer over 4000 years ago? Graft, extortion, corruption among officials, excessive taxation, almost all of the sins now known in our cities, were common practices. Two reformers, 400 years apart, claim to have swept them all away—for a period—just as reformers "clean up" our modern cities.[7]

Civilization owes a great deal to the Sumerians. Over 5000 years ago this farmer people, first made known to modern historians within a century, had produced the cuneiform script, one of the earliest and most widely used methods of recording men's thought, thus making human experience definitely transmittible and recorded history possible. They taught all of the Near East their letters. Theirs was the classical language and script of the Near East for perhaps 3000 years. They had produced a group of prosperous towns in southern Mesopotamia, with successful irrigation, wide commerce, and remarkable artisanship. The tombs of King Abargi and Queen Shubad have revealed to the astonished world the wealth of gold, silver, and copper and of artistic skill that had accumulated at the small city of Ur perhaps a thousand years before Abraham.

Even more astonishing than the gorgeous silver and gold jewelry, weapons, and vessels found in the royal tombs were the pathetic human sacrifices that accompanied the burials. In the tomb of King Abargi, besides two wagons with their asses, lay at least sixty-five persons, men and women, who accompanied him into the next world. His queen, Shubad, took thirty-five with her. In another death-pit six men and sixty-eight women had been buried. In still another lay a richly clad woman with four men, apparently servants, and a gold cylinder seal of "Meskalamdug, the king," evidently a parting gift from the monarch to his queen. At two different levels above there had been sacrificial ceremonies and a man buried in a coffin at each. In every case the buried retainers showed no sign of violence. Apparently they took a lethal drug and lay down quietly in close ranks to die with their master or mistress.[8]

This seems strangely out of keeping with other evidence regarding Sumerian culture. Their economy combined private ownership with state-controlled irrigation and apportionment of land, autocratic military rule and well-ordered legal codes with democratic judicial procedures. They prized their freedom and lived simply and laboriously at a rising cultural level, but with a wide and ever widening gap between the poor and the rich. With increasing wealth, greed and the lust for power bred rapacity within the little city-states and wars between them. Military leaders became monarchs, their henchmen petty oppressors. Social ills demanded reformation, for they had not only traditions but written accounts of their former freedoms.

From the death-pits at Ur, the ghosts of slain retainers rise in incongruous protest against a picture of ancient Sumer as a lost Eden. The very traditions to which Uru-kagina appealed cannot be taken as proving that the poor had ever been other than poor or had ever been effectively protected. The descriptions of Gudea's "Paradise" witness to the everyday evils that were to be momentarily forgotten. The terms the Sumerians used to describe their ideals of justice so impressed their wild nomadic Semitic conquerors, the Akkadians, that for over 2000 years the royal decrees of the Akkadians, the Assyrians, and, indeed, all Semitic-speaking peoples echoed their phrases about the rights that the laws of the gods assured the poor and the helpless. Ruler after ruler acknowledged his obligation to respect and uphold the rights of him that had no helper. Until the Greeks and the Romans appeared, men believed (although they did not practice the doctrine) that governments should protect the weak from the strong, the poor from the rich.

The Israelite prophets had taken up the tradition in its full literal sense, and the apocalyptists and Psalmists had echoed it, even though sometimes only as a slogan. For Jesus it had its full prophetic meaning once more. Unfortunately, except as recorded in the Bible, it disappeared when Jesus, the man from the country, the Jewish villager, was replaced by Paul, the city man, the Roman citizen. The record seems to exhibit a clear example of retrogression in ethical standards.

Yet, during the long centuries when the West was slowly living down the evils and growing out of the weaknesses of Roman imperialism and Hellenistic sophism, the social-ethical tradition was kept alive, in suspended animation, it must be granted, but still viable. The laws of heaven have never been observed in fact, but only professed in word. The poor have been remembered with charity, rarely with opportunity. But in that regard progress has been made, for opportunity, not merely charity, has become the goal of modern social ethics. Neither Christianity nor democracy has done away with poverty. Government by millionaires and churches built by their gifts promise little for the future. Two world wars have produced only that sardonic caricature of the social gospel, Russian communism, and in America a reaction to self-sanctified capitalism. Yet there has been progress. Who would go back to live in little Sumer of 5000 years ago?

CHAPTER XVIII

What Hope in History?

1. *The Processes of Progress*   Progress is possible because perfection is impossible. Progress is probable because it has always resulted from the struggles and conflicts of the past. Progress is inevitable because of the intrinsic urge of energy in the universe and man's insatiable curiosity and dissatisfaction.[1] But what kind of progress? What hope can be found in the paleontological and archaeological records of 500,-000 years and the written records of 5000?

Utopianism is a vain dream. Human perfectibility means going on toward perfection but never reaching it. The reign of God is never at hand; it never will come on earth. At times certain types of progress come rapidly, but none comes without effort. More often progress results from struggle and conflict. Destruction must precede construction. The overthrow of an extremely unsuccessful monarchy and then of a venal and selfish priesthood and its Temple had to precede the rise of a religious Judaism. Sumerians, Akkadians, and Assyrians, Babylonians and Persians, Macedonians and Romans, the Holy Roman Empire and medieval feudalism have had their day, their legacy not quite spent. Doubtless modern industrialism, capitalism, socialism, and communism will have to go the way of slavery, serfdom, and guilds. No social organization is perfect and permanent.

With no acceptance of the ancients' belief in fate and with no wanton interpolation of Freudian bestiality, the story of Oedipus is still the story of mankind. In spite of their best efforts to avoid the weaknesses and perversities that beget disaster, individuals and societies often bring tragedies upon themselves by a false step, a fatal error. The best of intentions cannot make up for mistakes of judgment or will.

285

In spite of the higher idea of God that Jeremiah and Ezekiel proclaimed, it is true that, when the fathers have eaten sour grapes, the children's teeth are often set on edge, not because the nomads' relentless God, like the ancient Furies, pursues the children unto the third and fourth generation, but because the laws of heredity, physical and social, which bring good, also bring evil. Weeds and briars grow by the same laws as wheat. Loss brings gain, but gain also brings loss. Progress in a new cultural activity often leads to neglect and deterioration in an older one. Society swings too violently from one extreme to another.

It is true that the values of culture accumulate from generation to generation as its evils do not. But all true progress in values increases sensitivity. Evils unrecognized by the fathers plague their children and demand redress. Therefore conflict, not against imaginary demons or with the aid of imagined angels, is always inevitable. The higher the progress, the more bitter the conflict. The atmosphere is rarer in higher altitudes. Conflict is grounded in man's double nature. He belongs to both the low levels and the high. History can promise neither peace on earth nor a paradisiacal end to its conflicts.

The mills of history grind slowly. Human emotional volatility and impatience are enemies of progress. The ancient apocalyptist always saw the end at hand. Proponents of the social gospel fondly thought the end was near. Their antagonists now deny the possibility of progress because the social gospel failed to produce what its leaders promised. The evidence for progress rests upon the course of history during the relatively brief period of only a few thousand years, when culture has increased both in quality and in quantity. Great changes could not be expected.

Some years ago Rabindranath Tagore wrote apropos of man's ambitious haste,

When God's will to create shook the sky into fiery whirls,
His power, in the beginning of years, built up its triumph in towering hills.
But his dream waited millions of barren nights before he smiled on his first
    shy flower.[2]

Human nature and the processes of history being what they are, simple formulas for progress are impossible to discover. Christian opponents of progress, who wish to avoid unsettling ideas of social morality, often call for an individual gospel, a simple gospel of repentance and conversion. Only saved men, they say, can save society. Impatient proponents of the social gospel insist that life cannot be good in an evil society; a changed society would change men. They have too easily fallen into legalism—the passage of a prohibition amendment would end all evil. They overlooked the fact that respect for law is in short supply in the United States and that it can arise only from a much sturdier temper in society. An unemotional conversion is demanded that does not place the highest value upon quick profits and sensuous, not to say sensual, amusements.

For progress, improvement must come to both individual character and social environment. It is not a matter of merely making laws and inculcating morals. Intelligence as well as good will is necessary. The laws of growth for both individuals and society must be known and used. Psychology, economics, and sociology, as well as morals and religion, are involved. There are no short cuts. Yet the equipment of human nature includes the good will and intelligence that make progress possible.

2. *Problems of Faith and Works* Certain disavowals and affirmations must be set down to prevent misunderstandings and prepare for a final synthesis. Past experience makes it indubitably clear that no one, whether Christian or atheist, should pin his faith to any particular known economic or political theory or social pattern as if it were perfect and final. None satisfies mature examination; none represents the reign of God. History has exhibited constant change—and progress—from cave and camp to village, from village to city; from city-state to empire; from slavery to feudalism, monarchy, democracy, state socialism—the changes, the combinations, have been almost infinite. Surely (to take one example) something better can be found than elected legislative bodies that allow usurpations of power by cantankerous old men, that easily yield to corruption, and that crown demagoguery with the highest honors. Neither Protestantism nor Catholicism is the final

288 *Man, Morals and History*

answer to men's religious needs. There is room for progress in every area of modern culture.

The glorification of wealth is in the sharpest antithesis to the gospel of Jesus and to the universal verdict of mankind in all ages, except under the intoxication of its superficial glamour. Great individual wealth brings more evil than good with it. Yet social wealth is essential to social health. The economic interpretation of history is as far from scientific objectivity as the heroic interpretation. Yet due weight must be given both to great men and to economic organization since they shape society in all its aspects. But an organization of society, such as ours, that glorifies the acquisitive instinct and the profit motive in the individual perverts the whole culture. Wealth, like health, is a prerogative of every individual. The socio-economic organization should provide for every individual the health and wealth suited to his needs and abilities. In a properly organized society there will be no poor and needy—a far-distant goal, yet an ideal to be maintained against all pessimists.

Recent discussions of history by well-known Christian leaders of various tendencies who try to be both orthodox and honest (a most difficult dialectic) reach the conclusion that there is no hope in history or in man because of man's inherent sinfulness. Yet they cannot in all good conscience abandon society to its evils. One of the best conservative statements is that of G. Ernest Wright.

The revealed order (Wright says) is eschatological and therefore its consummation is beyond history. Yet the Christian cannot retire from the evils and struggles of society. Why not? First, because the prophets and apostles set a high example of earnest struggle against evil [the latter on an individual level]. Second, because regard for his neighbor leads the Christian to a vital concern for justice. The Christian must attack the misuse of power and wealth and all forms of injustice, even accepting the role of suffering servant. Can the little flock of the elect, then, hope for success in their efforts? The Bible returns no certain answer, says Wright. But the destruction of Jerusalem and the cross of Christ indicate present defeat rather than victory —until, beyond history, there comes the new earth that "shall be full of the knowledge of the Lord as the waters cover the seas." [3]

As to the Christian's duties one can only agree. As to results—the destruction of Jerusalem was one of the great constructive catastrophes of history. It potentially emancipated both Judaism and Christianity from a barbarous cult of bloody sacrifices and all similar antispirituality in worship, as well as from bondage to an unholy city that stands in history as a symbol only of crass racialism, political intrigue, military force, and murdered prophets. Its destruction enforced the command, "Go out into all the world and preach good news," as Christian missionaries had already begun to do.

As the destruction of Jerusalem represented progress, not retreat, so the cross of Christ is a symbol, not of defeat, but of victory. The early Christians said that the demons overreached themselves in destroying Jesus, for his crucifixion broke their power over men. Not in fancy but in reality, the very effort of the Palestinian authorities to silence Jesus' voice and extinguish his movement established it as an undying, world-wide force that appropriated Israel's promised prophetic mission to all the nations and eventually assisted in destroying the Roman Empire.

Jacob Burckhardt remarked that the evidence for real greatness in a historical character is "a magical after-effect" of the whole personality that reaches across the peoples and the centuries to project itself upon us. When (he says) "an individual entirely forgets himself and his own existence for the sake of a great purpose, such a man at such a moment seems sublime." Jesus, at the end, standing upon the record of his message and trusting God's will rather than his own desires and hopes, faced his prejudiced judges without attempt to escape and without whining or whimpering. He trusted God, and history has given him his portion with the great.

The ancients' "revealed eschatological order" and the moderns' "consummation beyond history" belong to a prescientific cosmology that is based on now-impossible assumptions and interprets nature and history in now-unintelligible terms. Are history and society hopeless, doomed to endless and fruitless frustration and, finally, to a most emphatic and miraculous *finis?* Such a consummation is a *non sequitur* from a dramatic, a logical, and a moral point of view, for it introduces quite literally a *deus ex machina.* As to the future—and the end—the biblical writers knew no more than moderns (which is nothing), very much less indeed, for they had no conception either of the beginning and the continuing processes of creation, or of evolution and progress. The terms in which the prophets, apocalyptists, and even Jesus state their remarkable faith are helplessly inadequate to express a faith for today. Which faith can best produce works?

3. *Action* What hope is there then in history? Only conflict, struggle, tragedy? All that, but not only that! The Hebrew God, like Ahuramazda, was a God who acted. The Christian God is also an active God, participating with intense interest in human affairs. He is also a just God and merciful, just and merciful not only to a Chosen People or a little flock of Christian "elect," but to all men without distinction of race or previous condition. He desires good for all men.

In ancient times God's supposed action merely portrayed the beliefs of the age. He tormented the Egyptians with plagues as the Hebrews would like to have done; he fed his people in the desert; he sent storms to destroy their enemies; he opened up the Red Sea for them and drowned their pursuers; he dammed up the Jordan for their crossing; he warned them by signs and portents; he sent pestilence and famine as punishments for their sins; he used foreign nations to chastise them. In a miraculous world he was a God of miracle. Can a modern, scientific world trust such a God? Hardly; except those who keep science and religion strictly sundered in departmentalized minds. Fortunately God and science are not at war.

How then, actually, has God acted and how does he work today? He has always been the same, though men apprehend him differently from age to age. He works in history, not by miracle but by men. The miracles are wrought by men who do his will. He works, not in place of men but through them, by inspiring and empowering them to do his deeds of justice and mercy. Men are the discoverers of his truth and justice. There is no propositional revelation. He does not reveal already-formulated fact or truth by speaking to men, whether from the skies or within the heart; but, like a true teacher, he leads them to discover it for themselves in the uses of nature and the experiences of history. So also he inspires men with courage, patience, endurance, and moral strength; by his presence in willing hearts he steels them against their enemies and strengthens them against their own weaknesses and fears.

Jeremiah's experience is typical. He was to be a "fortified city, an iron pillar, and bronze walls." [4] Yet no miracle saved him. He suffered everything but death. His hopes for his people were never realized—except in ways far beyond his wildest dreams. He was the "suffering servant" in Old Testament story, as Jesus became for the early Christians.

Aristotle almost rises to the level of a Christian ideal of service when he says that "the purpose of the state is the good life," that is, "a happy and honorable life." "Political society exists for the sake of noble actions," and "those who contribute most to such a society have the greater share in it." [5] The Christian, if he will follow his teacher, cannot stand at one side as a mere aloof and critical observer. He must take his part in the task of improving society, always with his reasonable, non-utopian, but lofty criteria of what the world needs: individual freedom and opportunity; equal justice, political, social, and economic, for all; control of the strong by society for the protection of the weak and needy; above all, opposition to the reign of wealth and power and pride. He must remember that the reign of God is always coming but never arrives. It will never come down out of heaven but, like all living things, aspires toward heaven.

Without any question, the view that makes men partners with God and names them his agents in spreading knowledge of his laws, carries a far greater and more virile incentive for men to struggle and suffer than the hope of heaven, the uncertain pessimism of Orthodox views, and the frustrating tensions of Neo-orthodoxy. To that incentive there is a further addition, quite in contrast to the doctrine of original sin and total depravity.

Julian Huxley, who carries some weight in biological circles (although not all biologists agree), argues that, according to the present evidence, man is the final outcome of biological evolution and that man stands alone as the bearer of further social and ethical progress.[6] With even greater emphasis it may be said that men devoted to the will of God stand alone. They are the heralds of the "good news of God."

God depends on men, as of old he called the prophets and Jesus summoned the fishermen of Galilee to become fishers of men. There are no demons fighting against the good, but only men. As there were no angelic archers at Mons to steady the British line, so there are no angelic messengers of the gospel, but only men who stand alone—with God.

To believe that men, working together with God, can achieve progress, not downward toward a final catastrophe, but upward toward an ever better life for all men—that is surely a profound and moving reason for enduring whatever must be endured. History exhibits men sinning but repenting and continually rising out of their dead selves to larger lives. Not Satan and his demons, but God reigns in the world. With no pride of self but joy in God and his work and world, man can remake his cosmos.

Every achievement means a further advance. True progress does not result when men are coaxed, like a donkey with a wisp of hay tied in front of its nose. We do achieve. We enjoy the fruits of victory. There is joy in doing, not in having; in going on, not in arriving. Edwin Markham wrote of "the press of endless passion" that makes

> . . . every goal
> A traveler's tavern, whence he must depart
> On new divine adventures of the soul.[7]

One of the basic characteristics of history is that it is a continuous process. It is like a stream in its course from the mountains to the sea. Its sources are under the mountainous debris of prehistory. It emerges into known history as the Jordan bursts forth from the base of Mount Hermon at Caesarea Philippi and wells up out of the valley floor at Dan. At times it floods all of its banks or subsides almost to a trickle. It has twisted and turned and returned upon itself. It has been swelled by tributaries and been almost lost in swamps. History has sometimes seemed to disappear in underground channels. It has been dammed by avalanches of destruction. But it has always come through to flow stronger than before. Unlike a river, history has flowed upward. It is still far from a Sea of Death.

The River Jordan comes suddenly to an end in a cul-de-sac from which there is no escape. Jewish national history also came to an end in 70 A.D. But the cultural values produced in the Near East and culminating in the Roman Empire could not be destroyed, even by the barbarian invasions. Moral and religious values represented in Judaism and artistic, intellectual, and philosophical values found in Hellenism did not cease to produce their fruits. Partly through Islam and rabbinic Judaism, partly through Christanity, the stream of Western culture, flowing underground for a time, was preserved and augmented. There is no reason—except mad unreason—why it should now come to an end. The future can rest in the hands of the God revealed by science and history.

In the hands of that same God as revealed by Jesus, history and mankind are safe. This is not a secure and easy world. Man is his own master and his own worst enemy. But God is not "on the side of the heaviest battalions." History is not a struggle for existence in which the largest and fiercest survive. The most enduring society is the one ruled by the spirit of co-operation, not by that of competition. Ashley Montagu, as a social anthropologist, has written that a "sense of mutuality and co-operativeness" is "part of man's protoplasm"; his "evolutionary destiny is integration and co-operation, *not* disintegration and antagonism. . . . In the profoundest sense of the word, greatness, both for the group and for the person, consists in service." [8]

It is in the nature of man and society that, as Jesus said, "He that wishes to be great among you must be the servant of all." [9] In his two basic principles, love for God and love for the neighbor, Jesus bound together recalcitrant human nature with God in a mutuality that is slowly but invincibly fruitful and progressive. The history that produced Jesus and the history that has flowered under his influence shine with hope in the impatient gloom of modern doubt and despair. Frederick L. Hosmer affirmed this hope:

> But the slow watches of the night
> Not less to God belong;
> And for the everlasting right
> The silent stars are strong.

CHAPTER XIX

The Meaning of Ancient Near Eastern History: A Summary

1. *The Nature of the Problem* Meaning is a much used and much abused word. Discussions of the "meaning of meaning" may leave the reader deeply puzzled as to the meaning of the proposed "meaning." As here used, it implies chiefly two questions: Does history "make sense"? Has it any value for us in the midst of our crises and confusions?

History is the life of men; it is human experience. Does the record of that experience in the ancient, formative periods of culture exhibit connections and continuities that prove it a reasonable process, or is the whole life of mankind only confusion and irrationality? That is the fundamental question. Its answer must be sought within the more definite frame of modern scientific and humanistic studies of the universe and of all cultural processes.

In summarizing and interpreting the results of this study of the history of the ancient Near East, several separate but related factors must be kept in mind: the nature of history in general; the particular course of Near Eastern history, especially its meaning in terms of morals and religion; the prospects of Western culture, the heir of Near Eastern and Mediterranean cultures; and the special contribution to Western culture made by the Bible, the most widely read and influential religious product of the Near East.

The study has been made as objectively as possible on the basis of those general principles and hypotheses which should govern any scientific investigation. Briefly they are that this is a rational universe; effect follows cause. Materials used as evidence must be critically but variously treated according to their character. Historical method is different only in detail from that of the physical scientist. History is unique in that human beings have a relative freedom and creativity to a much larger extent than is found in nature. Yet the whole universe exhibits a creative process, indeed a vast complex of processes of change. History is a process of change even more emphatically than, for example, geology is, yet the "eternal hills" change, not only outwardly through erosion and earthquakes but from within through the radioactivity of the apparently changeless rocks. Change is the essence of life and of history.

Man's psychosomatic constitution is not the subject of history but its basis, for it makes it possible for him to comprehend the processes of the universe of which he is a part, just as the fact that he is a historical being makes it possible for him to understand history. Man usually learns best from his own experience but, fortunately, he can learn also from the experience of others, for no one can undergo all possible types of experience. His imagination enables him to relive the experience of others. "Experience" covers knowing, feeling, and activity. History, therefore, is not mere knowing but also, as a matter of imagination and action, a highly dramatic process.

In order to understand history, another distinction is highly important. The word "history" has two meanings. On the one hand it is a series of external, cultural processes that provide experience, the two together making "history as such," "what actually happens." On the other hand, the word "history" is used for men's recollection, records, and interpretations of what has happened in society and in men's minds. This is history as known. History as the actual totality of any culture is one thing; history, or better, historiography, the account of known history, is quite another.

Hardly anyone will deny that historiography has progressed from the chronicles of Saul's and David's reigns, or from Herodotus and his interesting tales down to the twentieth century. History as such is also a process of development, just as truly as are the making of the physical world and biological evolution. That it is also a process of progress is demonstrated by a comparison of ancient history's achievements with its prehistoric beginnings and with the development of culture as now known—unless one sets up impossible standards of value. I submit to the reader's judgment that these principles and hypotheses are demonstrated to be correct by the history of the ancient Near East.

2. *The Interpretation of History*   There are four typical modern interpretations of history: the positivist-scientific, the mechanist, the supernaturalist, and the scientific-interpretive.

The first two readings are excluded by the very nature of history as a creative process. The positivist-scientific historian would be the last to find any real value in the biblical drama and the development of morals and religion. They are mere superstitions. For him history is a succession of interesting events, but there is neither process nor value. However, modern science and philosophy no longer deny the existence and importance of value. Science which recognizes no value has none.

The mechanist sees meaning in history in that it is a process in which one event inevitably leads to another. It is fully deterministic. Man "is what he eats"; he is merely a bundle of chemical and electronic reactions. The result is much like thoroughgoing Calvinism, except that economics or some similar impersonal, nonspiritual entity, instead of God, is the determinant. The economic interpretation of history was merely a one-sided mechanist exaggeration of the very important influence of economics in the historical process.

The Bible, with its supernaturalist interpretation of history, first told the story of the universe from Creation to Doomsday and thus gave it coherence and meaning. It was not originally intended as such; it was simply Hebrew history. But a priestly writer revised Babylonian myth into the myth of Creation magnificently told in the first chapter of Genesis. As R. G. Collingwood remarks, Hebrew myth "replaces theogony by ethnogony."[1] The Hebrew myth of the Chosen People and the Covenant then found the thread of continuity in the divine purpose. The prophets added the Day of the Lord and the apocalyptists expanded that Day into a final catastrophe and the Day of Judgment. The Hebrews (or possibly the Mazdians?) were thus the first to discover a thread of continuity running throughout. On this interpretation, the continuity is not within the process but is imposed from without by God—a perfect example of *deus ex machina*.

Collingwood has written an excellent description of the type of history accepted by both critical and uncritical conservatives. "Any history written on Christian principles [he says] will be of necessity universal, providential, apocalyptic, and periodized." By universal he means beginning with creation and including all nations and cultures. By providential he means that history is regarded as the working out of God's purposes through men and therefore has meaning. Apocalyptic, as he uses the word, implies an intelligible pattern with the life of Jesus at its center. History is then divided into two parts, B.C. and A.D. Usually other periods are discovered that are signalized by epoch-making events.[2]

This is a Christian idea of history in the sense that it is a simplified rendering of views that have reigned in catholic Christianity throughout the centuries and, as Collingwood goes on to show, have been in essence accepted by Eusebius, Augustine, and other Fathers down to the present day. Collingwood overlooks the significance of one characteristic feature. The catholic view always includes the Second Coming of Christ and the final Judgment as marking the end of history, the passing of "this age," and the onset of the next age. Christian history is also eschatological. As Collingwood remarks, "Eschatology is always an intrusive element in history."[3] Yet it is a part of the catholic view and has become the password of biblicism. Some, who would not insist on a spectacular, visible Second Coming, still insist that the New Testament promise must be fulfilled in some way.

No rapprochement is possible between the fundamentalist and a discussion such as this, which honors science. He has neither the frame of reference nor the apperceptive mass within himself by which to understand what the problems are. But there is a large body of scholars with a very considerable following who are not fundamentalists but are supernaturalists. Many of them claim to be critical scholars, and justify the claim, but fail to comprehend the basic implications of modern science, either natural or cultural. Outstanding representatives of Neo-orthodoxy belong to this class. They believe that God is the Lord of history, that he acts in nature and in history directly, not through natural law; that he speaks directly to men revealing truth in theological propositions. A prophet's "the Lord said to me" is to be taken literally, not understood as a metaphor, perhaps, or as an example of the well-known psychological phenomenon of clairaudience.

3. *Criticism and Its Misuse*   Unfortunately critical supernaturalists, like fundamentalists, fail to understand the modern scene; they do not breathe the atmosphere of science. This failure is strikingly demonstrated by a document widely distributed as an official publication of the Study Department of the World Council of Churches. These "Guiding Principles for the Interpretation of the Bible" correctly, if very briefly, set forth five necessary steps: the determination of (1) the original text; (2) the literary form; (3) "the historical situation, the *Sitz im Leben;* (4) the meaning which the words had for the original author and hearer or reader [thus outlawing allegorical interpretation]; (5) the understanding of the passage in the light of its total context and the background out of which it emerged." [4]

This, be it noted, was only "for the interpretation of a specific passage," not for the Bible as a whole. The catch is that the second section of the document with its critical principles is preceded by one entitled "The Necessary Theological Presuppositions of Biblical Interpretation." One can hardly believe one's eyes. That title of itself destroys all pretense of factual interpretation, let alone objective search for inner meaning. With a remarkable exhibition of the ecumenical spirit, the conference produced a creed for the World Council. It closes with a guillotine: "Any teaching that plainly contradicts the Biblical position cannot be accepted as Christian." [5] What of evolution? Must one believe in the Virgin Birth of Jesus? Certainly historical results determined by theological presuppositions can have no standing with historians. Supposedly the committee determines the Biblical position and so all Christian theology.

Conservative biblicism creates other difficulties. Historical criticism has come to be so generally accepted that even dogmatism must render it lip service, while its supposed results are misused. Slanted history, propagandist history, is universally damned as malpractice and taken as evidence of a weak case. Those who use it, no matter how sincere and convinced of the truth of their opinions, are doing Christianity and the world a decided disservice.

Equally serious is the partisan use of uncertain or ill-digested results of exaggerated criticism. A dangerous example is the claim that modern criticism has discredited liberalism and the search for the historical Jesus. When Emil Brunner says that we must pass over Jesus as an uncertain quantity for the Acts and Paul, he is perhaps relying on Rudolf Bultmann's form criticism. But a vast number of New Testament critics in all Western lands have never accepted Bultmann's results. When recently, in an American lecture, Martin Niemoeller repeated the canard that Albert Schweitzer had pointed out the definite failure of criticism "to find out the facts about the historical life of Jesus," he was going far beyond the facts. The fact that criticism now admits the Gospel writers to have been writing not as historians but as evangelists does not prove that they gave no attention to facts or seriously distorted them.

Having used criticism to set himself free from fact, Niemoeller proceeded to quote Paul in a wrong sense and to allegorize—quite uncritically—the story of Peter's walking on the waves of the Sea of Galilee.[6] Is such use of the Bible legitimate? Dodd, Brunner, and others display the same kind of unhappy example, but with greater skill, when they set aside the Gospel accounts of Jesus' life and teachings to make the early Christian *kerygma* (evangelistic preaching) of Acts the norm, and from it go on to expound Pauline doctrine. Many scholars doubt the authenticity of Luke's speeches in Acts. Written toward the end of the century, how can they command more historical respect than the Synoptic Gospel account of Jesus' words? Very generally, however, the Gospels are rightly regarded as a main stream of early Christian *kerygma* and more authentic than Acts, more authoritative than Paul.

It is clear that no set of rules can render interpretation truly scientific unless they are consistently applied in a truly scientific spirit. Interpretation depends upon the interpreter's scientific standards and intellectual conscience, upon his conception of the world in which he lives and his ability to relate his facts to his scientific principles. If he believes in the reign of law and not caprice in the universe, he will reach conclusions that are intelligible to the modern mind. If he believes in miracles, in divine caprice, he will see and interpret the Bible as the ancients saw it and be incapable of making his religious faith intelligible to his modern contemporaries.

The Bible as a whole, not merely isolated passages, must be seen in its *Sitz im Leben,* "in the light of its total [cultural] context and the [unscientific] background out of which it emerged." He who cannot discriminate between this age and that ancient one is hopeless as a leader in the modern world and only adds to its confusion and hopelessness.

4. *Confused Thought Categories* The Orthodox and Neo-orthodox, following the simple early Christian principle of discovering in the Old Testament types and prophecies of Jesus and the early church, add thereto their own penetration into the meaning of the Scriptures and combine antique categories of thought with their early Protestant credal dogmas. They are like the movie architect and property men who built a medieval castle to represent a corner in the wall of ancient Jerusalem, clad Joab's soldiers in medieval helmets, and graced David's apartment with Louis XV furniture. Much of our modern mass Christianity is like a movie's ancient Israelite crowds dressed in modern Arab garments from North Africa. Better so, perhaps, than medieval and Renaissance Italian, Spanish, and Dutch crowds, but still true to no historical facts. Even Tissot's highly praised Palestine and Jesus were modern Arabs and Ashkenazi Jews from Poland.

The combination of the antique and outmoded in the thinking of multitudes today even of educated Christians is well illustrated by the cinema *David and Bath-sheba,* which was popular in its year. It was designed not to be spectacular like its predecessor and rival, *Samson and Delilah,* but definitely historical. But it had to be sufficiently attractive not to lose money for the producer; actually it was both artistically and financially successful. But in both script and production there was a disturbing mixture of ancient and modern.

Goblets, torches, and similar accessories were modeled after objects excavated at Mizpah and Megiddo from buildings of David's and Solomon's times. But, characteristically, they had to be twice the original size to equal the magnificence of David's supposed palace. In the story David has serious question as to miracles. Did God's hand cause the death of Uzzah when he touched the Ark, or was it to be explained as due to combined anxiety and fear of "the holy"? More than once he voiced very modern doubts.

Gregory Peck's rendering of the Twenty-third Psalm, harp in hand, was beautifully done. David's final prayer of penitence and pleading for the rescue of his people from the drought and famine brought on by the king's sin was put together out of phrases from the Psalms and, as rendered, was a moving religious experience, much more so in the live production in the bare and disordered sound stage than on the screen. But he prayed to a vengeful God who was punishing the people for the king's sin. How could God's answer be given? Actually a clap of thunder and a heavy downpour were used as symbols— modern doubt removed by ancient miracle worked by push button. Antique and confused—yet within the narrow framework of typical modern religious thinking! How else could it have been done? The problem of communicating the old values with modern language is indescribably difficult.

Categories of thought change tremendously as man learns more and more about the universe in which he lives. How can those of 3000 years ago give any logical arrangement and consistency to minds living in the twentieth century? How can the prescientific biblical modes of thought appeal to men in a world of chromosomes and genes, of protons and neutrons?

5. *Myth and Symbol* In the interpretation of nature, history, and human nature, myth and symbol play a most important role. Beyond the factual and objective lies a vast area to which experience points and within which man's adventurous imagination seeks to penetrate. Language serves the objective world poorly enough. For the world

of feeling and abstract ideas man must use the same poor counters
in figurative senses to describe the subjective. This is true especially
of art, philosophy, morals, and religion. There lies the realm of myth
and symbol.

A myth is essentially a story that embodies supernaturalism and
miracle, that depends upon a *deus ex machina*. "Myth" is also used
of the personification, or hypostatization, of abstract ideas (i.e., the
"myth of the state," or "racial myth"). A symbol may be an object or a
verbal expression that represents an abstract idea, as a flag represents
the state or a cross stands for suffering and service, or as the "reign of
God" implies a society where righteousness prevails. Both myth and
symbol usually embody anthropomorphisms. As hardly need be said,
a story that involves supernaturalism or miracle is not a statement of
historical fact. The question is whether myths and symbols are recognized as such and give some adequate, impelling expression to truth.
All myths, Babylonian, Greek, Jewish, Christian, or any other, must
submit to the test for adequacy and spiritual appeal.

The value and use of myth and symbol are a bone of contention
between scientific liberalism on the one hand and conservatism, Neo-
orthodoxy, and similar modern trends on the other. History cannot
ignore myths, symbols, legends, mistaken science, and other furnish-
ings of the ancient mind that, taken literally as they were originally
intended, have no meaning for the world of today. They cannot be
allegorized with honesty or with success. They once explained the
problems and eased the anxieties of multitudes because they were
literally believed. Ancient myths were the imaginative responses of
primitive minds to the problems that arose in their physical and
historical experience. They reflect the beauty and fecundity of the
earth, tragic catastrophes in nature and society, the conflicts of "great
souls struggling with the crises of their fate." They explained or
explained away the mysterious and awesome that would have made
life unbearable. For centuries they steeled minds and souls to meet
opposition, danger, and disaster, and warned men against weakness,
selfishness, and crime. They had their values, small and great.

The genealogical tables in the Bible gave the individual a sense of belonging to history, to both past and future, to an enduring entity, and to lasting values. The racial, national, and Covenant myths enlarged the Jews' felt grasp on reality and life; so also, when allegorized, they served the earlier and later church under oppression and persecution. Belief in the direct providential action of God was a constant solace to the Jewish national community and to the embattled church as well as to the family and the individual. Men could always hope for a miracle to save them. But have such myths permanent value?

Thinking of religious myths, George Santayana said that religion and poetry consist "in what the imagination adds to science, to history, and to morals." Greek religion was "nothing but poetry." The religion of the Hebrews also was poetry. But the Hebrews' "sense for conduct" and their vivid nationalism carried them beyond any prosaic record of events or cautious ethical and social theory. Their "bold dramatic theory of their race's covenant with Heaven" was exactly the tragic motif to "portray with awful acceleration the ways of passion and fate," [7] luridly illustrated (it may be added) in the Babylonian conquest of Judah and the Exile and in the Jewish War of A.D. 66-70.

Nearly sixty years ago (history continues, rather than repeats) Santayana pointed out the dangers of denying that the poetry of ancient dogma, its myths and symbols, were poetry and of insisting that they were matters of fact. "Imaginative significance was the touchstone of orthodoxy," he insists in his essay on "The Poetry of Christian Dogma." [8] Facts do not move men to action. Moral significance is the touchstone of religion as it is of historical progress.

However deeply the disintegration and the harmful effects of antiquated forms of thought with their myths and symbols may be regretted, the replacement of them is a difficult and dangerous operation. The fact that the new point of view is established by evidence and logic does not guarantee it any effective appeal to the emotions such as is required for religious devotion and moral action.

Ernst Cassirer's thorough and illuminating discussion of "symbolic forms" reaches the conclusion that "every religion comes to a period of crisis where it must . . . break loose from its mythical foundations." [9] When the mythical images no longer adequately express reality, the necessary change introduces new relations that react upon both the mythical forms and the concepts of reality. After tracing the growth of Hebrew religion and the prophetic clarifications of reality that accompanied its various crises, Cassirer turns to Christianity. Quoting Harnack, he notes that for the primitive Christians the antithesis was not between the symbolic and the objective, or empirical, but between "the God-wrought *mystérion*" and "the natural, the profanely clear." [10]

Cassirer fears that the ancient symbolism has entered so fully into the texture of Christian thinking that it cannot be disentangled. Reinterpretation or replacement seems impossible. One must agree. That there must be a "Copernican revolution" cannot be denied. The myths of Creation, the Fall, the Flood, and all those connected with the idea of the Chosen People down to apocalyptic eschatology no longer represent either fact or truth and they are so strange to modern thought as to have no meaning. They are not even mysteries, but only mystifications. Likewise the myths of *Heilsgeschichte,* of revelation and "God's Word," and its corollaries of biblical unity and biblical theology as a coherent system, are not true to fact. The myth of the Virgin Birth, of the Incarnation, of the substitutionary atonement and redemption, and of bodily resurrection have become a dead weight on the wings of faith.

Granted that, variously allegorized and misinterpreted, they still interest and sustain multitudes, they baffle many others. What can be done to maintain allegiance to the basic morality and religious devotion that these terms expressed? Let no one say, "Go to now! I will invent new myths and symbols." Society does not admit of such a procedure. They must come spontaneously. But let no one say, "Let us embalm the old ones and entomb them, like Lenin and Stalin(!), for the multitude to adore, even though they are dead." On the contrary, let them die a natural death. If there is life enough in Christianity to make it of value to mankind (and I believe there is), new inspiration will come to breathe life into symbols of a living faith.

Are there any of the ancient symbols that can be saved and are worth saving? While the conception of God as king and of the reign of God refers to an institution that is almost no longer in existence,

I doubt if the "democracy of God" is a proper substitute. However, the phrase "kingdom of Heaven" is not admissible because it is a false, though literal, translation of the Aramaic phrase that Jesus would have used. The Aramaic word for "heaven" was simply a pious substitute for "God," and the word translated "kingdom" meant "dominion," with the emphasis not on a place or territory but on the "rule" or "reign" of God. "Thy kingdom come," meant "thy will be done." Those who do God's will are under the reign of God. Until the meaning of the phrase is clear the symbolism will mislead rather than help in the understanding of Jesus' teaching. It implies a state of mind, but one in which the whole man is included, "body, soul, and spirit," intellect, emotion, and will, fidelity and social action, all oriented toward God.

All depends on the accepted conception of God. The myth of total depravity has remarkable repercussions. "Present theological trends," that Hydra-headed monster in a liberal Eden, seem to be poisoning the mental atmosphere. A former student returned from a year in one of the large theological schools of eastern America where Neo-orthodoxy is in the ascendant. In a chapel talk he ranted madly over man's sinfulness and God's vengeance upon it. One could only feel that if Christianity had such a God, it would be better to be an atheist.

God may still be called king, but Father is certainly the least objectionable symbol. It discreetly suggests nothing as to the ontological nature of deity. But no term is universally satisfactory. A friend of mine had a father who was so heartlessly cruel to him and his mother that he could hardly repeat the Lord's Prayer. Conversely it is easy to imagine a father so weak and sentimental that the word makes the whole universe a tawdry summer resort. But a father who is impartially and infinitely just, kind, and intelligent may stand as a partial symbol for the God of Jesus. Whether in an imperfect universe, such as ours certainly is, he can be absolutely perfect may be questioned.

To call God the "Wholly Other" is a worse heresy than pantheism. Religion is not a lonely encounter with this "Wholly Other," but what man does in his encounter with his total world under the eye of a heavenly Father. It is not merely "what the individual does with his own solitariness," but the value the spirit discovers when "it has merged its individual claim with that of the objective universe. Religion is world-loyalty." [11]

6. *Perspectives* History is life. Written history is a record and inevitably an interpretation of life as each person sees it. The historian of the pure science school boasts of being color-blind. The existentialist turns everyone's coat "seamy side out." The humanist chooses for his hero the best-dressed man. The conservative tears the clothes off and exposes man in the filthy rags of his sins. The liberal realist sees man as an animal that has learned to think, to discriminate between good and bad, and that in other areas than those of physical satisfactions— an animal, but one with an insatiable urge to learn and to go on from good to better, one whose conscience troubles him when he fails to follow the urge of the universe toward progress.

In the long perspective of history, man is not a helpless insect, baffled and battered by the winds of fortune, but a man, who falls but rises and faces into the storm, who falls but rises again and again. There is nothing in either nature or history to suggest that men have the right to make ease and comfort the goal of life. Nature is not man's enemy; neither is it an indulgent parent. Western civilization developed first in lands that demanded the labors of irrigation and, as it expanded, concerted communal action, on the banks of the Nile, the Tigris-Euphrates Valley, and the Indus. Then, as men increased their mental and emotional capacities, the torch passed to lands with a harder aspect, where, as Deuteronomy (11:10) remarks in comparison with Egypt, a man could not water his seed by working with his foot, but depended on the whims of the clouds. In sterner surroundings, a hardier individual independence, a more fertile imagination, and greater initiative developed, to produce Israel, Greece, and Rome. The still more difficult Temperate Zone produced still hardier races and higher cultures. Challenge and response, to quote Toynbee, are the secret of progress.

In the other great culture lands of southern and eastern Asia, analogous developments have taken place and progress has been made. It does not appear that any of those cultures is ready to assume the leadership of the world. One could imagine China following the example of the Teutonic hordes in Europe, taking Western culture to itself and building a new world. But in the perspectives of past history there is nothing to encourage definite or detailed predictions as to the future, even though "Westward the course of empire takes its way." That another act, a horrendous one, will "close the drama with the day," as so many now fear, is extremely unlikely if one may judge by the darkly pessimistic anxieties that have so often been happily disappointed in the past.

What may reasonably be inferred from past experience is that humanity will go on to implement its realizable ideals and even many that may now seem to lie far below the horizon of possibility. What most of all is needed in society is faith in human potentialities and flexibility in the approach to the problems of the day. Inventive ingenuity needs to be centered, not on gadgets for the house or the family car, but on the problems of personal character, social structure, and moral ideals. The invention and realization of ideals and the means of communicating them to other people is the business of leaders. The study of present problems in light of the ideal leaders of the past is one of the chief sources of inspiration.

For the Christian the leadership of the historical Jesus is the supreme inspiration. Dogmatism has dimmed and distorted his figure. Theology (necessary as it is) does not create and vitalize realizable ideals but fossilizes them. That is the greatest crime of Neo-orthodoxy and Orthodoxy. Good men can do an immense amount of harm by pressing a partial truth too far, as Albert Schweitzer did in his *Quest of the Historical Jesus*. His ideal, which he has fulfilled more inspiringly than any man in our generation, was taken from the Jesus of the Gospels. Those who take Schweitzer too literally and discard the historical Jesus have turned the clock back to the confused theology of Paul and the early Christians who were struggling with a problem similar to ours: the effort to communicate the truths of Jesus' faith to a pagan world. Jesus, fortunately, was not concerned with Jewish theology (though he spoke its language), but with morals and religion: the highest ideals of personal devotion and moral conduct. His summation of ideals developed through 3000 years can be the inspiration of ours.

In the vast perspectives of the universe, in the long perspective of history, whether atheist or agnostic, humanist or theist, the individual can find no promise of a stagnant, peaceful Paradise on earth. Popular Christianity makes prayer a gadget and God the supreme gadgeteer. When serious disappointments or crippling accidents come, God is blamed, and faith, such as it was, is swamped in complaints.

In this world of ours men must follow the Stoic ideal, but not with mere stubborn, hopeless, self-conscious resignation, nor with unchristian otherworldliness, but with some purpose of service to individuals and society. Some goal, not centered in oneself and success and happiness, but in areas of mind and spirit where "the whips and scorns of time, ... the slings and arrows of outrageous fortune," can never reach, will give life zest and value. It can never be a final goal, but one that always moves.

Man must "accept the universe." Kant was right in discovering the evil in nature and man to be the cause of his efforts toward a better world. Whether one call it a selfish or a divine discontent, the challenge of difficulties, of obstacles to be overcome, is necessary to arouse man to effort. The semiarid mountains and gorges of Palestine are eternal witnesses to the value of hardship. The potentialities of response are built into man's nature, and the divine impulse of energy in the universe is on the side of him who bravely responds.

GENERAL BIBLIOGRAPHY
WITH
ABBREVIATIONS

Selected literature frequently used or of general value in this context, whether favorable or unfavorable to the interpretation here presented

AASOR Annual of the American Schools of Oriental Research.

Abel, le Père F.-M. Histoire de la Palestine depuis la conquête d'Alexandre jusqu'à l'invasion arabe. Vol. I. Paris: Librairie Lecoffre, 1952.

Adams, Henry. The Education of Henry Adams. Boston, New York: Houghton Mifflin, 1918.

AJSL American Journal of Semitic Languages and Literatures.

Albright, William Foxwell. *AP* The Archaeology of Palestine. London, etc.: Penguin Books, 1954.

———. *APB* The Archaeology of Palestine and the Bible. New York: Revell, 1932.

———. *ARI* Archaeology and the Religion of Israel. 2nd ed. Baltimore: The Johns Hopkins Press, 1946.

———. *BP* Biblical Period. Pittsburgh, 1950. (Reprinted from Finkelstein, *The Jews*, pp. 3–65; see below.)

———. *FSAC* From the Stone Age to Christianity. 2nd ed. Baltimore: The Johns Hopkins Press, 1946.

———. *RDBL* Recent Discoveries in Bible Lands. Pittsburgh: Biblical Colloquium, 1955. (Reprinted from *Young's Analytical Concordance;* see below.)

Alt, Albrecht. *KSGI* Kleine Schriften zur Geschichte des Volkes Israel. 2 vols. München: Beck, 1953.

ANEP See Pritchard.

ANET See Pritchard.

BA The Biblical Archaeologist.

Badè, William Frederic. *OTLT* The Old Testament in the Light of Today. Boston, New York: Houghton Mifflin, 1915.

Baillie, John. The Belief in Progress. New York: Scribner's, 1951.

Baron, Salo W. *SRHJ* A Social and Religious History of the Jews. 3 vols. New York: Columbia Univ. Press, 1937.

Bartholomae, Christian (tr.). *GA* Die Gatha's des Awesta. Zarathushtra's Verspredigten. Strassburg: K. J. Trübner, 1905.

Barton, George A. *AB* Archaeology and the Bible. Philadelphia: American Sunday-School Union, 1937.

BASOR Bulletin of the American Schools of Oriental Research.

Bousset, Wilhelm. *RJ* Die Religion des Judentums im späthellenistischen Zeitalter. 3rd ed. Hugo Gressmann, ed. Tübingen: Mohr, 1926.

Breasted, James H. *Dawn* The Dawn of Conscience. New York, London: Scribner's, 1937.

Butterfield, Herbert. Christianity and History. New York: Scribner's, 1950.

———. History and Human Relations. London: Collins, 1951.

CAH Cambridge Ancient History. Cambridge: The University Press, 1923–39.

Cameron, George G. Persepolis Treasury Tablets. Orient. Inst. Publications, No. 65. Chicago: Univ. of Chicago Press, 1948.

Case, Shirley Jackson. The Christian Philosophy of Religion. Chicago: Univ. of Chicago Press, 1943.

Cassirer, Ernst. An Essay on Man: An Introduction to a Philosophy of Human Culture. New Haven: Yale Univ. Press, 1944.

———. Language and Myth. Tr. by Susanne Langer. New York: Harper, 1946.

———. The Myth of the State. New Haven: Yale Univ. Press, 1946.

Causse, Antonin. Les dispersés d'Israël. Paris: F. Alcan, 1929.

———. Du groupe ethnique à la communauté religieuse. Paris: F. Alcan, 1937.

———. Les "pauvres" d'Israël. Strasbourg: Istra, 1922.

Charles, R. H. (ed.). *APOT* The Apocrypha and Pseudepigrapha of the Old Testament in English. 2 vols. Oxford: Clarendon Press, 1913.

Conant, James B. On Understanding Science: A Historical Approach. New Haven: Yale Univ. Press, 1947.

Cook, Stanley A. The Religion of Ancient Palestine in the Light of Archaeology. Schweich Lectures, 1925. London: Published for the British Academy by H. Milford, Oxford Univ. Press, 1930.

Cowley, A. *APFC* Aramaic Papyri of the Fifth Century. Oxford: Clarendon Press, 1923.

Cronbach, Abraham. The Bible and Our Social Outlook. Cincinnati: Union of Amer. Hebrew Congregations, 1941.

Cullmann, Oscar. Christ and Time: The Primitive Christian Conception of Time and History. Tr. by F. V. Filson. Philadelphia: Westminster Press, 1950.

Danby, Herbert (tr.). The Mishnah. London: Oxford Univ. Press (Humphrey Milford), 1933.

Dentan, Robert C. (ed.). *IHNE* The Idea of History in the Ancient Near East. American Oriental Series, Vol. 38. New Haven: Yale Univ. Press, 1955.

Dodd, Charles Harold. The Authority of the Bible. New York: Harper, 1938.

———. The Bible Today. Cambridge: University Press, 1947.

———. History and the Gospel. New York: Scribner's, 1938.

Duchesne-Guillemin, Jacques. *Zor* Zoroastre: Étude critique avec une traduction commentée des Gatha ("Les dieux et les hommes"). Paris: Maisonneuve, 1948.

Falkenstein, A., and von Soden, W. (tr.) *SAHG* Sumerische und Akkadische Hymnen und Gebete. Zürich, Stuttgart: Artemis-Verlag, 1953.

Finkelstein, Louis (ed.). The Jews: Their History, Culture, and Religion. 1 vol. in 2. New York: Harper, 1949.

———. *Phar* The Pharisees: The Sociological Background of Their Faith. 1 vol. in 2. Philadelphia: The Jewish Publication Society of America, 1940.

Fosdick, Harry Emerson. Christianity and Progress. New York: Revell, 1922.

Frankfort, Henri. *BC* The Birth of Civilization in the Near East. Bloomington: Indiana Univ. Press, 1951.

———. *KG* Kingship and the Gods: A Study of Near Eastern Religion as the Integration of Society and Nature. Chicago: Univ. of Chicago Press, 1948.

Frankfort, H. and H. A. (eds.), *et al.* *IAAM* The Intellectual Adventure of Ancient Man. Chicago: Univ. of Chicago Press, 1946.

Gaster, T. H. Thespis: Ritual, Myth, and Drama in the Ancient Near East. New York: Schuman, 1950.

Ginsberg, H. L. The Ugaritic Texts (Hebrew). Jerusalem, 1936.

Gordon, C. H. *IOTT* Introduction to Old Testament Times. Ventnor, N.J.: Ventnor Pub. Co., 1953.

———. *UHB* Ugaritic Handbook (Analecta Orientalia, 25). 3 parts. Roma: Pontificum Institutum Biblicum, 1947.

———. (tr.) *UL* Ugaritic Literature. Roma: Pontificum Institutum Biblicum, 1949.

Graham, William C., and May, Herbert G. Culture and Conscience, Chicago: Univ. of Chicago Press, 1936.

Grant, Robert M. *MNL* Miracle and Natural Law in Graeco-Roman and Early Christian Thought. Amsterdam: North-Holland Publishing Co., 1952.

Gressmann, Hugo (ed.). *AOTB* Altorientalische Texte und Bilder zum Alten Testament. 2 vols., 2nd ed. Berlin, Leipzig: de Gruyter, 1926–27.

———. Der Messias. Göttingen: Vandenhoeck und Ruprecht, 1929.

———. *MsZ* Mose und seine Zeit. Göttingen: Vandenhoeck und Ruprecht, 1913.

Guignebert, Charles. The Jewish World in the Time of Jesus. London: K. Paul, Trench, Trubner and Co., 1939.

Heidel, Alexander. *BG* The Babylonian Genesis. 2nd ed. Chicago: Univ. of Chicago Press, 1951.

———. *GE* The Gilgamesh Epic and the Old Testament. Chicago: Univ. of Chicago Press, 1946.

Hocking, William Ernest. What Man Can Make of Man. New York: Harper, 1942.

Horton, Walter M. Theism and the Scientific Spirit. New York: Harper, 1933.

HTR Harvard Theological Review.

Huxley, Julian. Evolution: The Modern Synthesis. New York: Harper, 1942.

———. *MMW* Man in the Modern World. (Mentor Book.) New York: New American Library, 1948.

———, *et al.* Evolution as a Process. London: Allen and Unwin, 1954.

IAAM See Frankfort, H. and H. A.
IHNE See Dentan, Robert C.

James, Fleming. *POT* Personalities of the Old Testament. New York, London: Scribner's, 1939.
JAOS Journal of the American Oriental Society.
JBL Journal of Biblical Literature.
JEA Journal of Egyptian Archaeology.
JNES Journal of Near Eastern Studies.
JPOS Journal of the Palestine Oriental Society.
JR Journal of Religion.

Kent, Roland G. *OP* Old Persian: Grammar, Texts, Lexicon. American Oriental Series, Vol. 33. New Haven: Am. Oriental Soc., 1950, 2nd ed., 1953.
Kohler, Kaufmann. *OSC* Origins of the Synagogue and the Church. Ed. by H. G. Enelow. New York: Macmillan, 1929.
Kramer, S. N. Sumerian Mythology. Memoirs of the American Philosophical Society, Vol. XXI. Philadelphia, 1944.
———. *FTS* From the Tablets of Sumer. Indian Hills, Col.: Falcon's Wing Press, 1956.
Kroeber, A. L. *Anth* Anthropology. New York: Harcourt, Brace, 1948.
———. Configurations of Culture Growth. Berkeley, Los Angeles: Univ. of Calif. Press, 1944.
———. The Nature of Culture. Chicago: Univ. of Chicago Press, 1952.
———, and Kluckhohn, Clyde. Culture: A Review of Concepts and Definitions. Papers of the Peabody Museum of American Archaeology and Ethnology, Harvard University, Vol. XLVII, No. 1. Cambridge: Peabody Museum, 1952.
———, et al. Anthropology Today. Chicago: Univ. of Chicago Press, 1953.

Langdon, Stephen. Babylonian Wisdom. London: Luzac, 1923.
Langer, Susanne K. Philosophy in a New Key. (Pelican Book.) New York: Penguin, 1948.
Lieberman, Saul. Hellenism in Jewish Palestine. New York: Jewish Theological Seminary of America, 1950.

Linton, Ralph (ed.). The Science of Man in the World Crisis. New York: Columbia Univ. Press, 1945.

Lloyd, Seton. Foundations in the Dust: A Story of Mesopotamian Exploration. London: Oxford Univ. Press, 1947.

Lods, Adolphe. *Isr* Israel from Its Beginnings to the Middle of the Eighth Century. Tr. by S. H. Hooke. New York: Knopf, 1932.

————. *PRJ* The Prophets and the Rise of Judaism. Tr. by S. H. Hooke. New York: Dutton, 1937.

Lommel, Herman. *RZ* Die Religion Zarathushtras nach dem Awesta dargestellt. Tübingen: Mohr, 1930.

Luckenbill, Daniel D. *ARA* Ancient Records of Assyria and Babylonia. 2 vols. Chicago: Univ. of Chicago Press, 1926, 1927.

McCown, C. C. *GSG* The Genesis of the Social Gospel. New York: Knopf, 1929.

————. *LPP* The Ladder of Progress in Palestine. New York: Harper, 1943; 2nd ed., 1944.

————. *SRJ* The Search for the Real Jesus. New York: Scribner's, 1940.

————, *et al. TN* Tell en-Nasbeh, Excavated Under the Direction of the Late William Frederic Badè. 2 vols. Berkeley, New Haven: The Palestine Institute of Pacific School of Religion and the American Schools of Oriental Research, 1947.

Malinowski, Bronislaw. The Dynamics of Culture Change. Ed. by Phyllis M. Kaberry. New Haven: Yale Univ. Press, 1945.

————. Magic, Science and Religion and Other Essays. (Doubleday Anchor Books.) Garden City: Doubleday, 1954.

————. A Scientific Theory of Culture and Other Essays. Chapel Hill: Univ. of No. Carolina Press, 1944.

Matthews, I. G. The Religious Pilgrimage of Israel. New York: Harper, 1947.

May, Herbert G., and McCown, C. C. (eds.). *RMBW* Remapping the Bible World; Nelson's New Bible Maps. New York: Nelson, 1949.

Meland, B. E. Seeds of Redemption. New York: Macmillan, 1947.

Milburn, R. L. P. Early Christian Interpretations of History. The Bampton Lectures of 1952. New York: Harper, 1954.

Miller, Hugh. Christian Truth in History. New York: Harper, 1941.

———. History and Science: A Study of the Relation of Historical and Theoretical Knowledge. Berkeley: Univ. of Calif. Press, 1939.

Minear, Paul S. Christian Hope and the Second Coming. Philadelphia: Westminster Press, 1954.

Moffatt, James. *Mof* The Holy Bible . . . A New Translation. New York: Harper, 1934.

Montagu, M. F. Ashley. *DHD* The Direction of Human Development: Biological and Social Bases. New York: Harper, 1955.

Moulton, James Hope. *EZ* Early Zoroastrianism. London: Williams and Norgate, 1913.

Mowinckel, Sigmund. Prophecy and Tradition: The Prophetic Books in the Light of the Study of the Growth and History of the Tradition. Oslo: J. Dybwad, 1946.

Muller, Herbert J. Science and Criticism: The Humanistic Tradition in Contemporary Thought. New Haven: Yale Univ. Press, 1943.

———. *UP* Uses of the Past: Profiles from Former Societies. New York: Oxford Univ. Press, 1953.

Niebuhr, H. Richard. Christ and Culture. New York: Harper, 1951.

———. The Meaning of Revelation. New York: Macmillan, 1941.

Niebuhr, Reinhold. Faith and History: A Comparison of Christian and Modern Views of History. New York: Scribner's, 1949.

———. The Irony of American History. New York: Scribner's, 1952.

———. The Nature and Destiny of Man: A Christian Interpretation. 2 vols. in 1. New York: Scribner's, 1946.

North, Christopher R. The Old Testament Interpretation of History. London: Epworth Press, 1946.

Noth, Martin. Die Welt des Alten Testaments. Sammlung Töppelmann II, Theologische Hilfsbücher, Bd. 3. 2nd ed. Berlin: Töppelmann, 1953.

Nyberg, H. S. *RAI* Die Religionen des alten Iran. Tr. by H. H. Schaeder. Mitt. der vorderasiat.-aegypt. Gesellschaft, Bd. 43. Leipzig: Hinrichs, 1938.

Olmstead, A. T. *HA* History of Assyria. New York, London: Scribner's, 1923.

———. *HPS* History of Palestine and Syria to the Macedonian Conquest. New York, London: Scribner's, 1939.

316 Man, Morals and History

——. *HPE* History of the Persian Empire. (Achaemenid Period). Chicago: Univ. of Chicago Press, 1948.

Pfeiffer, Robert H. *HNTT* History of New Testament Times with an Introduction to the Apocrypha. New York: Harper, 1949.
——. *IOT* Introduction to the Old Testament. New York: Harper, 1941.
Pritchard, James B. (ed.). *ANEP* The Ancient Near East in Pictures Relating to the Old Testament. Princeton: Princeton Univ. Press, 1954.
——. *ANET* Ancient Near Eastern Texts Relating to the Old Testament. Princeton: Princeton Univ. Press, 1950; 2nd ed., 1955.

RinL Religion in Life.
RMBW See May and McCown.
RSV The Holy Bible: Revised Standard Version. Toronto, New York, Edinburgh: Nelson, 1953.
Robinson, H. Wheeler. Redemption and Revelation in the Actuality of History. New York: Harper, 1942.
Rowley, H. H. *FJJ* From Joseph to Joshua: Biblical Traditions in the Light of Archaeology. Schweich Lectures, 1948. London: The British Academy, 1950.
——. The Relevance of Apocalyptic: A Study of Jewish and Christian Apocalypses from Daniel to Revelation. 2nd ed. New York: Harper, 1946.

Simpson, George G. The Major Features of Evolution. New York: Columbia Univ. Press, 1953.
Smith, Maria Wilkins. *GZ* Studies in the Syntax of the Gathas of Zarathushtra Together with Text, Translation, and Notes. Linguistic Dissertations, No. IV. Philadelphia: Linguistic Society of America, 1929.
Social Science Research Council. Theory and Practice in Historical Study. New York: SSRC, 1946.
Söderblom, Nathan. The Nature of Revelation. Tr. by F. E. Pamp from the 2nd ed. of 1930. New York: Oxford Univ. Press, 1933.
SYR Syria.

Tax, Sol, *et al.* An Appraisal of "Anthropology Today." Chicago: Univ. of Chicago Press, 1953. (See Kroeber, above.)

Tillich, Paul. Biblical Religion and the Search for Reality. Chicago: Univ. of Chicago Press, 1955.
——. The Interpretation of History. New York: Scribner's, 1936.
Toynbee, Arnold. Civilization on Trial. New York: Oxford Univ. Press, 1948.
——. *GHT* Greek Historical Thought. (Mentor Book.) New York: New American Library, 1952.
——. The Prospects of Western Civilization. New York: Columbia Univ. Press, 1949.

Ungnad, Arthur. *APE* Aramäische Papyrus aus Elephantine. Leipzig: Hinrichs, 1911.

Von Soden, W. See Falkenstein.

Wach, Joachim. Das Verstehen. 3 vols. Tübingen: Mohr, 1926, 1929, 1933.
Wallis, Louis. The Bible Is Human. New York: Columbia Univ. Press, 1942.
——. God and the Social Process. Chicago: Univ. of Chicago Press, 1935.
——. The Sociological Study of the Bible. Chicago: Univ. of Chicago Press, 1912.
Wallis, Wilson D. Culture and Progress. New York: McGraw-Hill, 1930.
——. Religion in Primitive Society. New York: Crofts, 1939.
Ware, Caroline F. (ed). The Cultural Approach to History. New York: Columbia Univ. Press, 1940.
Whitehead, Alfred North. *AI* Adventures of Ideas. New York: Macmillan, 1933.
——. Modes of Thought. New York: Macmillan, 1933.
——. Process and Reality. New York: Macmillan, 1929.
——. Religion in the Making. New York: Macmillan, 1926.
——. Science and the Modern World. New York: Macmillan, 1925.
——. "The Study of the Past—Its Uses and Dangers," *in* Essays in Science and Philosophy. New York: Philosophical Library, 1947, pp. 151–65.
——. The Philosophy of Alfred North Whitehead. Ed. by Paul Arthur Schilpp. 2nd ed. New York: Tudor Pub. Co., 1951.

318   *Man, Morals and History*

Wieman, Henry N. The Directive of History. Boston: Beacon Press, 1949.

——. The Sources of Human Good. Chicago: Univ. of Chicago Press, 1946.

Willoughby, Harold R. (ed.) The Study of the Bible Today and To-morrow. Chicago: Univ. of Chicago Press, 1947.

Wilson, John A. *BE* The Burden of Egypt: An Interpretation of Ancient Egyptian Culture. Chicago: Univ. of Chicago Press, 1951.

Wood, H. G. Christianity and the Nature of History. Cambridge: The University Press, 1934.

Woolley, Sir Leonard. A Forgotten Kingdom. (Pelican Book.) Baltimore: Penguin Books, 1953.

——. Ur of the Chaldees. (Pelican Book) London, etc.: Penguin Books, 1929, 1954.

Wright, G. Ernest. *BDMS* The Biblical Doctrine of Man in Society. London: SCM Press, 1954.

——. *CIF* The Challenge of Israel's Faith. Chicago: Univ. of Chicago Press, 1944.

——. *GWA* The God Who Acts. Studies in Biblical Theology. London: SCM Press, 1952.

——. *OTAE* The Old Testament Against Its Environment. London: SCM Press, 1950.

Young's Analytical Concordance to the Bible. New York: Funk and Wagnalls, 1955.

Zeuner, Frederick E. *DP* Dating the Past: An Introduction to Geochronology. London: Methuen, 1946, 1950; 3rd ed., rev., 1952.

SPECIAL BIBLIOGRAPHIES
AND
NOTES

PART 1 THE CUP OF LIFE

CHAPTER I IN THE BEGINNING

1. Human Beginnings

Garrod, Dorothy A. E., and Bate, Dorothea M. A. *The Stone Age of Mount Carmel*. Vol. 1, *Excavations at Wady el-Mughara*. Oxford: Clarendon Press, 1937.

McCown, T. D., and Keith, Sir Arthur. *The Stone Age of Mount Carmel*. Vol. II, *The Fossil Human Remains from the Levalloiso-Mousterian*. Oxford: Clarendon Press, 1939.

Albright, *FSAC*, pp. 3, 90–91; McCown (C. C.), *LPP*, pp. 18–38; Kroeber, *Anth*, pp. 98–99.

2. What Is History?

Kroeber, *The Nature of Culture*, pp. 152–66, esp. p. 165.

3. History and Time

Zeuner, *DP*.

CHAPTER II WHAT HAPPENED IN THE BEGINNING

1. The Making of the World (Cosmogony)

Gamow, George. *Biography of the Earth*. (Pelican Mentor Book.) New York, 1941, esp. pp. 155–80.

'Simpson, George G. *The Meaning of Evolution*. (Mentor Book.) New York: New American Library, 1953, esp. pp. 13–26.

Blum, Harold P. *Time's Arrow and Evolution*. Princeton: Princeton Univ. Press, 1951, esp. pp. 8–59.

2–3. The Fact and Nature of Evolution

Simpson, *op. cit.*, chiefly followed in this sketch; cf. also Huxley, *Evolution*, and *MMW*, pp. 162–76.

Zeuner, *DP,* chap. XII.
Montagu, *DHD,* pp. 24–34.
Morgan, C. Lloyd. *Emergent Evolution.* New York: Holt, 1923.
Rall, Harris Franklin. *Christianity.* New York: Scribner's, 1940, pp. 71–72.
Blum, *op. cit.,* pp. 60–86, 156–202.

4. Criteria of Progress
Simpson, *op. cit.,* pp. 110–15.
Kroeber, *op. cit.,* (above, chap. I, sec. 2), pp. 152–54, 318, 402–8.

5. The Superiority of Man
Huxley, J. *Evolution,* pp. 573–74; Montagu, *DHD,* pp. 42–58.
Huxley, Aldous. *Ends and Means.* New York: Harper, 1937, pp. 306–7.

6. Evolution and Culture
Childe, V. Gordon. *Man Makes Himself.* (Thinker's Library, No. 87.) London: Watts, 1948, pp. 17–21.
Cassirer, *An Essay on Man,* p. 228.

7. Progress a Reality
Simpson, *op. cit.,* pp. 107–23; Montagu, *DHD,* pp. 288–315.
Dewey, John. *Reconstruction in Philosophy.* (Mentor Book.) New York: New American Library, 1952, pp. 102, 108–12, *et passim.*

CHAPTER III PALESTINE: THE TWO CUPS

1. The Inner Cup: The Land as a Whole
Benedict, Ruth. *Patterns of Culture.* (Mentor Book.) New York: New American Library, 1953, p. 19.

2–4. Regional Differences, Climate, Resources
McCown, *GSG,* pp. 37–74; "Geographic Conditioning of Religious Experience in Palestine," in Willoughby (ed.), *The Study of the Bible Today and Tomorrow,* pp. 231–46; *JBL,* LXVI (1947), 425–36, with references.

[1] Lev. 26:34–36; 2 Chron. 36:21.

CHAPTER IV THE CONTENTS OF THE CUP: CULTURE IN THE MAKING

1. At the Center

Lloyd, Seton. *Foundations in the Dust.*

Woolley, Sir Leonard. *Digging Up the Past.* (Pelican Books.) Harmondsworth: Penguin Books, 1937, 1949.

Albright, *AP*, pp. 1–48, and *FSAC*, pp. 1–47; McCown, *LPP*, pp. 1–17.

2–4. Prehistory

Albright, *FSAC*, pp. 88–105, and *AP*, pp. 49–79; McCown, *LPP*, pp. 18–84.

Childe, V. Gordon. *Dawn of European Civilization.* New ed. New York: Knopf, 1939.

———. *New Light on the Most Ancient East.* 4th ed. London: Routledge and Kegan Paul, 1952.

———. *What Happened in History.* (Pelican Books.) New York: Penguin Books, 1946, pp. 1–105.

———. *Progress and Archaeology.* (Thinker's Library, No. 102.) London: Watts, 1945.

Braidwood, Robert J. *The Near East and the Foundations of Civilization.* Condon Lectures. Eugene: Oregon State System of Higher Education, 1952.

———. *Matarrah; A Village of Early Farmers in Iraq.* Chicago: Oriental Institute, Univ. of Chicago, 1952.

Frankfort, *BC.*

Coon, Carleton S. *The Story of Man.* New York: Knopf, 1954, pp. 3–180.

Wilson, *BE*, pp. 8–68.

CHAPTER V THE HEBREWS: RACIAL AND CULTURAL INHERITANCE

1. Artifact and Tablet

The Alphabet: Albright, *BASOR*, 110 (Apr., 1948), 6–22, and *AP*, pp. 185–96; McCown, *LPP*, pp. 100–117 (needs revision); see below, chap. XII, sec. 1.

Artifact: Albright, *ARI*, pp. 64–67.

2. Language and Race

Albright, *FSAC*, pp. 105–89, *ARI*, pp. 36–67, and *AP*, pp. 45–109, 175–203; Wilson, *BE*, pp. 230–31, 234–35, 239–59.

Gurney, O. R. *The Hittites.* (Pelican Books.) Harmondsworth: Penguin Books, 1954.

3. Egypt and the Hebrews

Wilson, *BE*, pp. 134–36, 154–65, 177–205.
Steindorff, George, and Seele, Keith C. *When Egypt Ruled the East.* Chicago: Univ. of Chicago Press, 1942, pp. 24–29, 47–60, 103–15, 248–54.
Albright, *ARI*, pp. 49–54, 61–64; Gordon, *IOTT*, pp. 41–60, 75–80, 120–36.

4. The Philistines

Wilson, *BE*, pp. 244–46, 258–60; Gordon, *IOTT*, pp. 108–9; Alt, *KSGI*, I, pp. 216–30.

5. Syrian Neighbors

Albright, *ARI*, pp. 37–44, 68–94; Gordon, *IOTT*, pp. 81–99.

6. Nomadic Neighbors

Montgomery, J. A. *Arabia and the Bible.* Philadelphia: Univ. of Pennsylvania Press, 1934; Alt, *KSGI*, I, pp. 203–15.

PART 2 WHAT THE MOVING FINGER WROTE: WHAT ACTUALLY HAPPENED

CHAPTER VI WHO WERE THE HEBREWS?

1–2. The Problem: Hebrew People and Language

On the patriarchal age and the "Conquest": *RMBW*, pp. 7, 8.
Alt, *KSGI*, I, pp. 1–192; Gordon, *IOTT*, pp. 100–136; Albright, *FSAC*, pp. 179–96, 210–14, *BP*, pp. 13–17, and *AP*, pp. 205–8, 209; Rowley, *FJJ*, pp. 12–37.
On the 'Apiru (Khabiru): Albright, *FSAC*, pp. 182–83, 211, 326, n. 54, 330, n. 6, and *ARI*, p. 200, n. 8; Rowley, *FJJ*, pp. 37–56; Wilson, *BE*, pp. 201, 230, 255–256, 257; *per contra*, Gordon, *IOTT*, p. 76, and n. 2.

3. Nomads and Peasants

McCown, *GSG*, pp. 133–45; Albright, *ARI*, pp. 96–102; Alt, *KSGI*, I, pp. 140–43; Olmstead, *HPS*, pp. 35–42; Pfeiffer, *IOT*, pp. 30–31, 162–63, 166–67, 218–20, 274.

On nomadism and Yahweh: Lods, *Isr*, pp. 308–25; Olmstead, *HPS*, pp. 245–56; Gressmann, *MsZ*, pp. 409–24, 431–48; Albright, *FSAC*, pp. 194–210, 214; Rowley, *FJJ*, pp. 105–08, 147–56; McCown, *GSG*, pp. 134–47.

[1] Josh. 12:7–24; Judg. 1:22–33; see May in May and McCown, *RMBW*, pp. 6, 9, 10.

[2] Judg. 1:16; 4:11; 5:24; 1 Sam. 15:6; 2 Kings 10:15–17, 23; 1 Chron. 2:55; Jer. 35:1–11, 16–19. See below, chap. XI, secs. 2–3.

5. Mesopotamian Relations

Albright, *FSAC*, pp. 179–84; *BP*, pp. 3–13; Gordon, *IOTT*, pp. 75–80, chaps. VIII–IX; James, *POT*, pp. 1–44.

[3] Badè, *OTLT*, pp. 187–217.

CHAPTER VII FROM TRIBE TO NATION

1. The Times of the Judges

Albright, *FSAC*, pp. 210–20; *BP*, pp. 17–23; Gordon, *IOTT*, pp. 137–44; *RMBW*, pp. 8–14.

[1] Judg. 8:30; 12:14; cf. 2 Kings 10:1.

2. The United Kingdom

[2] Jer. 7:12–15; 26:6–9.

[3] 1 Kings 11:29–40; 14:1–16.

[4] 1 Sam. 10:1–13.

[5] Albright, *FSAC*, pp. 232–33; Wilson, *BE*, p. 290; Olmstead, *HPS*, pp. 288–92; *ANET*, p. 26b; Alfred Haldar, *Associations of Cult Prophets Among the Ancient Semites* (Uppsala: Almqvist and Wiksells, 1945), pp. 114–19, 144–45.

[6] 1 Sam 19:18–24; 1 Kings 20:35–43; 2 Kings 2:3–7, 15; 4:1, 38.

3. Israel and Judah: A Divided People

Albright, *ARI*, pp. 142–68; Gordon, *IOTT*, pp. 178–96, 203–24; *RMBW*, pp. 15, 16.

[7] 1 Kings 14:31; 15:10, 13; 16:31; 2 Kings 8:26; 11:1–20. Cf. Albright, *ARI*, pp. 157–59.

[8] Jer. 26–28; cf. 1 Kings 22:1–28; 2 Kings 3:15; McCown, *GSG*, pp. 166–70.

On places and remains of cult: McCown, *BASOR,* 98 (1945), 2–15, *JBL,*
LXIX (1950), 205–19, and *TN,* I, pp. 206–12, 233–48, 204, fig. 50c;
pls. 84:15–20, 23; 85; 86; 87:2; with refs. to literature.

4. *Judah Alone*

Albright, *BP,* pp. 39–48; Gordon, *IOTT,* pp. 225–56.
The inscriptions of Assyrian monarchs that illuminate much of biblical
history during this period are most conveniently found in Barton, *AB,*
Luckenbill, *ARA,* and now *ANET; RMBW,* p. 17.

[9] So Albright, *BP,* p. 40; Gordon, *IOTT,* p. 218, nn. 14, 15, denies this
identification, as do others.

[10] 2 Kings 16:1–20; Isa. 7:1–17.

[11] Isa. 37:9–37.

[12] *KSGI,* II, pp. 250–75.

CHAPTER VIII FROM NATION TO CULT COMMUNITY

1. *A Critical Period in Jewish History*

Albright, *FSAC,* pp. 240–47, and *BP,* pp. 45–47; Gordon, *IOTT,* pp. 257–
68; Olmstead, *HPS,* pp. 517–75, and *HPE,* pp. 135–43, 465–67; Baron,
SRHJ, I, pp. 85–107; *RMBW,* p. 21.

2. *A Complicated Situation*

[1] Albright, *BA,* V (1942), 49–55, and *BP,* pp. 47–48, n. 115; *ANET,*
p. 308b.

[2] R. P. Dougherty, *Nabonidus and Belshazzar* (*Yale Or. Series, Re-
searches,* XV; New Haven, 1929), pp. 105–60; Montgomery, *Arabia*
(above, chap. V, sec. 6), pp. 64–67; P. K. Hitti, *History of the Arabs* (4th
ed.; London: Macmillan, 1949), pp. 39–43; C. C. Torrey, *JAOS,* 73 (1953),
223–24.

On the Elephantine colony see Albright, *FSAC,* pp. 286–87, and *ARI,* pp.
168–75; Olmstead, *HPS,* pp. 598–610; Lods, *PRJ,* pp. 304–12; Barton,
AB, pp. 486–90; Ungnad, *APE;* Cowley, *APFC; ANET,* pp. 222–23,
491–92 (Ginsberg); see also

Kraeling, A. E. *The Brooklyn Museum Aramaic Papyri.* New Haven:
Yale Univ. Press, 1953.

Driver, G. R. *Aramaic Documents of the Fifth Century B.C.* Oxford:
Clarendon Press, 1954.

4. The Exile
[3] 2 Kings 25:22–26; Jer. 40:7–42:7; McCown, *TN*, I, pp. 118 (3), 163 (4), 169–70; pl. 57:4.
[4] Alt, *KSGI*, II, pp. 327–37; cf. Ezra 5:4–5.

5. The Day of Yahweh
[5] Quoted by Olmstead, *HPE*, p. 435, n. 13.
[6] Isa. 44:28–45:13.
[7] *ANET*, pp. 312–16; Barton, *AB*, pp. 484–85; Olmstead, *HPE*, pp. 51–56; cf. below, chap. XIV, n. 27.
[8] Isa. 40:1–2, 10–11; Ezra 4:1–4; 5:1–2.
[9] Hag. 2:6, 7, 21–23, all dated within four months, 29 Aug., 16 Oct., 18 Dec., 520 (1:1; 2:1, 10, 20); after that, silence. Cf. Albright, *BP*, pp. 49–50.

CHAPTER IX THE HIEROCRACY OF THE SECOND TEMPLE

1. Problems of the Restored Community
Albright, *FSAC*, pp. 246–55; Alt, *KSGI*, II, pp. 316–62; Olmstead, *HPS*, pp. 531–75, and *HPE*, pp. 304–7, 313, 465–67; Baron, *SRHJ*, I, pp. 85–127; Lods, *PRJ*, pp. 185–99; *RMBW*, p. 22.
[1] *Ant.* xi. 8 (i. 3).

2. The Second Restoration
[2] On the disputed date see Albright, *BP*, pp. 50–54, 64, n. 113, and *FSAC*, pp. 248, 335 (n. 67), 366; James, *POT*, pp. 462–69; Pfeiffer, *IOT*, pp. 818–28.
[3] Neh. 5:1–5; 13:23–24; Ezra 9:2.
[4] McCown, *TN*, I, pp. 164–65, 171b–72a, 185b, 186, 227a, pls. 56, 57.
[5] Neh. 8:1–8; 9:38–10:38; 2 Kings 23:1–3; Neh. 13:23–29; Ezra 9:1–10:44.

3. Society and Politics
[6] Neh. 7:5–69 and Ezra 2:1–67 are taken as a census of the population in Nehemiah's time; cf. Albright, *BP*, pp. 62–63, n. 122.
[7] See Albright, *JBL*, LI (1932), 79 ff., and cf. the seal of Jaazaniah (*TN*, I, pl. 57:4); see above, chap. VIII, n. 3.
[8] Ungnad, *APE*, No. 1, l. 29; No. 3, l. 1; Cowley, *APFC*, Nos. 30, 32;

ANET, pp. 491–92. Lods, *PRJ*, p. 291, n. 1, thinks Geshem also a Yahwist.
⁹ Josephus *Ant.* xi. 306–12 (viii. 2); Pfeiffer, *IOT*, pp. 101, 809–11; Baron, *SRHJ*, I, pp. 214–17, and III, pp. 54–55, n. 18; Finkelstein, *Phar* (II), pp. 547–62; Lods, *PRJ*, pp. 317–19.
¹⁰ Josephus *Ant.* xi. 297–301.
¹¹ S. A. Cook in *CAH*, VI, p. 176.
¹² Olmstead, *HPE*, pp. 434–35, 436–37.

4. The Story of the Tobiadae
On the Tobiads: Josephus *Ant.* xii. 154–245 (iv. 1–xii. 2); *Josephus*, R. Marcus (ed. and tr., Loeb Classical Lib.; Cambridge and London, 1943), VII, 80–125, 767–68, notes and bibliography; Albright, *AP*, pp. 25, 149–50, *APB*, pp. 170–71, 221–22, nn. 108–11, and *BP*, pp. 52, 63, n. 129; Père H. Vincent, *JPOS*, III (1923), pp. 55–68; Finkelstein, *Phar* (II), pp. 574–87.
¹³ C. C. Edgar, *Zenon Papyri*, I (*Cat. gen. des antiq. du Musée de Caire*, I, Caire, 1925), nos. 59003, 59075–76.

5. Hellenism in Judea
¹⁴ McCown, *TN*, I, pp. 175–78, "Greek Pottery," by Dietrich von Bothmer.
¹⁵ O. R. Sellers, *The Citadel of Beth-Zur* (Philadelphia: Westminster Press, 1933), pp. 71–90; cf. pp. 10–13.
¹⁶ C. H. Kraeling, ed., *Gerasa, City of the Decapolis* (New Haven: American Schools of Oriental Research, 1938), pp. 28–33, 460–61; C. S. Fisher, *BASOR*, 45 (1932), pp. 7–8. C. C. Edgar, *Zenon Papyri in the University of Michigan Collection* (University of Michigan Studies, Humanistic Series, XXIV; Ann Arbor, 1931), pp. 16–18.
¹⁷ McCown, *LPP*, pp. 299–325.
¹⁸ See Edgar, *locc. citt.*, nn. 13, 16, above.

6–7. The Maccabean Revival and Roman Rule
¹⁹ Isa. 19:18–25; 42:1–4; 49:1–6; 56:3–8; T. Levi 18:9.
²⁰ 1 Macc. 14:8–12; cf. Mic. 4:4; Zech. 3:10; 1 Kings 4:25.
²¹ Josephus *Ant.* xiii. 299–300 (x. 7); *BJ* i. 68–69 (ii. 8); T. Levi 8:11–15.
²² Josephus *BJ* ii. 118–61, 254–55, 651 (viii. 1–13; xiii. 3; xxii. 1); vii. 253–54, 265 (viii. 1); *Ant.* xviii. 11–23 (i. 6).
²³ Pliny *Hist. nat.* v. 17.

On the Hellenistic and Early Roman period: *RMBW,* pp. 39–44.
Guignebert, Charles. *The Jewish World in the Time of Jesus.*
Mathews, Shailer. *New Testament Times in Palestine.* New York: Macmillan, 1934.
Oesterley, W. O. E. *A History of Israel.* Vol. II of Oesterley and T. H. Robinson, *A History of Israel,* 2 vols., Oxford: Clarendon Press, 1939, pp. 175–301.
Klausner, Joseph. *Jesus of Nazareth.* New York: Macmillan, 1944, pp. 121–228.
Baron, *SRHL,* I, pp. 128–224; Finkelstein, *Phar* (II), pp. 570–625.
Abel, *Histoire de la Palestine,* Vol. I.

PART 3 WHAT THE RUNNER READS: THE INTER-PRETATION OF HEBREW HISTORY

CHAPTER X THE HAND OF GOD IN HISTORY

An undogmatic study of the Hebrew conception of history is difficult to discover; but now see
Burroughs, Millar, in Dentan, *IHNE,* pp. 101–31, with an up-to-date bibliography—an excellent survey; cf. Schubert, in *ibid.,* pp. 342–45.
Per contra see
Piper, Otto. *God in History.* New York: Macmillan, 1939.
Wright, G. Ernest, *BDMS, CIF, GWA, OTAE* (credal coloring).
Dodd, C. H. *The Bible Today.* Cambridge: Univ. Press, 1947, pp. 1–14, 50–64, 70, 98–121.
On creation: Heidel, *BG,* pp. 1–81; *IAAM,* pp. 50–61 (Wilson), pp. 168–83 (Jacobsen); *ANET,* pp. 3–10 (Wilson), pp. 60–100 (Speiser); Barton, *AB,* pp. 279–308.

1. The General Framework of Hebrew Thought

[1] Deut. 32:8; Isa 40:23.
[2] Hab. 1:6; 2:12–14; Isa. 45:1–4.
[3] Pfeiffer, *IOT,* pp. 190–92.
[4] See Jer. 43–44; Ezek. 11:14–21.
[5] See Pss. 31:17; 39:12–13; 88:3–5, 10–13; 89:48; Isa. 38:18–19.
On "soul" *(nephesh)* see Pss. 30:3, 9; 49:8–15; Job 33:18, 22, 28, 30.
[6] Deut. 28.
[7] 1 Sam. 16:14–16; 18:10; 19:9; cf. 1 Kings 22:19–23.

328   *Man, Morals and History*

⁸ Deut. 13:1–5; 18:15–22; Isa. 7:7–17; 38:7–8; Jer. 28:1–17.

2. The Hebrew Theory of History
⁹ *Isr*, pp. 314–15.
¹⁰ Exod. 19:5; 24:1–8; 34:10–28; Josh. 24:25; Deut. 29:1–28; 2 Kings 11:4, 17 (2 Chron. 23:16); 2 Kings 23:3 (2 Chron. 34:29–32); Neh. 9:38; Pfeiffer, *JBL*, LXX (1951), 4, 6; the Josiah covenant crucial.
¹¹ Gen. 12:2; 13:14–17; 15:1–21; 9:8–17; 17:1–19; Exod. 31:12–17; 2 Sam. 7:8–16.

3. Hope and Frustration
¹² Pss. 11:3; 79:10; 44 and 74; Gen. 18:23.
¹³ Ezra 33:21; 36:24–26; James, *POT*, pp. 346–49.

Chapter XI God's Education of the Hebrew People

1–2. The Unique Conditions; Nomadism
See chap. III and chap. VI, sec. 3, above.
¹ Josh. 22:4–8; 1 Sam. 4:10; 13:2; 2 Sam. 18:17; 2 Chron. 25:22; *et passim*, translated "home" in *RSV*.
² 1 Sam. 22–25; 1 Macc. 9:33.
³ Hos. 2:14–15; 12:9; Isa. 1:26.

3. The Pastoral-Agricultural Ideal
⁴ 1 Kings 4:25; 2 Kings 18:31=Isa. 36:16; Mic. 4:4; 1 Macc. 14:12.
⁵ Sir. 7:15; T. Iss. 5:3; Letter of Aristeas 107–8, 112–15.
⁶ See chap. X, sec. 1 and n. 6.
⁷ Prov. 13:11; 10:15; 13:8; 18:11; 22:1; 3:13–16; Pss. 1:1–3; 112:3; 128:1–6; 37:11.
⁸ Deut. 8:11–14; 31:20; 32:15; Neh. 9:25–26; Hos. 13:6.

4. Commerce in Hebrew History
⁹ Josephus *C. Ap.* I. 60 (12).
¹⁰ Sir. 26:29; 27:2. (E. J. Goodspeed *et al.*, *The Complete Bible: An American Translation*. Chicago: Univ. of Chicago Press, 1939).
¹¹ 1 Kings 7:46; 10:28–29.
¹² 1 Kings 22:39; Amos 3:15; 6:4; McCown, *LPP*, pp. 196–98, 357.
¹³ 2 Kings 14:22; 16:6; see McCown, *LPP*, pp. 297–99.

5. The Social Structure
See the works of S. W. Baron, L. Finkelstein, W. C. Graham and H. G. May, and Louis Wallis in the General Bibliography, above, and the bibliographies in Pfeiffer, *IOT,* pp. 861–62.

[14] Cf. Lods, *Isr,* p. 397; Baron, *SRHJ,* I, pp. 46–48, 56–64.

[15] Pss. 12:5; 10:2–16, *et passim;* Mark 11:15–18; 12:38–40.

[16] Finkelstein, *Phar* (I), pp. 4–5, 7–42.

[17] *Ibid.,* pp. 43–72; (II), pp. 619–22, 637–45; Baron, *SRHJ,* I, pp. 213–24.

7. Three Unusual Educational Institutions
[18] Cf. Joachim Wach, *The Sociology of Religion* (Chicago: Univ. of Chicago Press, 1944), pp. 346–57.

[19] *Ibid.,* pp. 360–68.

9. The Scriptures
[20] Ps. 40:6–8; 1 Sam. 15:22; Isa. 1:10–17; 58:1–8; 66:3.

[21] Heinrich Graetz, *History of the Jews* (Philadelphia: The Jewish Publication Soc. of America, 1940), II, p. 324.

[22] Finkelstein, *Phar* (II), pp. 581–83; Josephus *Ant.* xii. 142 (iii. 3) and R. Marcus, *ad loc.*

[23] Finkelstein, *Phar* (II), pp. 576–80, 709, n. 12, citing Mishnah, Aboth 1:1.

10. The Synagogue
See Finkelstein, *Phar* (II), pp. 563–69; Guignebert, *JWTJ,* chap. VI, sec. 3; Kohler, *OSC, passim;* Bousset, *RJ,* pp. 108, 172 (no definite evidence for it before 250 B.C.), 173–76, *et passim;* cf. Lods, *PRJ,* p. 350 and n. 6.

CHAPTER XII WHAT THE HEBREWS LEARNED

1. The Components of Hebrew Culture
[1] Albright, *FSAC,* pp. 179, 226.

[2] Kroeber, *Anth,* pp. 368–70, and, indeed, chaps. VII–XIV.

2. Hebrew Advantages
[3] Quoted by H. J. Muller, *Science and Criticism* (New Haven: Yale Univ. Press, 1943), p. 125.

3. The Long Perspective
See now *IHNE,* ed. Dentan, esp. Speiser, pp. 37–76 (Mesopotamia); Burrows, pp. 101–31 (Israel); Dinkler, pp. 171–214 (Christianity).

⁴ C. Ap. i. 58 (11); cf. Toynbee, *GHT,* pp. 60–69.

⁵ Well set forth in Toynbee's selections, *GHT,* pp. 117–34. I do not see that Welles (*IHNE,* pp. 147–61) or Schubert (*ibid.,* pp. 332–70) has proved that there was a sense of a historic process or a divine plan, as with the Hebrews.

5. Varied Currents of Thought

⁶ Whitehead, *AI,* pp. 353, 366–69; cf. Schilpp in Whitehead, *Philosophy* (ed. Schilpp), pp. 563–65.

CHAPTER XIII WHAT THE HEBREWS CREATED

1. Relations with Other Literatures
See Albright's summary, *JBL,* LIX (1940), 85–112.

¹ Albright, *ARI,* pp. 68–94, 110–19, 157–60, *et passim; BP* pp. 10–11, 14; *ARI,* pp. 68–94.

² See publications and discussions by MM. F. A. Schaefer, Ch. Virolleaud, R. Dusseaud, and others in *SYR* and elsewhere, esp. C. H. Gordon, H. L. Ginsberg, and T. H. Gaster in the General Bibliography, above, and Albright, *FSAC,* pp. 11–12; McCown, *LPP,* pp. 104–7.

³ Ps. 18=2 Sam. 22; Pss. 29; 45; 68; 88; 89; *ARI,* pp. 117, 128–29; see now *RDBL,* p. 90.

⁴ Albright, *FSAC,* p. 243; Gaster, *Thespis,* includes Pss. 29; 65; 66; 68; 74:12–17; 76; 89:2–19; 93, and with less certainty, 47; 48; and 96–98; other use of Canaanite myth, pp. 145–50, 208–10.

⁵ See below, sec. 2.

⁶ See Lloyd, *Foundations,* pp. 164–66.

⁷ The various sources and points of view in Gen. 1-11 are taken here as the untutored reader would see the whole; cf. Pfeiffer, *IOT,* pp. 130, 160–62, 188–97; S. Mowinckel and Albright, *JBL,* LVII (1938), 230–31; LVIII (1939), 87–103.

⁸ Pfeiffer, *IOT,* pp. 204–5; *ANET,* pp. 265–66 (Oppenheim); Barton, *AB,* 317–26; T. Jacobsen, *The Sumerian King List* (Orient. Inst. Assyr. Stud., No. 11, Chicago, 1939).

⁹ Albright and Mowinckel, n. 7, above.

[10] Heidel, *GE*, pp. 80–88, Tablet xi, 1–196; pp. 224–69; Barton, *AB*, pp. 327–36; *ANET*, pp. 42–44 (Sumer, Kramer); pp. 93–95 (Akkad, Speiser); in Sumerian King List, Barton, *AB*, p. 317, I, 40; *ANET*, p. 265b (Oppenheim); Jacobsen, *IAAM*, pp. 126–27; Woolley, *Ur*, pp. 17–26; Pfeiffer, *IOT*, pp. 161–63, 205; Kroeber, *Anth*, p. 545.

[11] See now Wilson in *ANET*, pp. 421–24, esp. n. 46; Breasted, *Dawn*, pp. 370–81; Pfeiffer, *IOT*, pp. 647–48; *per contra*, R. O. Kevin, "The Wisdom of Amen-em-apt and its Possible Dependence on the Hebrew Book of Proverbs" (thesis), Philadelphia, 1931. Cf. McCown, *GSG*, p. 110; *HTR*, XVIII (1925), 363–67; and see chap. XIV, sec. 2 (end), of the present book.

[12] Albright, *FSAC*, pp. 282–89; Ungnad, *APE*, pp. 62–82; Cowley, *APFC*, pp. 204–48; *ANET*, pp. 427b–30 (Ginsberg); Prov. 23:13–14 seems to come from Akhiqar, Eleph. frags., Cowley, vi. 81–82; Ungnad, No. 55, Pap. 53:2–3; Charles, *APOT*, II, pp. 778–79 (Agnes Smith Lewis).

[13] See Pfeiffer, *IOT*, p. 649.

[14] Breasted, *Dawn*, pp. 363–64; so also Eduard Meyer, *Die Israeliten und ihre Nachbarstämme* (Halle: Niemeyer, 1906), pp. 451–55; McCown, *GSG*, pp. 213–26; *HTR*, XVIII (1925), 367–86.

[15] Breasted, *Dawn*, pp. 281–86, 366–70; against direct influence of the Aton hymn on Ps. 104, but not of Egyptian syncretistic henotheism upon the Hebrews and indirectly on the Psalm, Wilson, *BE*, pp. 224–29; cf. Albright, *FSAC*, pp. 165–70.

[16] See Breasted, *Dawn*, pp. 364–66; McCown, *GSG*, pp. 110–11; *HTR*, XVIII (1925), 364–65; Frankfort, *KG*, pp. 311, 468, nn. 67–68; *ANET*, p. 422, chap. iv (Wilson).

2. Archaizing Revivals

[17] Olmstead, *HA*, pp. 489–94.

[18] Albright, *FSAC*, pp. 241–44; Wilson, *BE*, pp. 294–96.

[19] Jer. 10:1–10; Isa. 44:9–20; cf. Pfeiffer, *IOT*, pp. 449, 482.

[20] Well described by Wright, *OTAE*, pp. 77–102, but without reference to the demonology of 1 Enoch 6=10, of Tobit, and other noncanonical works (see Charles, *APOT*, II, Index, s.vv. "Demonology" and "Demons"), the Gospels, and the early church (on the latter, McCown, *The Testament of Solomon*, Leipzig: Hinrichs, 1922).

[21] Typical objective discussions: M. Dibelius, *Die Geisterwelt im Glauben des Paulus* (Göttingen: Vanderhoeck und Ruprecht, 1909); Bousset, *RJ*, Index, s.vv. "Dämonen, Engeln, Geister"; R. Grant, *MNL*, pp. 74, 77, 85,

96, 98, 206; R. Bultmann, *Das Urchristentum im Rahmen der Antike* (Zurich: Artemis Verlag, 1949), pp. 173–74, 211–13; McCown, *op. cit.* in n. 20. See *ANEP*, figs. 644–71.

[22] E. R. Goodenough, *Jewish Symbols in the Greco-Roman Period*, IV (Bollingen Series, XXXVII; New York: Pantheon Books, 1954), esp. pp. 54–55.

3. Ritual, Civil, and Moral Law

[23] Pfeiffer, *IOT*, pp. 210–70; Albright, *FSAC*, pp. 204–6; Alt, *KSGI*, I, pp. 278–344.

[24] Lev. 19:17, 34; Deut. 10:19; Lev. 20; 24:10–23.

[25] *Origin and History of Hebrew Law* (Chicago, 1931), p. viii.

[26] On slaves and masters and sale for debt, note Exod. 21:26–27; Deut. 15:12–18 and the Code of Hammurabi; G. R. Driver and J. C. Miles, *The Babylonian Laws*, I (Oxford: Clarendon Press, 1952), pp. 217, 408–9. On savagery to enemies and heretics, see Num. 25:1–5; 31:17; Deut. 20:12–18. On *lex talionis* see Alt, *KSGI*, I, pp. 341–44.

4. The Psalms: Lyrical Ideology

[27] S. Mowinckel, *Psalmenstudien*, 6 vols. (Kristiana: J. Dybwad, 1921-24). Lods, *PRJ*, pp. 347–48; Gaster, *Thespis*, pp. 73–97; Pfeiffer, *IOT*, pp. 624, 636, hymns in Temple worship after 400.

[28] Pss. 34:11–22; 37; 49; 73; 127; 128; 133.

[29] Ps. 18:7–15; 2 Sam. 22:8–16; Ps. 19:1–6; 29; 89:5–12; 97:1–5; 104.

[30] Pss. 8:1; 19:1; 25:7; 103:13, 17; 107:8; 147:6–9.

[31] Pss. 37:8; 139:7, 21.

[32] Pss. 30:3, 9; 49:7–20; 88:10–12; 89:46–48; 115:16–17; Prov. 30:8–9; Eccles. 3:18–22; 9:3–6. Pfeiffer, *IOT*, pp. 778–79.

PART 4 IDEALS—ACHIEVEMENTS—HOPE: THE OUTCOME

CHAPTER XIV ANCIENT HOPES AND SOCIAL IDEALS

See Breasted, *Dawn;* McCown, *GSG*, pp. 187–291.

ANET, passim; IAAM, pp. 93–121 (Wilson); pp. 202–19 (Jacobsen); R. R. Marett, *Faith, Hope, and Charity in Primitive Religion.* New York: Macmillan, 1932.

1. Beginnings of the Social Conscience

[1] *IAAM*, pp. 106–8 (Wilson); pp. 128–29, 135–36, 187 (Jacobsen); Jacobsen, "Primitive Democracy in Ancient Mesopotamia," *JNES*, II (1943), 159–72; Frankfort, *BC*, p. 61, and *KG*, pp. 215–21; see above, chap. IV, sec. 4.

2. The Social Conscience in Egypt

[2] Breasted, *Dawn*, pp. 13, 18–21; Wilson, *BE*, pp. 47–49; Frankfort, *KG*, pp. 157–58; *ANET*, pp. 213a (Wilson).

[3] Breasted, *Dawn*, p. 316; McCown, *GSG*, p. 254.

[4] Breasted, *Dawn*, pp. 186, 206, 313–19; McCown, *GSG*, p. 251.

[5] See above, chap. XIII, n. 11.

3. The Social Conscience in Babylonia

[6] See McCown, *GSG*, pp. 188–198, 245–59, and above, chap. IV, sec. 4. Cf. now Kramer, in *Archaeology*, 7 (1954), 145–46, and *FTS*, pp. 41–46.

[7] McCown, *GSG*, pp. 189–94; Frankfort, *KG*, p. 274 (Jacobsen); Falkenstein, *SAHG*, p. 180.

[8] Kramer, *op. cit.*, pp. 143–44, and *FTS*, pp. 47–51; Falkenstein, *SAHG*, pp. 87–90; Hymn for Ur-Nammu (Ur-Engur).

[9] *IAAM*, p. 194 (Jacobsen); Falkenstein, *SAHG*, pp. 115–16, 124–25, 371; McCown, *GSG*, p. 247.

[10] Von Soden, *SAHG*, pp. 240–47 (n.b., 242–45); McCown, *GSG*, pp. 194–95.

[11] *ANET*, pp. 164a, 178a (Meek); McCown, *GSG*, pp. 228–29; Smith (*op. cit.* above, chap. XIII, n. 25), pp. 181, 219.

[12] Luckenbill, *ARA*, II, §§92, 104, 118–20, 156, *et passim*, 233, 256 (269), 344, 656, 659E; 954, 957, 962.

[13] Kent, *OP*, pp. 132, 140, 142; DB. iv. 65 (§63); DNb. 8–11 (§8a); DSe. 39–41 (§44).

4. The Social Conscience in Ugarit

[14] Gordon, *UHB*, p. 164, and *UL*, p. 82; Text 127, ll. 29–34, 42–50; *ANET*, p. 149a (Ginsberg).

[15] Gordon, *UHB*, pp. 182, 179, and *UL*, pp. 88, 94; Text 2 Aqht, V, ll. 4–8; 1 Aqht, ll. 19–25; *ANET*, pp. 151a, 153a (Ginsberg); Gaster, *Thespis*, pp. 279, 296; *The Oldest Stories in the World* (New York: Viking, 1952), p. 201 (the significant words omitted, pp. 176, 182).

[16] See, e.g., Deut. 21:19; 22:15; 25:7; Job 5:4; 31:21; Prov. 22:22.

[17] For parallels cf. Ps. 140:12 (13); Prov. 29:7; 31:8–9; Jer. 5:28; 22:16; 30:13.

5. The Return of Paradise

[18] Luckenbill, *ARA*, II, §§987, 769, 935, 970. Gressmann, *Messias*, pp. 204–6. See above, n. 7.

[19] *Op. cit.*, pp. 1–63. See the Prologue to Hammurabi's code for an earlier example, n. 11, above.

[20] McCown, *GSG*, p. 256; G. A. Cooke, *A Textbook of North-Semitic Inscriptions* (Oxford, Clarendon, 1903), pp. 159–61, 171; Albright, *JPOS*, VI (1926), 84–85. Olmstead, *HPS*, p. 409, has a very different translation.

6. A Divinely Chosen Ruler

See McCown, *GSG*, chap. VIII, "The Perfect Prince."

[21] McCown, *GSG*, pp. 231–37.

[22] Luckenbill, *ARA*, I, §§20, 30, 43A, 209, 217, 356, 437, 498, 714; II, §§137, 180, 407, 577, *et passim*.

[23] *Ibid.*, II, §233.

[24] *Saturday Review*, 24 July, 1954, p. 13.

[25] Luckenbill, *ARA*, II, §§1138, 1153.

[26] McCown, *GSG*, p. 236; cf. Gressmann, *Messias*, p. 211.

[27] Barton, *AB*, pp. 484; see above, chap. VIII, n. 7.

7. Pride, Catastrophe, and Humility

[28] E.g., Luckenbill, *ARA*, I, §§437, 522; II, §§156, 648; Albright, *FSAC*, p. 254.

[29] Wilson, *BE*, pp. 294–304. See below, chap. XV, n. 2.

[30] Luckenbill, *ARA*, I, §§437, 481, 497, 125, 240, 787, 806; II, §§104, *et passim;* I, §745, II, §§1000, 1008.

8. Pessimism and Life's Problems

[31] *IAAM*, p. 208.

[32] *Ibid.*, p. 212.

[33] Breasted, *Dawn*, pp. 163–65.

[34] *Ibid.*, pp. 168–78.

[35] *Ibid.*, pp. 178–81; cf. McCown, *GSG*, pp. 111–12, 213–25.

[36] Jacobsen, *IAAM*, pp. 216–18; Langdon, *Babylonian Wisdom*, pp. 67–81; Albright, *FSAC*, p. 253; *ANET*, pp. 437b–440b (Pfeiffer).

9. The Righteous Sufferer

[37] Langdon, *Babylonian Wisdom*, pp. 35–61; Jacobsen, *IAAM*, pp. 212–16; Barton, *AB*, pp. 491–94; Albright, *FSAC*, p. 253; *ANET*, pp. 434b–437b (Pfeiffer).

[38] Olmstead, *HA*, pp. 73–74; Von Soden, *SAHG*, pp. 264–68; Gressmann, *AOTB*, I, pp. 248–50; cf. McCown, *GSG*, p. 234.

[39] Luckenbill, *ARA*, II, §984; Von Soden, *SAHG*, pp. 269–70.

[40] Quote, P. A. Schilpp, *Philosophy of George Santayana* (Evanston, Chicago: Northwestern Univ., 1940), p. 282.

CHAPTER XV THE HEBREW HOPE

Badè, *OTLT*.
Causse, A. *Les "pauvres" d'Israël;* Smith, J. M. P., *The Moral Life of the Hebrews* (Chicago: Univ. of Chicago Press, 1928); McCown, *GSG*, pp. 259–91.

1. The Problem of Justice

[1] 1 Kings 18:5–6.

[2] McCown, *GSG*, pp. 113–14, 202, 251–55; B. Gunn, *JEA*, III (1916), pp. 81–94; Wilson, *BE*, p. 299.

2. The Hebrew Social Conscience

[3] Quoted by Harold L. Ickes, *Secret Diaries*, II (New York: Simon and Schuster, 1954), p. 550.

[4] Amos 2:6; 3:1; Mic. 3:1.

[5] Mic. 2:2, 9; 3:3, 11; Isa. 1:2–5, 16, 17, 23; 5:8, 20–23; 9:17; 10:1–2.

[6] Jer. 1:18; 2:26; 4:9; 13:13; 23:1–2, 9–22.

[7] Jer. 22:1–17; 21:12; cf. 2 Kings 22:1–23:27; 2 Chron. 34:1–35:19; Jer. 7:1–7.

[8] Ezra 16:49; 18:12–13, 16–17; 22:12, 29.

4. Postexilic Problems and Ideals

[9] Isa. 42:3–4; 56:1; 58:6–7; 59:3–4, 11, 14; 61:1, 8.

[10] Isa. 11:3b–5; 25:4; 26:6; 29:18–21; 32:7.

[11] Neh. 5:1–13; cf. above, chap. IX, sec. 2, n. 3; sec. 3.

[12] Cf. Hillel (30 B.C.–20 A.D.), *Pirḳe Aboth* 2:6: "No *'am-ha-arets* can be saintly." See Danby, *Mishnah*, p. 693.

[13] Amos 4:4–5; 5:21–24; Pss. 40:6–8; 50:7–15; 51:16–17; 1 Sam. 15:22.
[14] Mic. 2:1–11; 6:9-7:6; James, *POT*, pp. 270, 280–81; Pfeiffer, *IOT*, pp. 593–94.

5. Mythological Motifs

The problem of demythicization or the reinterpretation of myth, as discussed by Rudolf Bultmann, Ernst Cassirer, Susanne Langer, *et al.*, although pertinent, is too complicated to be considered here, or in the next chapter. See above, chaps. VIII, sec. 5; X, sec. 3; XIV, secs. 5–7; *IAAM*, pp. 3–27 (H. and H. A. Frankfort), Gressman, *Messias*, pp. 1–192; and below, chap. XIX, sec. 5.

[15] E.g., Gunkel and Mowinckel; cf. Albright, *ARI*, pp. 128 f., but Pfeiffer, *IOT*, pp. 629–32, and many others place all, or nearly all, after the Exile. For Albright the Canaanitish Psalms may be either early or postexilic; for Gressmann (*Messias*, pp. 195–98) the "royal Psalms" are pre-exilic.
[16] Pss. 9:17–20; 37:11, 25.
[17] See, e.g., Pss. 40:17; 69:20, 32–33; 70:5; 72:12–14; 86:1–2; 109:22; cf. McCown, *GSG*, pp. 259–74.

Chapter XVI The Neoprophetic Hope

Pfeiffer, *IOT*, pp. 875, 878, 881–83; *HNTT*, pp. 538–40.
Rowley, H. H.   *The Relevance of Apocalyptic: A Study of Jewish Apocalypses from Daniel to Revelation.*   2nd ed.   New York: Harper, 1946. A scholarly but conservative discussion, with extensive bibliography, pp. 179–95.

1. The Apocalypse a New Type of Prophecy

[1] See Ps. 74:9; 1 Macc. 4:46; 9:27; 14:41; Josephus *C. Ap.* I. 37–41 (7–8); cf. Zech. 13:2–5; Jer. 23:13–17, 25, 33–34.
[2] "Party" is not used to imply organization; cf. McCown, *GSG*, pp 271–72; *per contra*, A. Causse, *Les "pauvres" d'Israël*, pp. 95–96. See chap. XV, n. 17.
[3] Deut. 28:13; 1 Enoch 103:11.

2. Evolutionary Stimuli

[4] See above, chap. XIII, sec. 4, esp. n. 32.

[5] For an example of Hellenistic influence see Paul's term, "spiritual body," 1 Cor. 15, and below, sec. 4.

[6] See above, chap. XIII, sec. 2, nn. 20–21. Not to be overlooked is the evidence of the magic papyri; Karl Preisendanz, *Papyri Graecae Magicae* (2 vols.; Leipzig, Berlin: Teubner, 1928, 1931), esp. Jewish motifs: I, Pap. iv, 850, 1010, 1484–85, 1538, 1568–69, 1628, 3019–20, 3040, Iaō, Sabaōth, Jesus god of the Hebrews, Solomon, etc.; II, Pap. vii, 311, 626, 1012, etc., p. 53, Sabaōth, Adōnai, archangels. J. A. Montgomery, *Aramaic Incantation Texts from Nippur* (Philadelphia: Univ. Museum, 1913).

[7] Gordon, *UL*, pp. 42, 44; *UHB*, pp. 149, 137; texts 67 VI, ll. 9–10; 49 I, ll. 13–15. Beelzebul is neither "lord of flies," nor "lord of dung"; cf. *zbl*, "raise," in Akkadian and Arabic. See Albright, *ARI*, pp. 61, 73, 195, nn. 11–12; *JPOS*, XVI (1936), 17–18; in John 12:31; 14:30; 16:11, "ruler of this cosmos"; in 1 Cor. 2:6, 8, "ruler of this age." Albright translates *aleyan* as "he who prevails," *zebul* as "the exalted one."

3. Stimuli from Mazdaism

Söderblom, Nathan. *La vie future d'après le mazdéisme*. Angers: A. Burdin, 1901.

Scheftelowitz, J. *Die altpersische Religion und das Judentum*. Giessen: Topelmann, 1920.

Gressmann, Hugo. *Die orientalischen Religionen im hellenistisch-römischen Zeitalter*. Berlin, Leipzig: de Gruyter, 1930, pp. 124–38.

Duchesne-Guillemin, Jacques. *Ormazd et Ahriman: L'aventure dualiste dans l'antiquité*. Paris: Presses Universitaires de France, 1953.

[8] Kent, *OP*, pp. 130, 132. DB. iv. 88–92, §70.

[9] There being no consensus of opinion as to Zarathushtra's date, the only certainty is Nyberg's conclusion (*RAI*, pp. 31–47): before *c*. 485; possibly after 550.

[10] Gressmann, *op. cit.*, pp. 128–33; Albright, *FSAC*, pp. 278–80.

[11] It begins six inscriptions of Darius, eight of Xerxes, and one (out of two found) of Artaxerxes I.

[12] Kent, *OP*, pp. 151–52, XPh. 46–56; *ANET*, pp. 316b–317a (Akkadian text, Oppenheim); cf. Cameron, *AJSL*, LVIII (1941), 319–25.

[13] DB. V. corrected to conform with Kent, *OP*, p. 134, rev. ed.; cf. Nyberg, *RAI*, pp. 364–68. See Ys. 46:10–11; 48:1–9; 51:13–15; 53:1, 9.

[14] Kent, *OP*, p. 140, DNb.

[15] See above, n. 12.

[16] See Bousset, *RJ*, pp. 342–57.

[17] Dan. 7:16; 9:21; 10:13, 18, 20–21; 12:1; cf. Moulton, *EZ*, chap. VIII (pp. 254–85).

[18] 1 En. 46–48; 51; 61:8–62:16. See E. Herzfeld, *Zoroaster and His World* (Princeton: Princeton Univ. Press, 1947), pp. 833–34; Mark 12:35–37; 14:61–62; Pss. 2; 110; cf. Mark 8:29–33.

[19] See Gressmann, *Messias*, pp. 401–14; Bousset, RJ, pp. 262–68, 351–55; C. H. Kraeling, *Anthropos, Son of Man* (New York: Columbia Univ. Press, 1926), pp. 85–109; Albright, *FSAC*, pp. 290–92.

4. Judaism and Mazdaism Contrasted

[20] Ys. 30:4–9; 31:20–22; 48:2; 51:1. The best scholars differ as to the translation of crucial phrases (*frasha* in Ys. 30:9, and *aḵereti* in 48:2) but agree that a better world was to come and men had a part in making it so.

[21] See above, chap. XIV, n. 13.

[22] See Ys. 30:2, 8, 10, 11; 31:14, 15, 20, *et passim*. The wicked must be punished as evidence of Ahura's power and justice.

[23] 1 En. 50:1; 51:1, 2, 5; cf. 2 Macc. 7:9–14; 14:44–46.

[24] Ys. 30–34; 48.

On the above see the following, listed in the General Bibliography: Bartholomae, *GA;* Duchesne-Guillemin, *Zor;* Lommel, *RZ;* Nyberg, *RAI;* M. W. Smith, *GZ;* Moulton, *EZ.*

5. Christian Hopes

[25] Out of the large and growing literature, see, as the best and most comprehensive to date, Millar Burrows, *The Dead Sea Scrolls* (New York: Viking Press, 1955); T. H. Gaster, *The Dead Sea Scriptures* (Anchor Book, Garden City: Doubleday, 1956).

[26] Luke 12:31; Matt. 6:33; Luke 6:20–21, 24–25; 19:1–10; 18:13–14; Mark 8:30–31; 9:31; 10:33–34; 14:62. See McCown, "Reign of God," in *RinL*, XVIII (1949), 211–13; "Jesus, Son of Man, a Survey of Recent Discussion," *JR*, XXVIII (1948), 3–6; argument based on Mark as the least revised and interpolated of the Gospels.

[27] As the writer of the fourth Gospel saw from his later perspective; John 14.

[28] See 1 Thess. 4:15–16; 1 Cor. 15:23–25; Phil. 2:10–11; Eph. 6:12.

[29] John 11:25; 12:31; 3:19.

Various discussions have arisen around the problems here considered:
Dibelius, Martin. "Die sociale Motiv in Neuen Testament," in *Botschaft
u. Geschichte*, I. Tübingen: Mohr, 1953, pp. 178–203. (Objective)
Wilder, A. N. *Eschatology and Ethics in the Teaching of Jesus.* 2nd
ed. New York: Harper, 1950. (Objective)
Cullmann, Oscar. *Christ and Time.* Tr. by F. V. Filson. Philadelphia:
Westminster Press, 1940. (Dogmatic)
Minear, P. S. *Christian Hope and the Second Coming.* Philadelphia:
Westminster Press, 1954. (Biblicist)

CHAPTER XVII HOPE IN HISTORY

1. History as Adventure
    [1] The meaning in history as here presented finds its theoretical justifica-
tion in Whitehead's organismic philosophy; see his *AI*, pp. 53, 207, 303,
330–32; *Modes of Thought*, pp. 39, 142, *et passim*. The evidence is to be
seen in an objective appraisal of what has actually happened in the agelong
process.
    [2] *De anima* 402b.

2. *Ancient and Modern Misconceptions*
    [3] Whitehead, *Modes of Thought*, p. 3; cf. McCown, *HTR*, XXXVIII
(1945), 158–60.
    [4] *De anima* 418b–20b.
    [5] William Temple, *Nature, Man, and God*, Gifford Lectures (London:
Macmillan, 1934), pp. 317, 322; B. H. Streeter, *The God Who Speaks* (New
York: Macmillan, 1936); Georgia Harkness, *Foundations of Christian
Knowledge* (New York, Nashville: Abingdon Press, 1955), pp. 81–85.

3. Positive Conclusions
    [6] See above, chap. II.

4. Social and Economic Morality
    [7] See above, chap. XIV, sec. 3.
    [8] Woolley, *Ur*, pp. 34–56.

CHAPTER XVIII WHAT HOPE IN HISTORY?

1. The Processes of Progress
    [1] See chap. XVII, sec. 1, Whitehead.

[2] Translated from the Bengali, *Manchester Guardian Weekly* (June 12, 1925), p. 490.

2. Problems of Faith and Works
[3] *The Biblical Doctrine of Man and Society* (Ecumenical Biblical Studies, No. 2; London: SCM Press Ltd., 1954), pp. 165–69.

3. Action
[4] Jer. 1:7, 18–19.
[5] *Pol.* 1280b–1281a.
[6] *Man Stands Alone* (New York: Harper, n.d.), pp. 1–33; *MMW*, pp. 4–28, 146–61; *Evol*, pp. 556–78.
[7] From "The Mighty Hundred Years."
[8] Montagu, *DHD*, pp. 247, 190, 174; cf. Mark 10:43–44.

CHAPTER XIX THE MEANING OF ANCIENT NEAR EASTERN HISTORY: A SUMMARY

The special bibliography for this chapter is unusually long since the summary covers nearly all phases of the total subject. Some of the books listed are of recent date and were not available when the previous chapters were written.

Brunner, Emil. Christianity and Civilisation. 2 vols. Gifford Lectures, 1947, 1948. London, New York: Nisbet & Co., Scribner's, 1948, 1949.

Bury, J. B. The Idea of Progress. London: Macmillan, 1921.

Collingwood, R. G. The Idea of History. (Galaxy Book.) New York: Oxford, 1956.

Conant, James B. On Understanding Science. New Haven: Yale Univ. Press, 1947.

Dodd, C. H. According to the Scriptures. New York: Scribner's, 1953.
———. The Bible To-day. Cambridge, New York: Univ. Press, Macmillan, 1947.

Fitch, Robert Elliot. The Kingdom Without End. New York: Scribner's, 1950.

Harkness, Georgia. Understanding the Christian Faith. New York, Nashville: Abingdon Press, 1947.

Horton, Walter Marshall. Christian Theology. New York: Harper, 1955.

Otwell, John H. Ground to Stand On. New York: Oxford, 1957.

Richardson, Alan, and Schweitzer, W. (eds.). Biblical Authority for Today. Philadelphia: Westminster Press, 1951.

Robinson, H. Wheeler. Inspiration and Revelation in the Old Testament. Oxford: Clarendon, 1953.

Santayana, George. Interpretations of Poetry and Religion. (Torch Books.) New York: Harper, 1957.

Tillich, Paul. Dynamics of Faith. New York: Harper, 1957.

Trueblood, D. Elton. The Predicament of Modern Man. New York: Harper, 1944.

Whitehead, Alfred North. The Aims of Education. (Mentor Book.) New York: New American Library, 1955.

Wilder, Amos N. (ed.). Liberal Learning and Religion. New York: Harper, 1951.

———. New Testament Faith for Today. New York: Harper, 1955.

———. Otherworldliness and the New Testament. New York: Harper, 1954.

[1] Collingwood, *The Idea of History*, p. 17.

[2] *Ibid.*, pp. 49–51.

[3] *Ibid.*, p. 54

[4] Richardson and Schweitzer, eds., *Biblical Authority for Today*, pp. 240–44.

[5] *Ibid.*, p. 241.

[6] Published in *The Divinity School News* (Univ. of Chicago), XXIV, no. 1 (1957), 1.

[7] *Interpretations*, pp. 24–25.

[8] *Ibid.*, p. 109.

[9] *The Philosophy of Symbolic Forms*, II (New Haven: Yale Univ. Press, 1955), p. 239.

[10] *Ibid.*, II, pp. 248–49, quoting Harnack, *Dogmengeschichte*, I, p. 198.

[11] Whitehead, *Religion in the Making*, pp. 16, 60; cf. J. S. Bixler in *The Philosophy of A. N. Whitehead*, ed. Schilpp, p. 502.

Index

Aaronic priesthood, 84, 87, 171
Abargi, King, 282
Abdi-khipa (Abdu-kheba), 61 f.
Abel, 83, 197
Abraham, 78, 85 f., 142, 149 f., 155, 159, 189
Abu Shahrein (Eridu), 51
Acts, and criticism, 299
Adams, Henry Brooks, 12
Adaptation to environment, 22 f.
Aeschylus, 188
Agur, 200
Ahab, 63, 70, 94 f., 98 f., 164 f., 225, 238
Ahaz, 70, 95, 99 f., 112
Ahijah, 92
Ahuramazda, 109, 113, 258, 260 ff., 290
Akh-en-Aton, 84, 201
Akhigar, 194 f.
Akkadia, 283, 285; cuneiform, 58, 61; law codes, 221; tablets, 57
Albright, W. F., 80, 85 f., 118, 196, 198, 202, 228
Alcimus, 131
Alexander Janneus, 132
Alexander the Great, 133
Alphabets, development of, 58 f., 185; South Arabian, 72
Alt, Albrecht, 100
Amalekites, 71
Amarna letters, 80, 86 f.
Amaziah, 95
Amen-em-ope, 199 ff., 219 f., 228
'Am ha'-arets, 135, 177, 243, 266
'Amman (Rabbath-Ammon), 33, 128
Ammon, 70 f., 90, 110, 119 ff., 125
Amorites, 56, 60 f., 70, 72, 78; names, 86
Amos, 98, 102, 109, 143 f., 151, 162, 165, 170, 176 f., 238 f., 244 f., 267, 269
Anathoth, 83
Anau, 51
Animistic personalism, 145
Antigonus, 133
Antiochus III, 178
Antiochus IV Epiphanes, 125 ff., 130
Antipater, 132

Antony, 133
'Apiru, see Khabiru
Apocalypticism, 153 ff., 250 ff., 266 ff.
Apollonius, see Zeno
'Aqabah, Gulf of, 31 f., 40
Arabian Peninsula, 42, 60 f., 71 f.
Arabs, 71 f., 120, 125
Arad, 83
Aram, Kingdom of, 70, 90; Plain of, 86
Aramaic, 70, 78, 107, 119, 152, 189, 201
Arameans, 72, 78
'Araq el-Emir, 124
Arauna the Jebusite, 63
Archelaus, 133
'Areboth Moab, 36
Aristobulus, 132 f.
Aristotle, 269, 274, 278, 291
Ark, 90 ff., 173
Arpachiyyah, 51
Arsames, 107
Artaxerxes I, 259
Artaxerxes II, 117, 123, 260
Artaxerxes III, 123
Ashdod, 119 ff., 128
Asher, 79, 81
Ashkelon, 64, 128, 164
Assuan (Elephantine), 107, 109
Assur, 109
Assurbanipal, 202 f., 222 f., 225, 232 f.
Assur-nasir-pal I, 227 f., 232
Assur-nirari, 229
Assyria, 83, 90, 94, 98 ff., 104 f., 114, 151, 191, 222 f., 247, 283; influence on Hebrew literature, 199; palaces, 57
Athaliah, 95 f., 149
Athlit, 5
Aton, cult of, 108 f., 144; hymn to, 201
Augustine, 143, 297
Augustus, 133, 269
Azariah (Uzziah), 40, 95, 98, 164 f., 247
Azariah of Judah, 99
Azekah, 127

Baal worship, 70, 73, 93, 95 ff., 101, 112, 161, 252

343